KT-196-857

DOG

The definitive book for dog lovers

BRUCE FOGLE

MITCHELL BEAZLEY

DOG: The definitive book for dog lovers
Dr Bruce Fogle

First published in Great Britain in 2010 by Mitchell Beazley,
an imprint of Octopus Publishing Group Limited,
Endeavour House, 189 Shaftesbury Avenue, London, WC2H 8JY
www.octopusbooks.co.uk

An Hachette UK Company
www.hachette.co.uk

Distributed in the US and Canada by Octopus Books USA
c/o Hachette Book Group USA
237 Park Avenue South, New York, NY 10017
www.octopusbooksusa.com

ISBN: 9781845334796

A CIP catalogue record for this book is available from the British Library.

Commissioning Editor: Helen Griffin
Senior Art Editor: Juliette Norsworthy
Designer: Phil Gilderdale
Project Editor: Georgina Atsiaris
Copy Editor: Candida Frith-Macdonald
Proofreader: Elaine Koster
Indexer: Hilary Bird
Production: Caroline Alberti

Typeset in Perpetua
Printed and bound in China

Contents

Introduction

This book is about dogs, those noble, honest, and immutably faithful companions so many of us feel compelled to live with. It's about how and where they evolved, why we let them live with us, what roles they have played in our lives, and how we have changed their colours, shapes, attitudes, and abilities. It's about the dog's cycle of life, from birth through a surprisingly short puppyhood and sometimes exasperating adolescence into calmer adulthood, and inevitable geriatric decline. It is also, needless to say, about us, about our enduring relationship with our canine companions.

As I've lived with dogs all my life, you'd be right to assume I like their company. Even filled with people, my home feels sterile and empty unless something covered in hair is stirring up the air. During my life, many dogs have arrived, matured, aged, and eventually died. Recently, the life of one of my dogs ended and another began. At the time of writing, I have a young Golden Retriever named LL Bean, and for the past few months I've been a bystander once more to the fascinating early development of a dog's responsive behaviour. Let me introduce Bean, as an example of just how well dogs and humans understand one another.

Potent symbol A retrieving breed may carry the lead to you, another may sit and stare at it hanging by the door, and virtually all will bounce to their feet when you pick it up. To a dog a lead means a walk, so much so that you never even need to say the word.

After I showered this morning Bean ambled over and licked my leg. I said "No", and she stopped. Later I prepared Bean's breakfast, and she lay quietly on the floor, intently watching each aspect of the food preparation routine. As I mixed it, Bean stood up so I gave her a hand signal – pointing down. She sat back down until I put her food bowl on the floor and said "OK", and when she heard that, she got up, went across to her bowl, emptied it, and licked it dishwasher clean.

Sometimes I take Bean for her morning run in the park, and sometimes my wife, Julia, does. Bean may be no more than a pup, but she easily "reads" when I'm not going to take her for her walk; on those days she just lies there looking mournfully at me. (Your dog doesn't practice that doleful look in front of a mirror. It comes naturally, and we're all suckers for it.) Today she knew I was going to take her out. She ambled into the hallway, picked up her lead, pranced back to me with the pride of the best-trained Lippizaner horse, went to the front door, and waited for me to open it. Like all dogs, she's superb at watching what I'm doing, reading my "intention movements". This morning she saw me put on my walking boots rather than my work shoes, so rather than the despondent routine, there was joy in her eyes. Dogs read us well, but we're pretty good at reading their feelings.

My veterinary clinic is in town but I write in the country. This morning, because I'm writing, I took her for a walk in the adjacent fields and woods. The local farmer has ploughed deep furrows in preparation for potato

Keeping in step Walking your dog is life-affirming. It's as if you are plaited together into one extended consciousness. I might see a squirrel before she does, then she will spy one before I do. We share the walk and the world.

planting, and Bean burned off some of her pent-up energy by using one of these furrows as a race track, attempting (unsuccessfully) to break the land speed record. With that out of her system, we walked through the next field, where potatoes were planted last year. Bean found an absolute treasure, one of last year's rotten potatoes, and started to eat it. I took a step towards her, to get near before telling her to "drop it", but seeing me move, she ran away, her normally horizontal tail waving excitedly at twelve o'clock high. I didn't want to turn this into a game, so I turned my back and walked away until I could hide behind a tree, then I called her name. Because Bean's a sociable creature, she came running, and I rewarded her with some roughhousing.

Back home, seeing me sitting at the computer, Bean has climbed onto a comfortable chair (I'll sort that out later!) and gone to sleep. She's read my intentions again, knows I'll be here for some time and, sociable individual that she is – and dogs are amongst the most gregariously sociable of all species – she's decided to doze off.

Everything Bean and I did this morning stems from our mutual ability to read each other's body language and intention movements. Don't look for anything more complicated than that simple fact to explain the relationship dogs and humans can develop. We don't need words, and neither do dogs. A mute understanding of each other is at the very core of why people and dogs have been "best friends" for millennia. I don't say that simply because I'm a dog fan. Of course I appreciate dogs, but I didn't appreciate them half as much when I started working with them almost 40 years ago. My admiration for their skills has simply increased year on year, as I've met more of them and seen what they're capable of. Science backs me up.

The feeling is mutual

Most of this book is devoted to dogs, but first I'll briefly spend a little time on the species at the other end of the leash – us. We know, through recent and repeated studies, that if we point or even nod towards something, dogs are better at working out what we're pointing at than any other species. They are better than cats, better than wolves, they are even better than our closest relatives, chimpanzees, at reading our intention movements. Dogs have an uncanny ability to share our thoughts, but that knack is mutual. Nobel Prize-winning ethologist Konrad Lorenz wrote in 1950 that some time during our ancient history we evolved an equal ability to read dogs. We read them with almost as great precision as they read us, because we share a wide range of behaviours and body language, a rare set of circumstances in the animal world. Our relationship with them is reciprocal. We understand each other.

Wonder dog It's all too easy to mock the absurd qualities of the *Lassie* films – "What's that, Lassie? His heart rate's down to 30 beats per minute?" – and dogs need serious training to become real lifesavers. But what's impressive is that with the right training, they do become lifesavers, or almost anything else we need.

But we can make mistakes and misinterpret subservient behaviour for love. During my time in practice, dogs have been increasingly "Disneyfied", portrayed as simple stereotypes of loyalty and affection. In fact, the affection that our dogs give us is often triggered by our own needs or experiences, and varies considerably from person to person. How your dog behaves with you and with others is intricately interwoven into the mutual bond of respect and affection you have for each other.

Of course, there are also problems associated with our close relationship with dogs – bites, transmissible diseases, allergies, and emotional and financial strains when they are unwell. But dogs remain the most wonderful species for giving affection because of their gregarious sociability, because their attachment behaviours are so similar to ours. With that similarity comes an emotional bond, and that bond is at the core of this book.

Constancy in a changing world

I've been a clinical vet for nearly four decades. I try to be an unbiased observer of our relationship with dogs, but that's tough; I've lived with dogs since the day I was born, with only a short gap at university, so I've already been won over. However, there is an undisputed fact upon which my veterinary colleagues agree, and that is that the intensity of our emotional relationship and interaction with our dogs has increased during the time I've been in practice. Some people feel that this is a consequence of how Western culture is developing, and a sign of the weakness of modern society, but the deep feelings we have for our dogs are neither new nor unique. The bond of friendship that we have with them has been an integral part of our history ever since wolf-dog pups were first raised in human settlements as much as 40,000 years ago.

There was a time in the very recent past when most dogs had practical and utilitarian values, but in an affluent, urban society, few dogs now serve any of their traditional roles. We house them in our homes simply because we feel better for doing so. Dogs give us social and psychological rewards, and if I were to encapsulate in a single word the reason we enjoy living with dogs, that word would be *constancy*.

Generation by generation, life has become more hectic, and cultural values are evolving faster than ever before. The three-generation family living under the same roof, where grandparents shared child-rearing responsibilities with the parents, is now rare. Even the nuclear family of two biological parents, two-point-three kids, and a Volvo in the drive no longer represents even half of family units. Many couples both work, and postpone parenthood by almost ten years compared with just three decades ago. Gay partnerships are common, and there are more "empty nesters" who no longer have any living things other than their houseplants or gardens to look after. Young people move to where work is and often live alone, as do many more when marriages dissolve or when partners die, and in some cities the majority of households contain a single person.

Through all of this the dog remains immutable. Always there. Always responding the same way. Always honest with feelings and emotions. Your dog doesn't care one bit about the stock market, or politics, or terrorism, or taxes. It's just reliably ever present, waiting for a touch, or a walk, or some play. Dogs make us feel good, because however fast the world changes, they remain the same, a constant in our lives.

Why we live with dogs

The most common value people attribute to dogs is protection. It's a favourite fantasy that our dogs will protect us from harm and bring help when it's needed. My mother-in-law's Lhasa Apso/Staffordshire Bull Terrier cross certainly did when she collapsed in the garden. Tied by his leash, Bill howled and howled until neighbours arrived. But Bill had been trained to do this through Hearing Dog training, part of which is to get help when the deaf owner needs it. Would any dog naturally do this?

Researchers in the Department of Psychology of a Canadian university had dog owners either collapse in an open field with a feigned heart attack, or appear to become pinned behind a fallen bookcase indoors. In not a single instance did a pet dog understand the nature of the emergencies and go to get help. Similarly, while trained dogs will protect you if you are physically attacked, an untrained dog is as likely to think it's a game as it is to confront the attacker. The only genuine way a dog actually protects you has nothing to do with physically defending you: burglars say that if they are given a choice they target homes that don't have dogs. Some police forces say that simply having dog food visible through the kitchen window is as good a burglar deterrent as a standard alarm system.

Bill and Hillary Clinton's White House dog, Buddy, epitomized in his name the second most common reason people give for acquiring a dog: companionship. (Barack and Michelle Obama's daughters practically made their dog Bo part of a family tree: Bo is also the name of a cousin's cat as well as their grandfather's nickname.) Before our security-conscious times, this was the number one reason. Rationally, a successful household doesn't need a dog to provide companionship, but after getting a dog, 70 per cent of families surveyed reported an increase in family happiness. Dog-owning children are more involved in activities such as sports, hobbies, clubs, or chores than children who don't live with pets, and score significantly higher on empathy and social orientation scales. For many of us a dog is a cultural part of the family, and nuclear families consisting of two parents and growing children make up the largest individual group of dog owners, but they are not the majority. I'm an empty nester, and we make up the second largest group. Other large groups of dog owners are single people living alone and childless couples, whether they are postponing child-rearing or don't want or can't have children.

Lifelong lessons Dogs are good for growing kids. When you're the one being looked after, having a dog is a way to learn to look after someone else. And when your parents, or teachers, or just the whole world don't understand, a dog will (or will do a good enough impression of it).

All of us talk to our dogs, but large numbers of us confide in them too. Have you ever, in exasperation, turned and uttered an expletive to your dog? "Oh $%&@!" If so, you're guaranteed that your thoughts and feelings went no further. The non-judgmental dog, the buddy who is there to listen, is a little like a non-intervening psychiatrist who just listens and nods, letting you say what you want to say, what you need to say. Dogs don't criticize, and that makes them great companions. In a study of people given trained Hearing Dogs, the dogs fulfilled the owners' primary expectation of alerting them to sounds, and addressed the concern of security, making owners feel safer than they did before obtaining their hearing dog. But companionship was just as important to these individuals, who said they were significantly less lonely after receiving their dog. Virtually all studies on dog ownership produce similar findings.

Many of us also enjoy being seen with certain types of dogs, breeds that make a statement about us. Paris Hilton's Chihuahuas are as much an extension of her image as black Labradors are for the CEOs of Fortune 500 companies in the United States. Tough-looking dogs, especially tough-looking male dogs, give street kids status. Where I live, Bull Terrier-type dogs are an absolute must street accessory for guys in their late teens and early twenties. For my more affluent, middle-class clients, other crossbreds, particularly Labradoodles but also Cockerpoos, Goldendoodles, and Puggles, are fashionable. For some people a dog is almost a brand, and the brand you choose says something about you. My own brand loyalty to Golden Retrievers is not immutable. When we were in the market for our current dog, I suggested that we get a couple of Jack Russell Terriers that we could dribble as basketballs by day and use as pillows by night, but my commander-in-chief, Julia, vetoed the suggestion.

Dogs are good for us

Studies in the United States and Australia have found that dog owners contacted their doctors less often over a one-year period than people without pets. Pets seem to help their owners in times of stress. Johannes Odendaal at the University of Pretoria in South Africa found that we experience an increase in dopamine, a brain chemical associated with a feeling of well-being, when we stroke our own dog. We also experience a drop in the stress hormone cortisol, and women experience an increase in prolactin, a hormone of well-being that stimulates the release of milk.

American data published well over 20 years ago indicated that social support and owning a pet were the greatest predictors of one-year survival after a major heart attack, regardless of any other factor, including the severity of existing disease or the demographics of the patient. In another study, pet ownership was associated with lower levels of perceived or subjective stress, regardless of objective stress or social support levels. Medics say dogs reduce subjective stress by offering companionship and an acceptable object of attachment. The reasons why aren't fully understood, but there are many examples in studies from science journals:

- The presence of a dog reduces the stress of children during a visit to the dentist or a physical examination at a doctor's office.
- People with borderline hypertension have lower blood pressure on days they take their dogs to work.
- Seniors who own dogs visit their doctor less than those who do not, and cope better with stressful events without entering the healthcare system.
- Medication costs dropped by over 50 per cent per patient per day in nursing home facilities in New York, Missouri, and Texas that added animals and plants as an integral part of the environment.

It seems only logical that dog owners get more exercise than people who don't own dogs, and this has been confirmed most recently in a Canadian study showing they increase mild to moderate physical activity. But not by much. A Norwegian study found a typical owner walked his dog for half an hour or less each day, but even that time (nowhere near enough, in my opinion, for the physical needs of a dog) is enough to improve our health. That small amount of exercise is what is probably at the root of why pet owners have better physical health and fewer prescriptions written for them than their pet-free peers.

Healing touch We like to think we're a civilized species, that primitive needs such as regular touch are no longer vital to our wellbeing. Dogs have no such illusions, and this is perhaps one reason why they are good for our health. They walk straight into the heart of our personal space and ask to be stroked. There's no fear of rejection here.

Art is as compelling as science

Scientific studies quantify how dogs are good for us, but dogs were iconic companions long before their value was articulated in medical journals. Countless tributes to their value have been written, and the one I like most is Senator George Graham Vest's ornate purple prose. Senator Vest addressed a jury in Missouri in 1870 on behalf of a plaintiff claiming $50 for the shooting of his hound, Old Drum. Without so much as a scribbled note, he said this:

The best friend a man has in the world may turn against him and become his enemy. His son or daughter that he has reared with loving care may prove ungrateful. Those who are nearest and dearest to us, those whom we trust with our happiness and our good name, may become traitors to their faith. The money a man has, he may lose. It flies away from him, perhaps when he needs it most. A man's reputation may be sacrificed in a moment of ill-considered action. The people who are prone to fall on their knees to do us honour when success is with us may be the first to throw the stone of malice when failure settles its cloud upon our heads.

The one absolutely unselfish friend a man can have in this selfish world, the one that never deserts him, the one that never proves ungrateful or treacherous, is his dog. A dog stands by him in prosperity and in poverty, in health and sickness. He will sleep on the cold ground, where the wintry winds blow and the snow drives fiercely, if only he may be near his master's side. He will kiss the hand that has no food to offer; he will lick the wounds and sores that come in encounter with the roughness of the world. He guards the sleep of the pauper master as if he were a prince.

When all other friends have deserted, he remains. When riches take wings, and reputation falls to pieces, he is as constant in love, as the sun in its journey through the heavens. If fortune drives the master forth an outcast in the world, friendless and homeless, the faithful dog asks no higher privilege than that of accompanying him, to guard him against danger, to fight against his enemies. And when the last scene of all comes, and death takes his master in its embrace and his body is laid away in the cold ground, no matter if all other friends pursue their way, there by the graveside will the noble dog be found, his head between his paws, his eyes sad but open in alert watchfulness, faithful and true even in death.

The jury stayed out for just four minutes before awarding the plaintiff five hundred dollars in damages. Wouldn't you have done the same? The judge had to explain that they couldn't give more than the original demand of fifty dollars. Today there's a statue of Old Drum on the lawn of that courthouse.

We dog owners want to believe what Vest said, but is it true? Are dogs capable of noble thoughts? Are dogs part of their own natural world, or a misbegotten part of human culture? And what is it about dog owners that makes us behave in the ways we do, letting dogs become obese or (like mine) sleep on the bed? What makes us feel so relaxed, so secure in the company of our dogs? Why do we think we can talk to them, and that they understand us just as well as we understand them? These are topics I'll touch on in the following pages.

I'm sure you're just as aware as I am that not all dogs are lucky enough to be treated humanely. Far from it. Those that are in our homes are the fortunate ones, with conscientious and curious owners who are willing to invest time and money to care for them and learn more about them. We're lucky too, that we can share such a wonderfully honest, uncomplicated, and rewarding relationship with this kindred species.

Best friends forever A dog may be a loyal companion in a solo life, a playful character who enlivens an adult home before, after, or just without kids, or a vibrant addition to a boisterous family. Different dogs suit different people, but they are all capable of being unshakeably on your side.

CHAPTER ONE

How Dogs became Dogs

Dogs are what they are because of where they've come from. That may sound trite, but to understand and fully appreciate the unique place of dogs, it helps to know how they came to look and behave the way they do today. That means looking at their origins, at the prehistory and the family of the dog.

Amongst the mammals of the world there is a large family of hunting carnivores called the Canidae. Until recent genetics studies triggered a re-evalution of relationships, this family was divided into 14 subgroups or genera. Thirteen contained the dog's distant but still-living or very recently extinct relatives, including the foxes, the bush dog, the raccoon dog, the African wild dog, the short-eared dog, the maned wolf, and the Indian dhole. The fourteenth genus, *Canis*, contained the dog's very closest relatives: the coyote, three types of jackal, and the wolf.

Redrawing the family tree

Recent genetic analyses have modified this classification, showing only six distinct genera within the Canidae family. Three are minor, each containing just one isolated species (the grey fox, bat-eared fox, and raccoon dog), and three major. One major group consists of the fox-like canids, and a second includes all the South American canids. The third includes the wolf-like canids – the dog, the wolf, and the coyote – but also, at increasing genetic distance from them, the Simien jackal or Ethiopian wolf and the golden jackal, then the black-backed and side-striped jackals, and finally the African wild dog and the dhole.

Black-backed (*Canis mesomelas*), side-striped (*C. adustus*), and Simien (*C. simensis*) jackals exist only in Africa. The last, a species at risk of extinction, behaves much like the grey wolf, hunting in small packs. Genetic studies suggest that it may be a living remnant of an invasion of North Africa long ago by the grey wolf or its immediate ancestor. The golden jackal (*C. aureus*) thrives from the Balkans and Turkey to Myanmar (Burma), and is probably the model for the head of the Egyptian god Anubis. Like the coyote, golden jackals hunt singly or in pairs. This is the jackal that the Nobel laureate Konrad Lorenz thought some breeds of dog are descended from, a suggestion now ruled out by DNA evidence.

Closest cousins

Of the dog's closest relatives, the coyote (*C. latrans*) is increasingly successful. In the last century, this lone hunter expanded its territory from western North and Central America across the continent to the eastern seaboard, to include turf until recently occupied by the wolf. As its territory changed, so too did its kinship behaviour. Coyotes are becoming more sociable with their own kind, more willing to form small packs of blood relatives to defend territory or food sources. According to the fossil record, the coyote diverged from the wolf approximately a million years ago.

A varied family The dog's closer relations include the jackal (top left), resident of graveyards and guardian of the underworld to the ancient Egyptians, and the coyote (top right), the "trickster" of folklore in North America. Both will hunt, but are also scavengers, and adapt quite easily to living near humans. The dog's closest kin, the grey wolf (bottom right) is less adaptable. In Australia, dogs have returned to the wild as dingoes (bottom left). The DNA of dingoes shows they originated 5,000 years ago from a very small population of East Asian dogs, perhaps even a single female.

Coyotes can and do successfully interbreed with both wolves and dogs, producing "coy-dogs" that can only be accurately differentiated by genetic analysis. Some biologists claim that the coyote's increasing sociability is a result of interbreeding with wolves and dogs, but there is no genetic evidence that this is happening.

Varieties of grey wolves (*C. lupus*) are distributed throughout the northern hemisphere, and have been under pressure everywhere within their range for centuries. The English grey wolf became extinct around 1500, the Scottish wolf before 1750, and the French, Belgian, Dutch, Danish, German, and Swiss wolves by 1800. The Japanese wolf ceased to exist in 1905. In Europe and Asia, the grey wolf usually survives only in isolated remnant populations such as those in Spain, Italy, and Scandinavia. In the Baltic states, where wolf conservation is well developed, numbers are increasing, with over 400 in Latvia alone. Carpathian wolves are also being successfully conserved, particularly in southern Poland and Slovakia, but in Russia their numbers remain unknown. DNA analysis comparing prehistoric canine bones up to 12,000 years old found in Italy with modern eastern-European grey wolves indicates that these surviving wolves may still carry the genetic diversity of Europe's founder-dog population.

Regional breeds of grey wolf survive from Bulgaria and the Balkans into and throughout Asia, from Turkey in the west, northward to Arctic Siberia, southward to the Arabian peninsula and eastward through Iraq, Iran, Pakistan, India, and all the "stans" to Nepal, Tibet, China, and the shores of the Pacific. It is somewhere in this Asian region that the dog as we know it today evolved from this canine family.

Within the lower 48 states of the United States, the wolf was driven to virtual extinction in the course of the 19th and early 20th centuries, surviving only in Minnesota on the Canadian border. The Newfoundland white wolf became extinct in 1911, the Alaskan Kenai wolf in 1915, the Florida black wolf in 1917, the Great Plains Lobo wolf in 1926, and the last Cascade Mountains wolf died in 1950. Surviving examples of the smaller red wolf (*C. rufus*) of the southeastern United States are in fact hybrids with both coyotes and grey wolves. Conservation in Minnesota and reintroduction of Canadian grey wolves in other northern states have been remarkably successful. There are now over 2,600 grey wolves in the lower 48 states, over 2,000 of which are in Minnesota. There is also an isolated and endangered remnant population in Mexico. The grey wolf remains secure in Canada, where there are over 50,000, and Alaska, home to another 6,000 to 8,000. But in Canada and the United States alone, there are in comparison over 70 *million* direct descendants of wolves – dogs.

The story of the modern wolf is one of threatened survival, while that of the dog is of unparalleled success. The dog moved into the human community. It lost its aloofness. Yes, it lost control over its own breeding, but from an evolutionary perspective this was a brilliantly successful tactic. The world's total wolf population today is probably around 150,000; at around 400 million, the total dog population is almost 3,000 times greater.

Complex cousins The small, sociable wolves of Asia are all classified as subspecies of the grey wolf. Recent DNA evidence is calling into question exactly how the wolves of Iran, India, and Tibet are related.

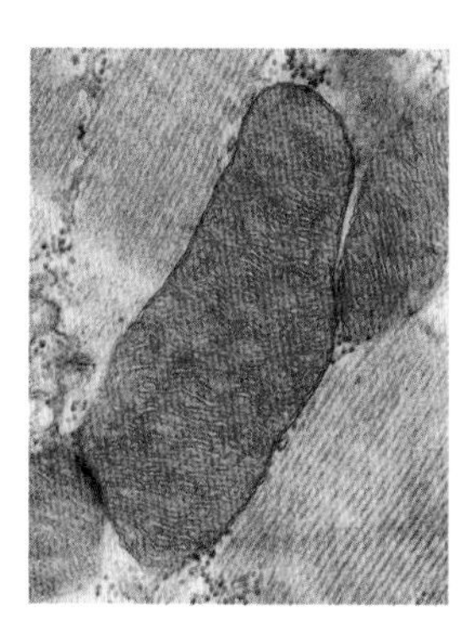

Truth will out They mean nothing to the untrained eye, but the microscopic revelations of DNA in mitochondria tell us the truth about the history of every species on earth. Earlier guesses based on morphology (how an animal looks) can prove to be embarrassingly wide of the mark.

DNA revelations

The true story of when and where the dog developed and how it spread has only become evident through studies of genetic material from ancient bones and modern dogs. Most have concentrated on mitochondrial DNA, mtDNA for short. Mitochondria are cells' power-plants, converting nutrients to energy, and they contain their own DNA, circular like that in bacteria, and completely different from the DNA in the cell's nucleus. Biologists hypothesize that early in evolution, over a billion years ago, bacteria invaded some single-celled microorganisms and eventually became incorporated into them as the mitochondria.

Your dog's genetic code is contained in nuclear DNA, the DNA in the nucleus that exists within most cells within its body. Your dog's mtDNA is different, and what makes it so fascinating is that over 99.9 per cent of it is inherited from the mother. This is because an egg cell contains around 100,000 mitochondria, but a sperm has only about 100, and these are carried on its tail, where the sperm needs its energy. Over time, copying mistakes (mutations) in mtDNA are inevitable, eventually producing divergent lines. The mutation rate over time remains constant, which means that studying mtDNA is like reading a written timetable of evolution.

Studies of mtDNA show that the dog diverged from its closest wolf relations between 40,000 and 100,000 years ago. Evidence published in 2004 showed that three out of four modern dogs share their mtDNA with a single female ancestor. In other words, three-quarters of all dogs today descend from one family of wolves. The rest are descended from just three other female wolf ancestors. If the studies are correct, there was one defining genetic event in which a line of wolves adapted to a life of cohabitation alongside humans; later on, but still in ancient times, other wolf lines were added on just three other occasions. No one knows exactly which wolves, and it's possible that the original wolf ancestor is now extinct. Genetic studies of ancient Italian dog and wolf skeletons indicate that the European wolf contributed in part to the development of dogs, but this is still very different from the historical belief that dogs in each region of the world descended from the local wolves of that region.

The studies confirm that the dog's primary origins are somewhere in Asia. The wolves of Asia, although all classified as part of *C. lupus*, look and behave considerably differently from their larger European and North American relatives. The fawn-brown Arabian desert wolf is roughly the size of a Brittany or English Springer Spaniel and weighs around 20kg (45lb), while the white or slate-blue Arctic tundra wolf can weigh in excess of 75kg (165lb). The largest wolves have specialized in capturing and killing big game; their shorter-coated Asian and Arabian relatives evolved as hunters of smaller game and also as efficient scavengers of carrion. These small wolves are sociable and adaptable, but size and sociability don't necessarily make them the modern dog's true ancestors. Studies of wolves in India revealed three genetically distinct groups, and only those wolves now living in the Himalayas and Tibet share common mtDNA with dogs. Other wolves from

Nepal, Tibet, and Himachal Pradesh have mtDNA distinct from that of both dogs and the wolves that do share their mtDNA with dogs.

An alternative ancestor

But was the ancestor of our dogs really a wolf? While most biologists are convinced that Bean, curled asleep on the sofa as I write, descends directly from an Asian wolf, and the genetic evidence points to a close relationship, a minority of experts argue for descent from an extinct canine species that was not a wolf, but was physically very similar to wolves. They point to physical and behavioural differences between dog and wolf, a lack of fossil evidence for transition, and practical difficulties that would be encountered in training proto-dogs descended from wolves.

A variety of wild animals have moved into the ecological niche created by humans, where they've found it possible to survive and reproduce: mice, rats, and more recently, raccoons, possums, and coyotes in North America and red foxes in Europe. Wolves have never been reported to inhabit a human settlement voluntarily, the way the ancestors of the dog did. Captive wolves can be tamed, because they are pack animals with a social hierarchy – but have you ever wondered why they have rarely been used to work, hunt, or perform in circuses? Wolves are much more difficult than many other animals to reliably train to command. They resist training to inhibit their natural behaviours, such as guarding kills, which is essential in sharing our lives with dogs. Wolf packs have a natural hierarchy, headed by the alpha male and alpha female; only this dominant pair reproduces annually. Other members of the pack will challenge the alpha pair, and eventually one then the other will be replaced, making challenge essential for reproduction and dangerously hardwired into the wolf mind. But dog packs, even feral packs, lack a wolf-like pack structure. Amongst the pariah dogs of Calcutta, several females may give birth around the same time to litters fathered by one or more males. Males fight with each other over females, but feral dog packs never revert to the classical dominance hierarchy of the wolf pack. Nor do feral dogs ever revert to a wolf-like appearance.

In *Anthrozoös*, a journal on which I was for a long time on the editorial board, Janice Koler-Matznick argued in 2002 in a piece called 'The Origin of the Dog Revisited' that dogs are physically and behaviourally different from wolves, but similar to an extinct canine species from China. This is presently classified as a wolf, *C. lupus variabilis*, but was previously called *C. chihliensis*. She argues that it could be wrongly classified, and may be a different species of *Canis* from which the modern dog descends.

This canine existed 200,000 to 500,000 years ago in large areas of China, where its remains have been found in layers of digs associated with our ancestor *Homo erectus* and *H. sapiens*. At Zhoukoudian, where Peking Man was found, *C. lupus variabilis* remains are four times more common that *C. lupus* remains, and Koler-Matznick points out they are in some ways more similar to dog than wolf skeletons: this diminutive canid probably weighed 13–20kg (29–67lb), roughly what a dingo weighs, and had a more slender muzzle than a wolf and more dog-like jaw bones. She argues that rather than

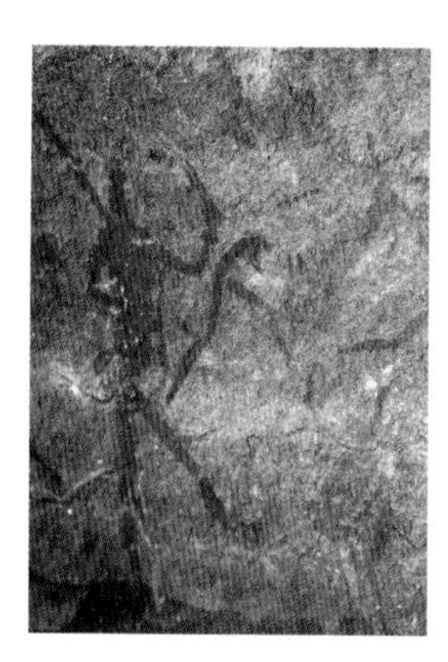

Hunting companion By the time cave paintings that show dogs assisting with hunting were made, the dog had been domesticated for tens of thousands of years.

hunting wolves shrinking and developing smaller and more crowded teeth to become scavengers, there was already a small canine scavenger with compact teeth. Koler-Matznick concludes that my pup Bean is "descended from a species of medium-sized generalist canid, a 'wild *Canis familiaris*,' that voluntarily adopted the pariah niche and remained commensal for an extensive period before some populations became truly domesticated."

Dogs emerge

I've read in many books that the first domesticated dogs were used in the hunt, but the more I think about that, the more impossible it becomes. Our ancestors had to sneak up on prey and spear it or club it. All a primitive dog would do is chase it away. Even today, Australian Aboriginal people prevent their dingoes from accompanying them when they hunt kangaroo, although they use them like terriers to locate prey that has gone to ground. I'm an adequate dog trainer and I've made life easy by living with Golden Retrievers – just about the easiest of breeds to train – but when my dogs see rabbits or squirrels it can be touch-and-go whether I can keep control. Can you imagine a wolf seeing prey to chase 15,000 years ago?

In *Dogs: A startling new understanding of canine origin, behavior and evolution*, Raymond and Lorna Coppinger argue, correctly I feel, that it's illogical to assume that Palaeolithic or early Neolithic people actively domesticated the wolf and created the dog. They explain how time-consuming this would be, how many wolves would be needed, and how much milk-feeding of wolf pups would be required. I like their conclusion, because it's so similar to one I reached with considerably less evidence almost 20 years ago.

The earliest shift from wolf to dog was not a physical change, identifiable from fossils or bones, but a hormonal one. The hypothalamus in the brain controls hormonal and emotional responses, and a change here triggers a cascade of effects, such as a reduction in the "fight or flight" response, an amelioration of fear. Swedish geneticists have found that while most of the expression pattern of genes in brains of dogs, wolves, and coyotes are similar, the pattern in the dog's hypothalamus is different. At the genetic level, this is at the root of what differentiates a dog's behaviour from a wolf's. A spontaneous shift in a gene affecting this part of the brain in an ancient wolf (or similar canine species) is all that was needed for one family to willingly live closer to humans: almost certainly, the dog's ancestors domesticated themselves.

When human campsites developed near canine families, these ancestors stayed rather than fleeing in fear, occupying this new ecological niche. They scavenged for food, bred, and produced descendants that did the same. These were the first proto-dogs, and their new living conditions led to a release from breeding constraints, allowing new mutations to flourish. Their small populations meant that those mutations accumulated faster, a trend called "genetic drift". This accelerated accumulation of mutations eventually changed their size and shape, producing the first true dogs we can identify from archaeological digs by their bone structure. The first dogs were all roughly similar, with smaller and more crowded teeth and narrower muzzles than wolves. The sinuses in the skull are larger, so dogs look brainer than wolves, but (don't let your dog know) the cavity in the skull for the brain is about one-third smaller. That doesn't mean your dog is less intelligent than a wolf – just different. Domestication reduced the need for some "learning centres", to do with territory and pack order, while putting new demands on others, to do with living and working with us, inhibiting predatory aggression towards our livestock, and understanding what we said with our voices or signalled with no more than a nod or a look in the eye. This is when the dog's destiny became wholly interwoven with our needs and whims.

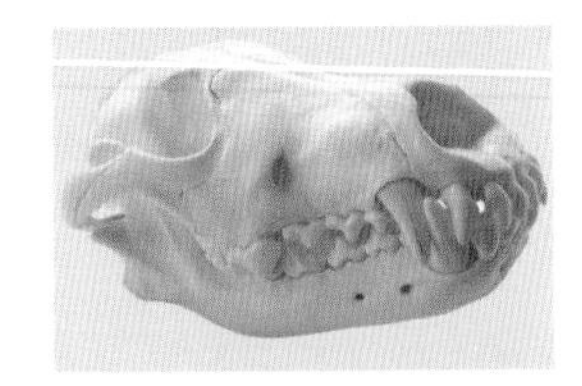

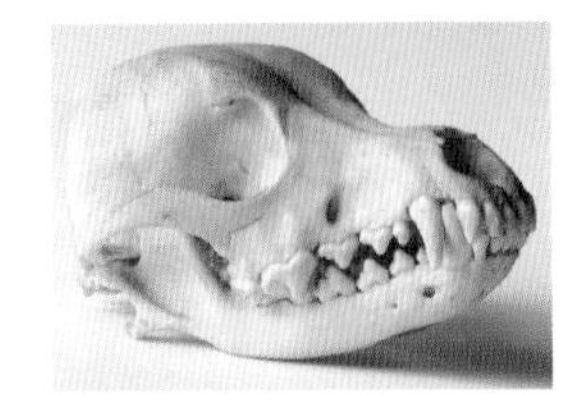

Bred in the bone Wolf and dog skulls are essentially similar but differ in the details. The narrower muzzle of the scavenging dog's skull (bottom) accomodates fewer and smaller teeth than that of the predator wolf (top).

I first became interested in the brain's hardwired "learning centres" when I read Stephen Pinker's *The Language Instinct*. If we're born with a hardwired brain circuitry to learn to speak, then it should be possible to calculate what learning centres dogs have in their brains, that we could modify or influence, but never add to or subtract from, by observing what they do. A dog knows what should and should not be eaten; naturally chases anything that moves quickly; knows how to choose where to live; understands danger and how to be cautious; understands the behaviour of other animals and can predict their actions from it; can mentally map large territories; intuitively patrols, investigates, and marks territory; understands motion, forces, and mechanics; understands the value of both kinship and dominance relationships, and bonds to its family early in life; intuitively needs to mate, knows the time to mate, and understands differences in sexual attraction.

Your dog's ability to think and to communicate with you is based on these discrete abilities. All dogs inherit hard-wired modules for each of these specific types of behaviour, but some behaviours are more efficiently wired than others in different types of dog, as a consequence of our ancestors preferring the looks or abilities of certain dogs and making sure that these dogs were allowed to breed.

Temperament influences appearance

For us, the most important difference between dogs and wolves is that the period during which pups learn to socialize lasts over four times longer in dogs than it does in wolves. Of course, modern dogs also look very different from wolves. They have unique coat lengths and textures, and colours such as fawn and piebald. They can have floppy ears and curly tails. Most have two fertility cycles each year, rather than the one that wolves have (although dogs do range from Basenjis with one yearly cycle to New Guinea Singing Dogs with up to four). It is tempting to think that our ancestors bred for all these changes, but surprisingly, the physical changes may have developed as an accidental side effect of selecting for that all-important extended infancy.

In the late 1940s, Russian geneticist Dimitri Belyaev embarked upon an experiment that should have made life easier for the fox farmers who produced pelts for the fur market. Adult foxes are vicious, and he was convinced that they could be made less so through breeding. Belyaev's discoveries did help farmers, but they have also helped to explain why my dog looks and behaves so dramatically different to any wolf.

Fast forward Belyaev's work created tame foxes within a single human lifespan. His experiments were much more intensive than early breeding of proto-dogs would have been, but they showed just how powerful selecting for a single trait can be.

Belyaev worked with individuals descended from foxes that had been bred in captivity for over 50 years. He offered cubs food while attempting to pet or handle them, continuing until they were physically mature, then classified them into three categories. Class I foxes actively approached him and allowed themselves to be handled, Class II foxes didn't approach people but allowed themselves to be touched, and Class III foxes remained fearful of people and didn't allow themselves to be touched. Belyaev bred from Class I foxes and repeated the process. Within six generations he had to create a Class IE, with the E standing for élite. These foxes not only approached people and allowed themselves to be petted, they actively sought out humans. They wagged their tails. They licked their people! After breeding these élite foxes for only 12 more generations, over one-third of all cubs born to them developed into élite adults. Within a few more years, three-quarters of Soviet farmed foxes were élites.

The experimenters carried out extensive measurements. They found that the skulls of élite foxes were shallower and narrower than unmodified foxes, while their muzzles were shorter and wider. The pituitary and adrenal glands were smaller in the élite foxes, and their levels of blood cortisol, an indicator of stress, were lower. Lyudmila Trut, who carried on Belyaev's studies, noted that the brains of domesticated foxes had a higher level of serotonin, related to a feeling of well-being.

These measurements were interesting, but even more fascinating was what spontaneously happened to the looks of the domesticated foxes. Some had mottled brown coats, while others were born piebald, or with blue eyes, or floppy ears, or curly tails. The researchers didn't breed for these characteristics – they were simply by-products of selecting for tameness, willingness to be handled, and an inclination to seek out human contact. They are strikingly similar to the changes that differentiate the dog from its wolf or wolf-like ancestor, and show that these changes can occur in a surprisingly short time.

Belyaev's domesticated fox cubs were different in other ways too. Their eyes opened sooner, and they responded to sounds earlier than the controls. They didn't develop fearful responses to unknown stimuli until weeks after the control cubs did, creating a larger window of opportunity to build social bonds. They started to bark, and continued doing so as adults. In many ways these foxes were lifelong cubs, perpetuating into adulthood a variety of physical and behavioural traits normally restricted to early life.

The same applies to dogs compared with wolves. Young wolves have floppy ears, but they inevitably become erect in adulthood. Wolf pups bark, but adults rarely do. Wolf pups carry their tails over their backs, but adults carry their tails horizontal. At first just by accident but later with intent, just like Belyaev, we prolonged not only the behaviour but the looks of youth into our adult dogs.

Dogs in our lives and languages

As people moved around the world, so too did dogs, first from Asia into Europe, but also to Africa and the Americas. Throughout the world, many of the words we use for "dog" have common roots in ancient languages,

URBAN FOXES

Today, city dwellers in Europe are well aware of the dramatic change in the lifestyle of foxes. In just three decades, a secretive, nocturnal, and rural animal became a confident, daytime, urban hunter, its diet changing from rural rodents to urban junk food, augmented by dew worms from manicured lawns. I live in the heart of the city, and more than once I've seen a fox contentedly sleeping on my garden table at high noon. When a garden fox sees me it does no more than look, sauntering off only when I open the door. Without the intervention of a Belyaev, the fox has successfully adapted to living in a densely populated human environment. Its "flight distance" when approached by something unfamiliar has suddenly diminished. This is what happened to dogs too: a reduction in fear, a willingness to live near humans, allowed the dog's ancestors to move into the new ecological niche created by human families. It's as simple as that. We didn't tame the wolf. The dog's ancestors chose to live in close proximity to us. They tamed themselves.

City slicker The urban fox, like the dog, is an evolutionary success story in Europe.

Island dogs Populations in islands – human or animal – can become isolated, frozen examples of their original founder populations. The genetics of the feral dogs of Bali tell us that they have developed in isolation for some 12,000 years, since dogs first arrived in the island.

from the ancient Chinese *k'iuon*, ancient Japanese *ken* to Indo-European *kuon*, ancient Greek *kun*, and the Latin *canis* and its variant *kani*. In some Asian languages, the Indo-European *kuon* became *shuon*, producing the Sanskrit *shvan* and Armenian *shun*. In the Germanic languages, it became *huon*, producing the German and Scandinavian *hund*, Dutch *hond* and English hound. The English word dog is an anomaly that might derive from the Old English *docga*, meaning a powerful type of dog.

Dogs spread around the world

Remains of early dogs are found throughout Eurasia. The oldest are two skeletons probably 14,800 years old found at Eliseyevichi, a very late Paleolithic settlement in Russia. They belonged to dogs the size of wolves, but with shorter and wider muzzles. Everywhere else, the oldest dog bones come from smaller, dingo-sized animals, and I'd like to see the wolf or dog identity of these Eliseyevichi bones confirmed by mtDNA analysis. The oldest evidence of a dog kept as a companion is a 14,000-year-old jawbone interred with a human at Bonn-Oberkassel in Germany.

By the Neolithic, beginning around 12,000 years ago in the Middle East and slightly later in Europe, dogs were an integral part of human culture. A Neolithic rock painting from Iraq shows people accompanied by dogs with curled tails hunting deer, while one from Algeria shows a man holding a spear and dogs with curled tails surrounding an ox-like animal. Remains interred during the next four thousand years turn up from Britain, Bedburg-Koningshoven in Germany, St Thibaud in the French Alps, the Russian Kamchatka peninsula, and northern China. In Israel, at a burial site at

Ein Mallaha dating back 12,000 years, a woman was buried with her arm around a young dog about the same age as my pup Bean, the oldest and most touching evidence that our ancestors could form emotional bonds with dogs. Further east, DNA evidence shows that modern Korean dogs such as the Jindo genetically resemble Siberian dogs; they arrived from northern East Asia, and moved on to Japan at least 8,500 years ago, where they became today's Akitas and Shibas. From the Malay peninsula dogs spread throughout the nearby islands, on to Australia, reaching the islands of the South Pacific, including New Zealand, only a few hundred years ago with Polynesian seafarers. The feral dogs of Bali are most closely related to the Australian dingo and the Chinese Chow Chow; they remain genetically distinct from European dogs.

God of the underworld
Anubis had the head of a jackal, not a dog, but ancient Egyptians do seem to have identified dogs with him. Dogs were buried in the Anubieion catacombs at Saqqara. The names of Egyptian dogs ranged from descriptions of their colour like "Blackie" or "Ebony" to qualities like "Brave One", "Reliable", and in one unfortunate (or perhaps humorous) case, "Useless".

The history of dogs in the Americas began some 12,000 years ago. Human mtDNA analysis indicates that this was the time of a human migration from eastern Siberia to North America; mtDNA studies of ancient American dog bones show that dogs, invited or uninvited, tagged along. The oldest American dog remains, around 10,000 years old, were found in Danger Cave, Utah. By the time Europeans arrived, most Indian dogs across North America were the size of dingoes, with one notable exception. On the northwest Pacific Coast there were also smaller "wool dogs", whose long hair was used to make blankets. Genetically speaking, long hair is recessive: only matings of two longhaired dogs guarantee longhaired pups, so the owners of wool dogs must have controlled their breeding. When brightly striped Hudson's Bay blankets became available in the early 1800s, the economic value of the wool dog was lost, and by 1858 America's first homegrown breed was extinct.

Considerable archaeological and pictographic evidence indicates that dogs moved from Asia through Egypt into Africa, with dogs similar to the Basenji present in Egypt almost 7,000 years ago, and dogs resembling the modern Pharoah Hound developing in the Dynastic era that began about 5,000 years ago. DNA evidence shows these dogs spread through regions north of the Sahara to produce the Sloughi and the livestock-guarding Aidi in Morocco. The indigenous breeds of Portugal are not genetically close to dogs from Morocco, Tunisia, and Algeria, so while the Moors introduced a variety of livestock from North Africa to the Iberian peninsula, there's no genetic evidence that they brought their dogs with them. Dogs spread rapidly along the Nile into the Sudan and eventually arrived in southern Africa with early Iron Age migrations along the Great Rift Valley and corridors through Zambia and Zimbabwe. The earliest dog remains in South Africa are dated to 570 AD; modern European breeds have now ousted indigenous African dogs, but some descendants are still found in areas where people maintain traditional lifestyles.

During these migrations, the pressures to survive in different climates and the effects of our selectively breeding for specific abilities produced dogs to suit both new places and new tasks. This is the basis for the enormous variety of dogs that exist today. From the beginning of their relationship with us, dogs served ever-changing and ever-increasing roles

Close companions Dogs have been essential to the Inuit. They traditionally roamed free, which the Inuit claimed was vital to their socialization, but civic authorites saw as a rabies risk. Protesting against culling of the dogs, one Salluit witness said "They were our only means of transportation, I don't think anyone would have survived without the use of dog teams. They were used for long-distance travel and hunting. Even when the Inuit were starving, we used to survive by eating our dogs".

and functions. In some circumstances, perhaps even in the very first Neolithic livestock-raising communities, dogs played a crucial role, and human history would not be what it is without the dog.

Man's best meal

You won't like this. According to an article in the Korean Journal of Food and Nutrition, 100g (3½oz) of young, farm-raised dog contains roughly 260 kcal, 60g (2oz) of moisture, 20g (¾oz) each of protein and fat, and reasonable quantities of B vitamins, a lesser amount of vitamin C, but no vitamin A. It's high in iron and phosphorus but low in calcium. Dog people don't like talking about eating dogs, because it seems almost cannibalistic, but even the DNA of the human tapeworm *Taenia solium* indicates that we acquired it by eating dogs. The dog's first role was to fill people's bellies. When we began to raise more energy-efficient herbivores, dogs became more of an emergency food supply, widely eaten in Europe during times of famine, by the Inuit when starving, and recently during the Russian Revolution and the two world wars.

Elsewhere, dogs were bred for their meat, fed on cooked taro root by the Polynesians or maize by the Aztecs. Hernando Cortes wrote in 1519 that "small gelded dogs which they breed for eating" were sold in the marketplace of Tenochtitlan. Chinese texts from 3,000 years ago list dogs as one of the "three beasts" kept for food, along with pigs and goats, and dogs are still eaten throughout southeast Asia. In the Philippines, eating dog meat started as a protective religious practice, a tradition also found in the Dog Feast among the indigenous people of North America. In China, where dog meat is sometimes euphemistically called "fragrant meat", eating it is a social display of wealth. Dog is said to increased positive *yang* energy, regulate circulation, and keep you warm. Korea remains the world's epicentre of eating dogs, with two to three million consumed each year, and for some Koreans it is a symbol of nationalism. But when I visited Seoul before the Olympics in 1988, dog restaurants in the city centre had been closed, and hotel staff and taxi drivers had been instructed not to take Westerners to those in the suburbs. My personal light on the horizon is that Korean editions of my books sell really, really well, although it will take a generation or more before younger Koreans gain influence and the number of dogs eaten starts to decline.

Dogs clean up

You're not going to like this one either. One day I took Bean out of our usual parks to a new location criss-crossed with bridle paths. On seeing horse manure for the first time, she picked some up and ran back to me to say "You have no idea how big the rabbits are around here!" Then, in a flash, it was gone. Down her gullet.

Dogs eat poop. It's wired into their brain circuitry. In some the instinct is firmer than in others; Bean's breeder warned us when we picked her up at eight weeks of age that she was a poop eater, the only one in the litter. This is another subject that books seem to shy away from, but I suspect that the dog's natural inclination to eat faeces is one of the reasons that our ancestors allowed them to hang around human settlements. Along with pigs, they were the local sanitation engineers, vacuuming up human waste. Parasitologist Christopher Barnard says that amongst the livestock-raising Turkana people of Kenya, mothers of newborn babies traditionally used a puppy as a living baby wipe, and anthropologists mention the trait almost in passing, as a natural assumption that this is what dogs do. Once our ancestors had settled permanently and began to store food, dogs also controlled vermin such as mice and rats that were attracted to the stores. Only much later, when the North African wildcat evolved into the domesticated cat, did the dog come to share its vermin-killing role.

Hunters and guardians

The first dogs passively helped people in other ways too, which we think of as their traditional roles today. Dogs readily and intuitively follow the scent trails of animals, but that doesn't mean that they helped us hunt at first.

Reliable ratters When early dogs killed small scavengers around human settlements, they fed themselves and helped our ancestors. This mututally beneficial relationship lasts to the present day.

Skilled worker The earliest livestock dogs were really just burly herd guardians. Later breeding saw the development of highly skilled collies that will gather, drive, and pen sheep. The "programming" that allows this sophisticated repurposing of their instincts is so strong that, if deprived of a job, these dogs may herd other dogs – or people – in open spaces.

That took much more breeding and training on our part. But dogs would have led us to animal dens, and probably to sources of water and through difficult terrain to where herbivores seasonally moved. They certainly helped us to find meat and survive.

One of the youthful characteristics that's perpetuated into adulthood in dogs is barking. Adult wolves seldom bark, but even an unowned, untrained feral dog naturally barks to guard its own territory and protect its own litter. If it shares its territory with people, its bark protects them too, so dogs naturally came to guard our homes.

Making them guardians of our livestock needed more intervention, but once achieved, the ability is impressive. A one-time classmate of mine ranched sheep in British Columbia, and to guard them imported two Komondor pups. They were raised from infancy with sheep, lived with them, were even shorn with them. He told me he was the only rancher in his valley not laying down poisoned bait to kill coyotes, and he hadn't lost a single head of stock. Virtually all guardian dogs are larger than dog-average and they probably evolved in Central Asia, coming west with Xerxes and Alexander the Great, and passing on through Europe with the Phoenicians. White, longer-muzzled dogs remained classical livestock guardians, while darker, heavier dogs were developed into fighting dogs and warrior dogs through selective breeding for massive size, ferocity, and obedience.

Warning sign This mosaic from Pompeii is one of many Roman examples that were laid in entrances. They usually showed a tied dog and sometimes included the words *"Cave canem"* or "Beware of the dog" to make the message crystal clear.

Dog fighting has existed as a "sport" for as long as we've lived with dogs. The Roman army used military dogs, the British-bred *Pugnaces Britanniae*, and when these dogs were not serving in wars they were used in dog fights. Although now technically illegal in most countries, dog fights are still widely organized around the world, even in Muslim countries. As in Europe and North America, young men primarily use Pit Bull Terriers and Rottweilers. In the Middle East the fighting dogs are caged, starved, and abused before they're used in fights. Someone who is familiar with dog fights in Oman tells me their wounds are seldom treated, and dogs that lose are brutally killed or left to starve to death in cages.

More positively, do you know the question dog trainers are most frequently asked? "How do I stop my dog from pulling on the lead?" No one knows for sure when we harnessed the pulling power of dogs, but Inuit folk history says it happened over 2,000 years ago, and the sled dog remained vital to their survival until well into the 20th century. Farther south, Native Americans on the Great Plains of Canada and the United States used dogs to pull their travois, or triangular sleds, while in Europe dogs also pulled carts, notably in Switzerland and Belgium. Big dogs have helped us travel or carried our loads for at least a thousand years, and they do so instinctively. That function has only disappeared in my lifetime.

Constantly companions

Many commentators believe it's a modern interpretation to claim that companionship was an early role for dogs. They say that it could only develop in a resource-rich environment, where there's surplus time to invest in emotional bonds. Balderdash! The hard-wired instincts of our ancestors were no different from ours, and nurturing is one of them. Virtually every single culture that anthropologists have ever studied keeps pets, and dogs are the preferred species when they're available.

In *Studies in Animal and Human Behaviour*, Konrad Lorenz said that juvenile features – such as a large head, large eyes, or clumsy movements – automatically trigger affection and nurturing in us. The adaptive value of this response is self-evident if we're to be successful raising our own young, but a young pup is also just about as cartoon babyish as you get. And we selected dogs to retain throughout life both physical and mental characteristics of youth – as we do ourselves. Over time, the dog became, as the cliché so aptly says, our best friend. You may not think so, but even your pet dog's got a job. It is social and psychological rather than functional and utilitarian, but that doesn't make it any less important or valuable.

Religious attitudes to dogs

Religious beliefs have profoundly affected how different peoples around the world live with dogs, and even whether they live with them. Most pet dogs today live in regions of the world where Christianity, Islam, Hinduism, and Buddhism dominate.

The dog has its day The Hindu festival of Kukur-tihar applies to all dogs, even those that work for bodies such as the army and police. It's just possible that the offerings of special foods impress them more than the marigold garlands do.

Christianity developed from Judaism, and the Jewish Old Testament is explicit that animals are part of God's creation and should be treated with compassion. It also gives clues about how dogs in the eastern Mediterranean behaved and were treated several thousand years ago. They are beaten with sticks in Samuel, and mentioned as urban scavengers in Kings and Psalms and as sheepdogs in Job. The Jewish Talmud, a collection of interpretations of the bible, mentions the dog just once, combined with an injunction on health and safety: "Breed not a savage dog, nor permit a loose stairway." The New Testament includes the dog just twice. One mention is in a parable, where the poor man at the gate "longed to be filled with what fell from the rich man's table, but instead the dogs would come and lick his sores." The other is from a Gentile woman, who persuades Jesus to heal her daughter even though she is not one of the children of Israel by saying that "even the dogs under the table eat the children's crumbs." Historical attitudes have, of course, modified over time: dogs have been integral in Christian households for millennia, while the companion dog in the Jewish home has become commonplace within the last few hundred years.

Islam has a more problematical relationship with dogs. The Qur'an says that all animals are made by Allah, that Allah loves all animals, and that they should be treated with kindness and compassion. Dogs are mentioned only five times, with no mention of them being dirty. But in the hadith, recorded oral traditions of Muhammad's actions, the dog has become dirty. Sometimes interpretation is problematic: one hadith states that if a dog drinks from your vessel, you must wash it seven times. Where saliva-borne rabies was endemic, this made perfect sense, but draconian interpretation has made it a need for ritual cleansing if you are touched by dog saliva. The commentator Abu Hurayra appears to have simply been a "cat person" rather than a "dog person". One fundamentalist British-based website issues

Year of the dog Chinese astrology attributes animal qualities to humans, a neat reversal of our tendency to anthropomorphize animals. So dogs are trustworthy and loyal, but unlike most real dogs are said to be compatible with rats and rabbits.

believers with instructions such as "Do not allow a dog in your house as a pet or for any other non-necessary reason", but religious scholars such as Qudrat Ullah Shebah in Pakistan have argued that pet dogs are perfectly acceptable within the tenets of Islam. Many Muslims (including some of my clients) are perfectly comfortable keeping pet dogs.

Chapter 13 of the Vendidad, part of the sacred texts of Zoroastrianism, is devoted to the dog. It says "A dog has the characters of eight sorts of people" and explains he's like a priest because he's patient and easily satisfied, like a warrior because he fights for the benefit of the cow, like a husbandman because he's first out of the house in the morning and last in at night. The analogies continue, and to me they reflect an excellent understanding of dog behaviour. A colleague in Mumbai put me in touch with Zoroastrian scholar Khojeste P. Mistree, who told me that even today at a traditional Zoroastrian funeral ceremony, a dog is brought into the room to view the corpse and accompany the soul of the deceased to judgment.

In Hinduism, dogs are said to protect homes and their inhabitants, and religious belief says that the dog is a messenger of Lord Yamaraj, the god of death, and dogs guard the doors of Heaven. In Nepal, the 14th day of the lunar cycle in November is Kukur-tihar, the dog's day, when dogs are garlanded with marigolds and offered special food, incense is burned, and a vermilion dot is applied to the dog's forehead.

The dog is one of the 12 animals featured in Chinese astrology, and those born in the Year of the Dog are, like the dog, faithful, courageous, clever, and warm hearted. The second day of the Chinese New Year is considered to be the birthday of all dogs, and the dog is an auspicious animal, a friend who understands the human spirit and obeys its master regardless of status. Chinese tradition says that if a dog comes to your house, you should adopt it, for it symbolizes the coming of fortune (or a meal on legs, of course).

In other religions throughout the world, dogs are often the companions of the dead, gatekeepers or guardians of the underworld, or intercessors with the gods. Three-headed Cerberus guards the entrance to Hades in Greek myth, the dog Garm heralded the end of the world in Scandinavian lore, and in the Americas the dog-headed Aztec god Xolotl led the sun through the nocturnal underworld until it was reborn with the dawn, while Mayan dogs carried human souls across the river of death. But in the Zoroastrian creation story, the dog is seen as the collaborator of Srosh, God's vice-regent on earth. And one Native American saying I like, be it genuine or the product of a modern mind, says "God made the earth, the sky and the water, the moon and the sun. He made man and bird and beast. But He didn't make the dog. He already had one."

The humble dog Alongside religious or symbolic images, art from ancient Egypt to the Mughal court or European medieval manuscripts show the dog as a part of everyday life. At the heel or beneath a chair, the dog is a small but essential part of the bigger picture.

CHAPTER TWO

How Dogs are Classified

Selecting for practical uses produced dogs with distinctive looks and behaviours. Some dogs are easier to obedience train than others, or naturally aggressive, or more fearful. Knowing these traits helps to ensure that living with a dog is as productive and as satisfying for you, your family, and your dog as it should be, and classifications give clues to behaviour. Dogs have been classified and reclassified since Roman times, usually by function, although by the end of the 20th century looks became, for many people, the paramount value of the dog. Now, geneticists have reclassified breeds again, this time according to their genetic relationship to each other and their progenitor, the wolf.

Unique coat The Dalmation may be descended from an Indian pointer or truly originate in Dalmatia (Croatia). It was used to run beside carriages, making classification tricky. Today, it is known more by its instantly recognizable spotted pattern than any past purpose.

The Romans had three basic classes of dogs: watchdogs, sheepdogs, and hunting dogs. The hunting dogs were sub-divided into attackers, trackers, and chasers. By 1570, Dr. John Caius, personal physician to Queen Elizabeth in England, had a more refined classification of five categories: game hunters, fowl hunters, companions, farm dogs, and mongrels. Some of his categories were subdivided. His game hunters (*Venatici* in Latin or Dogges in English) consisted of "Harriers, Terrars, Bloodhounds, Gazehounds, Grehounds, Lyemmers, Tumblers and Stealers" while his fowl hunters (*Aucupatorii* in Latin) were "Setters and Spaniels". In the original Latin version of his book, he called the spaniel *canis aquaticus*, but when the English-language version of the book was published in 1576, he used the term spaniel. Caius' third group, the companion dogs, consisted of two types, the "Spaniell Gentle" and the "Comforter". His fourth group, farm dogs, also consisted of the "Shepherd's Dogge" (*canis pastoralis*) and "Mastive" or "Bandogge" (*canis villaticus*). His final Mongrel section contained three varieties, the "Wapp, Turnespet and Dauncer".

Modern breed clubs

Most dogs today are defined by their breed, and I should define what that means. A breed is a group of similar-looking dogs, only permitted to breed within that recognized, closed group, never with dogs from outside it. The notion of selectively breeding dogs and competing for the right to claim that your dog was the closest to a breed ideal developed in Britain in the latter part of the 19th century. Since then, it has been done sometimes for money, sometimes for prestige, and mostly just for the fun of it all. The idea was so appealing that the concept of breed clubs spread worldwide, and today there are almost 400 organizations that ensure the genetic integrity of their breed by licensing puppies only if breeders show documentary evidence that only recognized, documented parents were used. In some countries the majority of owned dogs are pedigree breeds. In North America, Europe, and Australasia, they are so prevalent that there's been a small reaction; a new market has developed for intentional crossbreeds, individuals with parents from different breeds.

In the United Kingdom, the Kennel Club (KC) was formed in 1873 and has been recognizing dog breeds and groupings ever since. The American Kennel Club (AKC) followed shortly after, working to the same model. Although these registries use slightly different names for their groups, both clubs have seven classifications.

Kennel Club	American Kennel Club
1 Toy	1 Toy
2 Terrier	2 Terrier
3 Working	3 Working
4 Hound	4 Hound
5 Pastoral	5 Herding
6 Gundog	6 Sporting
7 Utility	7 Non-sporting

These classifications were based on the dogs' function (Working, Pastoral, Gundog), size (Toy), and even on the social class that owned them. Although terriers varied enormously in size and assisted in hunting, herding, and working, they were the dogs of "the common man", the working classes, and so in class-divided Victorian Britain, they were given their own group. Some breeds, such as Poodles and Dalmatians, simply didn't conform to any of these groupings, so, on the basis of "I don't really know what this dog is for, so let's put it here" they were given their own classification: this is the group with the name "Utility" in the United Kingdom, and the curious and somewhat pejorative "Non-sporting" in the United States.

Working dogs Many of the breeds now recognized in the show ring are still kept and bred as working dogs, but the lines have often diverged. In some breeds the show dogs are predominantly dark in colour, while the working dogs have more white in their coats, making them easier for hunters to spot in the field.

By the 20th century, national kennel clubs had developed throughout Europe, Asia, Africa, and the Americas. While the KC and AKC concentrated on existing breeds in their own countries, other kennel clubs created new groups to accommodate their own national breeds. Eventually, clubs from Germany, Austria, France, Belgium, and the Netherlands formed an umbrella organization, the Fédération Cynologique Internationale (FCI), sometimes called the World Canine Organization. While the AKC recognizes just over 160 breeds, and the KC just over 200, the FCI recognizes around 340 breeds, greatly expanding the variety of dog types bred to conform to written standards. It now has over 80 member countries, and uses these 10 groups to accommodate both national pressures and increasing knowledge about dogs:

- Sheepdogs and cattle dogs (except Swiss cattle dogs)
- Pinschers, schnauzers, Molossoids, Swiss mountain and cattle dogs
- Terriers
- Dachshunds
- Spitzes and primitive types
- Scenthounds and related breeds
- Pointing dogs
- Retrievers, flushing dogs and water dogs
- Companion and toy dogs
- Sighthounds

In all these classifications however, there is one serious anomaly. They disregard Dr Caius's fifth classification of dogs: mongrels. Breeding dogs from within closed pools of individuals enhanced the social value of dogs, but it also created a cultural antipathy towards mongrels that we are only now successfully overcoming.

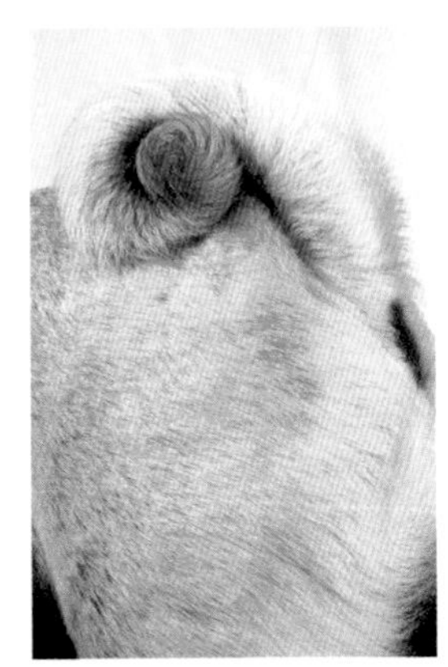

Extreme breed standards

One unpleasant quirk of breed standards is that it often was, and in some places still is, impossible for any member of particular breeds to meet them without surgery. Amputating tails, or docking, remains a common procedure in many breeds, even where it's explicitly against the law, as it is in most European countries. Breeders and lovers of a breed that's traditionally been docked will give many arguments for the procedure, and they're all spurious. People want tails docked simply because they like the look. It's no more complicated than that. Docking is usually done at a joint between two tail bones or vertebrae. The equivalent in humans would be making a depression in the skin on a newborn's baby finger then rotating it at one of the joints until you successfully removed the finger with minimal bleeding. Breeders are often much more adamant about tail docking than pet owners are. Once I docked tails if breeders asked me to, but I stopped over 30 years ago when I realized I was catering to human vanity, not the welfare of dogs. I have the same attitude to removing dewclaws, but this is in part because winters are mild where I live and snow is light. If a dog lives

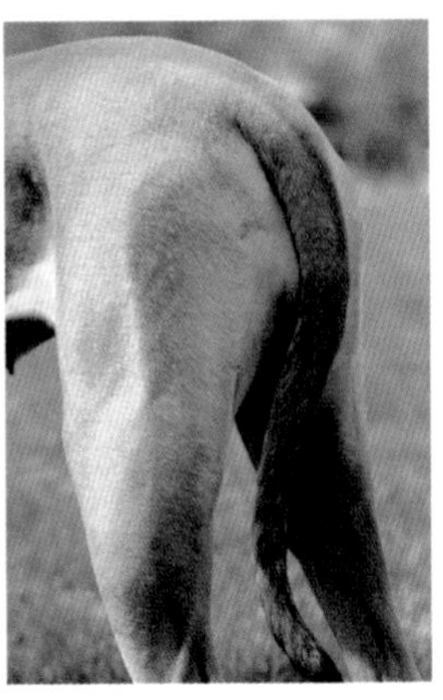

A tale of tails Upright tails – especially with a different colour to the tip, like the Beagle (top) were selected because they can easily be seen when a dog is hunting in vegetation. Some working spaniels historically had their tails docked, to prevent damage. This dog (second from top) conforms to the new ethical standards requiring a full tail. Left to their own devices, tails may be short and tightly curled as in the Pug and many "Nordic" breeds (third from top), or long and carried low as in many sighthounds and Great Danes (bottom). As it happens, I see more tail injuries in breeds with very long tails, usually from being caught in closing doors.

where dewclaw injuries from a paw going through ice-crusted snow are common, I don't have objections to dewclaw removal. As for amputating or cropping ears, this is by far the worst of the alterations we force defenceless dogs to endure. It's a grotesque mutilation, a wholly needless surgical procedure inflicted upon defenceless dogs because some people want them to look fiercer. Don't do it.

Unforeseen side effects

Restrictive breeding practices are needed to create a breed with specific looks, but they mean a loss of genetic diversity and increased genetic drift, the random increases in the frequency of certain genes. Dogs and humans have the same potential for genetic variation within their species, but the variation between dog breeds is far greater (over 27 per cent) than the variation found between distinct human populations (under 6 per cent). Conversely, genetic sameness (homogeneity) is greater *within* individual dog breeds (for example Weimaraners) than it is within isolated human populations (for example Icelanders). That sameness enhances genetic drift. Geneticists can also calculate the size of the gene pool for a particular population through a measurement called linkage disequilibrium (LD). By 2005 it was known that LD in dogs is 25–50 times greater than it is in

A GREAT GENETIC EXPERIMENT

Few breeders knew that over the last two centuries they unwittingly carried out one of the most far-reaching scientific trials ever. Dr Elaine Ostrander at the National Human Genome Research Institute, part of the National Institutes of Health in Bethesda, Maryland, says that it "represents perhaps one of the greatest genetic experiments ever conducted by humans."

Let me give you an example. What's your dog's tail like? Breed standards describe tails that are curled or double curled, gay (upright) or otter (straight back and flat), sickled (arching) or whipped, ringed or plumed, screwed or snapped. That's just tails. Ears come in equal variety, as do eyes. Within dog breeds there's an 80-fold variation in size, from tiny toys to magnificent mastiffs. That's a greater range not only than any other mammal species but also than the extremes of the entire wild Canidae family. Can you imagine the amount of trial and error that was needed to select for the genetic make-up that consistently produced specific sizes?

Dog breeds are genetically closed populations. Once established, there's no genetic variation (other than rare spontaneous change) beyond that which existed in the original founders. Early breeders may not have understood the concepts of "founder effects" and "bottlenecks" but they did recognize the potential of breeding from a small community of dogs that were all of a similar colour or had dwarfed legs, squashed-in faces, or a willingness to go down a hole in the ground to kill whatever they find. Breeds are created from founding animals, and the "founding events" of breeds developed in the last 200 years usually involved only a few dogs. For example, the Malcolm family in Scotland created the West Highland White Terrier by selectively breeding from only the lightest-coloured Cairn Terriers. Herr Dobermann created the dog named after him from a small selection of Rottweilers, Weimaraners, German pinschers, English Greyhounds, and Manchester Terriers. Bean, my Golden Retriever now lying spatchcocked on the sofa behind me, descends from liver-coloured Flat-coated Retrievers crossed with (now extinct) Tweed Spaniels, with a dash of Irish setter. Many breeds, including older ones, have experienced breeding "bottlenecks". For example, few Polish Lowland Sheepdogs survived World War II, but those that survived are the source of all Polish Lowland Sheepdogs alive today.

Ancient breed The Lhasa Apso has existed for thousands of years in Tibet, but only a small number of dogs have been brought out of the country. This small gene pool puts western Lhasas at a disadvantage to their cousins at home: any harmful genes are more likely to increase in frequency here.

humans, and particularly high in breeds developed recently from a small gene pool, such as the Japanese Akita and the Pekingese in the West.

From a health perspective, this can be dreadful. As genetic drift increases in small populations, the genes that increase in frequency include dangerous ones. Unfortunately, the very reason for the existence of most dog breed clubs is to encourage genetic drift, although that isn't the way breeders would see what they do. Show breeders selectively breed to conform as closely as possible to written standards. If a certain individual wins a dog show because she conforms best to breed standards, she may be bred to a close relative, perhaps a grandfather, and in many if not most countries even to her father. This encourages genetic drift towards the breed standards –

something that breeders want – but it also inevitably increases the risk of all those breed-specific diseases.

That's why some inherited medical conditions (such as hip dysplasia, heart disease, or skin allergies) occur at a greater frequency in some breeds than in others or than in mutts, and more in those breeds with the smallest gene pools, where genetic drift is greatest. There are valvular heart disease and hindbrain prolapse in Cavalier King Charles Spaniels, pulmonary fibrosis in West Highland White Terriers, allergic skin and bowel conditions in Golden Retrievers, a tendency to put on weight in Polish Lowland Sheepdogs, and dilated heart disease in Dobermanns, to name but a few.

The homogeneity within breeds makes it easier to find the genetic cause of a disease in a dog than to find the genetic cause of the same disease in a human. One by one, the genetic causes of highly specific diseases such as narcolepsy in Dobermanns, copper toxicosis in Bedlington terriers, and progressive myoclonic epilepsy in Miniature Wirehaired Dachshunds are being discovered. Initially, this leads to genetic testing of parents for known inherited diseases within the breed, but eventually, knowing the genetic cause of a medical condition should lead to a treatment. (For an up-to-date list of all known inherited health problems in dog breeds, you can visit www.vet.cam.ac.uk/idid.) But of all the conditions that dogs (and people) suffer from, cancers are the most frustrating. Dogs develop cancers at around twice the frequency we do, and as a result significant research money is now being invested in studying canine cancers. Once the genes that increase a dog's susceptibility to common canine cancers, such as lymphoma and osteosarcoma, are discovered, the key to unlocking prevention and treatment is available, for them and for us.

Closer than you think Dogs share at least three-quarters of their genes with humans – and with mice. A relatively small number of genes account for huge physical differences.

Modern genetic classification

There are 19,000 reported canine genes. Dogs share at least 14,200 of them with the human. The differences between your dog and you reside in the remaining genes, and breed differences are found in minute variations in microsatellite DNA. Microsatellites are repeated snippets of DNA with known locations on a chromosome, and their sequences are shared among closely related individuals. Just as the greatest diversity in human genes exists in Africa, where our ancestors evolved, the greatest diversity in canine

GENETIC TRAITS REVEAL PARENTAGE

The anti-parasite drug ivermectin is safe and effective for most breeds but if injected may kill others, Collies in particular, due to a mutation in a gene called multidrug resistence gene 1 or MDR1. One in three Collies carries it, as do smaller numbers in related breeds, such as Shetland Sheepdogs, Australian Shepherds, and Old English Sheepdogs. Because the last breed existed in 1873 when the British Kennel Club was formed, it's safe to say that the mutation occurred in a British collie-type dog some time before 1873. The mutation is also found in three new breeds: the McNab, Longhaired Whippet, and Silken Windhound. Although Collies are not in the official ancestry of these new breeds, the kennels where the Longhaired Whippet was "restored" in the 1950s also kept Shetland Sheepdogs, and the Silken Windhound has Longhaired Whippet in its ancestry. The frequency of the MDR1 mutation can be expected in increase in these breeds.

genes exists in Asia, where dogs evolved. Recent research explored this diversity by studying microsatellite DNA of 85 dog breeds, plus wolves. It revealed four different breed clusters, considerably different from the KC and AKC groupings, but not from FCI groupings.

The oldest and genetically most diverse group contains 14 breeds, all either dogs of Asian origin, sled dogs, or known ancient hounds. It includes the Japanese Akita and Shiba Inu, the Chinese Shar-pei, Chow Chow, and Pekingese, the Siberian Husky, the Samoyed, and the Alaskan Malamute, the Afghan Hound and the Saluki, the Tibetan Terrier, Lhasa Apso, and Shih Tzu, and the African Basenji. Grey wolves from eight countries also fell into this first cluster; in other words, these are the wolf's closest canine relatives.

The next cluster consisted of mastiff-type or Molosser dogs. This group includes the Mastiff, Bull Mastiff, Bulldog, Boxer, Miniature Bull Terrier, French Bulldog, Rottweiler, Presa Canario, Newfoundland, and (rather unexpectedly) the German Shepherd Dog.

The third cluster includes working dogs such as the Collie, Shetland Sheepdog, Belgian Sheepdogs, and a subset of sighthounds including the Greyhound, Borzoi, and Irish wolfhound.

The fourth and final cluster contains the breeds most distant from the wolf, all European in origin. It is the largest group, and genetically the least diverse. It includes many gundogs – Labrador, Flat-coated, Chesapeake Bay, and Golden Retrievers, Springer, American Water, English and American Cocker, Cavalier King Charles, and Clumber Spaniels, the Irish Setter, and Pointers – and two scent hounds, the Basset Hound and Bloodhound. Terriers are represented by the Manchester, Australian, West Highland White, American Hairless, Airedale, Cairn, Bedlington, Kerry Blue, Soft-coated Wheaten, and Irish Terriers. Other more eclectic members are the Saint Bernard, Pomeranian, Pug, Komondor, Kuvasz, Beagle, Keeshond, Norwegian Elkhound, Standard Poodle, Bichon Frise, Dachshund, Doberman, Schnauzer, Great Dane, and Schipperke.

Unexpected relationships

There were surprises here – for example, that sighthounds such as the Greyhound and Borzoi are genetically closer to herding dogs than to hunting dogs, and that breeds regarded as ancient, like the Egyptian Pharaoh Hound, the Spanish Ibizan Hound, and the Norwegian Elkhound are, genetically speaking, not primitive breeds at all but recent recreations of ancient types. It may be that the modern Pharaoh Hound and Ibizan Hound are true descendents, but repeated accidental or intentional crosses with local European dogs have reduced the original elements that maintained their looks. This could be why Asian breeds close to Europe, like the Saluki and Samoyed, are "more European", while geographically remote breeds, like the Siberian Husky, retain their original wolf DNA. Only 85 breeds were examined in this study. I expect that many more Nordic and Asian breeds. such as the Greenland Husky and Canadian Eskimo Dog, will fall into the primitive category. I expect too that the Indian Pariah Dog, Dingo, and New Guinea Singing Dog will fall into this first category. Other breeds, including

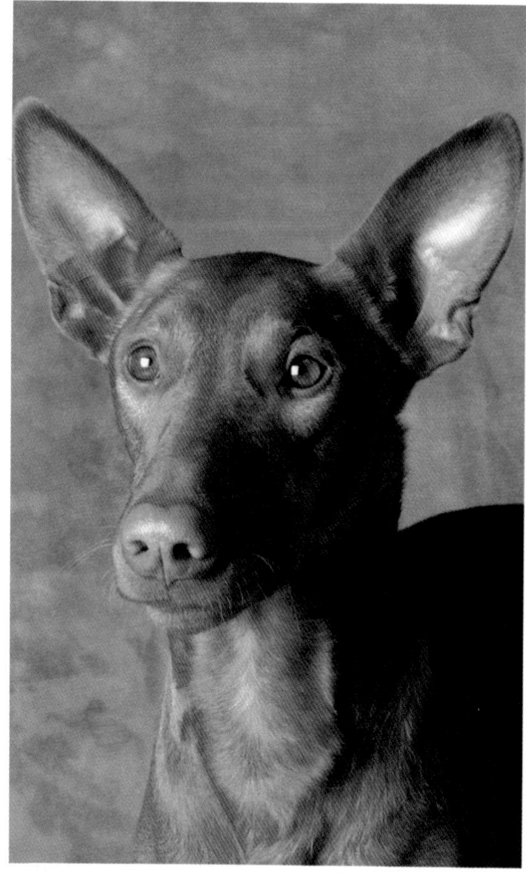

Looks aren't everything
Although the Pharaoh Hound resembles ancient Egyptian wall paintings of dogs, its genes show it to be a modern recreation. It is also claimed as the rabbit-hunting Kelb tal-Fenek on Malta, without any pretensions to ancient lineage.

the Canaan Dog and the various Scandinavian spitzes and Russian laikas, may also be truly primitive.

Continuing genetic research is also revealing which breeds are most closely related to each other. For example, DNA studies show that the Caucasian Shepherd, the Central Asian Shepherd, the North Caucasian Volkodav, and the Turkish Akbash and Kangal dogs are all a single group, with a gene contribution from Scandinavian dogs. Other genetic studies show differences within breeds. These results are useful when classifying breeds into groups, and I'll use this information in the next chapter, when I look at some pragmatic groupings of dogs.

Classification by lifestyle

Leave it to me and I'd put all dogs into three classes: ferals, strays (and their close associates, latchkeys), and owned dogs. You're probably most familiar with the last category. These are your dogs, those I see each day at work, dogs that live as honorary members of human families. These are the dogs I'm going to devote most of the rest of this book to, but they are a minority of the world's 400 million dogs. Many dogs are strays, but the largest category of dogs are ferals, dogs that survive by luck, intelligence, and wit, almost always in close proximity to us. Just as our use once defined dogs, these lifestyles can affect their behaviour.

Feral dogs

Throughout the world there are hundreds of millions of feral dogs perpetuating their lines without our intervention. They live as beach dogs in Mexico and Thailand, wadi dogs in the Middle East, village dogs in Africa, but most commonly as urban street dogs on all continents except Antarctica, surviving by scavenging. They are sometimes direct descendents of ancient dog types: the Australian Dingo and the New Guinea Singing Dog are both classic feral dogs. They can also be the desendants of modern dogs – strays, latchkey dogs, or dogs intentionally abandoned by their owners – that have learned to survive by their wits. The feral dog population of Romania increased massively in the early 1990s when pet dogs, often purebreds, were abandoned for economic reasons, and the survivors added their genes to the existing feral population.

In 2008 I helped fact-check *The Dogs of South Central*, a film about the feral dogs of South Central Los Angeles. These dogs are descendants of pet dogs. They look like crosses between American Pit Bull Terriers, Labradors, Rottweilers, and American Staffordshire Bull Terriers, with perhaps a dash of German Shepherd Dog and Akita. Los Angeles has thousands of stray and feral dogs. As with strays and ferals worldwide, a few are treated with a degree of kindness, given scraps of food and allowed to rest on private property, often in dens under wooden homes. Most are at best disregarded or, more commonly, treated as pests, and I'm sure you know that some stray and feral dogs are treated with the most malign barbarity.

Latin America has almost 70 million ferals, as many unwanted dogs as the entire owned pet dog population of the United States; in Mexico City alone there are a million ferals and strays roaming the barrios and boulevards. The city's municipal pounds kill a quarter of a million each year, and countless more die in road traffic accidents, but these losses don't even dent the population. Wherever they live, feral dogs are extraordinarily resilient. On Thailand's resort island of Phuket, most of the street dogs disappeared after the 2004 Boxing Day tsunami, but in less than a year their numbers returned to pre-tsunami levels. For the foreseeable future, the world's feral dog population will remain stable. I don't see that as wholly unfortunate. These dogs form a genetic bank that we'll be able to draw on in the future,

ISRAEL'S PARIAH BREED

Dr. Rudolphina Menzel began observing the feral dogs of the Negev Desert of Palestine in the 1930s. She classified the dogs as either heavy, sheepdog-like, dingo-like, collie-like, or greyhound-like, and selectively bred from chosen individuals to create the Canaan Dog, now recognized in the United States.

The entire breed is descended from the small gene pool of her breeding programme, with predictable consequences. Progressive retinal atrophy, hip dysplasia, osteochondritis dissecans, epilepsy, and hypothyroidism – all diseases with probable genetic origins – are prevalent within the breed. A larger gene pool would diminish the risk of these disorders but, even though kennel clubs allow the use of "country of origin" stock to broaden this breed's genetic base, the Canaan Dog's health can never be improved this way. In a bid to eradicate rabies from wildlife in Israel, the government destroyed most feral dogs in the Negev. The last two feral Canaan Dogs were captured and killed in the mid 1990s.

Hanging on Feral dogs are often malnourished, like these skinny examples from Calcutta, but they survive and reproduce in remarkably stable numbers as long as there is rubbish for them to scavenge from.

when we accept that we should be doing something to enhance the genetic quality of our purebred dogs.

Ferals can breed true

Feral dogs are known by different names around the world, but the feral dogs of India have historically been called "pariah dogs". Until recently, pariah was a derogatory word meaning an unwanted outcast, but it is taking on a new interpretation. Increasingly, when applied to dogs, the word is a synonym for primitive. Longstanding feral dog populations often breed true to type, producing pups that look like their parents and grandparents. "Pariah-type" is used to describe dogs of a certain size and shape, dogs that look similar to the feral dogs of India, Thailand, Sri Lanka, and Indonesia, all of which have a roughly comparable conformation. While most pariah-type dogs in south and southeast Asia descend from primitive dog stock, some also descend in part from imported European dogs. In the survival of the fittest, those that succeed are those that are mentally and physically best prepared for their environment.

The shanty districts and uncollected garbage of Mumbai support a large population of pariah dogs, many raised by street dwellers and then allowed to roam freely. These "pet" street dogs are cherished by their poor owners but disliked by more affluent city-dwellers. Dog welfare associations such as WSD Indian Pariah Dog Club (wsdindia.org) promote the indigenous pariah dog, recognizing it as India's most ancient breed. The typical Indian pariah or street dog is moderate in size, usually under 16kg (35lb), with short brown, fawn, or fawn-white hair. In Rajastan, tricolour pariah dogs are common, and in Tamil Nadu there are more black street dogs, perhaps as a result of previous crossbreeding with the black-coated European pet dogs that have lived in the area for centuries.

Some pariah-type dogs, such as the Israeli Canaan Dog (*see p.44*) and the Balinese Kintamani, are now recognized as purebreds with pedigree papers, and bred to conform to written, formal standards. Other examples of where we've intervened in natural selection, created breed standards, and given indigenous ferals an approved name include the Basenji (Africa), Xoloitzcuintle (Mexico), Carolina Dog (southeastern United States), Jindo Gae (Korea), Pero Sin Pelo (Peru), Dingo (Australia), and New Guinea Singing Dog. Other ferals may one day become purebreds, including the Bali Dog (Bali/Polynesia), Khoi/Hottentot Dog and Sica (South Africa), and Telomian (Malaysia).

Local type Ferals show the typical build and colour of a locality. Regional variation lies behind many established breeds: every region of France seems to have its own hunting dogs, and every valley in England once seemed to have its own terrier. There is no reason (other than snobbery) why the hardy, intelligent survivors of India could not achieve official status.

If you're interested in creating your very own breed, take a trip to southern Italy to collect a decent supply of the long-haired, short-legged, affable local dogs, or to a wadi in Oman for the less affable but equally distinctive pariah-type wadi dogs, or to the streets of Manila for some "Askal" dogs (a short form for *asong kalye*, Tagalog for "street dog") and embark on your breeding programme.

Stray and latchkey dogs

I've been in veterinary practice long enough to remember when it was culturally acceptable to let our dogs roam. These are what I call latchkey dogs, owned and homed but allowed to roam. Angus, the Scottie that lived in the home where I was born, travelled widely each day – I know this because when we shopped at a delicatessen about a kilometre (half a mile) away from our home, the shop owner would tell us he'd given Angus a bit of pastrami earlier. Letting your city dog roam was acceptable then, and it's still the norm in urban areas where poverty and lack of education are bedfellows, as well as in some rural areas.

Strays are dogs that once lived with people but have been either lost or abandoned. In most countries (except those in Scandinavia), strays are so common that dog shelters are necessary, and often full to capacity. There's an inverse relationship between education and affluence on one hand, and stray dogs on the other. England used to have a large stray and latchkey dog population, but the late 20th century saw a cultural change. Slogans like "A dog is for life, not just for Christmas" worked. More people thought carefully about acquiring a dog, and the stray population shrank. The largest and most efficient dog shelters found themselves with surplus space. They either diversified into housing unwanted cats or filled their kennels with dogs from the Republic of Ireland. There the annual stray dog count of 25,000 (of which 15,000 are annually killed) still vastly exceeds stray dog numbers for all of England, a country that has seven times the human population of Ireland.

I'm involved with the charity Hearing Dogs for Deaf People, which recycles unwanted dogs to act as ears for people who otherwise wouldn't know that someone's at the door, or their baby is crying, or a smoke alarm is ringing. Twenty-five years ago the sparky, friendly dogs we needed came from local shelters. They were mostly lost or abandoned but had been raised in home environments, and we developed techniques to train them. Today we're also using strays from Ireland, and we've had to modify our methods, because these dogs have a different culture. Often raised in a yard, with less human intervention, they have been independent since early puppyhood. They are freethinkers, independent spirits. They enjoy human companionship, but training needs extra effort, to make them feel part of their human family.

Freedom of the city The pampered dogs of wealthy north European and North American society tend to be kept indoors or in their gardens. But in many other places an owned dog may still go trotting through the streets alone on its own business or wait for its owner outside the front door rather than inside.

CHAPTER THREE

Modern Dog Breeds

All of us are influenced by fashion, by what we are most likely to see, so trends in breed popularity are self-perpetuating. We're more likely to admire a specific breed if we've seen or met some. Looks are, of course, a vital part of what we find alluring in a dog, but so too is behaviour, and the two are linked to some extent.

What a dog looks like is important for two reasons. The first, of course, is that it has to look like the type of dog you want to live with. Our dogs are extensions of our characters, either accentuating and emphasizing who we are (or at least who we *think* we are), or filling voids, augmenting our personality with traits we don't have. That's why it's not only thuggish guys who want to be seen with brutish dogs. Some mousey guys want to be seen with brutish dogs too. The second is that in some instances, but not always, looks give clues about personality and temperament. The dogs I see are purebreds, crosses between purebreds, or true Heinz-57 mutts, but even within muttdom it's not difficult to guess at the ancestry of an individual. A quick look at the size, coat texture, and dominant physical features will make it relatively easy to pigeonhole any dog's lineage. It may look primitive, or Nordic, or hound-like, or terrier-like, or any of a dozen more classifications. Once a dog is classified into a particular group, and you know what that group was originally developed for, you've got an idea about that dog's potential personality. Maybe.

Moving away from wolf behaviour

Researchers have studied different breeds to see if they all inherited the same level of wolf-like behaviour. Dogs signal each other by body language, but the body parts they use – the muzzle, the area around the eyes, the ears and the tail – have been intentionally altered in many breeds. The eyes and muzzle may be covered by long hair, the ears may droop, and the tail may

Sociable characters Many scenthounds were bred to live and work in packs. The advantage of this past is that they tend to be relaxed around other dogs and people; the disadvantage is that they really don't enjoy being left alone.

DNA PROFILES FOR DOGS

In 2005, I travelled around Europe with my Golden Retriever Macy, and we visited regions my ancestors left in the mid- to late 1800s for Scotland, then Canada, the United States, Australia, and New Zealand. Before that trip I had my DNA analysed and found that most of my ancestry is similar to that of the indigenous populations of Bavaria, Spain, and Portugal. As most of us are, I'm a human mutt with ancestry in a variety of populations. In 2007, a similar ancestral analysis was launched for canine mutts, initially only available in North America. DNA analysis of a cheek swab or blood sample sent to www.whatsmydog.com indicates which breeds contributed to your mutt, with an accuracy of over 84 per cent.

be naturally short or tight. We also surgically alter the ears and tails of some dogs, interfering with their normal body language. Scientists use the term paedomorphosis to describe the retention of juvenile looks into maturity, and the breeds with round heads and large, frontal eyes, such as the Pug, Pekingese, and Cavalier King Charles Spaniel, are the most paedomorphic. We intentionally bred some dogs this way, and intentionally or not we also selected for genes that lead to the adult retention of juvenile behaviours, such as the lower threshold for aggression. In the 1990s, animal behaviour psychologist Deborah Goodwin reviewed published material on how wolves communicate, using body language signals to prevent the escalation of aggression within the pack. She drew up these lists of common behaviours:

Threatening body language

- Growl
- Displace
- Stand over
- Inhibited bite
- Stand erect
- Body wrestle
- Aggressive gape
- Bare teeth
- Stare

Submissive body language

- Muzzle lick
- Look away
- Crouch
- Submissive grin
- Passive submit
- Active submit

Goodwin then investigated how many of these wolf signals were used by different breeds of dogs. She selected dogs from ten breeds, which lived in permanent groups or "packs" with breeders, and watched their normal social interactions to see if they used any of the 15 wolf behaviours.

She concluded that the further the domestic dog had diverged in appearance from the wolf, that is, the more paedomorphic the breed was, the more wolf body language it lost. Surprisingly at first glance, gundogs

Ancestral ways The wolf behaviours that we never want to face in our dogs are the snarls, gapes, and challenging glares (below). One we encounter only in a few breeds is the howl (below right); while some dogs do howl when left alone, for wolves howling is everything from a social glue to a broadcasting system. We are likely to come across a couple of the submissive wolf behaviours, like looking away from trouble or licking the lips (below right), in any dog.

WOLF BEHAVIOURS IN TEN SELECTED BREEDS

Breed	Score
Siberian Husky	15
Golden Retriever	12
German Shepherd	11
Labrador Retriever	9
Large Munsterlander	7
English Cocker Spaniel	6
Shetland Sheepdog	4
French Bulldog	4
Norfolk Terrier	3
Cavalier King Charles Spaniel	2

Breeds scored one point for each of the wolf-like behaviours used

retain more wolf behaviour than their avuncular looks suggest, but the circumstances in which retrievers use these signals differ from those in which wolves use them. Unlike wolves, or Siberian Huskies, they used them not during conflict but during play activity, in a more fossilized form. I've watched Bean's body language, and she scored 14 at six months old, typically using wolf signals in play with other dogs or with inanimate objects like her tennis ball. She would gape and bare her teeth at her tennis ball before leaping on it, but she never growled at it.

I'm happy to allow Bean to stand erect and stare at other dogs, to stand over them, to push them away when they come to me, to body wrestle with them and to play bite them, because she's not using these signals as a ladder of aggression as wolves or Huskies do. In other words, a breed may have wolf-like body language, but that doesn't mean it uses that body language in the same way a wolf does. So body language is not a very effective way to calculate how wolf-like a dog really is. If a Golden Retriever has something really valuable to protect, its food or a favourite toy, its wolf signals are used against another dog or a person, with intent; possessive aggression is the most common type of aggression in Golden Retrievers.

Changing breed temperaments

Categorizing dogs gives general clues about personalities. For example, terriers are excitable, scent hounds are laconic, gun dogs are highly trainable, and guarding dogs are potentially dangerous. All of these statements are by and large true, but it takes surprisingly little intervention – often no more that seven generations of selective breeding – to turn a truth into a falsehood. Let me give you an example. In the 1960s, when Pyrenean Mountain Dogs and Bernese Mountain Dogs were first bred as pets in significant numbers, they were tough and unpredictable guardian mastiffs. A Pyrenean once cornered me at the clinic, and it was a seriously intimidating experience. A Bernese that belonged to a client, a recently retired US Navy Seal, hospitalized him for three weeks when she attacked him for no apparent reason. Yet today, I'll confidently open the mouth of any Pyrenean or Bernese and use my finger as a tongue depressor to check the tonsils. That's because the small number of breeders who had imported these breeds knew they had an aggression problem. They agreed amongst themselves to breed only from dogs with calm personalities, and in less than twenty years, both breeds had become more like Golden Retrievers; they were relaxed, gentle, and equable. This was only possible because the small number of breeders agreed on a joint action plan. Similarly, Scandinavian Rottweiler breeders have produced a consistently reliable line of dogs; in the United States and United Kingdom, not all Rottweiler breeders were interested in breeding out the "unreliability" factor, so it still exists in those countries.

Classification used in this book

Each dog has its own potential, and part of that comes from its ancestry. British and American kennel club divisions provide quite decent guidelines, but in some ways are set in a Victorian aspic. The more recent FCI lists are more extensive and informative, but occasionally as much about dog-world politics as they are about dogs. Now, exciting new genetic information on dogs adds scientific weight to our understanding of when and where each breed developed. I've combined all of these factors to produce my own list of dog groups (*see box opposite*). Although the divisions are mine, the names, translations, and (sometimes idiosyncratic) capitals are from the registries.

Remember, any breakdown of breeds into a manageably small number of categories is arbitrary, especially that last group, "Toys and Companions". Virtually all our dogs are kept as companions, so that word could be added to the previous seven categories, but I've used it for breeds that were developed solely for companionship. Many of these are especially small.

Popular breeds

Certain breeds are very popular and the easiest way to look at breed popularity is to analyze yearly registration numbers at the world's largest canine registries. Combined statistics from British, American, Australian, Japanese, and European dog registries show that the world's most popular two breeds are the Labrador Retriever and the German Shepherd Dog.

Constant companions Some breeds are tricky to keep track of, being listed in one group by one registry and placed in a completely different group by another. Most of the breeds that were created specifically as companions, however, are classified in the same way by registries the world over, like the Pug.

POPULAR BREEDS ARRANGED BY GENETIC GROUP

1 **Primitive and Nordic or Spitz breeds**
- Siberian Husky

2 **Mastiffs and livestock guardians**
- Rottweiler
- Great Dane
- Boxer
- Bulldog
- Dobermann

3 **Sighthounds**
- Whippet
- English Greyhound

4 **Scenthounds**
- Beagle

5 **Livestock herders and shepherds**
- German Shepherd Dog
- Shetland Sheepdog

6 **Gundogs**
- Labrador Retriever
- English Cocker Spaniel
- American Cocker Spaniel
- Golden Retriever
- English Springer Spaniel
- Standard Poodle

6 **Gundogs (continued)**
- German Pointers
- Weimaraner

7 **Terriers and Dachshunds**
- West Highland White Terrier
- Border Terrier
- Staffordshire Bull Terrier
- American Staffordshire Bull Terrier
- Dachshunds

8 **Toy and companion dogs**
- Cavalier King Charles Spaniel
- Yorkshire Terrier
- Chihuahua
- Pug
- Boston Terrier
- Miniature Schnauzer
- Miniature and Toy Poodles
- Lhasa Apso
- Shih Tzu
- Pomeranian
- Maltese

Above are 35 of the world's most popular breeds, divided into my eight categories: their exact position varies by country. The greatest variety of popular breeds, 11 of them, come from the Toy and Companion category, but the actual number of dogs in the 8 breeds of the Gundog class is much larger, simply because Labrador and Golden Retrievers, Cocker Spaniels, Poodles, and German Pointers are so overwhelmingly popular.

Finding the right breed

The following pages carry a chart of breed characteristics. On the basis of daily grooming and need for exercise, I've included how time- and space-consuming a breed is. Behaviour is more subjective, but in the 1980s, Ben Hart, Professor of Animal Behaviour at the University of California's veterinary school, asked show judges to fill out questionnaires about breed behaviour. A few years later I asked breeders showing at Crufts to answer a modified questionnaire. Both questionnaires covered ease of training, natural excitability, and barking. The results were broadly similar and, on the basis of those I've also indicated whether a breed is good for a first-time owner or with kids.

BREED TRAITS SCORED 1 (Low) to 5 (High)

Breed	Size	Space needed	Good with kids?	Good first dog?	Trainability	Excitability	Daily care	Noisy?
Afghan	4	5	2	no	1	2	5	2
Airedale	3–4	4	3	no	2	4	3	4
Akita	5	4	2	no	3-4	1	3	1
Alaskan Malamute	3–4	3	3	possibly	3	2	3	1
Australian Shepherd	3	2	5	yes	5	1	3	1
Basset Hound	4	2	5	possibly	1	1	2	2
Beagle	3	4	4	yes	1	4	1	4
Bichon Frise	2	1	5	yes	4	4	5	5
Bloodhound	4	1	5	possibly	2	1	1	1
Border Collie	3	5	2	no	5	4	3	3
Boston Terrier	2	1	4	yes	3	4	1	4
Brittany	3	4	5	possibly	4	3	2	2
Bulldog	3–4	1	4	possibly	1	1	2	2
Boxer	3–4	5	4	possibly	3	4	1	2
Cairn Terrier	2	1	4	yes	3	4	2	4
Cavalier King Charles	2	1	5	yes	4	3	3	5
Chesapeake Bay Ret	4–5	4	5	yes	5	1	1	5
Chihuahua	1	1	2	no	2	5	1–2	2
Chow Chow	4	2	1	no	1	1	4	1
Cocker Spaniel	3	2	5	yes	3–5	3	3–4	5
Collie	4	3	5	yes	4	2	1–3	5
Dachshunds	1–2	1	2	possibly	2	3	1–2	2–3
Dalmatian	4	4	2	no	3	3	1	3
Dobermann	4	4	3	possibly	5	2	1	2
English Springer Spaniel	3	5	5	possibly	5	3	3	3
Fox Terrier	2	3	1–2	no	1	5	1–2	5
German Shepherd Dog	4–5	4	3	no	5	3	3	3
German Pointers	4	4	4	possibly	3–4	3	1	3
Golden Retriever	4	3	5	yes	5	1	3	1
Great Dane	5	4	4	no	3	1	1	1
Hungarian Vizsla	3–4	3	5	yes	4–5	2	1	2
Jack Russell Terrier	2	3	1	no	2	5	1–2	5
Labrador Retriever	4	4	5	yes	5	2	1–2	1
Lhasa Apso	2	1	4	yes	3	4	2	3
Maltese	1	1	4	yes	3	5	4	4
Newfoundland	5	1	5	no	3–4	1	5	1
Norwegian Elkhound	4	4	4	yes	3–4	2	3	2
Old English Sheepdog	5	4	3	no	2	2	5	1

Breed	Size	Space needed	Good with kids?	Good first dog?	Trainability	Excitability	Daily care	Noisy?
Pekingese	1	1	4	maybe	2	3	3	3
Pomeranian	1	1	5	yes	3	4	3	3
Toy/Miniature Poodle	1–3	2	5	yes	4–5	4	3	5
Standard Poodle	4	3	5	yes	5	2	4	3
Pug	2	2	4	yes	1	3	1–2	4
Rottweiler	5	4	2	no	3–4	1	1	1
Saint Bernard	5	4	4	no	2	1	5	1
Samoyed	4	3	3	possibly	2–3	2	4	3
Miniature Schnauzer	3	2	4	yes	3–4	5	3–4	5
Scottish Terrier	3	2	2	possibly	2	5	2	4
Shar Pei	4	4	2	no	2	3	5	3
Irish Setter	4	5	4	yes	2–3	5	3	4
English Setter	4	5	4	yes	3	4	3	4
Shetland Sheepdog	2–3	2	4	yes	5	3	3	4
Shih Tzu	1–2	1	5	yes	3	5	2	3
Siberian Husky	4	4	2	no	3	3	2	3
Staffordshire Bull Terrier	3	2	4	possibly	3	4	1	4
Weimaraner	4	4	3	possibly	4	2	1	4
Welsh Corgis	3	2	2	possibly	3	3	1	3
West High White Terrier	2–3	2	1	possibly	1–2	5	4	5
Yorkshire Terrier	1	1	1	yes	1–2	5	4	5

The two most popular breeds worldwide, based on survey results, are the German shepherd (above left) and the Labrador retriever (above right). Both have lines bred primarily either for working or for companionship.

Group 1: Primitive and Nordic dogs

If there's one characteristic that unifies most of the truly primitive and even the Nordic breeds, it's their independence. Dogs in this group march to their own drum and are perhaps least open to advanced training. Virtually all dogs, even the most primitive, can be obedience trained, but don't expect a Basenji, a Greenland Husky, or a Korean Jindo to take much interest in agility trials or retrieve work.

Aside from their personalities, potential owners should be aware that another factor uniting these breeds is the amount they shed. These dogs are great if you've got a spinning wheel and enjoy knitting. The amount of hair Akitas shed twice yearly is truly stupendous, while the copious down of a Samoyed spins into wonderful angora-like wool. Seriously. One Samoyed can provide you with a pair of warm gloves or mitts each year. Nordic dogs look (and shed) the way they do because they are adapted for cold climates, with long hair and an insulating, waterproof undercoat. Small ears help to reduce heat loss and the risk of frostbite, and thick fur between the pads protects the paws.

Seldom seen Many primitive dog breeds are popular and numerous, but the curious New Guinea Singing Dog remains extremely rare. The most primitive of all breeds, the Australian Dingo, never kept as a pet, survives in greater numbers.

PRIMITIVE AND NORDIC DOGS

Primitive type breeds

Africa Basenji
Australia Dingo
India and southeast Asia Pariah dog
Israel Canaan Dog
Mexico Xoloitzcuintle (Mexican Hairless Dog, in Standard, Intermediate, Miniature)
Papua New Guinea New Guinea Singing Dog
Peru Perro sin pelo del Perú (Peruvian Hairless Dog, in Large, Medium-sized, Miniature)
Thailand Thai Ridgeback Dog, Thai Bangkaew Dog

Primitive Asian Nordic breeds

China Chow Chow, Shar Pei
Korea Jindo Dog
Japan Akita, Hokkaïdo, Kai, Kishu, Nihon Supittsu, (Japanese Spitz), Sanshu, Shiba, Shikoku

Nordic watchdogs and herders

Finland Suomenlapinkoira (Finnish Lapphund), Lapinporokoira (Finnish Reindeer Herder)
Iceland Islenskur Fjárhundur (Icelandic Sheepdog)
Norway Norsk Buhund (Norwegian Buhund)
Sweden Svensk Lapphund (Swedish Lapphund), Västgötaspets (Swedish Vallhund)

Nordic hunting dogs

Norway Norsk Elghund Grå (Norwegian Elkhound grey), Norsk Elghund Sort (Norwegian Elkhound black) Norsk Lundehund (Norwegian Lundehund)
Russia Russko-Evropeïskaïa Laïka (Russian-European Laïka), Vostotchno-Sibirskaïa Laïka (East Siberian Laïka) Zapadno-Sibirskaïa Laïka (West Siberian Laïka)
Sweden Jämthund (Swedish Elkhound), Norrbottenspets (Norrbottenspitz)

Nordic sled dogs

Canada Canadian Eskimo Dog
Finland Karjalankarhukoira (Karelian Bear Dog), Suomenpystykorva (Finnish Spitz)
Greenland (Denmark) Grønlandshund (Greenland Dog)
Russia Samoiedskaïa Sabaka (Samoyed)
United States Alaskan Malamute, Alaskan Husky, Alaskan Eskimo Dog, Siberian Husky

European spitzes

Germany Deutscher Spitz (German Spitz), Eurasier (Eurasian), Großspitz, Mittelspitz, Kleinspitz (Giant, Medium, and Miniature Spitz), Zwergspitz (Pomeranian)
Italy Volpino Italiano
Netherlands Keeshond

Recent genetic studies have confirmed the relationship between primitive breeds, including the Dingo and the Basenji, and Asian "Nordic" breeds, such as the Chow Chow. Nordic breeds is a bit of a misnomer: these types originated in Asia, but Westerners have always associated their conformation with dogs from Nordic countries. Kennel clubs usually classify the prick-eared Basenji with its tightly curled tail as a sighthound, but I've placed it here with its genetic relatives. Basenjis tend to be climbers and yodel rather than bark, although those raised with other dogs copy their barking.

As a general rule, Nordic dogs are suspicious of the unknown (especially unknown people), and don't have to be trained to be aggressive. They need to be intensively socialized with other dogs when very young if they are to mature into adults that are reliable with other dogs. Travelling through the Karelia region of Finland, I once asked a Finnish frontier guard who bred Karelian Bear Dogs why he didn't use those instead of a German Shepherd Dog when patrolling the Russian border. He grinned as if I'd asked the dumbest question imaginable, which I had, and replied "Impossible to train".

SHIBA

Height: 35–40cm (14–16in)
Weight: 8–10kg (18–22lb)
Life expectancy: No accurate statistics
First use: Hunting dog
Country of origin: Japan
Colour: Wide range

Japan's indigenous breeds

Nordic Spitz-types migrated or were transported from northeast Asia into China, then Korea, and eventually to Japan. All of Japan's indigenous breeds have classic Nordic characteristics: solid, robust bodies, wedge-shaped heads, small, densely furred, upright ears, and curled tails. They don't make overt displays of emotion and are inclined to be quiet, barking only when there's something really worth barking at.

These dogs were historically seen as a single group, divided according to size and region of origin. The large were Akitas, the medium-sized were Kai, Shikoku, and Kishu, and the small ones Shiba. (The Tosa fighting dog is the product of crossing large indigenous dogs with western mastiff breeds.) Only Akitas and Shibas are common outside Japan. Due to dog-world politics, there are technically two different Akita breeds: the Japanese Akita with no black hair on the mask or body, and the larger, more heavy-boned American Akita. Regardless of its forename, the Akita is a calm, quiet but assertive breed that demands less vigorous exercise than many other breeds.

Shibas are increasingly popular, although most that I see are rarely let off their leads because of "training issues". These are classically bold, quiet, fastidiously clean little hunters with a curiously high-pitched shriek, used both when annoyed and when overjoyed. I hear it when I take a blood sample from a Shiba, but also when it races to greet its owner.

CHOW CHOW

Height: 45–56cm (18–22in)
Weight: 20–32kg (44–70lb)
Life expectancy: 13.5 years
First use: Guard and sled dog
Country of origin: China
Colour: White, cream, fawn, red, blue, black

Nordic dogs in Europe and America

How Nordic breeds spread from Asia into Europe remains a mystery, but it's realistic to assume that they travelled through Arctic regions, and probably southward from the Nordic regions of Russia and Scandinavia into central Europe in ancient times. Skeletal remains of Nordic-type dogs around 2,000 years old have been found in Switzerland, and these were almost certainly ancestors of the German Spitz-type dogs.

While the primitive breeds of Asia were never put to consistent practical use, their European and American cousins were developed through selective breeding to hunt, herd, and pull sleds. The largest, most powerful breeds, such as the Karelian Bear Dog and Norwegian Elkhound, were and still are used for moose and elk hunting. Smaller breeds, such as the Finnish Spitz and the Lundehund, were used in Scandinavia to hunt birds and small mammals. The Inuit used the largest of all the Spitz types, the Canadian Eskimo Dog and the Greenland Dog, to pull sleds, but 19th-century trappers found that size didn't equate with endurance, and instead they imported and extensively used the smaller Siberian Husky. The Lapphund served a similar purpose for the Sami people of Scandinavia.

Nordic breeds need to work

SIBERIAN HUSKY

Height: 51–61cm (20–24in)
Weight: 16–27.5kg (35–60lb)
Life expectancy: No accurate statistics
First use: Sled dog
Country of origin: Siberia
Colour: Any colour

SAMOYED

Height: 46–56cm (18–22in)
Weight: 23–30kg (51–66lb)
Life expectancy: 11 years
First use: Sled dog
Country of origin: Asia
Colour: White, cream, white and biscuit, silver tipped

Because they have natural dignity, gloriously thick coats, and penetrating eyes, several Nordic breeds have become widely admired. The Siberian Husky may be the most popular worldwide, even where it is poorly adapted for living happily, such as urban Italy and Japan. Originally used as a sled dog by the Chukchi people of eastern Siberia, it outshone the indigenous breeds when it was imported into Alaska and the Yukon in the late 19th century to work in the Nome and Klondike gold rushes. The Husky's instinctive desire to run and its strong-willed independence makes training one harder than average. Quiet, athletic, and quite reliable with people, this breed is a challenge, especially for city dwellers; if you're looking for a housedog, look elsewhere. Siberian Huskies are great at finding open gates, gaps in fences, other dogs to challenge, flower beds to dig , and cats to chase, but they aren't inclined towards intense shows of loyalty, and they're about on a par with Golden Retrievers when it comes to guarding instinct. The larger Alaskan Malamute has a similar personality. Both need intensive socializing as young pups and go through a rebellious adolescence between one and two years of age. Neither should be housed permanently outdoors. They need the joy of outdoor activity and thrive in cool and cold climates, but they can become morose and unreliable without constant human companionship. The smaller Samoyed shares some of these characteristics, but I find them more responsive to command, more akin to the Scandinavian Spitz mindset.

A few Nordic breeds have never been bred for any purpose other than companionship, so I've included them both here and in my Toy and Companion group. During the 19th century, the Pomeranian was bred down to its present small size from larger German Spitzes. While the Giant, Middle, and Small German Spitzes are all in decline, even in Germany, the toy Spitz or Pomeranian has become one of the world's most popular micro-dogs, outnumbered only by Yorkshire Terriers and Chihuahuas. Poms are wonderful companions if you're willing to live with yapping and (even with good early socializing) occasional snapping. This is a classic bantam Spitz, with a wide range of Nordic characteristics and an added feisty confidence. In the 20th century, North American breeders shrank the American Eskimo Dog too, creating the still-uncommon Alaskan Klee Kai.

Group 2: Mastiffs and guardians

Mastiffs or molossers are massive compared with other dogs. Dog breeds descended from mastiff ancestry include livestock guardians, from the powerfully built, tough Russian Ovtcharkas and the much more amenable Komondor of Hungary to bull-baiting breeds. They also include the problematic fighting dogs, from the Japanese Tosa to the Fila Brasileiro.

Genetic studies show that most mastiffs belong to a closely related and ancient family: some feel that the Tibetan Mastiff may be ancestral to the entire group, while others say that the smaller Turkish Kangal is more typical of their origins and their descendents, the guardian and shepherd dogs.

The Kangal Dog is interesting. Native to the Sivas region of Turkey, it is a classic example of a natural, working mastiff, powerfully built, with pendant ears and a relatively short, heavy neck, but lacking the exaggerated body proportions of many of the modernized breeds. These natural livestock guardians have no-nonsense approach to work and are also used in Turkey as military dogs. The Turkish government sponsors several breeding facilities for Kangal Dogs and limits their export.

Odd one out Most mastiffs come with a label that says "Not suitable for children" but J.M. Barrie immortalized the character of a Newfoundland in Nana, the dog that acts as a devoted nursemaid to the Darling children in *Peter Pan*.

MASTIFFS AND GUARDIANS

Mastiffs
Argentina Dogo Argentino
Brazil Fila Brasileiro
Denmark Broholmer
France Dogue de Bordeaux
Germany Deutscher Boxer (Boxer), Deutsche Dogge (Great Dane), Rottweiler
Great Britain Bulldog, Bullmastiff, Mastiff
Italy Mastino Napoletano (Neapolitan Mastiff), Cane Corso Italiano (Italian Corso Dog)
Japan Tosa
Portugal Cão Fila de São Miguel
Spain Perro dogo mallorquín/Ca de Bou (Majorca Mastiff)

Mountain mastiffs
Canada Newfoundland
France Chien de Montagne des Pyrénées (Pyrenean Mountain Dog)
Germany Hovawart, Leonberger
Hungary Komondor, Kuvasz
Italy Cane da pastore Bergamasco (Bergamasco Shepherd Dog), Cane da pastore Maremmano-Abruzzese (Maremma and Abruzzes Sheepdog)
Macedonia/Serbia and Montenegro Sarplaninac (Yugoslavian Shepherd Dog)
Morocco Chien de Montagne de l'Atlas/Aïdi (Atlas Mountain Dog/Aidi)
Poland Polski Owczarek Podhalanski (Tatra Shepherd Dog)
Portugal Cão da Serra da Estrela (Serra da estrela Mountain Dog), Cão de Castro Laboreiro (Castro Laboreiro Dog), Rafeiro do Alentejo (Alentejo Mastiff)
Russia Kavkazskaïa Ovtcharka (Caucasian Shepherd Dog), Sredneasiatskaïa Ovtcharka (Central Asia Shepherd Dog), Ioujnorousskaïa Ovtcharka (South Russian Shepherd Dog), Tchiorny Terrier (Black Terrier)
Slovenia Kraski Ovcar (Karst Shepherd Dog)
Slovakia Slovensky Cuvac (Slovakian Chuvach)
Spain Mastín Espanol (Spanish Mastiff), Mastín del Pirineo (Pyrenean Mastiff)
Switzerland St. Bernhardshund (Saint Bernard), Appenzeller Sennenhund (Appenzell Cattle Dog), Berner Sennenhund (Bernese Mountain Dog), Entlebucher Sennenhund (Entlebuch Cattle Dog), Grosser Schweizer Sennenhund (Great Swiss Mountain Dog)
Tibet Do-Khyi (Tibetan Mastiff)
Turkey Coban Köpegi (Anatolian Shepherd Dog), Kangal

Mastiff breeds in Europe

The earliest mastiffs contributed to the French Dogue de Bordeaux, the Italian Neapolitan Mastiff, and the Spanish and Pyrenean Mastiffs. Some of the Roman mastiffs transported into the Swiss Alps moved on to Germany, eventually leading to the Great Dane (or more accurately the Deutsche Dogge). Similar mastiffs existed in Denmark and Sweden but became extinct. The Danish mastiff, the Broholmer, has recently been recreated using local Danish dogs and Spanish Mastiffs. I visited a Broholmer breeder in northern Denmark recently, and while my Golden Retriever Macy was at first intimidated by their size and confidence, I found them both immensely handsome and reliable.

In mountainous regions and high plains from Central Asia through Asia Minor, Eastern Europe, and Western Europe to the Pyrenees of France and Spain, shepherds found that mastiffs were ideal livestock guardians. The descendants of those long-coated and often white-haired dogs still exist as the Akbash Dog of Turkey, the Polish Tatra, the Slovenian Kuvac, the Hungarian Kuvasz, the Italian Maremma, and the French and Spanish Pyrenean. Darker or parti-coloured livestock guardian mastiffs, such as the Sarplaninac, also exist throughout the Balkans.

GREAT DANE

Height: 71–76cm (28–30in)
Weight: 46–54 kg (101–120lb)
Life expectancy: 8.4 years
First use: War dog, hunting dog
Country of origin: Germany
Colour: Fawn, black, blue, brindle, harlequin

German mastiff breeds

The Great Dane, Rottweiler, and Boxer are the world's most popular members of this group. Great Danes were developed in the 16th century, probably by crossing English Mastiffs with existing large greyhound-type stock, and are the national dog of Germany. The breed's French and English names (Grand Danois, Great Dane) are courtesy of the French naturalist the Comte de Buffon; from the late 19th century the German name was politically unacceptable abroad. Although some males can assert themselves in a dominant manner, this is, in essence, a quiet, calm, and intensely affectionate breed. Anxious Great Danes comically back up to sit on their owners laps when they visit me at the clinic, like the cartoon Great Dane Scooby Doo. Surprisingly, you don't need much room to house this large breed, but a good sturdy sofa is useful, and a nearby open space for some leisurely ranging around. The unpleasant custom of amputating most of their pendulous ears to make them appear more dominant and aggressive is banned throughout Europe and is, I'm happy to say, gradually dying out in the rest of the world too.

ROTTWEILER

Height: 58–69cm (23–27in)
Weight: 41–50kg (90–110lb)
Life expectancy: 9.8 years
First use: Herd guardian, police dog
Country of origin: Germany
Colour: Black and tan

Rottweilers probably descend from mastiffs crossed with local southern-German herding dogs. Once used as herders, they began to be bred for police work in the early 20th century, and they're now kept solely for companionship or guarding. This is a problematic breed. On the one hand, Rotties are affectionate, exuberant, cuddly companions. On the other hand, American statistics show that only the American Pit Bull Terrier is responsible for more human deaths. While it is easy to obedience train, the Rottweiler needs intensive early socializing, and this breed can be a cocked gun in the wrong hands. Their ears have always been left natural, but their tails are still needlessly docked short in many countries, including the

Pulling power Newfoundlands still swim, Ovtcharkas still guard herds, and Bernese Mountain Dogs still pull carts across the world, usually in competition. Carting evens can seem a little surreal: far from the Alps, you may find dogs and owners in full traditional Swiss costume.

United States. Tails help dogs convey what they're thinking, and this is vital if you're to house one.

Boxers are direct descendants of German and Dutch bull-baiting mastiffs crossed with English bulldogs, and are the world's most numerous "mastiffs", if you're happy to accept their classification under this heading. While some are circumspect and suspicious of other dogs or strange people as adults, most of those I see are perpetually smiling juvenile delinquents, dogs that never accept that they have to grow up. Females and neutered males can be energetic fruit-baskets, boisterous clowns guaranteed to make you smile. Like so many other German breeds, Boxers have historically had their ears and tails amputated. Removing the ears now occurs in significant numbers only in the United States, but tail docking is still widespread outside Europe, where mutilations for purely cosmetic reasons are banned. If you're getting a Boxer, make sure it retains all its body parts: an x-ray of a six-year-old Boxer's back will show you the arthritic damage than occurs when a dog is left with only a short metronome of a tail to wag.

Popular but problematic mastiffs

Four other mastiffs are also popular pets. During the 20th century, the English Bulldog became hideously distorted in shape, with a head so massive that a large proportion of pups could only be born by Caesarian section. The consequences were severe breathing problems and the second-shortest median life expectancy of all breeds, a mere 6.7 years (only the Irish Wolfhound has a shorter life). Some breeders are now trying to breed back to the Victorian standard, when legs were straighter, heads were smaller, and Bulldogs still had necks.

The Newfoundland, geneticists tell us, is a truly ancient mastiff, but this is the soppy, sloppy member of the group. Males from any breed can be dominant, even the occasional Newfie, but I've never met a Newfoundland that didn't have a sweet and gentle disposition. They are, however, prone to a number of serious health problems and are seemingly magnetically attracted to any body of water.

A Newfie can be a large, drooling presence, but if there were canine drooling Olympics, the Saint Bernard would be the outright winner. Geneticists tell us that the Saint Bernard is a modern herding dog that has been bred up in size, rather than part of the family of truly ancient mastiffs. Breeding for increased size during the 20th century means that they can now weigh up to 90kg (200lb), which has increased health problems and reduced life expectancy. Similar concerns affect the Bernese Mountain Dog, another teddy bear of a dog with a median life expectancy of only 7.0 years. All these breeds thrive in the fresh air but also need to be treated as members of the human family.

ST BERNARD

Height: 60–70cm (24–28in)
Weight: 50–91kg (110–200lb)
Life expectancy: No accurate statistics
First use: Hauling dog
Country of origin: Switzerland
Colour: White and brown

Group 3: Sighthounds

Generally speaking, sighthounds are benign of temperament, not overly demonstrative, and not very territorial. Many are life-long lounge lizards, happy to snooze the days away until they are taken outdoors for activity. And there, the most amazing transformation takes place. The deferential, quiet sighthound sparks into the most graceful of all dogs. There is absolutely nothing more impressive than seeing a sighthound racing across open terrain at full speed.

Track and field Greyhounds, once used for coursing rabbits, were perfectly adapted for modern dog racing, an activity that developed in the 1920s, first in the United States and then a few years later across the Atlantic.

Sighthounds are, according to the geneticists, truly ancient breeds. There's little doubt that the shape originated at least 5,000 years ago in Asia. In ancient Persia there were 16 different varieties of sighthound, and remnants of these graceful dogs can still be found in Kazakstan, Uzbekistan, Turkmenistan, and the Tien Shan mountains of the Kyrgyz Republic. The future of these vestige populations is uncertain, although the Russian Cynological Federation recognises the Tasy and Taigan and is actively encouraging breeders to save isolated populations. In the Ukraine, north of the Black Sea, the Chort or Hortaya Borzaya was used to hunt hares, foxes, Saiga antelopes, and even wolves on the steppes; Ukrainian breeders are now attempting to restore and preserve that breed.

Ancient sighthounds still exist in Africa, in Mali, Niger, and Burkina Faso. The Azawakh, a primitive sighthound of the sub-Saharan Sahel belt, is disregarded by the Tuareg and Fula people, but used to protect livestock, while north of the Sahara, from Libya through Tunisia and Algeria to Morocco, the Sloughi both guards and hunts. Farther east, the Saluki has special status in the Muslim Middle East, where dogs are thought of as unclean. The Arabic word for dog is *kalb*, but the word for a Saluki is *saluki*: this ancient sighthound is not quite as doggy as other dogs are.

SIGHTHOUNDS

Afghanistan Afghan Hound
Great Britain Deerhound, Greyhound, Whippet
Hungary Magyar Agar (Hungarian Greyhound)
India Banjara Hound, Chippipari Hound, Poligar hound, Mahratta Hound, Mudhol Hound, Rampur Greyound
Ireland Irish Wolfhound
Italy Piccolo Levriero Italiano (Italian Greyhound), Cirneco dell'Etna
Mali Azawakh
Malta Kelb tal-Fenek (Pharaoh Hound)
Middle East Saluki
Morocco Sloughi (Arabian Greyhound)
Poland Chart Polski (Polish Greyhound)
Portugal Podengo Português (Portuguese Warren Hound or Portuguese Podengo)
Russian Federation Russkaya Psovaya Borzaya (Borzoi), Tasy, Taigan, Russian Steppe Hound
Spain Galgo español (Spanish Greyhound), Podenco Canario (Canarian Warren Hound), Podenco Ibicenco (Ibizan Warren Hound or Ibizan Podenco)
Ukraine Hortaya Borzaya (Chort)

Western influences

The sighthounds still found in Asia differ radically from their Western relatives, bred to Western kennel club standards. The Afghan Hound is a classic example. The British Natural History Museum has a branch in Tring in Hertfordshire, and there, in a long, glazed cabinet, are 87 stuffed dogs from the 19th century. One of them is an Afghan Hound, and it's not because this example of late-Victorian taxidermy has been attacked by moths that it looks to Western eyes as if it's been barbered. That's just what Afghan Hounds looked like when they first arrived in the West at the end of the 19th century, with thickly insulating but only moderately long hair. Breeding produced a flowing, high-maintenance, fashion-model coat, but otherwise this elegant dog remains as it was in Afghanistan and southern Russia, independent and not easy to obedience train.

Varieties of coursing sighthounds developed throughout many regions of India, but it was in Europe that sighthounds evolved into their greatest variety of sizes, from the 55kg (122lb) Irish Wolfhound down to the 3kg (7lb) Italian Greyhound. After arriving in Europe from Asia they spread throughout the Mediterranean and then deep into the continent. Varieties developed in all regions: the Podencos and Podengos of the Iberian peninsula, the Maltese Pharaoh Hound, the Italian Cirneco dell'Etna, Hungarian and Polish Greyhounds, and that most elegant of all sighthounds, the Russian Borzoi. In the British Isles some sighthounds were bred with mastiffs to produce the giant Irish Wolfhound and Scottish Deerhound, both of which became extinct and were recreated as the breeds we know today.

GREYHOUND

Height: 69–76cm (27–30in)
Weight: 27–32kg (59–70lb)
Life expectancy: 13.2 years
First use: Hunting dog
Country of origin: Great Britain
Colour: Black, white, red, blue, fawn, fallow, brindle, solid or with white

Racing dogs

Ancestors of the coursing and racing English Greyhound, the dog world's thoroughbred racing champion, may have been introduced to Britain by the Celts, but DNA analysis has shown the modern Greyhound is not a direct descendent of Asian sighthounds, but rather a close relative of herding dogs like the Smooth Collie. Modern racing lead to a massive increase in Greyhound breeding and to the great welfare problem that exists today. A conservative estimate is that over 10,000 adult greyhounds are killed each year in the United States alone, because they're not fast enough on the track and nobody wants to have them as pets. That's a pity because, big as they are, Greyhounds are couch potatoes. It's a misconception that they're highly energetic and need to run miles each day. Once a Greyhound has adopted a human pack, it becomes a dedicated family member, usually amicable with children but always a potential concern with any small animals.

ITALIAN GREYHOUND

Height: 33–38 cm (13–15 in)
Weight: 3–3.5kg (7–8lb)
Life expectancy: No accurate statistics
First use: Hunting dog
Country of origin: Italy
Colour: Cream, fawn, blue, black

In the last two hundred years, some sighthounds shrank. The Italian Greyhound was reduced to the size of a toy dog, but the Whippet, three times bigger than the Italian Greyhound but often three times smaller than the Greyhound, became the world's most popular sighthound. Whippets were once the common man's thoroughbred. Today, these gentle, trusting and surprisingly obedient dogs make affectionate, if somewhat fragile, companions. Their lean limbs and thin skin are both susceptible to damage. Most of the Whippets I see lead hedonistic lives acting as hot water bottles on cold nights for their owners. But be wary if something furry comes in the garden – Whippets are on sighthound autopilot and will chase any mammal that moves, including the neighbour's cat.

Too much of a good thing
Some Whippets can run at close to 64kph (40mph) due to a mutation in a gene that produces muscle protein. One copy of the mutation increases racing ability, but two copies produce heavily muscled "bully" Whippets, prone to cramp.

AFGHAN HOUND

Height: 64–74cm (25–29in)
Weight: 22.5–27.5kg (50–60lb)
Life expectancy: 12 years
First use: Hunting dog
Country of origin: Afghanistan
Colour: Any solid or shaded colour

IRISH WOLFHOUND

Height: 71–90cm (28–35in)
Weight: 40–55kg (88–122lb)
Life expectancy: 6.2 years
First use: Hunting dog
Country of origin: Ireland
Colour: Range of brindled shades

THE FIRST CLONED DOG

In early 2005, a team of Korean geneticists, lead by Hwang Woo-Suk successfully cloned a dog using DNA taken from an Afghan Hound named Tei. The cloned egg was implanted in a Labrador Retriever who carried "Snuppy" (an acronym for Seoul National University Puppy) to term. Later in 2005 it was discovered that Hwang Woo-Suk had fabricated evidence in another of his stem-cell research projects, but when independent investigators studied his work on cloning Snuppy they confirmed that it was accurate, and that the world's first cloned dog was truly an Afghan Hound.

Group 4: Scenthounds

The unifying factor in scenthounds is the long nose. Inside that nose is an enormous amount of nasal membrane, with a surface area usually greater than that of the dog's entire body, and that's why they're so superb at following scent on the ground or in the air. It shouldn't come as a surprise that France, the country that perfected perfume, is in a class on its own when it comes to the variety of its scenthounds.

SCENTHOUNDS

Austria Brandlbracke (Austrian Black and Tan Hound), Steirische Rauhhaarbracke (Styrian coarse-haired Hound), Tiroler Bracke (Tyrolean Hound)
Belgium Chien de Saint-Hubert (Bloodhound)
Bosnia Bosanski Ostrodlaki Gonic Barak (Bosnian coarse-haired Hound/Barak)
Croatia Istarski Kratkodlaki Gonic (Istrian short-haired Hound), Istarski Ostrodlaki Gonic (Istrian coarse-haired Hound), Posavski Gonic (Posavaz Hound), Dalmatian
France Poitevin, Billy, Français tricolore, Français blanc et noir, Français blanc et orange, (French Tricolour, White and Black, and White and Orange Hounds) Grand anglo-français tricolore, Grand anglo-français blanc et noir, Grand anglo-français blanc et orange, (Great Anglo-French Tricolour, White and Black, and White and Orange Hounds) Grand bleu de Gascogne (Great Gascony Hound), Gascon saintongeois, Grand Gascon saintongeois, Grand griffon vendéen, Anglo-français de petite vénerie, Ariégeois, Beagle-Harrier, Chien d'Artois (Artois Hound), Porcelaine, Petit bleu de Gascogne (Small Blue Gascony Hound), Gascon saintongeois, Petit gascon saintongeois, Briquet griffon vendéen, Griffon bleu de Gascogne, Griffon fauve de Bretagne, Griffon nivernais
Finland Suomenajokoira (Finnish Hound)
Great Britain English Foxhound, Otterhound, Harrier
Greece Hellinikos Ichnilatis (Hellenic Hound)
Hungary Erdélyi Kopó (Transylvanian Hound)
Italy Segugio Italiano (Italian Hound)
Norway Dunker (Norwegian Hound), Haldenstøvare (Halden Hound), Hygenhund (Hygen Hound)
Poland Ogar Polski (Polish Hound)
Serbia and Montenegro Srpski Trobojni Gonic (Serbian Tricolour Hound), Srpski Gonic (Serbian Hound), Crnogorski Planinski Gonic (Montenegrin Mountain Hound)
Slovakia Slovenski Kopov (Slovakian Hound)
Spain Sabueso Español (Spanish Hound)
Sweden Hamiltonstövare (Hamilton Hound), Schillerstövare (Schiller Hound), Smålandsstövare (Småland Hound)
Switzerland Schweizer Laufhund (Swiss Hound, divided into Bernese, Jura, Lucerne, Schwyz)
United States American Foxhound, Black and Tan Coonhound, Treeing Walker Coonhound, Coonhound

Small-sized hounds

Austria Alpenländische Dachsbracke (Alpine Dachsbracke)
France Basset artésien normand, Basset bleu de Gascogne (Blue Gascony Basset), Basset fauve de Bretagne (Fawn Brittany Basset), Grand Basset griffon vendéen, Petit Basset griffon vendéen
Germany Deutsche Bracke (German Hound), Bayrischer Gebirgsschweisshund (Bavarian Mountain Scenthound) Westfälische Dachsbracke (Westphalian Dachsbracke), Hannover'scher Schweisshund (Hanoverian Scenthound)
Great Britain Basset Hound, Beagle
Sweden Drever (Swedish Dachsbracke)
Switzerland Schweizerischer Niederlaufhund (Small Swiss Hound, divided into Bernese, Jura, Lucerne, Schwyz)
Southern Africa Rhodesian Ridgeback

Scenthounds are by nature most adept at living compatibly with other dogs. After all, this was almost as important for their survival as their ability to follow ground or air scent trails. Generally speaking, scenthounds don't have the killer instinct, which is why they are such good family dogs.

Midsummer Night's hounds
Shakespeare's hounds "With ears that sweep away the morning dew/Crook-knee'd, and dew-lapp'd like Thessalian bulls" still exist today.

Throughout Europe they remain the hunter's companion, more commonly found in the field and woods than in the show ring. That's good. It means that many of these family-oriented breeds continue to be bred for their working ability, not just for their looks.

French hounds

The grandparent of all scenthounds is the Bloodhound. Crusaders brought greyhound-type dogs back from the Middle East to Europe, where they were further developed in the Balkans, probably by crossing them with local dogs of mastiff ancestry. The Balkan dogs were eventually taken to northern France and Belgium where the Bloodhound or *le chien de St Hubert* was developed in its present form by the monks of the Benedictine Abbey of St. Hubert in Belgium. Bloodhounds are unflappable but large and wilful. They have one of the highest frequencies of life-threatening twisted stomachs, or gastric dilatation volvulus (GDV), also called gastric torsion or bloat. As a consequence of this, they have one of the shortest life expectancies of all breeds.

Elsewhere in France, aristocratic landowners produced an enormous variety of other large, scent-following pack hounds, from wirehaired griffons to short-legged bassets. These dogs were kept in hundreds of packs throughout France and used for hunting in forests and parkland. Breeding in France came to a halt during the French Revolution, but lines that had been developed there were smuggled out of that country, especially into Great Britain. Eventually, their descendants were returned to France and formed part of the root stock of today's French scenthounds.

BEAGLE

Height: 33–40cm (13–16in)
Weight: 8–14kg (18–31lb)
Life expectancy: 13.3 years
First use: Hunting dog
Country of origin: Great Britian
Colour: Lemon and white, orange and white, red and white, tricolour

Basset breeds

The Swiss appreciated the value of short legs on a dog, and from their range of already-small scenthounds, called the laufhunds, they created niederlaufhunds, a variety of "walking hounds" ideal for accompanying on foot while hunting in the mountains. The French created bassets, including the Basset Artesien Normand, Basset d'artois, Basset Bleu de Gascogne, Basset Fauve de Bretagne, and Basset Griffon Vendeen. The Petit Basset Griffon Vendeen is particularly popular where I work, and rightly so. This is a relatively compact dog with an avuncular disposition, excellent with children, easy to obedience train, but a law unto itself when it comes to tracking game.

The English Basset Hound has its origins in the smooth-haired bassets of Northern France, especially the Basset Artesien Normand. Goofy in appearance, this surprisingly large breed usually makes a fine children's companion, although its love of companionship means that a Basset left at home alone, wondering "Where is everybody?" tends to bay at the moon.

BLOODHOUND

Height: 58–69cm (23–27in)
Weight: 30–50kg (66–110 lb)
Life expectancy: No accurate statistics
First use: Hunting dog
Country of origin: Belgium
Colour: Black and tan, liver/red and tan, red

Beagles and brackes

Thanks in part to Snoopy, Charles Schulz's gentle and even-tempered cartoon dog, the Beagle is the world's most popular scenthound, especially so in the United States and Canada. When I was growing up, it was that continent's most popular breed. It wasn't until 2008, however, that a Beagle won Best in Show at the Westminster Kennel Club's annual canine beauty parade in New York city. Beagles are typical scenthounds – gentle with children, good with other dogs, and obsessive on a scent trail – but perhaps a little more open to obedience training than others. Their scenting abilities, small size, and unthreatening looks have made them the world's most popular food detectors, and they are used in Australia, New Zealand, the United States, Canada, Japan, and China to detect contraband food at ports of entry. Unfortunately, small size and ease of handling have also helped to make this the world's most popular canine laboratory animal. In the United Kingdom, where the most accurate records are kept, over 95 per cent of all dogs used in laboratory experiments are Beagles.

Curiously, Germany never produced an extensive variety of large scenthounds, but in the mountainous regions of the south, indigenous scent hounds, called brackes or Bracken, were crossed with large Dachshunds, producing the dachsbracke type, from which the Swedish Drever also evolved. The Dobermann, bred as a modern guard dog, also descends in part from now extinct black-and-tan German scenthounds.

Scandinavian hunters used stock from central Europe and Russia to develop an excellent range of scenthounds, of which the tricolour Hamiltonstövare is my favourite. This is a good, strong, uncomplicated breed, although epilepsy is a hereditary concern in some lines. Most of the Russian hounds were driven to extinction by the Russian Revolution, but the Norwegian Dunker is a living descendant of the extinct Russian Harlequin Hound.

PETIT BASSET GRIFFON VENDEEN

Height: 34–38cm (13–15in)
Weight: 14–18kg (31–40lb)
Life expectancy: No accurate statistics
First use: Hunting dog
Country of origin: France
Colour: White, white and orange, tricolour

New World, new tactics

European scenthounds were excellent at following the scent trails of game that went to ground, but were less useful in the United States, where raccoons and opossums took to the trees. A new variety of scenthounds, the coonhounds, were developed from French and English bloodhound and foxhound stock. Coonhounds track game until it takes to a tree, then bark themselves silly until the hunter arrives. There are six varieties of coonhound, named according to their coat colour (Redbone, Bluetick, and Black and Tan) their origins (English and Plott) or what they do (Treeing Walker). A Black and Tan Coonhound was the star of Christopher Guest's wryly accurate fake documentary film *Best in Show*.

Coonhounds are uncommon, but they have the typical attributes of scenthounds everywhere: an easy-going disposition, an affection for the human family, an enjoyment of the company of other dogs, and a convenient willingness to do nothing when there's nothing to be done. Like most other scenthounds, they take time to obedience train and once they get on a scent trail they're on autopilot until they finish the job. All coonhounds also drool impressively and, if you're willing to believe it, American president Thomas Jefferson once advised that "the way you deal with your coonhound's slobber can perhaps be the most telling way of how you handle your everyday problems."

SCHWYZER LAUFHUND

Height: 46–58cm (18–23in)
Weight: 15–20kg (33–44lb)
Life expectancy: No accurate statistics
First use: Hunting dog
Country of origin: Switzeland
Colour: Orange and white

Group 5: Herding, droving, heeling, and shepherd dogs

Livestock dogs were bred to work under instructions, rather than just use their native abilities. They need stamina and endurance to cope with their tasks, often in inhospitable terrain, combined with an easy willingness to listen and obey. And because most of the successful ones were developed in Britain, they need to be seriously waterproof. It's no wonder that this group includes the world's most popular working dog, the German Shepherd Dog, and the world's most successful canine thinker, the Border Collie.

Many of these herders and shepherds were developed from earlier livestock-guarding breeds, and so they combine a willingness to obey with a natural inclination to guard. The French, German, Belgian, and Dutch Shepherd Dogs are all prime examples of this type.

Other shepherd breeds, exemplified by the Border Collie and Shetland Sheepdog, evolved from sighthounds and so, while they work brilliantly as herders and drovers, they are not natural guards. The Border Collie is the world's most successful herder – so unbeatable that in modern agility trials and athletics, there is frequently one category for Borders and another for all the rest of the canine world.

Star performer Popularized in the 19th century by Queen Victoria, the Rough Collie was personified in the 20th century by the wonderdog Lassie. Today the breed is a popular companion, and rightly so, but those film-star looks do require film-star grooming.

HERDERS, SHEPHERDS AND HEELERS

Australia Australian Kelpie, Australian Cattle Dog
Austria Österreichischer Pinscher (Austrian Pinscher)
Belgium Chien de Berger Belge (Belgian Shepherd Dog, divided into Groenendael, Laekenois, Malinois, Tervueren), Schipperke, Bouvier des Ardennes (Ardennes Cattle Dog), Bouvier des Flandres/Vlaamse Koehond (Flanders Cattle Dog)
Croatia Hrvatski Ovcar (Croatian Sheepdog)
France Berger de Beauce (Beauceron), Berger de Brie (Briard), Berger de Picardie (Berger Picard), Berger des Pyrénées à poil long (Long-haired Pyrenean Sheepdog), Berger des Pyrénées à face rase (Pyrenean Sheepdog - smooth faced)
Germany Deutscher Schäferhund (German Shepherd Dog), Dobermann, Deutscher Pinscher (German Pinscher), Zwergpinscher (Miniature Pinscher), Affenpinscher, Riesenschnauzer (Giant Schnauzer), Schnauzer, Zwergschnauzer (Miniature Schnauzer)
Great Britain Border Collie, Rough Collie, Smooth Collie, Bearded Collie, Old English Sheepdog, Shetland Sheepdog, Cardigan Welsh Corgi, Pembroke Welsh Corgi
Hungary Mudi, Puli, Pumi
Netherlands Hollandse Herdershond (Dutch Shepherd Dog), Saarlooswolfhond (Saarloos Wolfdog), Nederlandse Schapendoes (Dutch Schapendoes), Hollandse Smoushond (Dutch Smoushond)
Poland Polski Owczarek Nizinny (Polish Lowland Sheepdog)
Portugal Cão da Serra de Aires (Portuguese Sheepdog)
Slovakia Ceskoslovensky Vlcak (Czeslovakian Wolfdog)
Spain Ca de Bestiar/Perro de pastor mallorquín (Majorca Shepherd Dog), Gos d'Atura Catalá/Perro de pastor catalán (Catalan Sheepdog)
United States Australian Shepherd

Because all breeds within this group are working dogs, they thrive on obedience training, and generally train easily and well. They need to let off steam through daily physical and mental activity, and are prone to make up their own activities – often destructive ones – when left with nothing to do. Within many of these breeds, and both Border Collies and German Shepherd Dogs are perfect examples, there are lines that are bred to work and other lines that are bred for family companionship. If you choose the wrong line of herder, drover, heeler, or shepherd, and let me stress this, you're in for a *very* tough time. But if you choose well and you're really lucky, you've added a wonderdog to your family.

British breeds and exports

The earliest ancestors of Britain's collies arrived over 2000 years ago, when Celtic tribes from the Iberian peninsula of Spain and Portugal invaded the British Isles, settling mainly in Wales and Ireland. Like most migrating and invading cultures, Celtic society was primarily based upon pastoralism, and wealth was measured by stock ownership, so hunting and herding dogs were of great importance. One charming theory claims that the name collie comes from the Celtic word for "useful", but the Oxford English Dictionary suspects it is more likely to come from "coal", for the predominantly black coat. The heelers, for their part, were not named for any talent in walking to heel, but for their role in driving cattle by nipping at their heels – a trait that is still noted today in Corgis.

Over the centuries, Romans, Angles, Saxons, and Vikings also settled in Britain. New types of herdsmen's dogs and livestock arrived with each new wave of invaders. By medieval times livestock was driven to and from ships, farms, and markets by drovers accompanied by a wide assortment of dogs. On the periphery of these herds were the "poachers' dogs", the lurchers, which were produced by breeding a collie-type dog with a deerhound or rough-coated greyhound type.

Until 1906, any black or brown dog with white feet and white tip to its tail was referred to as a sheepdog or collie, but a strain of versatile herding dog with a unique method of working had developed in the border counties between Scotland and England. Border collie-type dogs worked silently and low to the ground, using the power of their gaze to control the sheep, and were generally known as "eye" dogs. They became the most numerous of all sheepdogs in Britain, but their numbers went unrecorded because the Kennel Club first registered them only in 1976.

Other herding dogs were developed elsewhere in the British Isles. During the 8th and 9th centuries, Vikings from Norway invaded the Shetland Isles, bringing their horses, sheep, cows, and Spitz-like herding dogs with them. By the late 1800s, working collies were imported from mainland Scotland to improve their working abilities, producing today's small Sheltie, the world's most popular small herding dog. If breed history is correct, other foreign influences are seen in Bearded Collies, descended in part from Polish Lowland Sheepdogs that arrived in Scotland almost 500 years ago. Old English sheepdogs, once used as drovers rather than herders,

CATALAN SHEEPDOG

Height: 45–55cm (18–22in)
Weight: 17.5–19kg (39–42lb)
Life expectancy: No accurate statistics
First use: Herding dog
Country of origin: Spain
Colour: Mixed fawn, reddish-brown, grey, black and white; no solid white or black

BRIARD

Height: 58–69cm (23–27in)
Weight: 34–34.5kg (74–76lb)
Life expectancy: No accurate statistics
First use: Herding dog
Country of origin: France
Colour: Fawn, grey, or black

are said to have been developed by crossing shaggy English sheepdogs with Ovtcharkas, shepherds' dogs from the Russian Caucasian regions.

In North America, crossing British collies with dogs from the Basque region of Spain produced the Australian Shepherd, so named because of its connection with the sheep-hands who came from Australia to California. In Australia itself, the small, prick-eared, smooth-coated, black-and-tan Kelpie is probably descended from herding dogs that originated in the Orkneys and Hebrides off the west and north coasts of Scotland. Australian Cattle Dogs, also known as Blue Heelers, Red Heelers, or Queensland Heelers, were developed by crossing imported Scottish smooth-coated blue merle collies and the Kelpie to produce a small, stocky dog with enormous stamina, able to withstand the soaring temperatures of the outback.

AUSTRALIAN CATTLE DOG

Height: 43–51cm (17–20in)
Weight: 16–20kg (35–44lb)
Life expectancy: No accurate statistics
First use: Herding dog
Country of origin: Australia
Colour: Blue or blue speckled with black or tan markings, red speckle

BORDER COLLIE

Height: 46–54cm (18–21in)
Weight: 14–22kg (30–49lb)
Life expectancy: 13 years
First use: Herding dog
Country of origin: Great Britain
Colour: Black and white

Breed habits die hard

Border Collies win at just about everything, from sheepdog trials to agility trials, to intelligence tests, to flyball, but that doesn't make them ideal family companions. Left to twiddle their paws, it's almost guaranteed they'll become neurotic and destructive. In the United Kingdom, dog behaviourists see more Border Collies with behaviour problems than any other breed. This is a high-energy, mentally demanding breed, wonderful if you have ample time or work for them to do, but fraught with problems if you don't. They're also "nippy", especially those from classic working lines.

Two good alternatives to Border Collies are Shetland Sheepdogs and Australian Shepherds. Shelties are smaller, calmer, perhaps a little aloof by nature, but so easy to obedience train and great with kids if they meet them while they're still pups. Like Italian Greyhounds and Whippets, their thin leg bones are a little fragile. Australian Shepherds are more the size of Border Collies but, while energetic, live within the same range as active people do. Those specifically bred for agility trials or other work can be demanding, almost to the level of the Border Collie, but other lines bred primarily for companionship are well adapted to living a dog's life. They need only a couple of hours of outdoor activity each day, some distracting toys to play with at home, activities with the kids, and the rest of the time on the couch

A MEASURE OF INTELLIGENCE

Stanley Coren asked experts to rank breeds according to their "communication intelligence" or willingness to work and obey.

The "most intelligent" were:	The "dumbest" were:
1 Border Collie	1 Afghan Hound
2 Poodle	2 Basenji
3 German Shepherd Dog	3 Bulldog
4 Golden Retriever	4 Chow Chow
5 Dobermann (right)	5 Borzoi
6 Shetland Sheepdog	6 Bloodhound
7 Labrador Retriever	7 Pekingese

watching Animal Planet. Australian Shepherds are uncommon outside North America (although one did win Crufts dog show in Britain in 2006), but this is a dog that deserves more notice throughout the world.

MINIATURE SCHNAUZER

Height: 30–36cm (12–14in)
Weight: 6–7kg (13–15lb)
Life expectancy: No accurate statistics
First use: Herding dog
Country of origin: Germany
Colour: Black, black and silver, pepper and salt

Shepherds come in many varieties

Across the English Channel, stockmen in northern France, the low countries, and northern Germany used a wide variety of local dogs both to guard their livestock and to herd them. These evolved into today's Briard, Beauceron, and Picardy Shepherd, four varieties of Belgian Shepherd, three varieties of Dutch Shepherd, and of course the German Shepherd Dog, the world's most successful working dog.

The millions of German Shepherds that live as working dogs or companions across the world today descend from a breeding programme begun in the late 1800s by one man, Max von Stephanitz. His brilliant public relations move was to offer his dogs for free to the German military service during World War I. They quickly replaced all other breeds, and at the end of the war, returning soldiers took German Shepherd Dogs to the United Kingom, the United States, Canada, and elsewhere, while Hollywood spread the breed's reputation worldwide through film characters such as Strongheart and Rin Tin Tin. In Britain, post-war feelings meant the breed

What's my line? The modern Australian Shepherd is, like many dogs, splitting into working and companion lines. Those bred for working are likely to have higher energy levels and guarding instinct than show lines, making them a more challenging proposition for owners.

GERMAN SHEPHERD DOG

Height: 55–65cm (22–26in)
Weight: 22–40kg (48–88lb)
Life expectancy: 10.3 years
First use: Herding and guarding dog
Country of origin: Germany
Colour: Black with reddish-brown, brown, yellow to light grey markings, black, grey; white appears but is not shown

POLISH LOWLAND-SHEEPDOG

Height: 41–51cm (16–20in)
Weight: 14–16kg (31–35lb)
Life expectancy: No accurate statistics
First use: Herding dog
Country of origin: Poland
Colour: Any colour

was known as the Alsatian, after the French province of Alsace, until 1977. In Germany, many lines of German Shepherd Dogs are bred both for their looks and for their ability to work. Elsewhere, their immense popularity means they have been bred less scrupulously, simply because there's a market for them. As a result of this, nervousness and fearfulness became established within the breed. While a good German Shepherd Dog is one of the most reliable of dogs, there are equal numbers of unreliable fear-biters. Breeding for the show ring, especially in North America, also exaggerated a curious physical characteristic, the sloping back. Mainland European lines of dogs, especially those from the former Soviet countries, have more naturally level backs. American standards also disqualify longhaired German Shepherds, while these are intentionally bred for throughout Europe. In my experience, the solid black, longhaired German Shepherd Dogs are less inclined to fearful behaviour, while cream or white individuals are more likely to be nervous and highly strung.

Occasionally I meet a perfect German Shepherd Dog. They are easy to housetrain and obedience train, loving, stable and friendly, reliable with kids, playful and non-aggressive with other dogs, while at the same time they remain alert and watchful, fearless when confronted with threat, and reliable in doing whatever they're trained to do. When I meet one of these, especially if it has a sumptuous long coat, I want to steal it. Unfortunately these superb dogs are a minority of those I see. Many more, through either breeding or early learning, are unreliable. This breed naturally feels most comfortable in its own "den". If that's your home, fine, but if it's under a table, under a bed, or hiding from strangers, you've got potential problems. The German Shepherd Dog may be the world's most popular working dog, but that doesn't mean it's the best dog in the world.

In the shadow of the German Shepherd

Some German dog owners will tell you there are other candidates for best dog in the world, and point with pride to their pinschers and schnauzers. All of these breeds started life as large working dogs but now come in a variety of sizes. The smallest pinschers – the Miniature Pinscher and the Affenpinscher – have been diminished to the realms of toydom, and are listed both here and in that group. The smallest schnauzer, the Miniature Schnauzer, remains a larger and more robust breed. It has become popular worldwide, but especially in North America and continental Europe.

As with so many other German breeds, the Miniature Schnauzer has had to suffer the indignity and pain of having both its ears and tail amputated. Ear cropping stopped in many countries well over 50 years ago but remains common in the United States, while tail docking continued in some regions of Europe until early in the 21st century. I find Miniature Schnauzers funny, friendly, and trainable, especially when taught from an early age. I know a pair that accompanied their owner and the family Labrador pheasant shooting. After watching the Lab bring back pheasant on numerous occasions, the Miniature Schnauzers joined in, each successfully bringing birds back. The owner claims they didn't even chew them a little!

Group 6: Gundogs

Here's a declaration of interest: I live with gundogs. These days there are no fewer than six of them sleeping over at my place when my family gathers together at Christmas. One of them is a sane and sensible Golden Retriever. That's my Bean, of course. The others are Labrador Retrievers. Sane and sensible aren't the adjectives that instantly come to mind when I think of some of the things they get up to. But even so, because gundogs are "family" to me, there may just be a slight bias perceptible in what I've written about them here.

Masked braque The pointers of Europe share their heritage and their looks, with pendent ears, neat, strong muzzles, long legs, and typically parti-coloured coats that are easily seen. Although it was created from a mix of European pointing breeds, the Braque St Germain has developed a distinctive look with a divided orange "mask".

GUNDOGS

Water dogs
France Barbet (French Water Dog)
Germany Poodle
Ireland Irish Water Spaniel
Italy Lagotto Romagnolo (Romagna Water Dog)
Netherlands Wetterhoun (Frisian Water Dog)
Portugal Cão de agua Português (Portuguese Water Dog)
Spain Perro de agua español (Spanish Waterdog)
United States American Water Spaniel

Pointers and setters
Denmark Gammel Dansk Hønsehund (Old Danish Pointing Dog)
France Braque de l'Ariège (Ariege Pointing Dog), Braque d'Auvergne (Auvergne Pointing Dog), Braque du Bourbonnais (Bourbonnais Pointing Dog), Braque français, type Gascogne (grande taille) (French Pointing Dog, Gascogne type), Braque français, type Pyrénées (petite taille) (French Pointing Dog, Pyrenean type), Braque Saint-Germain (St. Germain Pointing Dog)
Germany Deutsch Kurzhaar (German Short-haired Pointer), Deutsch Drahthaar (German Wire-haired Pointer), Deutsch Stichelhaar (German Rough-haired Pointer),Pudelpointer, Weimaraner
Great Britain English Pointer, English Setter, Gordon Setter
Ireland Irish Red Setter, Irish Red and White Setter
Italy Bracco Italiano (Italian Pointing Dog)
Hungary Drotzörü Magyar Vizsla (Hungarian Wire-haired Pointing Dog), Rövidszörü Magyar Vizsla (Hungarian Short-haired Pointing Dog)
Portugal Perdigueiro Português (Portuguese Pointing Dog)
Spain Perdiguero de Burgos (Burgos Pointing Dog)

Spaniel type pointers and setters
France Epagneul bleu de Picardie (Blue Picardy Spaniel), Epagneul Breton (Brittany), Epagneul français (French Spaniel), Epagneul picard (Picardy Spaniel), Epagneul de Pont-Audemer (Pont-Audemer Spaniel)
Germany Kleiner Münsterländer (Small Munsterlander), Grosser Münsterländer (Large Munsterlander), Deutsch Langhaar (German long-haired Pointer)
Netherlands Drentse Patrijshond (Drentse Partridge Dog), Stabyhoun (Frisian Pointing Dog)

Griffon-type pointers
Czech Republic Cesky Fousek (Bohemian wire-haired Pointing Griffon)
France Griffon d'arrêt à poil dur Korthals (French wire-haired Korthals Pointing Griffon)
Italy Spinone Italiano (Italian Wire-haired Pointing Dog)
Slovakia Slovensky Hrubosrsty Stavac (Ohar) (Slovakian Wire-haired Pointing Dog)

Flushing Dogs
Germany Deutscher Wachtelhund (German Spaniel)
Great Britain Clumber Spaniel, English Cocker Spaniel, Field Spaniel, Sussex Spaniel, English Springer Spaniel, Welsh Springer Spaniel
Netherlands Kooikerhondje (Small Dutch Waterfowl Dog)
United States American Cocker Spaniel

Retrievers
Canada Nova Scotia Duck Tolling Retriever
Great Britain Curly-coated Retriever, Flat-coated Retriever, Labrador Retriever, Golden Retriever
United States Chesapeake Bay Retriever

Trainability takes another leap forward with the development of gundogs. These are almost always thoughtful and responsive breeds, which is why they are amongst the world's most popular family companions. The Labrador Retriever, the most popular of all breeds in the United States, Canada, the United Kingdom, Australia, and New Zealand, is four times more numerous than the next most popular breed. That's also a gun dog, the Golden Retriever in the United States and the Cocker Spaniel in the United Kingdom. Elsewhere, gundogs are just as popular; in Germany, the German Pointer is exceeded in numbers only by the German Shepherd Dog. If you are willing to accept the Poodle in the gundog category – and I've placed it here with all the other water dogs – then this is the most successful of all the breed groups.

Gundogs came before guns

Gundogs come in five varieties: water dogs, pointers, setters, flushing dogs, and retrievers. Water dogs existed well before the advent of hunting with guns, and in medieval times were used to retrieve arrows shot during hunting and also in times of war. Pointers were probably developed in Spain (as so many other hunting dogs were) to follow the scent of game then to stand rigidly still, often with a forelimb raised, so that their movement didn't trigger the game to dart for freedom. Hunters would then move forward with nets and capture the game. Setters behaved in the same way, except instead of "pointing" they crouched down or "set". Spaniels, or flushing dogs, flush birds from undergrowth towards hunters.

Gundog breeds proper have their origins in the 1700s, using the genetic base that already existed plus herders and hounds. The use of firearms in sport hunting, a new activity of the land-owning classes, required dogs to behave in new and more complicated ways. They had to learn to follow a sequence of instructions, not just to chase game, follow scent trails, or swim, but also to listen to and obey instructions before and during these activities. The retriever must learn to "wait", "go", "pick up", "hold", "carry back", and "drop". To work to the gun, dogs needed strong instinctive hunting abilities combined with a willingness to be trained and to obey command; to stay perfectly still, to jump into water when told to do so, to bring back game and never, ever eat it, not even chew on it!

STANDARD POODLE

Height: over 38cm (15in)
Weight: 20.5–32kg (45–70lb)
Life expectancy: 12 years
First use: Hunting dog
Country of origin: Germany
Colour: Any solid colour

Poodles and water dogs

The Portuguese and Spanish Water Dogs are amongst the most ancient breeds, as are the German/French Poodle, French Barbet, and Hungarian Puli. Most European countries had regional water dogs, and their descendants include the Irish Water Spaniel, the Dutch Wetterhoun, the English Curly-coated Retriever, and the American Chesapeake Bay Retriever and American Water Spaniel.

One of the most ancient of all water dogs is the Poodle, whose name derives from the German Pudelhund or "splash dog". Poodles come in three sizes – standard, miniature, and toy – if you live in the English speaking world, and four sizes – standard, medium, miniature, and toy – if you live

GERMAN POINTER

Height: 60–65cm (24–26in)
Weight: 27–32kg (59–70lb)
Life expectancy: 12.3 years
First use: Hunting dog
Country of origin: Germany
Colour: Brown, brown or black roan with white, light roan

in continental Europe. The European system is better, because it allows dogs larger than "miniature" but smaller than "standard" to still be appropriately classified. Interestingly, geneticists have discovered five distinct genetic groups within the breed. Parti-coloured Poodles were common until the beginning of the 20th century, but they virtually disappeared once breed standards banned the registration of anything other than a solid-coloured dog. Now that pet owners are interested in poodle crosses, some are also interested in parti-coloured purebred ones, and I've seen a few at the clinic.

I'm sure the reputation of Poodles suffers because of their demeaning (at least in my eyes) show cuts, which are stylized equivalents of old clipping methods designed to reduce drag in the water while keeping the chest and the leg joints insulated. A monthly all-over "pet cut" or a "lamb cut" shows off just how athletic these dogs are. The Poodle's role as yesterday's news in canine fashion isn't deserved. After they dropped from their height of popularity in the 1950s and 1960s, dedicated breeders regained control of their breeding. In my experience, they have successfully reduced the incidence of nippy or nervous individuals within the miniatures and toys; standards and mediums never had this problem. The Standard Poodle is one of the most underestimated of all breeds, a superb, wonderfully athletic family companion. Train one from puppyhood and it can be skilful at obedience, agility, and even scent tracking.

LABRADOR RETRIEVER

Height: 54–57cm (20.5–22.5in)
Weight: 25–34kg (55–74lb)
Life expectancy: 12.6 years
First use: Hunting dog
Country of origin: Great Britain
Colour: Golden, chocolate, black

Pointers

Spanish pointers were exported throughout Europe and formed the founder stock for the English Pointer, the Italian Bracco, the Danish Pointer, and similar pointers in Germany. Unaffected by revolution or war, Britain and Ireland's selection of pointers and setters date back many centuries, but the revolutions of 1848 lead to the disappearance of many of middle Europe's pointers. At the end of the 19th century German, Czech, Slovakian, and Hungarian breeders embarked upon a flourishing period of activity, creating new and rightly popular breeds such as the German Shorthaired, Wirehaired, and Roughhaired Pointers, and the Munsterlander, Visla, Weimaraner, Slovakian Pointer, and Cesky Fousek.

GOLDEN RETRIEVER

Height: 50–60cm (20–24in)
Weight: 27–36kg (59–79lb)
Life expectancy: 12 years
First use: Hunting dog
Country of origin: Great Britian
Colour: Golden, cream

Pointers can be shorthaired, wirehaired, or longhaired. To complicate matters, many longhaired pointers, such as the German Munsterlander and Dutch Drentse Partridge Dog, look like large spaniels. In France, these spaniel-type pointers are actually called spaniels: the Epagneul Picard, Epagneul de Pont-Audemer, and the Epagneul Breton, the last more commonly known as the Brittany in North America and Britain. The highly energetic German Wirehaired Pointer is enormously popular in Germany, while the German Shorthaired Pointer is the most popular of continental pointers in the English speaking world.

All of these fine dogs share a common attribute. They get "spooked" easily. From an evolutionary point of view, it's unnatural for a dog to freeze in mid-hunt and not go in for the kill. This contradiction is perpetuated today in the edgy personalities of pointers in particular. More than other gundogs, these are natural worriers unless extremely well socialized as youngsters, a little aloof with strangers, wary of the unknown. Some are highly strung, prone to their own neuroses. Because of this, they are better with older rather than younger children.

One exception is the Irish Setter, the one pointer from the British Isles that is widely known beyond its homeland. Its outstanding grace and beauty make it a world favourite, but having been bred for the last half century for companionship rather than for work, the breed has also become somewhat scatty. The cartoonist Gary Larson's "Six moods of the Irish setter", showing six identical goofy images of a smiling setter, remains a perfect description of this happy breed.

Spaniels

The British Isles are home to most of today's popular spaniels and retrievers. At one time all British spaniels were classified according to whether they flushed game from land, field, or water, but with the advent of breed clubs that changed. They began to be classified according to where they were bred, like the Sussex Spaniel, or how they worked, being "springers" or "cockers". Several are split into show lines and more high-energy working lines. In Britain, the English Springer Spaniel has become the country's most successful customs and police sniffer dog. These are high energy burners, especially working types, and will work themselves to exhaustion if given the opportunity. Springers aren't as obsessed as Border Collies, but this energetic and affectionate breed needs both open space to run in and mental stimulation when at home.

The English Cocker is, in essence, two breeds. Working Cockers, like Springer Spaniels, are gentle, affectionate, wound-up coils in constant need of something to do, and make superb agility dogs. At Hearing Dogs for Deaf People we're virtually guaranteed success when we acquire dogs that are even part working Cocker. American Cocker Spaniels, with more luxuriously lush, dense coats, were developed from more placid show lines of English Cocker Spaniels. Few are ever used for work, although they can be more work for you – those fine coats need constant attention.

One word of caution about Cockers, be they English or American. A behavioural trait called "avalanche of rage" or "Jekyll and Hyde Syndrome" is not uncommon in solid red or golden dogs. An affected individual behaves normally, suddenly becomes aggressive and then, just as quickly, reverts to its normal behaviour. This is a behavioural trait, possibly linked to hormonal characteristics unique to these individuals, and is also rarely reported in solid black Cocker Spaniels.

Why would a behavioural trait be linked to colour? Well, coat colour is controlled by genes affecting production of the pigment melanin, and one version of a gene called beta-defensin (oddly named because it was first wrongly assumed to help the body fight infection) produces yellow dogs, while a mutant version produces black dogs. As well as affecting melanin, the beta-defensin gene also plays a role in controlling the amount of cortisol produced by the body. Cortisol plays a central command role in how the body physiologically and behaviourally responds to stress. When I carried

IRISH SETTER

Height: 63–68cm (25–27in)
Weight: 27–32kg (60–70lb)
Life expectancy: 11.8 years
First use: Hunting dog
Country of origin: Ireland
Colour: Red

out a survey amongst thousands of professional dog breeders with a variety of solid-coloured breeds such as Labrador Retrievers, Poodles, and English Cocker Spaniels, they reported that black or brown dogs were easier to train, more reliable, and better with children than were blond, yellow, or apricot members of the same breed. Behaviourists at Cornell University's veterinary school report that chocolate and black Labradors were "under represented" in dogs referred to their behaviour clinic for aggression problems, compared with yellow Labs.

Labradors and retrievers

While cockers and springers were being perfected, aristocratic British breeders were also taking an avid interest in dogs arriving at fishing ports from Newfoundland. Greater and Lesser St. John's Dogs worked well in water, were amenable to training, and were the right size to retrieve game from land or water and return it to the hunter. They would instinctively carry gently, learn readily, and obey consistently. These dogs' ancestors may have arrived in Newfoundland as companions of Portuguese and Basque fishermen; in turn they were used to develop the English-speaking world's most popular family companion, the Labrador Retriever, and its similar but more avuncular buddy, the Golden Retriever. Two St. John's Dogs that survived a shipwreck in Chesapeake Bay formed the foundation stock for the Chesapeake Bay Retriever.

ENGLISH COCKER SPANIEL

Height: 38–40cm (15–16in)
Weight: 13–15kg (28–32lb)
Life expectancy: 12.5 years
First use: Hunting dog
Country of origin: Great Britain
Colour: Black, cream, red, brown, solid or with white, tan points

It isn't just at my practice that Labradors are the most popular of breeds. They're ubiquitous, and rightly so. Some pointers can be "glass-half-empty" individuals, but Labs eagerly anticipate life. Many breeds are mentally mature by two years of age, but Labs take three or more years to emerge from mental puppyhood (and some never, ever do). Popularity is inevitably accompanied by indiscriminate breeding and consequential health problems. There are more than 25 known inherited medical problems within the breed, and while there are certification programmes to diminish eye and joint conditions, there aren't similar programmes for other conditions, such as epilepsy (which is suffered by 3 per cent of all Labrador Retrievers in Denmark).

BRACCO ITALIANO

Height: 56–67cm (22–26.5in)
Weight: 25–40kg (55–88lb)
Life expectancy: No accurate statistics
First use: Hunting dog
Country of origin: Italy
Colour: White, white speckled or patched with orange or chestnut

There are two distinct types within the Labrador breed. Most family companions are box-shaped, 30–40kg (66–88lb) walking stomachs. Working labs are much smaller and leaner, often weighing around 23–25kg (51–55lb), with an even higher energy level than their larger relatives and more of a springer-type personality. They are excellent at field and agility trials and, of course, working to the gun. Labs are high octane dogs, and inclined to sing variations of the same song – "More!" "Again!" "Me!" Despite a deep, commanding bark, this affectionate breed makes a poor watchdog. I love them and think they're wonderful family companions, but the first few years of a Lab's life can be time consuming.

Golden Retrievers are the same size as their Labrador compatriots, and make equally wonderful family companions, but live life to lesser extremes. In this breed too there are working and show types, although the differences are not as dramatic as they are in Labradors. And there is a third category of Golden Retriever, which has been bred specifically to work as an Assistance Dog, as an aid for blind or disabled people. As might be expected, this is the calmest line of all Goldens. They are noble dogs, but as a result of breeding for such a calm and moderate disposition, their sense of humour has been displaced.

European breeds on the rise

Elsewhere in Europe, Dutch breeders developed the Dutch Partridge Dog, and dual purpose point-and-retrieve dogs were developed to work in fields and marshes in France. These were primarily in the northern regions, in Picardy, Normandy (Pont-Audemer), and Brittany. Brittanies have been exported to Canada and the United States, where they successfully work as triple-purpose dogs: pointing, retrieving, and playing with the kids.

European gundogs remain a wonderful resource, with several breeds that are still relatively uncommon but warrant wider recognition. The Small

Munsterlander is in fact the size of a large English Springer Spaniel and has a similar personality – energetic, alert, in need of both mental and physical stimulation. Hungarian Vizslas are slightly larger, a little prone to the pointer's typical worry of the unknown, but superb athletes and wonderful with the children of their own homes. Italian Spinones are laconic, goofy-looking, gentle slobs with, in my experience, a longer life expectancy than you'd expect for such big dogs, and an undiminished natural ability as pointer-retrievers. In town, they make loving pets, reliable with kids and laconic about life. In the countryside, their instincts take over and they transmogrify into intuitive workers. If visiting livestock-owning friends, tell them to hide their chickens and rabbits before you arrive.

Many gundog breeds are still used for their original purpose, some have become "dual purpose", and an increasing number serve the sole purpose of companionship. Their common denominator is a strong affiliation to people and particularly to the people they share their homes with.

Home turf This is where a gundog was meant to be. They adapt amazingly well to more sedate family life, but remember that they were bred to keep going all day. To give them what they need, most owners should probably stay out at least half an hour after they first feel inclined to head for home. Most dogs would choose to stay out even longer.

Group 7: Terriers and Dachshunds

I was raised in a home owned by a Scottish Terrier named Angus. He was succeeded by a series of Yorkshire Terriers, not the toy-sized types we see today but dogs double that size, which spent their indoor hours on their backs asking to be tickled and their outdoor hours chasing down any wildlife they encountered. It was the resulting frequent visits to the vet to remove porcupine quills from their faces or stitch up lacerations, not to mention my frequent responsibility for washing them in tomato juice in vain attempts to destroy the smell of skunk after they'd been sprayed, that made me consider veterinary medicine as a career.

Terriers are "earth dogs", originally bred for their feistiness, for a willingness to ruthlessly go to ground in a rabbit, fox, or badger tunnel and engage in head-on combat on their quarry's home turf. Any living thing – rats, ferrets, otters, weasels, mice, snakes – was fair game to a working terrier, and often still is to their companion descendants. However loveable they may be with people, never forget for a moment that these breeds are excitable, reactive, high energy burners, and bloodthirsty killers at heart. They will instantly pursue anything that is small and fast moving. In the terrier world, this tenacity is called "gameness".

The British Isles are home to almost all the terrier breeds, and provided the foundation stock for other country's terriers, like the Australian, Japanese, Brazilian, and Czesky Terriers. The one enormous exception to this rule is Germany, home to what is overwhelmingly the world's most popular ever terriers, the Dachshunds.

Little dog, big spirit Terriers sometimes act as if someone forgot to tell them they were small. It can seem that all the confidence and swagger of a large dog has simply been concentrated into the smaller packaging of these breeds, none more so than the feisty Smooth-haired Dachshund.

TERRIERS AND DACHSHUNDS

Large and medium-sized terriers
Brazil Terrier Brasileiro (Brazilian Terrier)
Germany Dachshunds (Smooth-, Long-, and Wire-haired), Deutscher Jagdterrier (German Hunting Terrier)
Great Britain Airedale Terrier, Bedlington Terrier, Border Terrier, Fox Terrier (Smooth and Wirehaired), Lakeland Terrier, Manchester Terrier, Parson Russell Terrier, Welsh Terrier
Ireland Glen of Imaal Terrier, Irish Terrier, Kerry Blue Terrier, Soft Coated Wheaten Terrier

Small-sized terriers
Australia Australian Terrier, Australian Silky Terrier
Austria Austrian Pinscher
Czech Republic Cesky Teriér (Cesky Terrier)
Germany Miniature Dachshunds (Smooth-, Long-, and Wire-haired)
Great Britain Cairn Terrier, Dandie Dinmont Terrier, English Toy Terrier (Black and Tan), Jack Russell Terrier, Norfolk Terrier, Norwich Terrier, Scottish Terrier, Sealyham Terrier, Skye Terrier, West Highland White Terrier, Yorkshire Terrier (now a Toy dog)
Japan Nihon Teria (Japanese Terrier)
Netherlands Smoushond

Bull-type terriers
Great Britain Bull Terrier, Miniature Bull Terrier, Staffordshire Bull Terrier
United States American Pit Bull Terrier, American Staffordshire Bull Terrier

Working origins

Both small and large terriers were developed in England, Ireland, Scotland and Wales. Small terriers are the yappy snappies of the dog world, great watchdogs but not necessarily the most trainable of breeds. They and their more recent, larger terrier cousins are probably the most modern of all groups of dogs, descendants of hounds that were dwarfed, miniaturized, or both, so that they could efficiently go to earth. The hound origin of terriers is most evident in the looks and appearance of the Dachshunds.

A 40-year-old *Encyclopedia of Dogs* I own says that, "Up to relatively recent times, terriers were bred principally by people of modest means." Bedlingtons and Dandie Dinmonts were developed by gypsies, and terriers were the dogs of commoners and farmers – practical, small dogs that helped rid buildings of vermin. Some, such as the Patterdale and Yorkshire Terriers, were used in sport, killing rats against the clock.

Until around the 19th century, short-legged, hard-nosed terriers existed throughout Britain and Ireland. With the advent of breed clubs, breeders began to produce distinctive regional varieties with regional names: Border, Lakeland, Manchester, Norfolk, Skye, Staffordshire, Scottish, Yorkshire, West Highland. Later, small terriers were crossed with hunting and retrieving dogs, producing faster dogs with greater stature: today's Welsh, Irish, Kerry Blue, and Airedale terriers. These terriers don't go to ground. They chase, capture, and kill. More recently, breeders have successfully bred the "terrorist" temperament out of many of these large breeds, producing dogs more interested in playing with other dogs than decimating wildlife.

BULL TERRIER

Height: 53–56cm (21–23in)
Weight: 24–28kg (53–62lb)
Life expectancy: 12.9 years
First use: Fighting dog
Country of origin: Great Britain
Colour: White, fawn, red, black brindle, with white or tricolour

Popular terriers

While some classic terriers, such as the Fox Terrier, have dropped from favour and others, such as the Glen of Imaal, are classified as endangered, four varieties thrive: the Jack Russell, West Highland White, Border, and Yorkshire Terriers. Because all registries now classify Yorkies as Companions and Toys, I'll leave them to the next group.

The Jack Russell is the most popular of all the true terriers I see. They have a well-earned reputation as little nippers, and let me tell you, their teeth are inordinately large for their size. They thrive on the companionship of people and of other dogs, but two of the same sex are likely to fight over who's top dog. Registry numbers don't tell the truth about Russells, because most aren't registered, and they come in a great variety of heights and coat textures. They're tough as walnuts and good healers as well as heelers.

Cairns, Westies, and Border Terriers filled similar roles. West Highland White Terriers were developed from the Cairns of southwestern Scotland, and both are robust bundles of fun, but Westies have a very high incidence of allergic skin disease and, later in life, breathing problems. Border Terriers have become enormously popular in the last decade, so much so they are now in the top ten most popular breeds in Britain, and a firm favourite as the British vet's small family companion. Most of the small terriers have longer than dog-average life expectancies.

DACHSHUND

Height: 13–25cm (5–10in)
Weight: 4–11.5kg (9–25lb)
Life expectancy: 12.2 years
First use: Hunting dog
Country of origin: Germany
Colour: Solid, solid shaded with black, two-colour, dappled, striped; no white

CAIRN TERRIER

Height: 25–30cm (10–12in)
Weight: 6–7kg (13–17lb)
Life expectancy: 13.2 years
First use: Hunting dog
Country of origin: Great Britain
Colour: Cream, wheaten, red, sandy, grey, brindled

JACK RUSSELL

Height: 25–30cm (10–12in)
Weight: 4–7kg (9–15lb)
Life expectancy: 13.6 years
First use: Hunting dog
Country of origin: Great Britain
Colour: Black and white, brown and white, tricolour

Bull terriers

The final category, bull-type terriers, were created by crossing tenacious terriers with aggressive mastiffs. They were once used in bull baiting because they didn't just bite, they bit and hung on. That's why breeds like the American Pit Bull Terrier are so dangerous, and why the Pit Bull is the flavour-of-the-decade fighting dog. Socialized early and raised as members of the family, Pit Bulls are rewarding but demanding companions. When they do bite, "accidentally" in the home or intentionally in premeditated dog fights, their terrier obstinacy turns them into lethal weapons. In the United States, Pit Bulls are responsible for more human deaths than any other breed. In the English-speaking world, Staffordshire and larger American Staffordshire Bull Terriers, always popular as family pets, have joined Pit Bulls as fashion statements for guys who feel that muscular dogs advertise who they think they are. The sad consequence is that these are amongst the most common dogs abandoned to shelters.

Dachshunds

It's only because their name ends in "hund" that these terriers are classified as hounds. They did work in packs – some still do – but Dachshunds are classic earthdogs, as fearless underground as the nippiest Jack Russell. They filled the same roles as small British and Irish terriers, while working pinschers and the Dutch Smoushond (*see pp. 74–79*) augmented the "attack and destroy" niche. Continental Dachshunds come in three sizes, measured by chest circumference: Toy or Rabbit at up to 30cm (12in), Miniature at 30–35cm (12–14in) and Standard at 35–45cm (14–18in). British and American Dachsies come in two weights, Miniature (under 5kg/11lb) and Standard. All come in smooth, long, or wire coats.

Visit the stuffed Victorian dogs at the Natural History Museum at Tring and look at the Dachshund. Only when you see what Dachshunds were like only a little over 100 years ago do you realise how dramatically their legs have been shortened for the show ring. There's no benefit in a dog being so close to the ground that walking rubs the hair off the chest, but that's what I see with some. These dogs need to flex their backs unnaturally just to climb stairs and are most susceptible to paralysis-threatening slipped discs. Dachshunds, especially long or wirehaired ones, are great family companions, but good leg length is vital for good health.

American humourist E.B. White once wrote of his insolent Dachshund Fred "when I answer his peremptory scratch at the door and hold the door open for him to walk through, he stops in the middle to light a cigarette just to hold me up". British dog behaviourist Roger Mugford once spent four full days at Cruft's staring at different breeds of dogs and noting their responses; the one most likely to bark at him was the Smooth-haired Dachshund.

Because many terriers were already small, they were prime subjects for further miniaturization. This is what happened to the Yorkshire Terrier, Miniature Pinscher, Toy Fox Terrier, English Toy Terrier, and Miniature English Bull Terrier. They're in my next group – companions and toys.

Group 8: Toy and companion breeds

All dogs give us companionship. People who own guarding breeds like German Shepherd Dogs, Dobermanns, and Rottweilers know that even these want to get on a lap and be stroked. Little dogs are no more than small versions of big dogs, but their small size has made them amongst the world's most popular pets. This category includes most of the exaggerated paedomorphs, breeds of infant looks with large, prominent eyes, relatively large heads, and small bodies.

TOY AND COMPANION BREEDS

European and European-derived breeds
Belgium Griffon belge (Belgian Griffon), Griffon bruxellois (Brussels Griffon), Petit Brabançon (Small Brabant Griffon)
Belgium/France Bichon à poil frisé (Bichon Frise), Epagneul nain Continental (Continental Toy Spaniel), Papillon, Phalène
France Caniche (Poodle), Bouledogue français (French Bulldog), Petit chien lion (Löwchen/Little Lion Dog)
Germany Affenpinscher, Kromfohrländer, Pomeranian, Zwergpinscher (Miniature Pinscher)
Great Britain Cavalier King Charles Spaniel, King Charles Spaniel, Pug, Yorkshire Terrier
Italy Bolognese (Bolognese)
Madagascar Coton de Tuléar
Mediterranean Bichon Havanais (Havanese), Maltese
United States Boston Terrier

Oriental and South American breeds
Tibet Lhasa Apso, Shih Tzu, Tibetan Spaniel, Tibetan Terrier
China Chinese Crested Dog, Pekingese
Mexico Chihuahua
Japan Chin (Japanese Chin)

The shrinking of dogs

Yorkshire Terriers, Boston Terriers, French Bulldogs, and Pugs were considerably diminished in size in the 20th century. So were Miniature Bull Terriers, Miniature Pinschers, and Affenpinschers. Small Poodles, small spitzes or Pomeranians, and small "comforter" spaniels were developed during the last 300–400 years, while genetic evidence shows that Lhasa Apsos and Shih Tzus have been small for at least 5,000 years. No one is yet certain when or exactly where Chihuahuas shrank.

It was first suggested as far back as 1984 that a gene called "insulin-like growth factor 1" gene or IGF-1 was involved with size in poodles, but studies of Portuguese Water Dogs, a breed with a variety of sizes, confirmed in 2007 that this single gene controls size. DNA analysis shows that the small size trait emerged 15,000 years ago, early in the history of domestic dogs. Doesn't it amaze you – it certainly amazes me – that the Shih Tzu, Lhasa Apso, and Tibetan terrier are truly ancient breeds, genetically closer to the wolf than the German Shepherd Dog is?

No one knows why little dogs weren't dropped from the early breeding pool, when they provided less dog meat and were no match for big game. I'd argue that shrinking in size was vital for the later success of dogs, because

Thinking small All heart, little dogs make great companions. The fashion for pint-sized dogs is nothing new – some small breeds go back centuries. Miniaturization can however have its drawbacks: Cavalier King Charles Spaniels are wonderful family pets, but their life expectancy is short compared to that of other small breeds, such as Miniature Dachshunds, due to inherited medical conditions.

it made it easier for the species to diversify early into a variety of types. Smaller dogs were also easier to maintain in villages, to transport for trade, and to take on migrations, and they sure were amusing to watch. I'm sure that our ancestors perpetuated these bantam dogs that seem to never grow up for the simplest of reasons: because they offered warmth, companionship, and amusement. And are those not still powerful reasons why we choose to live with them today?

Ancient little yappers no doubt acted as sentinel dogs, warning herdsmen and homesteads of approaching people or animals, and in Tibet small dogs also acted as good luck talismans for travellers. Eventually, they became companions of the aristocracy, first the Pekingese in China and the Japanese Chin in Japan, and later the King Charles Spaniel, Bolognese, Maltese, and Löwchen across Europe.

Size and health

Miniature and Toy Poodles, Miniature Dachshunds, and Yorkshire Terriers are the most numerous of today's toy breeds, and the first two have the longest life expectancies of all breeds. This may be in part because so many of them travel in shoulder bags from Starbucks to Starbucks, never setting foot where danger waits, but it's more likely that the relatively large organs of little dogs – the heart, lungs, kidneys, liver and digestive system – support their small bodies longer than do the relatively smaller organs of larger breeds. If your vet ever shows you an x-ray of your toy dog's chest you'll see what I mean. Little dogs are genuinely all heart.

While miniaturization of Poodles and Dachshunds has had benign or even positive effects on health, the same cannot be said for Yorkshire Terriers, Cavalier King Charles Spaniels, Boston Terriers, or Chihuahuas. Small Yorkies are particularly prone to soft tracheas – windpipes that will spontaneously collapse – with dire consequences. Some dogs need complex surgery in order to breathe easily once more. Chihuahuas have a similar problem and an increased incidence of epilepsy. This is associated with the exaggerated roundness of the skull, and also a problem with round-skulled Bostons. Cavaliers make the most wonderful of small family dogs but commonly suffers valvular heart disease and syringomyelia, a brain condition in which the hindbrain partly prolapses out of the skull. For these reasons this breed's median life expectancy (*see p.334*) is much shorter than you'd expect for a dog this size. Shih Tzus, Lhasa Apsos, and Tibetan Terriers, on the other hand, have fewer serious inherited medical conditions.

SHIH TZU

Height: 25–27cm (10–11in)
Weight: 5–7kg (10–16lb)
Life expectancy: 13.4 years
First use: Companion
Country of origin: Tibet
Colour: All colours

PEKINESE

Height: 15–23cm (6–9in)
Weight: 3–5.5kg (7–12lb)
Life expectancy: 13.3 years
First use: Companion
Country of origin: China
Colour: Any colour

Fashion trends

In the 20th century, breeders took miniaturization to extremes. Because there was good profit in following fashion, breeders intentionally bred from the runts, individuals that they once carefully avoided breeding from. I now see Yorkshire Terriers, Pomeranians, Chihuahuas, and Pekingese that as adults weigh less than 1.5kg (3lb). This is terrible. Their personalities are often terrific, but invariably the medical problems these dogs have are challenging, and their life expectancies shortened. This is a pointless trend

Mini-mastiff The Pug has been a companion breed for thousands of years, first in the East and then as a royal pet in the West. Although its cobby build still recalls its larger ancestors, the opinionated and stubborn Pug rarely shows the overt aggression typical of many true mastiffs.

BICHON FRISE

Height: 23–30cm (9–12in)
Weight: 3–6kg (7–13lb)
Life expectancy: No accurate statistics
First use: Companion
Country of origin: Mediterranean region
Colour: White

CHIHUAHUA

Height: 15–23cm (6–9in)
Weight: 1–3kg (2–6lb)
Life expectancy: 13 years
First use: Companion
Country of origin: Mexico
Colour: Any colour

that I'll be happy to see the end of. There is a wonderful selection of portable dogs, without any need to make any of them smaller still.

In the 21st century, the range of toy and companion dogs is being actively expanded by intentional crosses of two breeds to create something new. Poodles are often used: the breed itself is out of fashion, but has the good health, attractive coat, and responsive disposition that we want in small companions. I now routinely see Cockerpoos, Pekapoos, Maltipoos, and Yorkiepoos, and unlike kennel clubs I don't consider crossbreeding to be dastardly miscegenation. Crossing dogs is almost always good. You know how the parent breeds behave, so you've got a reasonable idea of the potential of the youngsters. You also know that crossing two breeds reduces the risk that both parents are carrying a recessive gene for any medical condition that exists within one of the parent breeds. For example, crossing a Cavalier King Charles Spaniel with a Miniature Poodle or a Tibetan Spaniel reduces the risk that the progeny will develop the inherited medical conditions that are rampant in Cavaliers.

CHAPTER FOUR

What makes a Modern Dog

We're built from the same parts, our dogs and us: over 90 per cent of your dog's DNA is identical to yours, and your biochemistry, senses, organs, and emotions follow a common design. I'm sure that's why so many of us can't help but think of dogs as furry people in disguise, mute humans desperate to talk to us, to tell us how they feel and what they're thinking. Don't let the similarities fool you. Dogs' sensory abilities differ from ours, and their brains process information in a different way.

Memory matters If they watch you hide a treat, both dogs and cats can uncover it immediately. But make them wait just thirty seconds, and most cats forget where it is; most dogs can still remember as much as four minutes later. This superior memory is just one reason why dogs are top of the training class.

From my medical perspective, the physical similarities between dogs and us are outstanding. Virtually all the principles of human medicine, with the exception of psychiatry, apply to caring for dogs, either for preventing physical or mental conditions or for treating them when they occur. I use the same anaesthetics, painkillers, and therapeutic drugs as doctors do to treat anything from heart disease to hormonal imbalances. When dogs need medical or surgical attention, I use the same principles of critical care that are used on you or me when life is threatened.

Of course, there are also wonderful physical and mental differences between us and dogs. Some are subtle – for example, all livers serve to cleanse the blood, but a dog's takes twice as long as yours does to break down aspirin. Give aspirin to a dog as frequently as you take it yourself, and it can cause stomach inflammation, even ulceration. Other differences are more dramatic. Dogs scent the world around them in ways so radically different to how we smell things that their ability is simply beyond our comprehension, and we sometimes think dogs must have some sixth sense.

It may seen a bit dry to talk about how a dog's eyes work or how digestion functions, but understanding their physical and biochemical make-up makes us better at caring for them and recognizing when something goes wrong, and makes it so much easier to understand why our dogs behave as they do. Understanding what motivates dogs puts us in a better position to work with rather than against what's inherently there.

Just how intelligent is your dog?

Before getting to the specifics, it's worth thinking about exactly how dogs approach and experience life. I hear the word "intelligence" at least once a day from owners, but I wonder if you know exactly what you mean when you say "She's the most intelligent dog I've every had", or (as I also hear) "He's a bit slow off the mark". I doubt that there's a breed standard anywhere in the world that doesn't boast of the breed's "intelligence", but what does it mean? How do you compare the natural kinds of intelligence that made early dogs useful to us with those needed to herd, to point or retrieve, to follow commands, or to act as eyes or ears for people with disabilities? In a dog context, there are four types of intelligence: instinctive, working, learning, and problem solving, and they need to be seen separately.

Instinctive intelligence is hardwired into the learning centres of the brain (*see p.22*), and the wiring in some dogs is certainly better than in others. Natural pressures and selective breeding have modified the dog's inherited learning centres, enhancing and diminishing different behaviours in different groups of dogs: terriers are persistent and inveterate diggers, toy dogs bark territorially, and retrievers do what their label says.

Dogs must communicate well with each other to work harmoniously and avoid fighting, but they also have an unparalleled ability to communicate with us. This type of intelligence is variously called communication, working, or obedience intelligence, and some have a whole lot more of it than others. A dog needs a willingness, a desire, to take directions from a person and not be diverted by distractions, and dogs with longer attention spans and persistence are more capable of concentrating.

Learning intelligence enables dogs to use their skills to adapt to or alter their environment. I leave the back door off the latch so that Bean can go in and out, but she had to learn to use her nose to push it open from inside, and her paws to pull it open from outside when the wind almost closes it. She watched my daughter's visiting Labrador do these things and soon copied her. Generally speaking, dogs with good learning intelligence need only a few exposures to a situation to form stable responses.

Problem solving – mentally constructing your own solution when faced with a problem – is slightly different. For example, if you place a food reward on the far side of a barrier and attach it to a string running under the barrier, how long does it take the dog to understand that pulling on the string brings the reward? This experiment has been carried out on a variety of animals: compared with primates, dogs are not good at mental problem solving, but some are much better than others.

When dogs are ranked by "intelligence" the word often means a combination of learning intelligence and problem solving. Herding breeds such as the Border Collie have been selectively bred for these, and are also phenomenally good communicators, so come top in intelligence tests.

One factor that differentiates the capabilities of a dogs' brains from ours, whatever their intelligence, is the influence of culture. In us, behaviour spreads from person to person, almost like a contagion. This provides a basis for our religious beliefs, fashion sense, or food preferences. Beyond puppyhood, dogs may learn specific skills from other dogs, but they are relatively poor learners from the culture of other dogs.

How emotional is your dog?

Dogs and people share the same anatomical parts. Do we share the same feelings and emotions? More specifically, are dogs aware of their emotions? When researchers started mapping the brain, they found where the hard-wired instincts were located, but had more difficulty finding the locations of feelings or emotions. These "motivators" involve many different pathways, which seem to vary from one dog to the next.

Sentience is a term often used in animal welfare issues. It's defined as having perceptions and sensations: if my dog is sentient, she's aware of her

Familiar feelings Debate as to the exact nature of sentience or consciousness has gone on for centuries. Dogs may not have our sense of time, place, or self, which is why rewards and reprimands must be immediate, but any dog owner could tell any philosopher that our dog's experiences, emotions, and memories are as real as our own.

surroundings and aware of what happens to her. Needless to say, she's also capable of feelings and emotions, of pain and pleasure – although these capacities were once thought by many scientists, including many of my own veterinary professors, not to exist in dogs. I have no doubt that dogs are sentient, and able to both remember and anticipate events. Some shiver when they come to the clinic, because they remember that the last time they visited I stabbed them and it hurt. Others arrive with gormless grins on their faces – I may have stabbed them too, but they remember that I also handed out liver treats, and they anticipate I might dole out more. Dogs experience fear, frustration, anxiety, and boredom, and can be reduced to a state resembling human depression by chronic stress or confinement.

Dogs can maintain complex social relationships because they understand what another animal is going to do. Dogs act in ways that resemble human empathy, such as lying down beside an ill companion, or licking their face. I see dogs worry when they hear sounds of distress from other dogs at the veterinary clinic. Dogs in my extended family frequently lick each other in greeting, and when they rest, they rest together. When I sit down, the most humanized of these dogs comes over and lies down too, always making body contact with my leg. To me, all of these behaviours suggest that dogs feel better when they're near each other or us. If you have two dogs and one goes away, the two will usually greet each other warmly when they're reunited. (Cats do the exact opposite.) When you return after a holiday, your dog probably greets you rapturously but then may go off and sulk, as if remembering hurt feelings. Tender feelings are normal in elephants, in gorillas, in cattle, in virtually all mammals that thrive on social structure. To me it's no more than common sense that dogs and humans share many emotional abilities, simply because these abilities evolved in both of us for the same evolutionary benefits.

Brains and nerves

Your brain and mine were not completely developed (meaning that the 15 billion cells in each had not matured into their adult structure) until we were 18 years old. Your dog's brain reaches anatomical maturity when it is just 12 weeks old. None of us grow any more brain cells during our lives. At 12 weeks, your dog has more than it actually needs. Later in life, if your dog survives to a great age, their numbers will drop to a critical level, and your dog will become a true mental geriatric. For most of their evolution, dogs simply didn't live long enough for this to be a problem; today, geriatric conditions including senile behaviour are amongst the most common problems that confront vets and owners.

At birth my dog Bean's brain was able to interpret only touch and warmth. By three weeks it was sufficiently developed to control her body temperature and metabolism, and she could urinate and defecate without her mother licking her bottom. By four weeks of age she had a perception of space. By five weeks she could stay awake if she wanted to. At six weeks of age she understood the significance of different body postures. At seven weeks she was beginning to understand what fear was and what to do when she felt it. At eight weeks she was perfectly comfortable to leave the security of her biological home, and by nine weeks her brain could easily control her bladder and bowels for several hours to prevent her from soiling her nest. By ten weeks virtually all her senses had reached maturity and now only needed experience to refine them. By 11 weeks her brain was completely developed for a mature understanding of cause and effect – for example, that if she heard the word "come" and she went to the person who said it, she would get a reward. By 12 weeks of age all of her senses and her abilities to have feelings and emotions were completely matured. The clay was mixed, most of it was already moulded, and all that remained was to add fine detail. Refinement of her brain functions comes from experience, both random and planned. Training your dog is simply planned experience, and training is most successful when the "surface" is blank, when there's no need to obliterate previous experience.

Brain chemicals

Brain cells communicate with each other through messenger chemicals called neurotransmitters, and a single brain cell can have up to 10,000 connections with other cells. Jaak Panksepp, author of *Affective Neuroscience: The Foundation of Human and Animal Emotion*, says dogs always seek out what they need in life and that in the brain there is "seeking" circuitry connected by neurotransmitter chemicals. The excitatory neurotransmitter dopamine, the "pleasure chemical", is released when seeking circuits are activated, for example, when a dog watching you prepare its meal becomes excited. All dogs have the same neurotransmitters, but different breeds appear to have different quantities; it is here that the seeds of exaggerated, diminished, or ritualized behaviours are sown. For example, Border Collies and Nordic sled dogs have more dopamine than do livestock-guarding breeds.

DRUGS FOR DOGS

Drugs have been developed to stimulate or inhibit some neurotransmitters, and are licensed for treating dogs with certain emotional disorders. I wish it were that easy – give a pill and cure an emotional problem – but the brain is infinitely more complicated than the kidneys. For example, serotonin plays a role in emotions such as anxiety, and selective serotonin re-uptake inhibitors (SSRIs) such as Prozac (fluoxetine) can reduce anxiety. But serotonin does much more. Nobody knows all its roles, but we do know that it's also involved with memory, wakefulness or sleep, and temperature regulation. Drugs such as SSRIs don't cure emotional problems in dogs; just as often they affect other brain activities and create even more problems. At best, they can be used to dampen down excessive neurotransmitter activity and give you a temporary window of opportunity in which you can train your dog to behave differently.

Social attachment and companionship are just as vital in a dog's life. When a dog is touched, its brain releases neurotransmitters called endorphins, natural painkillers. Nick Dodman at Tufts University found that dogs with depressed endorphins wagged their tails more and became more sociable, methods by which they tried to raise their brain's endorphin levels. (Don't worry – happy dogs also raise their endorphin levels when they wag!) You could say dogs become addicted to touch, addicted to love, physiologically dependent on satisfying contact with you, and separation can be painful, agony, or torture, all of it related to neurotransmitter chemicals in the brain.

The parts of the brain

Anatomically, most large parts of the dog's brain – such as the cerebellum, which is responsible for motion, and the brain stem, which is connected to the spinal cord – are equal to ours. Only the frontal lobe of their cerebral cortex, the "thinking" part of the brain, is much less developed than ours (and the less developed the frontal lobes are, the more a dog plays). That single difference is important: it means that our dogs don't think like us.

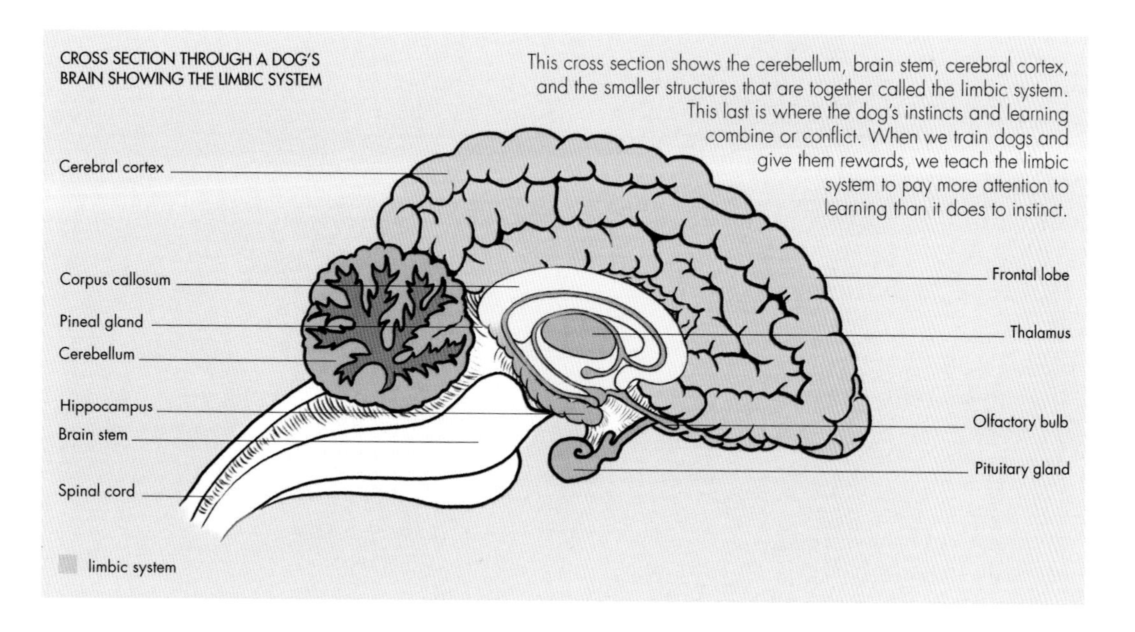

CROSS SECTION THROUGH A DOG'S BRAIN SHOWING THE LIMBIC SYSTEM

This cross section shows the cerebellum, brain stem, cerebral cortex, and the smaller structures that are together called the limbic system. This last is where the dog's instincts and learning combine or conflict. When we train dogs and give them rewards, we teach the limbic system to pay more attention to learning than it does to instinct.

Dogs don't push things from their conscious into their subconscious. Their emotions are cleaner and simpler than our mixed emotions, and they can't easily generalize the way humans can.

Temple Grandin, an autistic doctor of animal science, theorizes that both dogs and young children are like autistic people – straightforward and loyal – because their frontal brains aren't matured. Their emotions stay more separate and are compartmentalized, because their brain cells have fewer connections. She comments that "Strong emotions in animals are usually like a thunderstorm. They blow in and they blow out."

Grandin says that dogs, like autistic people, are "hyperspecific", seeing the differences between things a lot better than they see the similarities. For example, a dog can be relaxed with most people but be fearful of someone wearing a helmet, or limping, or carrying an umbrella, or of a different skin colour. She attributes this to dogs having less frontal cortex power to help them interpret the world and suppress fear. I'll come back to this, to the need for super-careful handling of high-fear dogs, when I discuss training throughout the second part of the book.

The limbic system and learning

Your dog's emotional development and responses are played out throughout all parts of the brain, in a complex of cells called the limbic system. If your dog can be said to have a value system, it's embedded in the limbic system, where information from and for the brain, the senses, and the body's hormones are integrated. The limbic system sends data to a part of the frontal cortex called the association cortex, which is where your dog decides whether to come to you when you command "come" or concludes "not this time" and runs off after something more exciting.

Learning through conditioning, learning to respond reflexively to a signal, occurs in the association cortex, and here is something we have great

PLAY FIGHTING IS HEALTHY

There's no connection between pups roughhousing with each other when they are young and winning fights as adults. The activities in play fighting and real fighting are different, as are the brain circuits that are activated (although if roughhouse play accidentally triggers pain it can develop into real fighting). Bigger dogs often handicap themselves when play fighting, intentionally rolling over and reversing roles. Some dogs sometimes intentionally lose when playing tug-of-war, in order to keep the game going. Play activity isn't just about winning, it's also about losing gracefully, about dominance and subordination, about integrating all of these facets of life. Play develops the young brain, improving its circuitry for handling novelty, surprise, or sudden loss of balance. Play helps dogs learn how to make predictions, set goals, and efficiently process incoming sensory data.

control over. If a young dog's association cortex is "superstimulated" between the ages of 6 and 12 weeks, it's possible to increase the number of interconnections between brain cells. You can superstimulate your pup's brain by safe, controlled exposure to as wide a variety of sights, sounds, smells, and textures as possible. Car rides. Public transport. Cyclists and joggers. Traffic noise. Construction sites. Thunder and lightning. Big dogs. Little dogs. Kids. Cats. Water. A dog that experiences a great variety of sights, sounds, smells, and other stimuli when very young will have a bigger, heavier brain than one that grows up isolated in the home and back garden. The brain doesn't have more cells, but the existing cells develop more connections with other brain cells, making actions and reactions more graduated and subtle. If you've missed the early puppyhood slot because you've rescued a bored or fearful dog from a dog shelter, experience still works. If you sensitively introduce an ever-increasing variety of sensory stimulation, that dog's brain will grow too. It just takes longer than it does in young dog and demands more patience on your part.

Jaak Panksepp says we should think of both dogs and us as having a variety of distinct core emotions embedded in the anatomy and chemistry of our brains. Four core emotions are rage, fear, curiosity/interest/anticipation and prey-chase drive. Sexual attraction/lust, separation distress, social attachment, and roughhousing play are the other four. As Panskepp puts it, "Cognitive thinking sits on top of our emotional value system". Dogs do less cognitive thinking than we do, simply because they've got less frontal cortex, but their emotional value system is still similar to ours.

The nervous system

Nerves connect the brain via the spinal cord to every organ and every single muscle in the body. Nerve cells can't repair themselves; if a nerve is severed its function is forever lost. This is why the spinal cord, where the bodies of

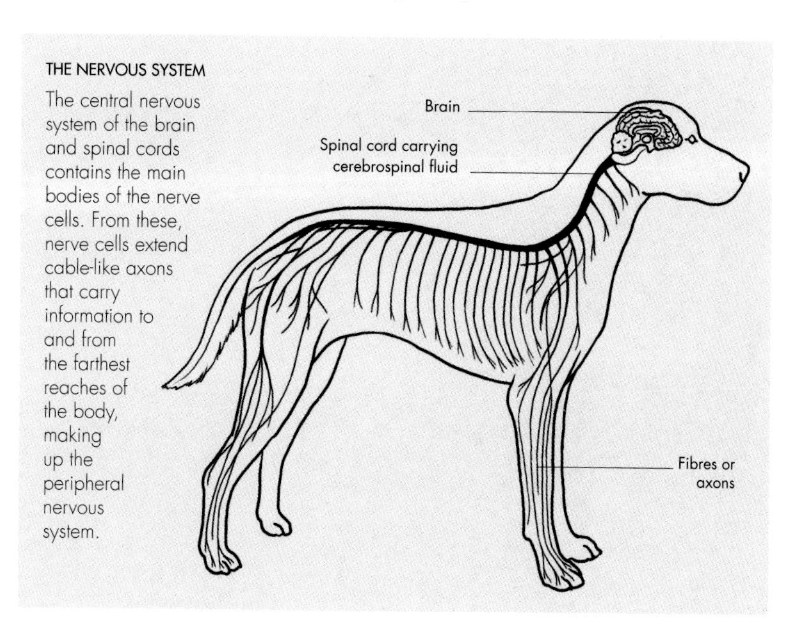

THE NERVOUS SYSTEM
The central nervous system of the brain and spinal cords contains the main bodies of the nerve cells. From these, nerve cells extend cable-like axons that carry information to and from the farthest reaches of the body, making up the peripheral nervous system.

nerves are located, is protected by the bony vertebral column that extends from the base of the brain almost to the tip of the tail. The spinal cord is also constantly bathed in shock-absorbing cerebrospinal fluid, but even so, a slipped disc between vertebrae or physical injury such as a road traffic accident can permanently damage it. The fibres of nerve cells, called axons, extend from the spinal cord to the most distant skin and muscle. An axon from the spinal cord to the tip of a Great Dane's toe can be over 1m (3ft) long. These too don't repair; if an axon is cut, and the muscle it feeds loses its nerve supply, that muscle shrinks and withers away.

The development of a spastic gait indicates damage to either the brain or the spinal cord. Inca, my son's epileptic Labrador, appears normal until she swims, when its obvious she has no natural coordination to her dog paddle. That's because one of her seizures damaged her cerebellum, responsible for motion, balance, and co-ordination. Trigger, a German Shepherd Dog I've known since a pup, now seems a little drunk on her hind legs. Her owner thought this was because of hip problems, but the true reason is an inherited immune condition called CDRM, similar to MS in people, which causes a gradual degeneration to the sheaths covering nerves in her spinal cord.

Dogs are very hormonal

Endocrine hormones are chemical messengers, like neurotransmitters. But while neurotransmitters exist only in the brain and nervous system and only in the tiniest quantities, endocrine hormones are manufactured by glands throughout the body in relatively large quantities, and travel via the bloodstream. Almost every single cell in a dog's body has receptor sites that can be switched on or off by one or more hormones. A modulated hormonal symphony is constantly played in your dog's body, orchestrated by the brain and the master gland at the base of it, called the pituitary gland.

The entire system is self-regulating. When the brain determines that a hormone is needed (by interpreting information from the senses and the rest of the body) it sends a signal to the brain's hormone-coordinating centre, the hypothalamus. This instructs the pituitary gland, the hormone

DOGS RUN LIKE CLOCKWORK

My dog arrives bright eyed and tail wagging at the side of my bed at six o'clock sharp each morning. I awake to her gaze and tell her to drop my socks. She does, then she hops on the bed, curls up, and goes to sleep until I get up a half hour later. She gets a little mixed up when the clock switches in spring and autumn, but otherwise her timing is perfect. It's the same at mealtimes. At the appointed hour, Bean comes and stares, then walks towards the kitchen, and if we don't follow, comes back, dances a little, may even give a command bark, and induces us to prepare her meal. At eleven o'clock at night if we haven't made a move, she does. She gets up, walks upstairs, gets into her bed and goes to sleep. Bean runs like clockwork because she has a 24-hour hormonal clock embedded in her brain, fuelled by the hormone melatonin and probably controlled by a single gene. In hamsters, a single genetic mutation around 25 years ago produced individuals with a 20-hour biological clock. Selective breeding produced some with 20-hour, some with 22-hour, and some with 24-hour biological clocks. Such genetic accidents rapidly disappear in nature; under our watch they lead at best to genetic discoveries and at worst to the perpetuation of freaks and misfits.

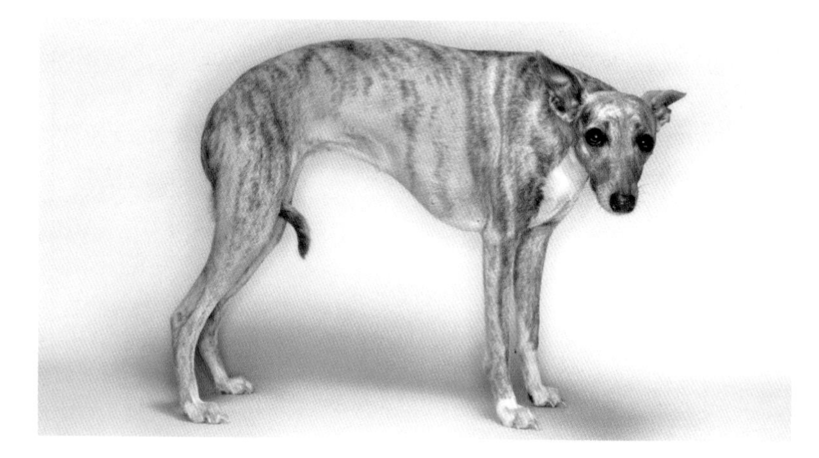

Stress test The hormonal response to stress is controlled by the adrenal glands. It is commonly called the "fight or flight" response, but in most situations it is actually more of a "snarl or cower" response. Sometimes dogs will do both, and defensive biters can be a real problem.

conductor, to send a stimulating hormone to one of the body's endocrine glands (testicles or ovaries, or adrenal, thyroid, or parathyroid glands) or to endocrine-producing tissue in the intestines, pancreas, or kidneys. The target gland responds by releasing a hormone into the bloodstream. This travels to where it's needed and acts on the relevant tissues, but also goes back to the pituitary. The pituitary stops secreting the stimulating hormone, and the target gland stops production. The entire cascade of events triggering hormone production takes a fraction of a second, but the hormonal production and hormone "biofeedback" to the pituitary lasts much longer. Certain hormones, including vasopressin, oxytocin, and prolactin, facilitate social togetherness. In human studies these are called the "Mom, Dad, and love" hormones. Dogs make social distinctions between "friend" and "stranger" as we do. When Bean does this with dogs in the park, when she forms companionable relationships with other dogs, her body is under the influence of her Mom, Dad, and love hormones.

The adrenal glands produce cortisol, the body's natural corticosteroid, and adrenalin, both of which are central to your dog's fight-or-flight response. A variety of medical conditions are controlled by cortisol; sometimes, when a condition is excessive or when the body doesn't produce enough natural cortisol, I supplement it with cortisone injections or tablets.

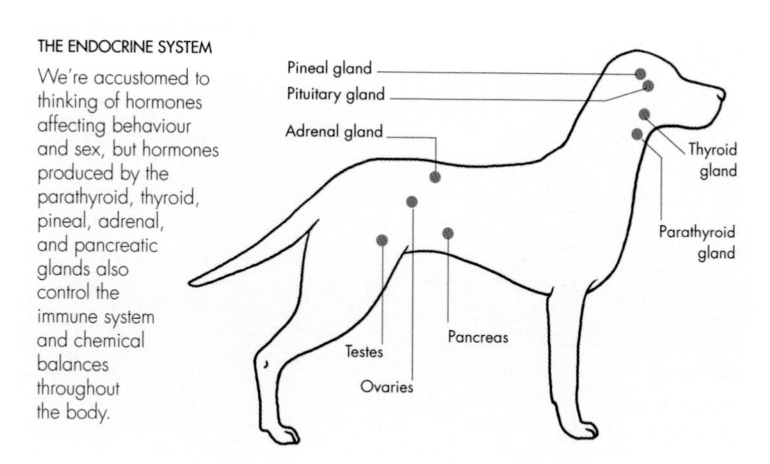

THE ENDOCRINE SYSTEM
We're accustomed to thinking of hormones affecting behaviour and sex, but hormones produced by the parathyroid, thyroid, pineal, adrenal, and pancreatic glands also control the immune system and chemical balances throughout the body.

Don't panic if your vet mentions cortisone – it's one of the greatest life-saving drugs available. Because it's a hormone, a sudden increase in it, through illness causing overproduction or through prescribing it to treat an illness, it can have an effect on a dog's temperament. This is usually a feeling of euphoria, but can sometimes be aggression.

The thyroid glands produce hormones associated with metabolism, and increasingly I see dogs with underactive thyroid glands. For unknown reasons, in some dogs (and some breeds, such as Cocker Spaniels) the immune system turns on and destroys the thyroid glands. Some researchers think that the reason lies in a variety of man-made chemicals in detergents, resins, plasticizers, herbicides, and pharmaceutical agents, which are "endocrine disruptors" and now permanently contaminate the environment. Many of these accumulate in the fat of animals we and our dogs eat, and may affect the health and behaviour of our dogs as much or even more than they do us. Dogs with underactive thyroid glands typically gain weight and have skin problems, but equal numbers experience behaviour changes that range from lassitude to inexplicable aggression. Professor Nick Dodman at Tufts University found that of 319 dogs referred for unexpected aggression, submissiveness, shyness, fearfulness, excitability, sensitivity to noise, anxiety, irritability, compulsiveness, moodiness, or apparent depression, 208 had thyroid disorders. Whenever a dog's behaviour seems out of keeping, it's prudent to consider that there might be a hormonal cause.

Sex hormones affect temperament and personality

If you have an intact female dog, you're probably aware of the effect of female hormone on behaviour. Usually twice yearly (in some less frequently, in others more frequently) the pituitary gland produces follicle-stimulating hormone (FSH) which triggers the ovaries to produce the female hormone oestrogen. During "heat" or oestrus, eggs are released from the ovaries, regardless of whether the female has mated or conceived, and the vacant sites on the ovaries produce progesterone, the hormone of pregnancy. Production continues for two months, then like clockwork it stops, and the female becomes hormonally neutral until her next heat cycle. The pituitaries

HORMONES AT HOME

An example of the refined subtleties of hormonal biofeedback and its influence on behaviour comes from recent sex hormone studies in men. It's been known for decades that the body "rewards" a winning athlete, male or female, with a boosted production of testosterone, but more recently a study of Canadian ice hockey players showed that teams playing at home received a testosterone boost before the match too. Playing at home triggers the pituitary to send signals to the testes and the adrenal glands (which are a woman's source of testosterone) and both increase their production. The advantage of playing at home isn't just psychological, it's also hormonal. This home advantage probably applies to dogs as well, which is why they're more confident on their home turf than when they're playing away from home.

Chemical conversation
When a female in the early stages of her cycle finds the testosterone-laden urine of a priapic male in the grass, broadcasting just how ready for action he is, her rising oestrogen level instructs her to leave her urine right beside it as a hormonal "Hello sailor". Her urine and even her anal secretions are affected by her hormonal status, broadcasting her forthcoming availability. This may focus a male's mind so much he refuses to eat – unless of course the male is a Labrador. A Lab can have sex, eat a pastrami sandwich, and watch football on television all at the same time.

of males, on the other hand, constantly produce leutenizing hormone (LH) which stimulates testosterone and sperm production in the testes. Males are hormonally ever ready to mate, while females will prevent males from inspecting their reproductive bits until their oestrogen level is at its highest, just after ovulating. But it's not quite that simple because, as I've mentioned, females also produce testosterone. After a male is neutered, the influence of testosterone drops, but after a female is neutered, the influence of her natural level of testosterone increases.

Testosterone is a fascinating hormone. It affects personality, mood, and aggression in both people and dogs. Just before birth, male pups produce testosterone, influencing brain development. Female pups don't produce female hormone until their first oestrus cycle, usually between five and twelve months of age, but exposure to their mother's testosterone before birth can affect their early development. In us, a man's ring finger is usually longer than his index finger, indicating a high exposure to prenatal testosterone, while a woman's ring and index fingers are usually equal. People who have had a higher exposure to prenatal testosterone than average score better on spatial tests and finding simple forms in large, complex pictures than people with a lower exposure; people with lower testosterone are those who provide the social glue in a group. Dogs exposed to high levels of testosterone in the womb mature into more dominant and assertive individuals than dogs exposed to lower levels. Dominant dogs probably have higher baseline testosterone than their peers (as power-hungry men do), and it's likely that, like high-testosterone men, the more they feel threatened, the higher their testosterone and aggression rise.

Here's some curious research. When they won, all owners who entered their dogs in a canine agility contest – male, female, average- or high-testosterone – treated their dogs the same way and hugged them. But high-testosterone men experienced a surge of testosterone after their dogs lost. They yelled at and shoved their dogs. Women and average-testosterone men, on the other hand, were sympathetic to their dogs, petting and hugging them. These results conform to previous research indicating that high-testosterone men become angry, excited, and cognitively-impaired when stripped of their status – that is, when they lose. Research in dogs also consistently confirms that an intact, high-testosterone dog is more difficult to obedience train than a low-testosterone or neutered dog. Managing testosterone level is certainly an effective way to manage the behaviour of high-testosterone dogs. Other researchers report that low-testosterone men become angry and impaired when they are placed in high-status positions that they don't want. They suggest that how we behave when authority or responsibility is either given to us or taken away from us is influenced by our inherent level of testosterone.

Tender touch Touches to the face are a powerful reward for dogs, but are also quite intimate. A dog needs to be relaxed to let you interfere with their sight or hearing by stroking near their eyes or around their ears – but most of them are, most of the time.

This applies to dogs as well. They have an innate, immutable hierarchy, intertwined with their testosterone levels, and a family group – you, your spouse, your kids, and your dog – is more stable and harmonious when hormone levels and social niches correspond. In an easy, well-functioning relationship, your dog should see you as someone with high status and be content with that. But each day at work, I hear a common comment from women owners of dominant dogs: "He pays attention to my husband, but not to me." The roots of this problem can be hormonal, and I'll come back to it when I discuss dog training.

Perfectly modulated senses

Because we share senses with dogs, it should be simple to understand how their senses work, but there are differences between them and us. Some are subtle, others so great it's virtually impossible for us to understand the sensations a dog experiences. Dogs share five major senses with us and have an additional scenting sense we lack. While much is written about the possibility that dogs have a "sixth sense", for example an electromagnetic sense through which they can predict earthquakes, all the scientific evidence suggests that they use their traditional senses to do things our own senses simply aren't sophisticated enough to do.

Touch sustains life

Touch is the most underappreciated and, in its own way, the most vital of your dog's senses. The reason dogs love to have their faces touched is because 40 per cent of all of their touch receptors, including infra-red heat receptors, are on the face. The rest are spread over the skin, and especially between the toes and on the pads of the feet. Just after birth a pup, swinging its head back and forth, uses those infra-red heat receptors to find its mother's body and crawl to her for warmth and nourishment. Given the chance, a dog will continue this comforting activity throughout life; putting its head on a person's lap is a primal reward.

Fine feelers Our brain devotes a lot of space to nerves from our fingertips; in animals like dogs, cats, and rats, the nerves from the whiskers take a similar priority. Some dogs dislike their whiskers being touched, or even eating out of a bowl where they touch the sides.

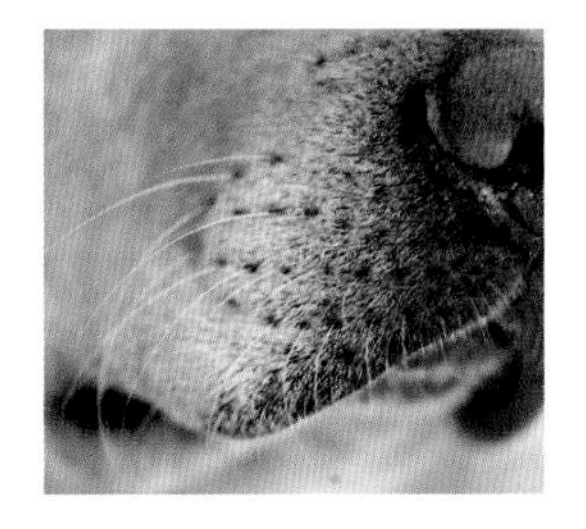

It's now over 50 years since distressing experiments on newborn macaque monkeys showed that young who are deprived of touch develop the most upsetting array of behaviour disturbances. They became fearful and withdrawn, mutilated themselves, and developed monotonously

SIGHTHOUNDS REALLY DO SEE BETTER

Colour- and detail-sensitive cones are concentrated in a region on the retina called the fovea. In us this is a circular pit, but in dogs it is more of a horizontal ellipse. This was no more than a curious anatomical detail until 2003, when scientists discovered that in dogs with long muzzles the ellipse is longer than it is in dogs with shorter muzzles. The longer the ellipse, the greater the number of cone cells it contains, and the wider the field of detailed vision. This longer fovea, called a "visual streak", is an anatomical reason why long-nosed sighthounds genuinely have better vision than other dogs.

repetitive behaviours such as banging their heads against walls. Touch is a powerful reward. That's why for many dogs touch is all that's needed to reward them for good behaviour. When dogs are trained using powerful food rewards, touch should be integrated into the reward so that it takes over as the primary reward and food can be dropped.

Touch is also used for investigating life. Whiskers or vibrissae above the eyes, on the muzzle, and below the jaw help to locate, identify, and pick up small objects that are too close for the eyes to focus on. These whiskers, which also pick up air currents, are in areas with extensive nerve endings connected to the same part of the brain as the eyes are, leading some researchers to say that dogs "see" with their whiskers. This may certainly be true of cats, who have more dramatically developed whiskers. The use of this sense is probably greater in dogs with short coats, whose whiskers don't get lost in a forest of long hair.

What's in the eye

Your dog is always watching you, even if only out of the corner of the eye. A dog senses not just what you're doing but what you intend to do, through your body language, your body orientation, your state of attention. It watches for eye contact from you, something it can respond to.

Are you as frustrated as I am that the "red-eye" eliminator function on cameras works so well on people but leaves you dog's eyes looking like two large, glowing blueberries? The reason is simple. Your dog has a mirror-like layer of cells called the tapetum behind the retinas on the inside back of the eye, which reflects light back to give the retina a second chance to register it. That's why your dog can see in one-quarter as much light as you need.

The retina is covered in two types of light-sensitive cells, rods and cones. Rods are sensitive to motion and light, while cones are sensitive to colour and detail. Dogs' eyes are dominated by rods. They have only one-tenth of the number of cone cells that we have, and their cones are tuned to two colours rather than our three, making dogs essentially red-green colourblind. That's not to say that they can't see colour. Like severely red-green colourblind people, they see in two colours, blue-violet and yellow, and shades of grey. One of the vets I work with is colourblind and can't differentiate green, yellow, orange, and red. Dogs are similar, so a trained guide dog doesn't guide a blind person across the road when a red light goes

Couch potatoes The refresh rates and screen definitions of televisions have always varied internationally, so what a dog got out of the television varied too. But about half do seem to be interested, principally in sports and nature programmes. The arrival of high-definition digital broadcasting may swell their ranks in coming years.

off and a green one comes on at a crossing, but when the top light goes off and the bottom light comes on, and when the traffic stops.

Dogs have relatively large eyes compared with us. The light-refracting surface, or cornea, and the pupil of their eyes are both larger, and the thick, light-gathering lens is much, much larger and heavier, which is why it took so long to develop replacement plastic lenses for dogs that have cataract surgery. These features let more light into the eyes, but reduce the ability to focus and the range of focus or depth of field. Dogs have difficulty seeing up close. A human baby can focus on something at 7cm (3in). A dog can't focus closer than 30–50cm (12–20in) away. Later in life, starting at around nine years of age, the lenses naturally harden or become sclerotic, and anything closer than about 1m (3ft) will be out of focus.

Dogs don't see like us

The set of a dog's eye dictates both its field of view and its depth perception. Predators like dogs and humans have eyes set relatively close together (prey species have wide-set eyes that can see almost completely behind them), but while human eyes face straight forward, the set of dogs' eyes varies considerably. Generally speaking they're around 20 degrees wider apart than ours, giving better peripheral vision than we have, but less depth perception. Depth perception is what your dog needs to jump, leap, or catch accurately. The relatively close-set eyes of Border Collies help to make them such brilliant catchers and Olympian agility performers.

In a standard sight test, a person with good eyesight or "acuity" can read to the bottom line at 6m (20ft) away; a dog would probably read only the top line. Acceptable human eyesight is best known as 20/20 (the metric equivalent is 6/6), which simply means you can distinguish at 20ft (6m) a letter or shape that a standard test says you should be able to distinguish at 20ft (6m). Average human vision is actually a bit better than this standard. In comparison, normal dog vision is between 20/50 and 20/100 (or 6/15 and 6/30). These numbers mean that a dog can see at 20ft (6m) what you can see from 50–100ft (15–30m) away. That's not terrible, but our dogs would all need glasses to drive or read a classroom blackboard. Interestingly, breeds such as the Labrador Retriever and Cocker Spaniel, selectively bred for good eyesight, see better than breeds such as the Rottweiler or Shar Pei, and Labradors selectively bred to be guide dogs have even better vision than regular Labradors. So it's possible to improve eyesight through breeding.

I occasionally meet a member of my family walking their dog or my dog in the park. If I stand still even just 100 paces from a dog that knows me, she doesn't recognize me – until I move. Dogs compensate for their poorer visual acuity through sensitivity to idiosyncrasies in our gait or movement. They are phenomenally good at seeing subtle differences in our bearing or posture, so my dog will notice my distinctive gait, recognize it, and run over to greet me. It's important to remember this when it comes to dog training. As well as recognizing you by your walk, dogs also classify your worth according to the slope of your back and the direction of your gaze. A dog's vision is terrific at recognizing authority, or lack of it, in your stance.

Moving targets While dogs may lack the long-distance focus and colour discrimination of good human sight, their ability to track movement and respond to it is razor sharp.

Sonar sweep The mobility of a dog's ears helps it to detect sounds from all directions. Dogs that can literally prick up their ears, usch as collies or primitive and spitz types, have better hearing than those that can't, like spaniels or hounds.

Dogs hear better than we do

There's been a lot of research into what dogs hear and what they understand when we speak. Much still isn't understood, such as why dogs are excellent at responding to spoken commands but not to recorded commands.

Sound travels in waves. The frequency of a sound wave is the number of sound wave cycles in each second, measured in a unit called a hertz (Hz). The higher the frequency (the more sound waves per second) the higher-pitched the sound. We hear sounds at frequencies of 20 Hz to 20,000 Hz. Below 20 Hz we can't hear sounds, but instead feel them as vibrations, for example from a hi-fi bass speaker. We neither hear nor feel sounds above the frequency of 20,000 Hz. Dogs probably hear sounds at frequencies of 40 Hz to 60,000 Hz, although there is considerable variation, partly because of the many shapes of dog ears, and not all studies agree. One recent report put dogs' hearing range at 67 Hz to 45,000 Hz. Whatever the specific figures are, the range and efficiency of a dog's hearing deteriorates with age just like ours. And ultimately, age-related deafness is not uncommon, especially in some breeds like Labrador and Golden Retrievers.

Because dogs hear things we don't, they can be intrigued or frightened by sounds we're not aware of. A high-pitched rodent squeak, inaudible to us, can trigger a pounce from your dog. The vacuum cleaner may simply produce noise to your ears but can be a frightening high-frequency sound to your dog. Pavlov was the first scientist to investigate pitch discrimination in dogs, and showed that a dog can distinguish two notes differing by one-eighth of a tone. My last dog, Macy, always knew when my son's car arrived in front of our house – she could differentiate the tone of his engine from that of other cars of the same model.

As well as hearing over a wider range of frequencies, dogs can hear quieter or more distant sounds than we can. They have mobile ears they can tilt and rotate to focus on a sound, and erect ears like the German Shepherd Dog's collect sound better than floppy ears like the Golden Retriever's. Differences in the intensity of the sound or its arrival time at each ear help to localize where that sound has come from. A dog takes only six-hundredths of a second to localize a sound, but they're not as good as we are at localizing the exact source of a sound. We can localize sound to within a degree of its source; dogs can do so only to within eight degrees.

The volume of a dog's ear increases directly in line with its weight up to 10 kg (22 lb), but over 11 kg (24 pounds) it doesn't increase with size at all. That's why little dogs often seem to have such goofy, big ears.

Dogs hear and understand each other

Dogs speak to each other with different tones of voice. I'll come back to this in the second part of the book, but in brief, submissive, care-soliciting, and pleasure sounds tend to be high-frequency, pure sounds. High-pitched sounds of short duration usually indicate fear or pain, while the same sounds repeated at a slower rate indicate playfulness or the anticipation of pleasure.

Threats, anger, and the possibility of aggression are delivered with noisy, low-frequency sounds – barks and growls. Sounds that are repeated quickly

SYNTHETIC PHEROMONES

A pharmaceutical company has used knowledge of pheromones and how the vomeronasal organ functions to produce a synthetic "Dog Appeasing Pheromone" (D.A.P.™). Scientists first isolated a pheromone from the sebaceous glands in the mammary tissue of lactating bitches that appeared to have a calming effect on their pups. This was then synthesized and packaged into a range of products, from a spray or a plug-in diffuser to a collar, for use in situations where dogs are anxious or distressed. In a number of clinical trials the pheromone has proved to be effective for reducing stress during fireworks or when visiting the vet, although the response varied with the individual dogs. Another clinical trial concluded that this pheromone was as effective as the anti-anxiety drug clomipramine in reducing the signs of separation anxiety in affected dogs.

convey a feeling of excitement and urgency, while single or widely spaced sounds are often used as commands. Generally speaking, sustained sounds such as growls indicate thoughtful intent, behaviour that is about to happen. They say "Take one step closer and you're mincemeat."

The incomprehensible world of scent

A dog scents life. Scent is the dog's most practical sense, but it is the most difficult for us to comprehend, because it is so utterly superior to our ability to smell things. My dog uses her extraordinary ability to smell things not just to follow the scent trails left by prey (or the modern equivalent, to awake from the deepest sleep several rooms away when I open the fridge door), but for an amazing variety of social purposes. She uses scent to recognize her family, determine the sexual status and receptiveness of other dogs, investigate and interpret scent marks on her territory, of course to follow scent trails but also, perhaps to scent emotion. Dogs are able to smell a variety of scents all at the same time and to grade them, to assign to them different priorities. A dog can concentrate on the most important smell first, and then switch its attention to the next most important.

Here are some statistics. I have around a half a square metre (or yard) of nasal membrane and 5 million scent receptors in my nose. Bean has up to seven square metres (or yards) of nasal membrane and 220 million scent receptors in her nose. I don't have a scent-capturing vomeronasal organ in the roof of my mouth. Bean does. And Bean's nose is wet for a reason. Moisture captures odour molecules, which are dissolved and concentrated in mucus. You and I produce around 600ml (1 pint) of nasal mucus each day, which sounds quite a lot, but our dogs produce oodles more. Just ask anyone with a Pug that sneezes when you say hello to it. Dogs also use that cartoon-like repeated sniff-sniff-sniff to maximize detection of smells. Repeated sniffing concentrates odour molecules in a nasal pocket that is not washed out by normal breathing, where they build up until there are enough of them for the brain to work on and recognize.

A keen sense of smell About 12 per cent of a dog's brain is devoted to the messages that come from the nose. The brain can discern whether a smell is stronger in the left or right nostril, and "sort" smells, so that sniffer dogs can find a target scent even if it is masked by other strong smells like coffee.

A dog can detect scents such as the smell of bladder cancer in urine or a corpse buried deep in the ground that even the most advanced scientific instrument can't detect. They track by comparing the concentration of odours from one footprint to the next. They work best when following discrete samples, for example footsteps, and need to smell only five steps to determine the direction in which the scent is moving. Dogs can follow the scent trail left by a bicycle, although they have great difficulty working out the direction the bicycle took. But when scientists glued a slice of bacon to a bicycle's tire, creating a discrete scent sample each time the bacon made contact with the ground, a trained dog was able to determine the direction that the bicycle had travelled in.

Odours play tunes in a dog's nose, triggering an orchestrated response of scent memories. They're better in some breeds than in others: it's over 40 years since it was scientifically noted that a Beagle took less than a minute to find a mouse in a field, Fox Terriers took 15 minutes, and Scottish Terriers took forever. Some breeds, such as Bloodhounds, are better at detecting and following ground scent; others, like Border Collies, are superior at following air scent. Medical conditions, such as epilepsy, diabetes, and of course upper respiratory tract infections, interfere with scenting ability.

Can dogs scent emotion?

The vomeronasal organ is a chemoreceptor organ embedded above the roof of a dog's mouth, separate and distinct from the nasal cavity. While the nasal membrane communicates with the region of the brain that interprets scent, the vomeronasal organ communicates directly with the parts of the brain associated with feelings and emotion, the amygdala and hypothalamus. Although there is some overlap, the nasal membrane is chiefly for "ordinary" smells, and the vomeronasal organ is chiefly for pheromones. Pheromones are scents that have evolved to act as chemical communication signals. Dogs produce pheromone scents in the sweat from their paws and other parts of the skin, in their urine, anal sac discharges, and scent from glands around their lips and on their cheeks. You may have seen a male dog licking at urine left by another dog. What he's really doing is capturing odour molecules to direct to his vomeronasal organ through the two small openings in the roof of his mouth. Your dog recognizes you by picking up your scent on its nasal membranes but also in its vomeronasal organ If your dog can sense your emotional state, and many people including me think that they can, it does so by reading your body language but also perhaps by detecting your emotional state through the vomeronasal organ.

Taste, scent, and texture in food

Taste is closely associated with smell, so much so that even pet-food manufacturers have trouble separating the value of one from the other. Dogs' sense of taste is not as good as ours, simply because they have fewer taste buds. While we typically have around 9,000 taste buds, dogs have fewer than 2,000. Our taste buds register sweet, sour, bitter, and salty, but dogs' are less sensitive, so much so that it's probably more accurate to say they register no more than pleasant, indifferent, and unpleasant.

Out of curiosity I've done taste tests on most of the dry foods that I've fed my dogs over the years, so I can report personally that dry dog food is often quite tasteless. If I hold my nostrils closed when I taste it, I get a hint of bitter and not much else. If I were a dog, I'd probably register the taste

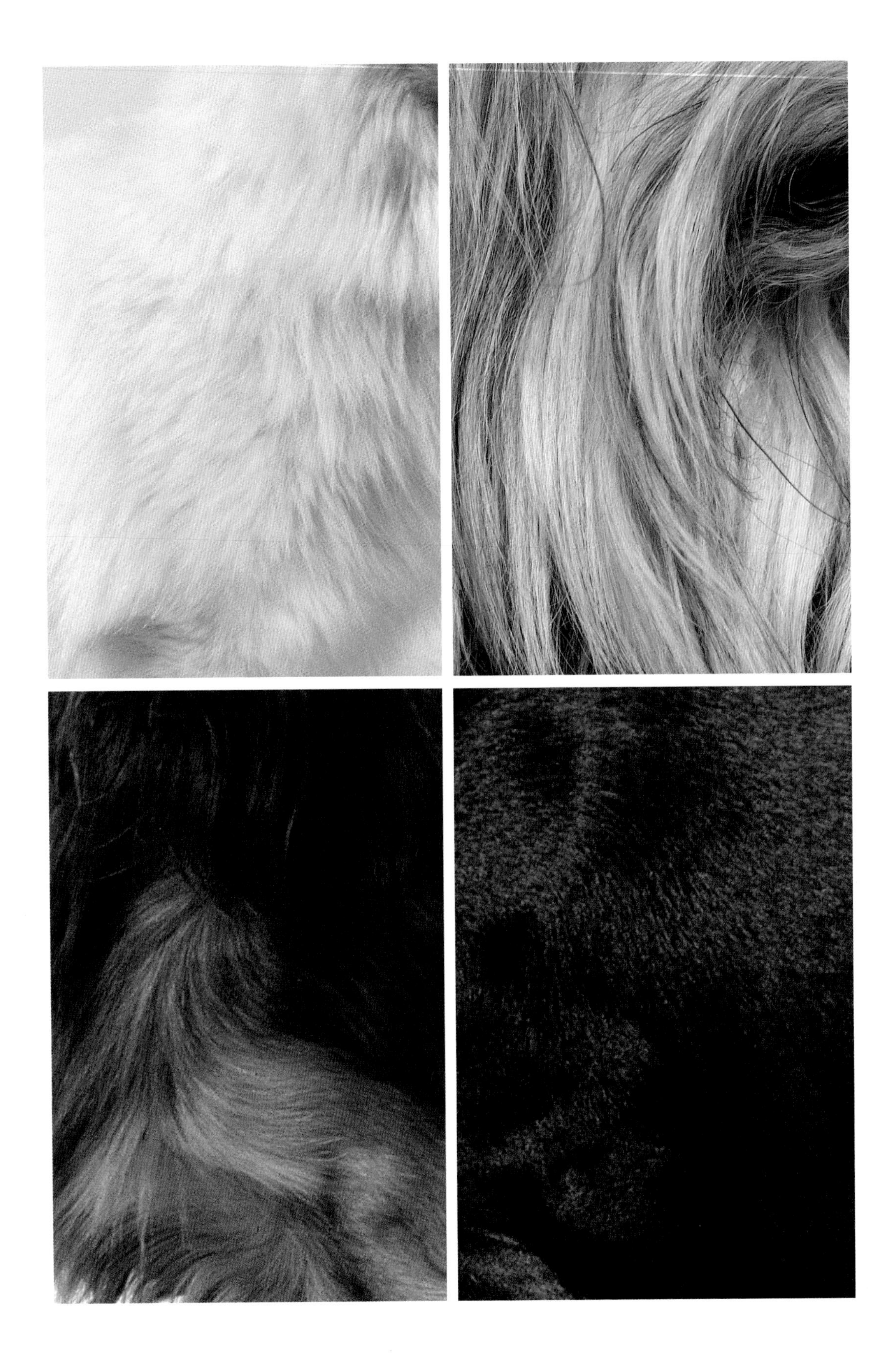

as indifferent. Manufacturers make their foods more attractive by spraying them with tempting animal fat. It's the aroma of this that attracts a dog to its meal and converts the event from indifferent to pleasant. Tastiness is irrelevant if a dog isn't attracted to the food in the first place by its smell.

Taste doesn't just depend on what's registered by the taste buds. Experience, even distant, forgotten experience, is just as important. For example, if a mother dog is given food containing aniseed around the time her pups are born, two months later her pups will show a preference for foods with aniseed. Feeding studies at Cornell University in the 1980s revealed that the food preferences of pet dogs are quite different from those of laboratory dogs. Just as the mother's eating habits affect her pups' preferences, our eating habits affect what our dogs like to eat.

Skin is a sensory organ

Your dog's coat isn't just for looking good. The skin is a true sensory organ. As well as keeping harmful microbes and chemicals out of the body, your dog's coat helps to regulate your dog's body temperature. Nordic breeds have immensely insulating coats, with up to 600 hairs per square centimetre (3,900 per square inch) while thin-coated breeds, such as Yorkshire terriers, can have fewer than 100 hairs per square centimetre (650 per square inch).

The coat is made up of different types of hair. All primary hairs, called guard hairs or the topcoat, are attached to erector muscles and can be raised in response to a range of sensory stimuli. The primary hairs along the back, for example, rise dramatically when a dog is excited. Each of these hairs also has an associated oil gland and sweat gland. Depending on the breed and type of coat, there are also secondary hairs, called the undercoat or "down". Rough-coated breeds, such as Wirehaired Dachshunds, have coats made up mostly of primary hairs, while those with silky soft coats, such as Smoothhaired Dachshunds, have mostly secondary hairs.

In most dogs the hair grows in cycles: an active period of growth, followed by a transitional period, then a resting period, then shedding. Changes in daylight hours and temperature trigger growth cycles, which is why dogs typically moult in autumn and spring. During winter the entire topcoat and half of the undercoat may be in the resting phase, but dogs living in heated homes often moult throughout the winter. Hormonal changes also affect the coat, as do nutrition, stress, and genetic influences. Some breeds, such as Poodles and Schnauzers, have continually growing hair like ours. You may read that if you're an allergic person you're less likely to be allergic to one of these breeds, but this isn't exactly true. Those of us who are allergic to dogs (and ironically, I'm one of them) react to a protein called "Can f1" in the skin and saliva. Dogs with constantly growing coats have just as much of this protein as other dogs do, but because of the way they're washed and groomed we unwittingly remove it. We're more likely to have an allergic reaction to a dog that has a thick coat, in which this protein (plus pollens and mould spores) accumulate, or to a dog prone to skin irritations that stimulate an increased production of the protein.

Coats for all seasons Spitz and Nordic dogs (top left) have exactly the kind of coat their native habitat demands: thick, insulating, and shed copiously in warmth. Yorkshire Terriers (top right) and other longhaired breeds have fine, silky coats, which contain few guard hairs and tangle easily. The tough coat of a breed like the Wirehaired Dachshund (bottom left) is protective and usually sheds water well. Dogs that have short, soft coats, like the Smoothhaired Dachshund (bottom right) or any of the Greyhound breeds, are vulnerable to injury and cold weather but carry the least "doggy" smell.

The anal sacs, on either side of the anus at three o'clock and nine o'clock, are a dramatically modified part of a dog's skin. Refined sebaceous and sweat glands secrete into each sac and, after the dog defecates, drops of this malodorous substance are squeezed out to anoint the faeces. French veterinarians investigating anal gland liquid found that it contains over 15 different fatty acids, so this "daily news" probably transmits 15 facts to the poop- or bum-sniffer, including who left the news, when they were there, even whether they are interested in sex.

In some breeds, especially spaniels, the anal sacs are poorly positioned and aren't emptied as easily as in other breeds. When the sacs are full, a dog drags its butt along in the grass (or carpet) or licks constantly, trying to empty them. A previous Golden Retriever of mine, Liberty, grabbed her own tail and gave it a sharp tug to empty full sacs, a manouvre that I thought was just brilliant but which my wife felt demanded my instant intervention.

Breathing and circulation

Like us, dogs breathe through their nose or mouth. Unlike us, they hang their tongues loose and pant a lot. Dogs pant when they're exhausted or worried or in pain, but also because they don't sweat efficiently through their skin the way we do. They pant to get rid of excess heat. Panting is usually a perfectly normal activity and only becomes significant and worth contacting your vet about when it's unexpected or inexplicably intensifies.

Dog snot has a purpose. There are antibody- and enzyme-rich secretions throughout your dog's respiratory tract, and these are used to help expel unwanted material from the system. In the distant past, viruses and bacteria hijacked these mechanisms as an ideal method for their own spread, so when you hear your dog coughing or sneezing, be aware that it might potentially be spreading transmissible disease to other dogs.

The dog's heart and lungs work much as ours do. Oxygen-containing air is automatically drawn into the expanding lungs as the diaphragm muscle involuntarily tightens. Inside the lungs, which have an area covering 50 square metres (60 square yards) – that's half a tennis court – in a dog like my Golden Retriever, red blood cells pick up fresh oxygen and discharge waste carbon dioxide. The lungs spontaneously contract, expelling the carbon dioxide from the dog's nose. (Yes, it's not just our cars: even our pets contribute to global warming.)

Seat of the problem Dogs that suffer from blocked anal glands develop a variety of strategies to deal with the problem. In all cases, it's fairly obvious where the issue is.

Circulation carries nourishment and waste

While 15–20 per cent of the blood pumped by the heart always goes to the oxygen-demanding brain, the rest goes wherever it's needed at the time. After eating, the flow of blood to the intestines increases, but when the muscles need energy, around 90 per cent of the available blood is diverted to them. This ability to carefully and constantly regulate blood flow is controlled by nerves (*see pp.105–6*) and hormones (*see pp.106–10*) that constrict or relax muscles in the walls of the tiniest arteries, called arterioles. Physiologists say that the potential flow of blood through an

Keeping cool A fur coat makes sweating impractical for most animals, so panting is the most practical way for dogs to regulate their temperature. The evaporation of water from the lungs and mouth acts in just the same way as the evaporation of sweat from our skin, only not quite as effectively.

arteriole can increase to 256 times the resting flow when needed. Dogs once did this chasing their meals; most now do so when chasing tennis balls.

Blood carries oxygen picked up from the lungs and nourishment picked up from the small intestines and transports them to virtually every cell in the body. It also picks up waste from muscles and organs and transports it to the liver for detoxification, to the kidneys for excretion, or back to the lungs where carbon dioxide is exhaled from the body. In pups, the oxygen-carrying red blood cells are manufactured in the liver and spleen, but by adulthood most red blood cells are manufactured in the bone marrow. The spleen acts like a blood-filled sponge, squeezing out an extra supply of red blood cells when they're needed. Splenic tumours are much more common in dogs than in humans, but if removal of the spleen is necessary a dog can survive nicely without that organ. The red blood cell level dips for a time then returns to its former level.

The dog's heart is similar to ours. Used blood from the body enters the right atrium at the top and passes through a valve to the right ventricle at the bottom and out to the lungs. Oxygen-rich, cleansed blood from the lungs enters the left atrium at the top and passes through a valve to the thick-walled left ventricle at the bottom, which pumps it throughout the body. Some breeds, such as Cavalier King Charles Spaniels, can inherit a predisposition to problems with leaking valves, called valvular heart disease. Other breeds, such as Dobermanns, can inherit a predisposition to problems with the contractility of the heart muscle itself, called cardiomyopathy. Dogs don't suffer from coronaries as we do – their coronary arteries don't get clogged with gunk, so they seldom die instantly from heart attacks. Canine heart disease is usually progressive rather than sudden. The two most common indicators that your dog's circulation is not efficient are a reduced tolerance for exercise and the development of a moist, continuing cough.

Eating and excreting

Comfort and eating Dogs know that food has emotional as well as nutritional value, for them and for us. When we train them with food treats (taken from a strict daily ration, of course) we take advantage of them. When they refuse all but particular foods as a form of emotional blackmail, they take advantage of us.

I have written before that a Labrador Retriever is not really a dog but a life support system for a stomach. Actually, I haven't, because my editor vetoed it then, but many of you know that the most direct route to your dog's obedience or affection is through its mouth. The large canine teeth are ideal for stabbing and holding prey, the side premolars and molars for shearing and cutting meat or grinding and chewing roughage and bone, and the small front incisors for nibbling meat from bones and grooming the coat. Few dogs use their teeth for these purposes. The most dramatic result is that gum and tooth problems requiring antibiotics, general anaesthetics, and dental procedures are amongst the most common conditions that vets treat. These can be prevented if dogs use their teeth to gnaw, chew, and scrape.

Dogs eat differently from us and this exasperates some people. Large dogs often eat quickly. "Taste it!" their owners shout at them (pointlessly – *see p.115*). Small dogs can be amazingly manipulative, convincing their owners they'll die if there's no seasoning on their breast of organic chicken. Basically, here is what happens when your dog eats: good stuff enters one end of a tube, and by the time it reaches the far end everything of value has been removed, leaving nothing but waste.

A moment on the lips

Food is picked up and, in what is sometimes the shortest of moments, bound together and lubricated by saliva to help it pass through the esophagus to the stomach. Saliva also keeps the mouth clean and the taste buds sensitive. The dog's pharynx and oesophagus are both very elastic, allowing them to swallow large hunks of meat and also (because they're dogs) bones, socks, and underwear.

Less digestion takes place in a dog's stomach than in ours. Compared with us, a dog has a very large stomach, in essence a holding tank, and relatively short intestines. The stomach secretes acid to help break down connective tissue and muscle fibres, but most of the enzyme activity that releases nutrients takes place in the first part of the intestines. The stomach lining is protected from the acid by mucus and a microscopically thin layer of a protective chemical; indigestible substances such as bones, twigs, or socks damage this protective film and lead to stomach inflammation and vomiting. Special receptors in the stomach detect certain natural but dangerous chemicals and signal a chemical recognition region in the brain (called the chemoreceptor trigger zone) which induces vomiting. Because dogs taste life they have a blunt ability to vomit easily. Stress can reduce the stomach's defences against its own acid, causing "acid rebound" and vomiting. Drugs originally developed to treat stomach ulcers in people are used to protect and restore the protective chemical lining of the stomach.

The chemical-cleansing liver

Any potentially damaging chemical that isn't immediately eliminated by vomiting is absorbed into the body, and it becomes the responsibility of the liver, the largest internal organ, to destroy it. Technically, the liver is part of the gastrointestinal system, and it has a tremendous ability to repair itself if damaged by chemicals or an infection. Your and your dog's liver both serve the same purpose: the production of bile to help emulsify fat and absorb fat-soluble vitamins, and the detoxification of dangerous substances. But they are not exactly the same and, in fact, sometimes behave very differently. For example, some people suffer from "attention deficit disorder" or ADD: they are easily distracted, unable to tell the difference between an important and unimportant pieces of sensory information. Some dogs behave the same way, and I thought a drug used as part of the therapy for ADD in humans might be useful for retaining the attention of dogs with wandering minds during obedience training. I contacted the manufacturer, who provided me with unpublished data on the drug, and discovered that while the drug survives intact to affect the brain in humans, in dogs it's immediately broken down by the liver and would never reach the brain. The liver is often the reason why drugs used for people either can't be used in dogs or must be used at significantly different doses or frequencies.

The intestines and nourishment

Waves of muscular contraction passing over the stomach help to mix food and pass it into the small intestines. Here digestive enzymes from the pancreas and liver are added to break protein, fat, and carbohydrate down into absorbable nutrients. Stomach acid is also neutralized, and fat-soluble vitamins are dissolved. Muscular contraction or peristalsis moves food through the small intestines and into the large intestine or colon, where excess moisture is removed. The large intestine is inhabited by billions of "good" microorganisms, usually belonging to over 400 different species or strains. These decrease the body's susceptibility to infection, synthesize vitamins, and break down waste material. Distension of the last part of the colon, the rectum, stimulates the dog's urge to defecate, and stool is discharged anywhere from once to four or five times daily, depending on your individual dog's bowel habits.

Problems in the intestines lead to diarrhoea more frequently than to constipation. Small intestine conditions produce watery diarrhoea, while large intestine problems can produce stringy stools often accompanied by mucus or sometimes blood. A simple diet change can alter the balance of the colon's natural digestive bacteria, leading to diarrhoea. Puppies produce copious quantities of lactase, an enzyme that breaks down lactose, the sugar in milk, but their lactase production drops as they grow. This is why normal milk can cause diarrhoea in some adult dogs (and people). Flatulence is caused by the build-up of gas manufactured by bacteria in the large intestines, and altering the diet is often all that's necessary to reduce gas formation. What goes on in your dog's intestines is subtly but sometimes significantly different to what goes on in your intestines. For example, bacteria in the large intestines produce a dog's own vitamin C, while we need to consume it in the food we eat. I'll explain more of these differences when I discuss nourishment for dogs at different life stages.

Poop to scoop Young and active dogs tend to defecate more often than old or inactive ones. The average output is estimated at 350g (12.5oz) a day, and it takes about a week to break down, making poop bags essential in most places.

Drinking and urinating are controlled by the brain

A thirst centre in the brain drives your dog's need to drink, responding to low water volume or chemical concentrations. Wet food is roughly 75–80 per cent water, so it provides large quantities of moisture. When fresh water is available, as it always should be, your dog naturally drinks enough to control its thirst. Clinically speaking, an increased thirst is always significant, and is an outward sign of a variety of potentially serious problems.

The kidneys are responsible for filtering the blood, retaining nutrients such as protein while discharging waste products. Urinating increased quantities may indicate the kidneys have lost their ability to filter well, or to concentrate urine. Urinating more frequently can be a sign of irritation in the urinary system. Difficulty urinating may mean there is damage, and pain, within the system. We urinate to get rid of waste liquid and completely empty our bladders when we do so. Dogs pass urine for the same reason but also to mark their territories, so they always keep a little in the tank. They have better staying power than we have, and a healthy young dog doesn't find it uncomfortable to build up a 12-hour supply before emptying it.

Born to run

A dog is a natural long-distance runner. Unless we've interfered through selective breeding and exaggerated or diminished various physical features, the dog has a wonderfully elastic and flexible body, nowhere near as graceful as a cat's but profoundly more adaptable than ours.

The skeleton, like all skeletons, consists of bony levers and lubricated joints. Unlike us, the dog has no clavicles, or collarbones; the front limbs and shoulder blades are anchored to the body by muscles. This gives them enormous flexibility when running. Bones are linked at cartilaginous joints which act like shock absorbers, each surrounded by a capsule filled with lubricating joint liquid. If your dog is limping, more often than not it has

HAPPY DOGS WAG THEIR TAILS TO THE RIGHT

If we are to believe research from Italy, happy dogs wag their tails to the right while dogs with negative feelings wag to the left. At first reading this may sound absurd, but it does fit with a large body of research showing emotional asymmetry in the brain. In most animals, including not only dogs and us but even fish and frogs, the left is associated with positive feelings such as safety, calm, attachment, and, in people, love. It is also associated with positive physiological states such as a slow heart rate. The right brain specializes in worry, fear, and depression, and is associated with a rapid heart rate and shutdown of the digestive system. Because the left brain controls the right side of the body and vice versa, the manifestations of left or right brain feelings are shown on the opposite side of the body. For example, birds look for food primarily with their right eye and watch for predators primarily with their left eye. Honeybees learn better when using their right antenna to touch. Male chameleons are more aggressive when they see something they don't like (another male chameleon) out of their left eye. So perhaps it's true that happy dogs wag to the right and fretful dogs wag to the left.

Dual purpose Urinating is not just for waste elimination. Male dogs tend to cock a leg to deposit urine on vertical surfaces, where it provides a marker for other dogs to read. Females are more inclined to squat, ideally where they can burn a large brown patch in a carefully tended lawn.

Little dynamo The dwarfing seen in many "earth dog" terriers is the type called achondroplasia, which affects only the leg bones. The result is a dog small enough to go to ground after prey, but with all the killing power of a bigger breed. Toy dogs tend to be miniaturized, which has the advantage of making them distinctly lighter on the lap.

injured a joint, which may become inflamed (arthritis) or may produce excess joint fluid (synovitis). Knee joints are particularly prone to injuries, particularly torn ligaments. Ligaments anchor bones to each other, permitting movement in specific directions while preventing excess movements that might injure delicate parts of the joint. Malformations of joints, usually called dysplasias, are common inherited conditions in dogs. Hip dysplasia leads to damage to the pearly, smooth, cartilaginous end of the femur and its socket in the hip. They become worn down to rough bone, leading to chronic inflammation and chronic pain. Similar inherited conditions can affect the shoulder and elbow joints.

We've reduced the size of the skeleton in two ways. Miniaturization proportionally reduces the size of every single bone, so an Italian Greyhound is a perfect small version of a Greyhound. Dwarfing reduces only the length of the long limb bones, so a Basset Hound is a naturally big dog with short legs. Some breeds have been both dwarfed and miniaturized, the most popular example being the Miniature Dachshund. Heads have also been radically altered. The head of the Saluki, a typical sighthound, is much longer and narrower than a wolf's, the Labrador's head, called mesocephalic, is slightly shorter, and dogs with squashed skulls are called brachycephalics. The Boxer is a moderate brachycephalic while the Pug and Pekingese are extreme brachycephalics. Most airlines will either not transport very brachycephalic breeds, such as Pekes, Pugs, Shih Tzus, and Bulldogs, in hot weather or simply not transport them at all. They've learned through unpleasant experience that these breeds are more prone to breathing problems and heatstroke than mesocephalic breeds.

Muscles join the bones together. All dogs, be they Whippets or St Bernards, have similar types of muscle fibres. While some people – sprinters for example – have a high proportion of fast-fatiguing muscle fibres that provide instant energy, a dog's muscles consist almost entirely of fibres that don't fatigue easily. That's why they are classic endurance athletes, capable of trotting, cantering, and running miles each day. That's also why a young dog taken for a walk off the lead will willingly cover four times as much ground as you do in the same time.

CHAPTER FIVE

Puppies in the Family Pack

I hope I've convinced you that dogs are different from us. Although we're both socially gregarious species that thrive on the presence of others, and although we both evolved as pack species with social hierarchies, we come from wholly different origins and have adapted to survive in quite different environmental niches. But, and there is a big but, in the very recent past, we changed the dog's niche. We took dogs out of the wild and brought them into our homes. They adapted amazingly well, but even now the attitudes, needs, and behaviours of the dogs we rear in constant contact with us from the day they're born are very different from those of dogs raised in the absence of early contact with people. Our pet dogs have unique needs, which differ from those of feral dogs. The most successful companion dogs are born into human households to mothers who were also raised as household companions. That gives them two advantages: they're reared in a human environment and reared by "humanized" dog mothers.

But we also play a unique role in our dogs' lives. In P.D. Eastman's wonderful children's book *Are you my mother?* the newborn bird asks everything he sees that simple but potent question. From birth a pup recognizes its mother but it also has another "mother", the breeder, the person who handles the pups each day, takes them from the nest while it's cleaned, talks to them, strokes them and, as they grow, starts to feed them. After the first two to three months, dogs join our homes, where we feed them, stroke them, comfort or reprimand them, and try our hardest to make them feel safe and secure. In developing the dog as a family companion we created a species that never really grows up, like Peter Pan. What we treasure in our dogs is that very fact – that they never mature, that their behaviour throughout life retains the curiosity and playfulness of youth. The only time in their lives when dogs live in a dog pack is a time that we seldom get a chance to see, the few short weeks after birth when young pups live with their mother and littermates. I'd like to describe here what few of us see: life with mother at the breeder's.

Meeting and mating

Even after thousands of years of human intervention, the dog's mating behaviour still remains physically and biologically that of a competitive pack animal. Females generally release eggs twice each year, although this varies considerably. Lola, my daughter's Labrador Retriever, has four seasons yearly, while Macy, my previous Golden Retriever, had one. As with most mammals, males are sexual opportunists. "If it stands still, hump it" is a universal evolutionary male mantra. Males will, of course, try to mate with females when they're in season, when they smell right, but they may also try

Single-parent family Wolves have the extended family of the pack, but a female dog usually has sole responsibility for protecting, feeding, cleaning, comforting, and disciplining her offspring. If you're serious about getting a pup, always take a good look at the mother first.

to mate with females who have odour-producing urinary infections, females who simply stand still, or neutered males who no longer have a strong male odour. In the absence of another dog, they may hump the kids, visitors' legs, big stuffed toys, or cushions. I'll explain how to overcome that perfectly natural behaviour later (*see p.274*).

Picking partners Unless chaperoned every second females are liable to hightail out an open door and find their own mate. Their choices are sometimes odd – dogs of either sex are no respecters of pedigree – and can even be physically improbable.

Left to themselves, who mates with whom depends upon opportunity, familiarity, and personal choice. In owned dogs, the females control when they will mate, but the breeder decides who with. Males are often more successful on their own turf, so females are sometimes brought to males, but the reverse is also common. Experience is important: males who have never mated before know what they want to do but often can't work out a successful approach, and need a helping hand from the breeder.

After mating, which is brief (there's little foreplay) dogs become stuck together or "tied", usually for 15–45 minutes. This is caused by a balloon-like swelling half way along the dog's penis, an evolutionary adaptation inherited from the wolf, which prevents other males from mating with the receptive female. This is apparent when a dog simply gets excited, and can be the reason a sexually aroused dog can't withdraw his penis back into its sheath. The male often swings a hind leg over his partner's back so that they are physically connected but up rump to rump, able to defend themselves.

Personality starts in the womb

Pregnancy lasts for two months. The physical development of the pups is directly related to their mother's health and nutrition, and there's good evidence that a dog's adult emotions are also affected by the womb environment. Mothers who are severely stressed during pregnancy may produce pups with more extremes in behaviour, reduced learning ability, and heightened emotional states. Well-nourished pups don't just crawl, walk, run, and play earlier than puppies from malnourished mothers, they also learn faster and have fewer emotional problems. These are powerful reasons why you should always get a pup from a hobby or obsessive breeder rather than from a commercial breeder.

The womb itself consists of two tubes called horns. Pups in the middle of each horn are likely to receive the best nutrition, a perfect head start in life. As I've mentioned (*see p.109*), females are hormonally neutral until

MOTHERS-TO-BE NEED EXTRA CARE

During the first five weeks of pregnancy, the mother needs only her normal amount of well-balanced nutrition. From the fifth week, her calorie intake needs to be increased by 10 per cent each week, either by increasing the quantity of her usual food or by switching to a more energy dense diet (*see p.305*) Mothers-to-be don't need calcium supplements: excess calcium can actually be harmful, interfering with the absorption of zinc and manganese from the diet.

Worming is also important, because many dogs carry latent roundworm larvae, which are activated by the hormonal changes of pregnancy. They pass from the mother both to developing pups across the placenta, and to newborn pups through milk. Worming pregnant females with a product such as fenbendazole daily from the fortieth day of pregnancy until the second day after birth reduces the numbers of worms transmitted to the pups by 98 per cent.

puberty, but the male pup's developing testes secrete bursts of the male hormone testosterone while still in the womb, which travels to the pup's developing brain and helps to shape future behaviour characteristics, like dominance. Some researchers suggest that female pups who develop between two males are also affected by minute amounts of male hormone, predisposing them to develop a more dominant personality.

Birth is usually uncomplicated

Pregnancy usually lasts 60 to 65 days, but can be four days shorter or longer. By 35 days, all of the pups' major physical characteristics are evident. By 40 days, the eyelids, claws, hair, even skin colour are apparent, and a few days later, skeletons are easy to see on x-ray. Good breeders know the signs that birth is imminent. The mother goes off her food and usually becomes restless before settling in the secluded nest the breeder has provided, and just before birth, her temperature drops a degree or more.

I've delivered quite a few pups, most recently a litter of seven from my daughter-in-law Marina's dog, but the most impromptu delivery was the litter of my son Ben's dog Inca. This fun-loving, happy-go-lucky comedian of a Labrador became restless and went off her food several days earlier than expected, 60 miles from her whelping box. I set up a make-shift whelping den from an unwanted duvet, but she found her own under a bed on the top floor of the house, so I slept in that room with her that night. At five in the morning she left her den, hopped up onto my bed, and on top of me, panting hot dog breath in my face. I stared nose-to-nose at her and she stared back at me, then I felt her abdomen contracting as she pushed to discharge her first pup. Inca was upset by what was happening as her contractions started, and had come to lie on top of me for security. I slid out from under her, spread the old duvet on the bed, and 30 seconds later she produced her first pup – Lola, my daughter's dog, the one with four oestrus cycles a year. Labradors are relatively large dogs that have large litters of fairly small pups, so birth is usually uncomplicated. After five pups emerged, Inca's biological clock told her it was breakfast time and, being a Labrador, that was more important than giving birth, so she left her litter and breakfasted before producing the rest of her pups.

Once the first pup is produced, others follow, usually at 10- to 45-minute intervals, and the entire process is normally over in less than six hours. Around 60 per cent of pups come out head first, the remainder tail and hindlegs first. Breech births – rump first – do occur, and are one of the reasons for veterinary intervention. Immediate help is needed if unproductive labour lasts more than an hour, if a fetus is visible but contractions stop for more than 10 minutes, if contractions continue for 20 minutes but the fetus is still not out, or if the number of afterbirths is fewer than the number of pups produced.

First moments The very first thing a mother does for each pup is lick it to remove the birth membranes and stimulate its first breaths.

Some dogs, especially terriers, will find earthy dens to have their pups in if given the chance. I've had to help one dog owner gently retrieve a newborn litter of Cairn terriers from a rabbit warren, where the mother had moved them the day after giving birth under the dining room table.

SCENT TRIGGERS EMOTIONS

Do you like the smell of newborn pups? If you do, the attraction may have ancient evolutionary origins. Research suggests that maternal behaviour is at least in part triggered by scent. There's no particular centre for maternal behaviour in either our brains or dogs' brains. Good mothering is mostly learned, and those who have been well mothered are likely to be good mothers themselves, but smell is certainly involved in the process. Maternal behaviour can be induced in virgin rats, and parenting behaviour in male rats, by the simple presence of newborn rats. In wolf packs, male wolves and "nursemaid aunts" will regurgitate food for pups, and adult dogs often allow pups to get away with behaviour they would never tolerate in adults. Some ethologists think that pups produce an appeasing pheromone that reduces dominant behaviour in adults.

In the mid 1990s, if you pardon the name-dropping, Crown Prince Naruhito and Crown Princess Masako of Japan proudly introduced me to their two Shiba-type dogs, born to a stray mother in an earth den in the grounds of Akasaka Palace in Tokyo. The litter of ten pups didn't emerge until they were five weeks old. Although they were late meeting people for the first time, all of them socialized to human life very easily and became companions of members of the Imperial Household. The "Crown Dogs" were sufficiently well mannered to become therapy dogs, visiting children in hospitals in the Tokyo area.

Nature is more likely to make mistakes when development is rapid, and dogs develop from eggs and sperm to fully formed animals in only two months. The obvious consequence of such rapid development is a relatively high frequency of developmental mistakes, some of which don't survive birth, while others die shortly after. Left to nature, about one out of seven pups doesn't survive; often the "runt" of the litter won't make it. But more often than not, we intervene, hand-feeding these pups and getting veterinary attention for physical problems such as large umbilical hernias. These special-needs pups require extra human attention to ensure their survival, but it's just as important to ensure they spend ample time with their mothers and littermates too, so that they not only survive but also develop their natural dog skills.

The first weeks of life

Good breeders ensure good nutrition before birth and safety during delivery but then, for the first three weeks of life, the pups are almost wholly the responsibility of their mother. This is the most natural period of their lives, a time when we are least important to them. Even so, handling a pup in the presence of its mother for 15 minutes each day during this time accelerates its physical and emotional development.

At birth the mother licked her pups and licked her teats, laying down a saliva scent trail for them to follow. If you are caring for a new litter of pups, don't go overboard with soapy hygiene. Pups need to smell their mother's teats to successfully find them. Contented pups spend 90 per cent of the first three weeks sleeping. Warmth is vital to them, so the room temperature should be 24°C (75°F) or more. If a mother leaves her pups for only a half hour their body temperature drops by 3°C (8°F). Shivering is a serious danger signal. A hot water bottle wrapped in an insulating towel makes a decent temporary mother-substitute when she leaves the nest.

During the first days, mothers instinctively understand how defenseless their pups are. Maternal aggression is perhaps the most fearsome of all forms of aggression, and a mother may risk death itself to defend her litter. But she also has subtler ways of defending them, and consuming their waste products is the most effective. Waste management reduces risk from disease microorganisms that may multiply in a contaminated nest, but eating her pups' faeces also removes many of the scents that predators might follow. Evolution has made this a simple process, ensuring that newborn pups empty their bladders and bowels only when their anogenital regions are licked by the mother. As the pup discharges, both solids and liquids are consumed by mother. This is an activity that some dogs that are not mothers also engage in, and I'm the owner of one of those dogs.

Supply and demand Dogs have from four to twelve teats, with smaller breeds having fewer teats. Not surprisingly, litter size is also related: the usual litter for a Chihuahua or a Yorkie contains just two to five pups, while a German Shepherd has four to nine, and a Labrador five to ten.

First feeding

During those first few weeks a good mother wakes her pups by licking them, cleaning them and stimulating them to feed. Breeders double the mother's food in the first week after birth, and increase it again during the

TYPICAL ENERGY NEEDS OF LACTATING DOGS (KCAL PER DAY)

Normal weight	Weeks 1–2	Weeks 3–4	Weeks 5–6
2–5kg (4–11lb)	370–735	555–1105	370–735
6–10kg (13–22lb)	845–1235	1255–1855	845–1235
11–20kg (24–44lb)	1330–2080	1995–3120	1330–2080
21–30kg (46–66lb)	2160–2820	3235–4230	2160–2820
31–40kg (68–88lb)	2890–3500	4335–5250	2890–3500
41–50kg (90–110lb)	3565–4135	5345–6205	3565–4135

following weeks, so that three weeks after birth, when the mother is producing her maximum amount of milk, she is consuming three times her normal amount of energy. But suckling is for bonding with mother, not just for filling the stomach. Good mothers find their pups' suckling activity both relaxing and comforting, and pups that need handfeeding due to maternal illness, insufficient milk, or rejection are likely to be delayed in developing social skills compared with those that have suckled normally. Finding and defending the most productive teat is also the behaviour of the most dominant pups in the litter: a knowledgeable breeder recognizes subtle puppy activities such as this, and can advise you about personality differences within a litter.

By two weeks of age pups start approaching their mother for a feed, but as their pin-sharp teeth develop and suckling becomes uncomfortable for her, she starts to reduce the frequency or length of her feeds. The pups would want to suckle forever, but she has other views. A good mother always loses weight, because producing milk is hugely energy demanding and physically drains her, so her evolutionary desire is to wean them on to solid food as soon as possible. She would wean pups onto solid food between three and six weeks of age if she were living rough, and breeders do the same. They mix equal parts of evaporated milk with crushed and moistened dry puppy food, baby cereal, prepared baby food, canned puppy food, scrambled egg, or cottage cheese. Pups start by licking the mix from a

Special care Breeders can sometimes find foster-mothers if a young or temperamental mother neglects her pups, or an older mother's milk fails, or the mother has an infection. A runt who is markedly smaller than its littermates, however, is at a huge disadvantage in the competitive crush to feed at the mother's teats, and may not survive without hand feeding.

ROLY-POLY PUPPIES

Breeders just love to send their pups off to their new homes looking like plump, shiny toys. These pups certainly are cute, but there's a hidden problem with early plumpness. Nutritionists suspect that the number of fat cells that a pup develops early in life – and don't kid yourself, plump means fat – is directly related to being overweight or obese later in life. Metabolically speaking, a dog may "defend" this initial number of fat cells. That's why losing weight later in life is so much more difficult for dogs that were fat puppies than for those that were once lean and became fat later in life. There's also research that indicates that skinny dogs live much longer – an average of 18 months longer in Labrador Retrievers – than littermates that are even slightly overweight. If a breeder has produced a litter of Humpty Dumptys, your first task will be to get that pup back to what its ideal weight should be.

finger, then from the finger in a saucer, and soon from the saucer itself. Some pups are quite sloppy eaters, while others are fastidious. Once a pup is an enthusiastic solid food eater – and this only takes a few days – breeders start to reduce the food they give to the mother and also control the pups' feeding, giving them access to their mother right after they've eaten. This ensures that they get warmth and comfort but don't stimulate milk production through industrial-strength suckling.

Some pups need hand feeding

If a litter is particularly large, or a mother is unwilling or unable to feed her pups, her milk can be replaced by commercially produced formula. Don't overfeed hand-fed pups; let them decide how much they want to accept. As a general rule in each 24-hour period a pup needs about 15ml or 15cc (1tbsp) of formula for each 50g (2oz) of body weight.

WEIGHT	FORMULA PER 24 HOURS
110g (4oz)	30ml (2tbsp)
225g (8oz)	60ml (4tbsp)
340g (12oz)	90ml (6tbsp)
450g (16oz)	120ml (8tbsp)
570g (20oz)	150ml (10tbsp)
680g (24oz)	180ml (12tbsp)
790g (28oz)	210ml (14tbsp)
910g (32oz)	240ml (16tbsp)

Social development

During the first few weeks after birth, the mother is the overwhelming influence on her pups, and the way she mothers them has long-lasting effects. Dogs that are vocal, for example, learned it from vocal mothers.

If you visit a litter and the mother grizzles and whines, don't be surprised if her pups grow up to do so too. Contact with people during the first two weeks of life stimulates a pup's development, but the absence of people at this stage doesn't create any irreparable damage. At around three weeks of age, pups begin to socially interact with their siblings, with other household dogs and cats, and with us. During the next few weeks, until a pup reaches 12 weeks of age, its eventual personality is formed; behaviourists call this time the "socialization period".

Most of that time is spent at the breeder's. The involvement of the breeder and activity with the littermates both have a profound influence on how a dog ultimately behaves. That's why it is so important that dogs who will live as pets are raised by their breeders in a home environment, not in a garden shed or in the garage, where there's little to stimulate their physical or mental development. Good breeders understand they should be involved in their puppies' play activity. A pup learns to inhibit its bite during play if its littermate squeals and stops play or bites back. Good breeders don't use excessive discipline when pups behave this way with them but instead withdraw rewards, stopping play when one of their pups goes over the top.

Dominance and submission are natural behaviours

I mentioned previously that some breeds of dogs, such as Huskies, use dominant behaviours they inherited from their wolf ancestors for real, while others, such as Golden Retrievers, may use the same dominant behaviours in a ritualized way when playing with other dogs (*see pp. 50–53*). During the socialization period, when pups are still with the breeder, dominant activities with littermates develop, and these include:

- Stalking, ambushing, chasing, or pouncing on littermates
- Standing over a littermate, especially with the head on the littermate's neck or with forepaws on the back
- Walking in a circle around a littermate, moving stiffly and with the tail wagging and raised
- Raising the hackles on the back
- Snarling, growling, or baring teeth
- Using a direct, concentrated stare
- Mounting a littermate, sometimes with pelvic thrusts
- Boxing
- Real biting

All of these behaviours are easy to interpret, and good breeders intervene before they get out of hand. But people often make mistakes about their dog's submissive behaviours. We often think submissive behaviours are "cute" and unwittingly reinforce them. Submissive behaviours (and common misinterpretations) include:

- Avoiding eye contact and turning the head away when looked at (sometimes interpreted as retribution or stoicism).
- Flattening the ears back, with head hung low and tail between the legs (often interpreted as guilt).

Role reversal In normal puppy play, there isn't a permanent "top dog". Games are only worth playing if they are dynamic, so all but the most dominant of pups – and dogs – will roll over and give someone else a chance to be boss. Even when it looks competitive, this play teaches puppies how to cooperate.

Don't push it Reactive terriers can be quick to rise to a challenge from another dog. Adults generally cut puppies a little slack – but only a little.

- Grinning with the lips retracted (mistakenly thought by many to be similar to a human smile).
- Licking the lips, sometimes sneezing, and in some breeds showing the incisors at the same time (misinterpreted as a dog trying to mimic a human smile).
- Rolling on the back, exposing the belly (often interpreted as no more than asking for a tickle).
- Urinating when greeting a person or another dog (wrongly thought to be a lack of toilet training).
- Remaining rock still when another dog circles, places a paw on the shoulders, or mounts (may be interpreted as being calm, but is more accurately interpreted as a submissive signal).
- Lying on the side and lifting a hind leg, exposing the genital region (usually accurately interpreted as a submissive signal).

Puppy play is vital for learning social skills

During the first eight weeks of life, when they live as a true pack, pups also learn how to engage in and enjoy group activities. They transfer these group activities to us when they move into our homes, and without them, lonesome pups howl or bark to get attention. Typical activities that our dogs want to continue with us include sleeping together – not just in the same room as us, but on our beds – eating together, lying, sitting, walking, running, or playing together, investigating the natural world together, sniffing, nosing, pawing, licking, and being stroked and groomed.

All of these behaviours are amazingly well developed by the time a pup is ready to leave its mother and siblings and join your family in its new home. The timing of that move is critical. Almost 30 years ago, an analysis of Seeing Eye guide dogs showed that while 90 per cent of dogs that left their mothers at eight weeks of age were succesfully trained as assistance dogs, the success rate fell to just 30 per cent among dogs who left their mothers at twelve weeks. Whenever possible, pups should move into their new homes at eight weeks of age. If this isn't possible, they should live inside the breeder's home and be exposed on a daily basis to what life is going to be like in your home – with young kids, cats, whatever – so that they learn about what life is like while their brains are still completely open to new experiences. If this doesn't happen, you'll have to undo previous learning as well as concentrate on new learning in your new pup.

LITTER SIZE AFFECTS PERSONALITY

Singleton pups, or those from litters of only two or three, have fewer opportunities to interact with a wide range of personalities and learn the fine nuances of body language. They may be less successful at developing the subtleties of canine social relationships later in life. This is one reason why small dogs, often from small litters, are frequently more inept at social relationships than larger dogs from larger litters. Another reason is that owners of small dogs more often cosset their dogs, preventing them from having normal interactions with other dogs.

CHAPTER SIX

Our Relationship with Dogs

Every aspect of the development of a dog's mind has a single natural purpose: to help it live a safe, secure, and satisfying life. That cute little bundle you bring home already has one aim in life: to be in control of its own life and maybe yours too! Feral dogs learn their limits from their canine pack, but our dogs have to learn from a human pack. It's up to you to ensure that your dog uses that wonderfully malleable and inventive mind in ways that are satisfying to you, your family, and your neighbours as well. For our part, dogs tell us what we want to hear. That might sound silly, especially considering they can't speak, but most of us think that we understand our dogs, and that life is rooted in reality when we live with dogs. They offer us reliable routines and something to love. Neurologist Robert Sapolsky says that "Something roughly akin to love is needed for proper biological development". From the time they arrive as pups until the heart-wrenching, life-or-death decisions of old age, there is certainly a feeling "roughly akin to love" in the relationships I've had with all my dogs.

Dogs go through passages of life, just like us, but their timescale is dramatically different. They're the equivalent of human infants for no more than the first three months of life, and personalities are moulded during this critical time. Puppyhood, or canine childhood, lasts from the end of infancy until puberty, which arrives as early as five months in very small breeds or as late as fifteen months in giant breeds. Then comes adolescence, the teenage years. Some dogs mature out of adolescence by one year, others not until they're three years old. And yes, some never grow up! Adulthood brings emotional stability and the reliability of set behaviours, and lasts until the onset of physical or mental decline. This can start as distressingly early as six or seven years of age in some giant breeds, usually somewhere over nine years in typical dogs, and as late as eleven or twelve years in some small individuals. In the following chapters I'll discuss these stages of life and how we should care for our dogs during each of them.

For us, life with a dog passes from the excitement of arrival through the exasperations and satisfactions of early training into the consistency and calm of a dog's adult years, when they are simply there, an icon of stability in the turbulence of life. You know what to expect from your adult dog just as you know what its needs are. Then suddenly your dog is no longer young, is no longer even middle-aged, but has entered the third passage of life and become an old dog. Having become accustomed to living with a life-long pup, you now find yourself living with a dependent geriatric, who needs a different diet, who has the aches and pains of arthritic joints, and whose toilet habits are no longer what they were. A dog's life is like a microcosm of our own lives – in little more than a decade it recapitulates ours from

Show you care A few years ago a popular television show pitted a sports car against a puppy to find which was the best "babe magnet". To the apparent dismay of the presenters, but probably of nobody else, the puppy won paws-down. We all recognize and respond to the love and committment that are implicit in a relationship with a dog.

birth to death. Our relationships with them can be emotionally fraught because we see the cycles of our own lives, the rapid passing of time.

Nurturing and being nurtured

At the very beginning of this book, I mentioned a raft of reasons why we think that life is better with dogs than without them, but really, it all comes down to this: most of us feel good not just when surrounded by life but when caring for living things. Forget about cause and effect or evolutionary selection, we simply feel mentally and physically better when we take a walk in the woods, visit a garden, watch livestock grazing in a pasture, see birds gliding in the air, catch a glimpse of a fish in a stream, chance upon a rabbit or a deer. In my nearby park, locals bring breadcrumbs to feed the birds, and tourists photograph squirrels coming to them for sandwich handouts. It's human nature. We're compelled to nurture, and what makes us so different from other species is that we feel this compulsion not only for our own children and grandchildren, but other people and animals too. Altruism, however it evolved, is part of what we are. That's why living with other animals is a universal phenomenon, as common amongst the world's remaining hunter-gatherers as it is for the tribes of the first world.

But dogs give us a unique form of love. Cultural anthropologist Constance Perin observed that dogs can be the "glue or the solvent" of neighbourly relations for middle-class Middle Americans. She wondered why dog owners sometimes blatantly lie, saying it wasn't their dog that messed on the neighbour's lawn when they really knew it was, or that their

Mutual benefit Just as our growing dogs have to learn their social skills from their human family, our growing kids can learn from their family dogs. Studies have found that regular contact with dogs improves the social skills an cooperative behaviour of pre-school children.

MEASURING YOUR ATTACHMENT TO YOUR DOG

Psychologists at the University of Kentucky in Lexington have produced a simple way to measure your attachment to your pet. The Lexington Pet Attachment Index is easy to answer: the higher your score, the higher your attachment to your dog. The role that a dog plays in the life of someone with a high score is very, very different to the role an identical dog would play in the life of someone with a low score. (In case you're curious, my own score is 30.)

Yes	Maybe	Don't know	No
5	3	1	0

- Do you consider your dog a friend?
- Do you talk to your dog?
- Would you say that owning a dog adds to your happiness?
- Do you talk to others about your dog?
- Do you often play with your dog?
- Does your dog know how you feel about things?

dog was perfectly reliable when they knew it was in fact potentially nippy. She wondered why people feel that their dogs will protect them, when factual evidence says the opposite. She became intrigued by the physiological and emotional rewards that we get from being near or touching our dogs – the drop in blood pressure and fall in heart rate, the way any agitation you're feeling diminishes in their presence.

One of the most moving displays of the calming influence of a dog I've witnessed was when I was handing out awards at a ceremony in Houston. One was to a young man in a wheelchair, born with multiple disabilities, and his service dog, a Golden Retriever. One of his disabilities was a speech impediment, so he rehearsed his lines, and he sounded good when I heard them. But when I announced the award he was overcome by emotion, and the only sound he could make was a sonorous and plaintive wail. For almost a minute he tried to make words but he couldn't, and the audience sat, silently unsettled. But then his service dog got up from where she was resting, walked over to him, sat down beside him, and put her head on his lap. At her touch he dropped his flailing right hand onto her head. His chin dropped onto his chest, and he sat motionless. Then I saw his hand press into her hair and he raised his head, inhaled, and (keeping his hand firmly on his dog) said clearly, "Ladies and gentlemen…"

Constance Perin says that the physiological rewards this man got from touching his dog are identical to the rewards we got from physical contact with our mothers when we were infants; both stimulate the same chemical pathways. We're outwardly and obviously care-givers to our dogs, but at a deeply submerged psychological level, we're also care-receivers. Perin coined the term "super-abundant" love for this love we felt when we were still "merged with mother", before we matured into the realization that we were unique, separate individuals. She says that people who have formed strong attachments to their dogs also experience this same feeling of super-abundant love for their pets.

Attachment can be intense

Each of us has his or her own reasons for wanting to live with a dog, as I mentioned in the introduction. The intensity of the relationships we have with our dogs is very personal, and speaking from my professional

experience I think it is deeply influenced by whether or not you have kids at home. I see the strongest attachment to pets in couples without kids: the postponers, the gay couples, and those who have never had children. Research backs me up: Lieta Marinelli at the University of Padua in Italy observed not only that people who have had dogs previously have greater affectionate bonds with their present dog than do first-time owners, but that people without children at home have stronger bonds with their dogs than families with children living at home.

The Pet Attachment Index (*see p.141*) is a rational way to measure your attachment to your dog, and I like a rational approach to what can be an emotional topic. If you're like me, you too may pride yourself in your ability to rationally think things through. But let's be frank. We are often unaware of how our emotions colour our thoughts, our decisions, and our actions. We may think we're using logic, but underlying our logic is instinct. As a slightly off-topic but personal example, when I hire new staff at the veterinary clinic, I select potentially suitable individuals from those who apply, then invite them to visit the clinic and meet us. My practice manager, my head nurse, and I each complete a form, grading such factors as the applicant's experience, eye contact, and response to hospitalized patients, concluding with the question "Would you trust this person with the care of your own pet?" But all of us acknowledge that within 30 seconds of meeting an applicant, our instincts already influence what we subsequently write. (The system still seems to work, however, because we rarely need to use it.) All of us are just as instinctive in our attitude towards dogs. We may give logical reasons why we choose to live with them, but the true reasons are often more emotional than logical.

Worry is an integral and painful part of our relationship with dogs, or with any animals we live closely with. Several years ago, I volunteered as a livestock inspector during a foot-and-mouth disease outbreak, and I met farmers who were emotionally devastated when their herds were slaughtered. Yes, they had raised their cattle to go to slaughter, but not then, not yet. While professional slaughtermen did most of the killing, it wasn't uncommon for me to be asked to personally kill with a lethal injection a bullock, or pig, or lamb that was more than an item of livestock. I wasn't surprised when I read about the high level of suicide in farmers who lost their stock in the outbreak.

The greater the level of attachment we have to our dogs, the more intense is the grief we feel when they die – and the suddenness of the dog's death and the role the dog played in life can exacerbate it. In a large study of adults in Ontario, Canada, over 30 per cent reported they experienced severe grief when their dog died. Not working through those feelings of grief can have long-lasting consequences, including depression, anxiety, social withdrawal, behavioral disturbances, and for kids, underachievement at school. I've seen clients who simply never get over the death of their dog. For many of us, a dog is an honorary member of the family, but society doesn't always acknowledge that. Never trivialize just how devastating the death of a dog can be to its owner.

A dog for all seasons Every person looks for something different in a dog. Some want a tireless travelling companion to share their adventures; at the other end of the spectrum, some seek a home companion when their horizons shrink. Intense attachments can form at both these extremes, and anywhere in between. They are naturally strongest in those who spend the most time with their dogs, regardless of how they fill that time together.

Problems with dogs

When we bring dogs into our homes, we usually think mostly about the positives, but there are negatives too, so let me mention the two most important. First, it is part of a dog's natural behaviour to bite. Dogs will sometimes bite by accident, but they also bite to make a point or simply out of fear. In the dog's world a bite is a guaranteed, effective form of communication, which is why they bite each other, but they also bite us. Second, dogs can be a health risk for some people. Zoonotic diseases, infections transmissible from dogs to us, are few in number (any species is more likely to contract infections from its own kind rather than a completely different species) but they do exist, and people with impaired immune systems are most susceptible to these. Allergy is a more common health risk in North America, Europe, and Australasia. Although dogs are a lesser cause of allergy than dust mites, cat dander, or pollens like ragweed, millions of people (including me) are allergic to them. So for those of you who have not yet brought your new dog from the breeder into your home, let's take a look at these two worrying problems.

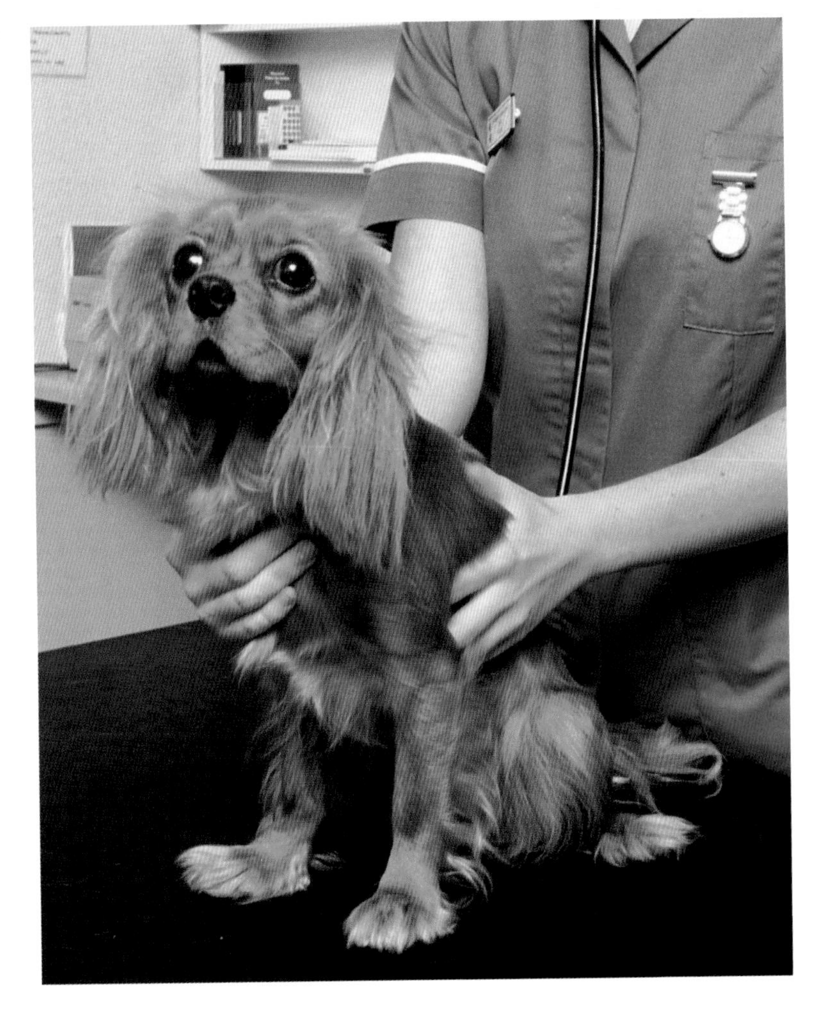

Health cheques Dogs do have health problems, but relatively few of them can be transmitted to humans. A dog's health is more likely to have a negative impact on your wallet than your health, which is why a health insurance policy is a useful accessory for any pet.

When the bite is worse than the bark

We trust dogs – predators – with our children's lives, quite a strange fact until you get past the horror statistics and see how rare it is that dogs cause severe or fatal bites. But they do. In the United States, 238 human deaths during the past 20 years have involved dogs from at least 25 breeds. More commonly, dogs simply bite. In the United States, it is estimated by the Centers for Disease Control that several million people are bitten each year, and a significant proportion need hospital treatment. While the physical injuries often heal quickly, the mental injuries take longer, and can last a lifetime. Here are some representative statistics from various countries.

In Berlin, Germany, 0.9 per cent of tax-assessed dogs were involved in "incidents" with humans in 2004. Rottweilers, Dobermanns, Pit Bull Terriers, German Shepherds, and American Staffordshire Terriers were responsible for a disproportionately high number of bites, most of which occurred on the dog owner's property. In Austria, which has stringent leash and muzzle laws, the annual incidence of dog bites is 0.5 per 1,000 children under 16; it is highest in one-year-olds and decreases with the child's age. The risk of an attack by a German Shepherd or a Dobermann is around five times higher than that of a Labrador Retriever or a crossbred dog, and the vast majority (82 per cent) of the dogs that bit were familiar to the children.

At a hospital in Cape Town, South Africa, bites accounted for 1.5 per cent of all trauma unit presentations, with boys making up 68 per cent of victims. Children under six years of age were more likely to have sustained injuries to the head, face, or neck, while older children more commonly received injuries to the buttocks, legs, or feet. Younger children were more likely to be attacked at home, older children outside the home.

In the United States, Pit-Bull-type dogs and Rottweilers were involved in more than half of all deaths due to bites, and of 227 reports with accurate data, over three quarters of fatal attacks involved dogs that were on their owners' property. The Centers for Disease Control estimates that half of all children under 12 years of age have been bitten at least once by a dog. In Pennsylvania, children younger than six years accounted for 52.8 per cent of dog bites, which were mostly inflicted by their own dogs and in their own homes. In Oregon, boys aged five to nine years have a higher rate of injury than girls, and biting dogs are more likely to live in areas where the residents' median incomes is less than the state's average income.

See the patterns here – the breeds, the location of attacks, the age of the victims? Selective breeding can enhance or diminish aggression or fear in dogs. While breeds like Golden Retrievers have been bred for low fear and low aggression, breeds like Pit Bull Terriers and certain large breeds, including many of the "attack" breeds, have been bred for low fear and high aggression. These breeds were created and prized for their tenacity during fighting and a high level of dominance. Some highly reactive breeds, such as Chihuahuas, Smoothhaired Dachshunds, and small terriers, are also more inclined to bite than are scenthounds, setters, or retrievers.

Dominant dogs of any breed like their own space, and because they share that space with us, the most aggressive of them may challenge us. Dogs also

Nobody's immune In many places "fighting breeds" are compelled to wear muzzles, but the truth is any dog can bite in the right – or wrong – circumstances. Even soft-mouthed retrievers can be liable to snap when guarding what is closest to their hearts – usually their food.

typically bite either because of fear or to defend their territory. According to a report in the British Medical Journal, young children were more likely to be bitten when dogs felt their food or other possessions, such as toys, were under threat, while older children bore the brunt of dogs' territorial behaviour. Behaviourist John Bradshaw says there are three underlying traits behind dog bites, which he has labelled aggressivity, reactivity, and immaturity. He rates male dogs higher than females in all three categories, and considers females easier to train than males. I agree with him.

Reducing the risks

It's impossible to eliminate dog bites, but not difficult to reduce the risk and incidence of this most common problem through early socialization, efficient obedience training, and neutering. Breed-specific legislation that bans the keeping of particular breeds misses the point if it doesn't address the problems of training dog owners to train their dogs. French legislation at least requires owners of dogs such as Pit Bull types, mastiff types, and fighting breeds to undergo training to educate them in the management of their dogs, as well as stipulating that these dogs must be muzzled in public, neutered, and owned only by people with no criminal record. Who does the training and what happens when an owner fails isn't clear.

Start early to socialize dogs to people of all sizes, colours, and appearances – people visiting your home and (if you're lucky enough to have one) your garden. Take the whole family and spend an hour a week at a good local dog club for six to eight weeks; you'll learn how to teach your dog basic obedience commands efficiently, and your dog will be exposed under controlled circumstances to other dogs and a variety of new situations. You'll also learn about what to look for in your dog's body language, the clues that it may bite. Be consistent, and always reward your dog's good behaviour when it meets other people or other dogs. Unless you plan to breed or your vet advises otherwise, arrange for the dog to be neutered. With females this reduces medical risks, and with males it reduces social risks. Games are great, and for most dogs even tug-of-war is a perfectly good game, but avoid rough and tumble games with potentially aggressive dogs. Don't encourage your dog to guard; leave that to professional guard dogs. Respect your dog's den: if it's under a table, don't reach in to get it out, but coax it out with a treat or a toy. Don't leave your dog unattended in the garden, and if there's even the slightest hint of an attempt to snap, nip, or bite, contact your vet. They will be able to determine whether there's a medical reason for the behaviour and when there's not, to refer you to a good dog trainer, who will show you how to use positive reinforcement training techniques to overcome or at least contain the problem. Remember, the great majority of dog bites occur at home and involve members of the dog's family.

Don't invite a bite

Never leave young children unsupervised with dogs, especially in the dog's own home. A dog may behave more dominantly with smaller individuals, especially if they squeal or scream. Everyone should learn the danger signs and the actions that may lead a dog to bite, but it is essential to teach children the following list.

- Signs of fear in a dog – flattened ears, averted gaze, cowering, tucked-in tail – may be followed by a defensive bite.
- Signs of overt aggression in a dog – a direct stare, alert ears, raised hair on the back, raised tail, bared teeth, barking, or growling – may be followed by an aggressive bite.
- Even if your own dog loves being petted, remember there are other dogs that are fearful and will bite if approached.
- Be calm and careful around dogs: do not shriek, scream, wave hands around, cry, or suddenly run.
- Never, ever touch any unknown dog without first asking the owner whether the dog can be petted.
- Never enter gardens in which there is a dog, especially a dog tethered by a chain or rope.
- Leave dogs alone when they are eating, sleeping, or playing with a favourite dog toy.
- Never take things such as toys, bones, or chews from dogs.
- Never sneak up on a dog, try to scare it, or force it where it doesn't want to go.
- Never bend over dogs, which can be interpreted as threatening.
- Always eat where dogs cannot try to grab the food.
- Children should not bury their faces in a dog's hair, even if the dog is the most gentle of individuals.
- Children, especially boys, should never play roughhouse games with a dog, even if adults do.
- Children, especially boys, must not tease a dog, because this can trigger both fearful and dominant dogs to bite.

Heed warnings Some snaps come with no advance notice, if a dog is suddenly thwarted or something is taken from it. But many come at the end of a series of warning behaviours that escalate from stares through growls to bared teeth. It's never worth "facing down" a strange dog in these circumstances; if the dog is your own, get help. Fast.

Deadly rage The name rabies is Latin for madness, and the virus causes anxiety, agitation, hallucinations, and inevitably biting, which transmits the saliva-borne virus to another victim. Many cities in China now enforce a one-dog rule, to match the one-child policy, after booming pet numbers were matched by a surge in rabies deaths. Elsewhere, vaccination has proved more effective in the long term.

Of course, unknown dogs and strays do bite too. Leave unknown dogs alone and never approach a stray, especially in countries where rabies is endemic. If a dog approaches you, don't run, yell, or scream; stand still and avoid eye contact with it. If a dog concludes you are not a threat it's more likely to just sniff you and walk away. If it still tries to bite you, protect yourself with whatever is available and quietly back away. If you fall, curl into a tight ball, protecting your head and neck with your arms, and lie perfectly still.

When dogs bite

If, despite all care, you are bitten, wash the wound immediately with antiseptic soap and warm water, and seek immediate medical treatment if your skin is punctured or torn. If you have not been vaccinated against tetanus in the last seven years, arrange for an immediate tetanus antitoxin injection. If you are bitten by an unknown dog in a country where rabies is endemic, arrange for immediate treatment with rabies antiserum – and if there's a choice between an inexpensive local product or a more expensive imported one, take the expensive option. If the dog that bit you was running loose, report the bite to the police or to animal control, with a description of the dog. If you are bitten by an owned dog, report the bite to the owners first, and if you are not satisfied with their response, to the police.

If your dog bites someone, take immediate responsibility. Restrain your dog and remove it to a secure location, such as a closed room or, if you are outdoors, your car. Check the degree of damage and arrange for any medical attention first. Give the victim your name and address, and if you live where rabies is endemic, information to confirm that your dog's rabies inoculation is up to date – if your dog is not inoculated, contact your vet and arrange for your dog to be put into quarantine. Report the incident to your insurer, and make an immediate appointment to determine the cause of your dog's aggression and arrange a plan of action to prevent further biting. Until the problem is overcome, don't take risks. Keep your dog muzzled except when it eats or drinks until a trainer tells you it is not necessary.

Rabies is a worldwide killer

The most horrific type of dog bite is one that transmits rabies. Each year over 50,000 people, mostly in Asia and Africa, die from rabies, and the most common way the disease is contracted is through dog bites. In Western Europe, North America (excluding Mexico), Australasia, and Japan, human deaths from rabies are rare. This is because so many dogs are vaccinated against the disease, and its incidence in wildlife is contained or even eliminated through schemes in which tasty treats containing vaccine are spread around target areas. Rabies can affect many animals. In the United States, dogs account for around 1 per cent of rabies cases in animals, 79 out of 6,940 in a recent year. Most cases are in livestock bitten by rabid wildlife, and the rare human cases are almost always contracted either from bats or from dog bites while travelling abroad.

Natural born biters?

Some dogs are born biters, but let me emphasize, some *dogs*, not some *breeds* of dogs. A good example comes from research undertaken into aggression in 1,053 English Springer Spaniels. A history of owner-directed growling or more intense aggression was reported in 510 dogs (48.4 per cent). Two hundred and seventy-seven (26.3 per cent) of these dogs had bitten a human, and 65.2 per cent of those bites were directed at familiar adults and children. But looking at the cases in more detail revealed not all Springers were equally likely to bite. Females were much less likely to than males, and, more interesting, Springers from lines bred for hunting work were much less likely to have a history of biting than those bred only for looks. Unwittingly, breeding for the show ring has somehow increased aggression in some lines of English Springers, while the level of aggression is lower in those lines still used for work.

Zoonoses and other shared problems

Living intimately with dogs, allowing them in our homes, on our sofas and beds, exposes us to other potential infections and infestations. Parasites such as fleas, ticks, and roundworms are the most common transmissible problems. Ticks can carry a range of unpleasant diseases, the most common of which is Lyme disease. We are more likely to pick ticks up from a walk in the woods or long grass than directly from our dogs, but dogs may bring ticks into our homes, or take us on walks to places where we pick them up.

DEALING WITH DUST MITES

Dust mites are one of the most common causes of allergy in both our dogs and us. If either you or your dog suffer, washing your laundry at 60°C (140°F) kills all dust mites. If you wash at 40°C (104°F) you kill just 6.5 per cent of dust mites. The research, conducted at Seoul University in Korea, found that hotter washing is also more effective at removing pollen and skin dander, be it yours or your dog's – and just as allergic people are commonly allergic to dog dander, allergic dogs are frequently allergic to human dander.

If you have any undiagnosed illness, be it a rash, joint pain, a fever, breathlessness, or fatigue, and this is a possibility, tell your doctor. Lyme disease is always in a vet's mind when a dog is presented with any of these symptoms, but it's an underdiagnosed condition in people and causes chronic disease if untreated.

There are other concerns. Infections that cause gastrointestinal disease – salmonella, shigella, and campylobacter – can be transmitted from dogs to us and vice versa, but in my experience, these are rare. Giardia, a single-celled intestinal parasite that causes diarrhoea, is more common, and its incidence is probably underestimated both in dogs and in us. The incidence of tuberculosis in people is increasing, and I've seen dogs that have contracted the infection from their owners. In each instance, once the diagnosis was made the infected dog was deemed a public health hazard and destroyed. The infamous MRSA (methicillin resistant staphylococcus aureus), once only a human hospital infection, has moved out of hospitals and into communities, and successfully migrated from humans to dogs. Now it is a potential zoonotic condition that can be transmitted from dogs back to the bacteria's original host, us. Therapy dogs that visit hospitals and residential care facilities should be tested for MRSA, and if anyone in your family has contracted this infection, either in hospital or elsewhere, your dog should be checked as well and treated with antibiotics if necessary.

Try before you buy It can be traumatic to find that your longed-for new puppy triggers sniffing, wheezing, or worse. If possible, borrow a dog first – and if somebody in the family does have a reaction, don't despair. Just be prepared to make a more careful choice of coat type – or if you're like me and still can't resist long blonde hair, reconcile yourself to sticking with a regular and thorough grooming regime.

Do dogs trigger allergy?

Dog lovers will tell you that living with a dog reduces your risk of developing allergies, but studies simply aren't consistent. In a large European study involving over 18,000 people, Norwegian doctors reported that living with dogs was associated with increased asthma among people without a history of atopic disease, but exposure to dogs during childhood resulted in decreased hay fever with no increased risk of asthma for people with a history of atopic disease. They concluded that exposure to dogs in childhood seemed to protect against adult allergic disease but promote nonallergic asthma. But German doctors following the health of over 3,000 children to two years found the opposite: decreased asthma and eczema among children in families without a history of atopic disease that owned a dog when the children were born, but increased prevalence in children whose families had both a history of atopic disease and a dog.

In the United States, test on six- and seven-year-olds in Georgia for common airborne allergens showed a reduced risk of allergic sensitization in those who lived with two or more dogs or cats in the first year of lives. In Arizona, tracking over 1,200 babies up to 13 years of age showed that among children of non-asthmatic parents those who had indoor dogs when they were born were less likely to develop frequent wheeze than those without dogs, but in children of asthmatic parents, living with a dog had no bearing one way or the other. The study concluded that dog exposure in early life might prevent the development of asthma-like symptoms in low-risk children with no family history of asthma, but does not significantly influence allergic sensitization. University of Cincinnati doctors found that infants in multiple-dog homes were less likely to develop wheezing in their first year than infants who were raised in dog-free homes. They found higher levels of endotoxins secreted by intestinal bacteria in multiple-dog homes; these may stimulate the immune system in a way that blocks the development of allergies early in life.

I interpret these results to mean that if there's no allergy in your family, exposure to dogs (and cats) early in life reduces your risk of developing allergies later in life, but if there is allergy in your family there still isn't good evidence of any effect either way. People who are allergic, like me, usually react to many allergens, one of which may be dog dander (*see p.117*). Doctors commonly recommend that pets should be removed from the homes of allergy sufferers – an apparently simple suggestion, but fraught with emotional complications that can be greater than the allergy problem. If your home is an allergic home, they may be alternatives. Allergy testing can give an idea of what you or your children may be allergic to, but is more reliable for telling you what you don't react to.

If you're getting a new dog, choose a breed or individual with a healthy, smooth coat and wash it regularly, at least twice each month. If you already have a dog and it's hairy, have the coat clipped regularly, at least once a month. Groom your dog at least weekly, always outdoors, and have your vet treat any skin conditions immediately. Don't allow your dog on furniture, or in the bedrooms of allergic family members, and wash your dog's bedding at least once a week. Dog dander (microscopic flakes of skin), easily builds up in fabric. If you have wall to wall carpets, vacuum them daily with a vacuum that filters dog dander and other allergens, such as pollens and dust mites. Lastly, don't let your dog lick people who are allergic to dogs, because dog saliva contains a protein that allergic people can react to.

Rapid response The skin allergy test is widely used to diagnose allergies of all kinds, to things that are touched, eaten, or inhaled. An allergy by its very nature provokes an immediate response, so this is a quick, simple, and safe way to identify, or at least rule out, a sensitivity to a substance.

CHAPTER SEVEN

Choosing a New Dog

We are the complex partner in the relationship we develop with our dogs. An eight-week-old pup is pretty much a blank canvas. Its feelings, emotions, and behaviours are in the process of being moulded, and you still have time – at least a month – to form them as you want them to be formed. Bringing an emotionally fully formed adult dog into your home is a different matter; inevitably you inherit unexpected problems or, to use a now-familiar term, "unknown unknowns", behaviours that will need to be unlearned before the behaviours you want can be learned. Many of us get personal satisfaction when we offer a home to an unwanted dog, but let's first look at the dog that's still putty waiting to be moulded into a contented canine member of a human family.

Good dogs come from good breeders

You can control the final third of a dog's socialization period, but it's up to the breeder to ensure that a pup has been raised in the best possible environment during its first eight weeks. Find a good breeder by word-of-mouth – ask veterinary clinic staff, friends, and neighbours. Amateurs, like me, sometimes breed from our own dogs because we, or friends of ours, want descendants. Amateurs often produce well-loved, well-socialized litters raised in their homes, but make sure that a vet has been involved, that the parents have been checked for inherited disorders, and that both mother and pups have been efficiently vaccinated and wormed.

Although professional breeders might be a bit quirky, a single-issue group of people who think only of their breed, many of them are a great source of purebred dogs. But while some are terrific, others breed just for profit, as a business, and they are dreadful. This is a greater problem when specific breeds are popular and in short supply, or in entire regions, such as Japan, where dog ownership is increasing and breeding an excellent commercial business. Tread carefully. Always visit the breeder and look for telltale evidence of obsession, like shelves of china dogs, dog door knockers, sofas covered in blankets for dogs to rest on, or show ribbons on all the walls. Be cautious if you are offered an older pup kept by the breeder "as a potential show dog". Many of these will have had little social experience outside the breeder's home or kennels, and may find it difficult to adjust to family life. The best breeders aren't there to make money, they breed because they obsessively love their breed. Good breeders will give you the third degree. They want assurances that you will provide a good home for their "babies".

Really good breeders know that some medical conditions have a genetic component and that the best way to reduce their incidence is by breeding from dogs free of these conditions. Screening tests for inherited eye or joint problems, such as progressive retinal atrophy and hip dysplasia, are routinely used by all conscientious breeders. The most efficient and concerned kennel clubs include the results of such tests in the registration documents for pups.

Stay in charge Of course the whole family will want to be involved in choosing a family dog, but a wise parent does some stage management. Whoever will take prime responsibility for the dog (and that's never one of the kids, whatever they promise) should choose a breeder and a litter they are completely happy with before getting democratic on the final selection.

If you are buying a purebred dog, check with your vet (or on the internet) for an update of what specific screening tests are available for that breed. Temperament problems, such as dominance aggression in English Springer and Cocker Spaniels, also run in families, and good breeders avoid using dogs with known inherited behaviour problems. Good breeders will also explain to you that generally speaking males are more dominant, more active, and more destructive, while females demand more affection and are easier to obedience and house train. Of course, early neutering, before puberty, perpetuates many aspects of a pup's youthful temperament and diminishes these differences.

Sources to avoid

Avoid dogs from commercial puppy farms or "mills", where pups are usually raised in medically and emotionally appalling circumstances without healthy socialization. Easily said, but how? For a start, be very wary of most pet shops. Some do source their dogs from reputable breeders, but according to surveys carried out by animal welfare organization, over 90 per cent get their pups from commercial puppy farms.

As for most things, the internet is either a wonderful source or a truly terrible one for finding a dog. Many dog shelters have superb sites, and breeder websites can be excellent, but they can also be dressed up to appear to be caring and conscientious when in fact they are fronts for commercial puppy farms. Be especially suspicious if a breeder, found on the web or any other way, offers to deliver your pup to you, either for your convenience or because they "just happen" to be in your vicinity, rather than letting you collect it from them. These people are often fronts for puppy farms.

Be equally wary of newspaper ads. Conscientious breeders rely on reputation and word-of-mouth to sell their pups, and the best breeders have

Keep your head Don't be seduced by the charms of the first pups you see. All pups are designed to be irresistable by nature. And don't feel compelled to "rescue" pups you feel sorry for. There are organizations to do that. Even in a shelter, it is in everyone's best interest – including the pups' – to make a head-over-heart choice that will lead to a stable, lasting partnership, not a head-over-heels one that could end in rehoming.

Nature and nurture Observe the puppy for a while to get a sense of its personality and habits. A pup may have a preference that shows at an early age, for digging holes or (like Bean) eating unsavoury items. You can change a lot, but forewarned is forearmed.

waiting lists and never need to advertise their stock. Newspaper ads for new litters are often fronts for puppy mills, and also the preferred sales method of "back-yard" breeders, people who breed their dogs primarily to earn a little extra income. Reliable amateur breeders usually have homes for their pups before their bitch is even bred; if they don't have enough homes, they will advertise on their vet's notice board.

And finally, should I even mention the local street corner? I'm afraid I should, because that's where teenage guys often get their thug dogs. Not that many teenage thugs will be reading this book, but street corners are where stolen dogs are exchanged. The breeds that are most likely to be stolen are those that can potentially be used for fighting or for breeding fighters, and also those that are fashion statements and easy to sell in the local drinking joint. Need I say more?

Choosing a recycled dog

If you're interested in a specific breed and are happy to give a home to an adult dog, all breed clubs have someone responsible for rehoming members of their breed that, usually for no fault of their own, need rehoming. When I was in the market for a new dog, the first person I spoke to was a Golden Retriever breeder who takes in retrievers for rehoming. She had a ten-year-old male "with barking issues" on hand, but my boss wanted a female, and a pup. A purebred may need to be rehomed because of a behaviour problem, but more commonly, a new home is necessary because of changed circumstances – a death, an illness, or a move into accommodation that prohibits pets. Breed club websites or your local vet will have e-mail addresses or telephone number of the nearest breed rescue secretary.

Well-run dog shelters are another fine source for the whole range of dogs from pups to the elderly, including purebreds, crossbreds, and randombreds. They often have excellent websites, showing the dogs needing homes and also describing their temperaments and the potential problems you inherit when you acquire one. Little dogs are increasingly uncommon at shelters; more common are varieties of bigger, tougher dogs: Bull-Terrier types, Rottweiler types, Husky types. These can be great dogs, but usually require experienced owners with the patience necessary to train them well. Don't set foot in a dog shelter until you have a firm idea of exactly what you want. I know that sounds harsh, but dogs behind bars, pleading with their eyes for you to rescue them, twist your emotions. When choosing a dog, make sure your head rules your heart.

Ask questions

Conscientious breeders are bound to interrogate you, so don't be bashful about doing the same to them. Ask them whatever questions come to your mind – these ones should always be on your list.

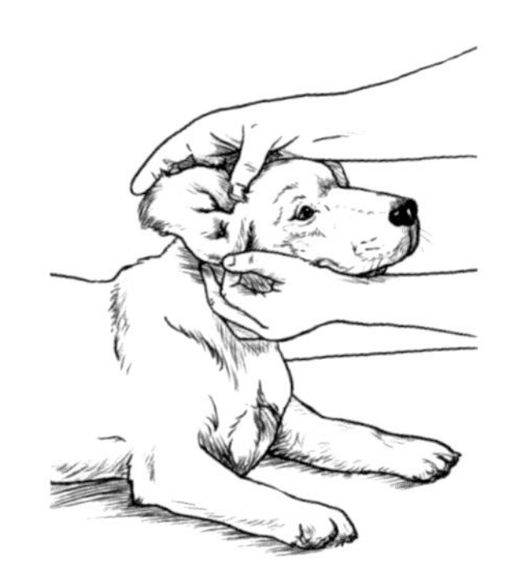

Take a good look Don't be afraid to examine your potential new pet. No breeder should be offended if you peer inside ears or under the tail – if they show their dogs, this is exactly what every judge will do in the ring.

Q ***How long have you been breeding this breed?***
A The longer the better.

Q ***Do you breed other breeds?***
A If more than one, the other breed should have attributes you'd expect the breeder to be interested in. For example, working Labradors and working Cocker Spaniels shoudn't ring alarm bells, but Chihuahuas and Akitas should. That might be a front for a puppy farm.

Q ***What's bad about the breed?***
A The more they tell you, the more honest they are.

Q ***May I see the father?***
A He may be a professional stud dog from another breeder, but expect your breeder at least to have a picture of him and put you in contact with his owner so that you can find out more about his personality.

Q ***Where do the dogs live?***
A Happy parent dogs live indoors in a home environment. They make the most sociable companions.

Q ***May I look around?***
A Conscientious breeders don't mind snoopers.

Q ***May I see your other dogs?***
A They should all be friendly and approachable.

Q ***May I return the pup if there's an unexpected problem?***
A The best breeders demand that their pup is returned to them if there's a problem.

Q ***May I speak to others you've sold pups to?***
A Good breeders are confident about the success of their dogs.

Q ***Has your vet examined the litter?***
A The breeder should be willing to give you the name and telephone number of the vet.

Q ***Do you participate in vet-supervised health monitoring schemes for the breed?***
A Good breeders ensure their dogs have been cleared by schemes to monitor inherited conditions such as eye and joint problems.

Q ***Do you register the results of these health surveys on your breeding stock with the kennel club?***
A Good breeders are proud of the quality of their breeding stock and register the results. In the most efficient countries, such as Sweden, the registration of test results isn't voluntary, it's a compulsory condition of puppy registration.

Q ***How often do you breed from the mother?***
A Good breeders follow kennel club regulations and limit the number of litters a mother can have, often to no more than four in a lifetime.

Care now saves trouble later

Choosing a puppy can be an intensely emotional experience, but you need to control your emotions and briefly examine the pup for any obvious problems. Here's a simple checklist.

- Eyes should be symmetrical and looking straight ahead, with no tear staining below them and no inflammation or discharge (conjunctivitis).
- The eyelids should be neither rolled in (entropion) nor hanging loose (ectropion), and should have no extra eyelashes. The third eyelid may be visible but neither inflamed or swollen.
- Ears should have no crust on tips or tenderness when touched, and good hair cover outside. Inside they should have clean, sweet-swelling ear canals with no wax visible. There should be no head shaking.
- The teeth should have a scissors bite, with the upper incisors fitting neatly over lower incisors; if they are too far forward, the bite is overshot. In some short-nosed breeds, like the Boxer, the lower incisors just overlap the upper incisors (reverse scissors or undershot bite).

Mix and match If your home already has pets, it can be helpful to gauge the response of a current dog to a new puppy, as well as that of a new puppy to an older dog. A grumpy oldtimer and a timid pup will never make a winnng combination in the home.

• Gums should be pink and healthy, although pigment spots are normal.
• Nose should be cool and moist, with decent nostril openings for easy breathing and no mucus when the nostrils are squeezed.
• Top of head should have no soft spot (fontanelle) present.
• Belly should be clean and smooth, without any bulge (umbilical hernia) at the navel.
• Anus should be clean, with no redness or hair loss.
• Coat should be bright and shiny, with a normal puppy smell. There should be no scale, dandruff, flaking skin, itchiness or obvious parasites, or moth-eaten appearance.
• Genitals should be clean. A female's vulva should have no inflammation, discharge, or "pasting" of hair, signs of discharge and vaginitis. A male's scrotum should have both testicles present and the foreskin (prepuce) should slide back and forth easily, with no adhesions.
• Legs and joints should be straight and well-formed. Have your vet check that the kneecaps (patellas) don't slip off, especially in toy breeds, and that joints are well-constructed and not loose, especially in large breeds.
• Feet must bear weight equally and not be splayed or flat-footed.
• Movement should be free and smooth, with no faltering or limping.

Before leaving the breeder, get the pup's pedigree and registration papers, its worming history (including product name), and its vaccination certificate

Perfect fit Try to imagine the puppy fitting in to your home environment. If you are busy working types, forget the high-input breeds from working backgrounds, and if you have young chidren choose the affable hunting types bred for low aggression.

showing when its next inoculation is due. Pick up a diet sheet. Check any guarantees before paying, and ensure that you have it in writing that your purchase is based upon the pup's good health and conformation, and that this will be determined independently by your own vet, who will examine the pup within 36 hours.

Assessing puppy personality

It's impossible to accurately assess a pup's character, especially on only one visit, and much still depends on future learning and experience. There is one exception: a pup that is dominantly aggressive at eight weeks of age, one that growls, snaps, and seriously tries to bite, is likely to mature into a dominantly aggressive adult that will require expert handling. Experienced breeders know the personalities of individual pups; take their advice about personality differences within the litter. The test below, carried out weekly from six to eight weeks in a quiet place, away from the mother and the littermates, can help a breeder to assess dominance fairly accurately.

Insecure or nervous pups have the lowest scores, confident and potentially dominant dogs the highest; both are best with experienced dog owners. You may instinctively be drawn to the underdog, the hang-back sad sack that gets trampled by the pushier pups, or be charmed by the little spark that barks at you when you try to examine it, but if you are a new dog owner, pups with middle scores are likely to be the easiest to manage.

ASSESSING DOMINANCE

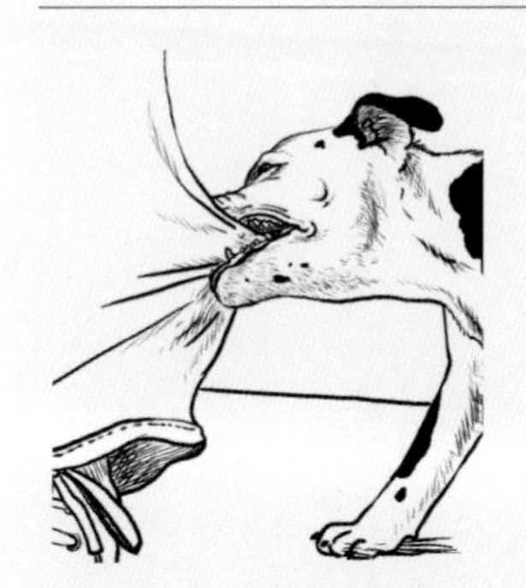

Sparky can become aggressive

Timid dogs can be destructive

The following exercise can be used to assess a puppy from about six weeks old. Try the following actions and score from one to five for the response seen.

PICK UP THE DOG

Shivering	Tentative	Relaxed	Resistant	Aggressive
1	2	3	4	5

PLACE THE PUP ON THE GROUND IN A NEW, QUIET AREA

Shivering	Tentative	Relaxed	Inquisitive	Exuberantly curious
1	2	3	4	5

ROLL THE PUP ON HIS BACK FOR A MINUTE

Shivering	Tentative	Relaxed	Wriggly	Aggressive
1	2	3	4	5

PLACE THE PUP 2M (6½FT) IN FRONT OF YOU, FACING YOU, KNEEL DOWN AND CALL

Doen't move	Tentative	Slow walk	Runs	Mows you down
1	2	3	4	5

Pups that amass a high score have strong, potentially dominant personalities, whereas those that score low are more likely to be on a nervous or submissive disposition. Both carry their own potential problems. The relaxed, positive, but sensibly cautious pups with mid-range scores are more likely to make good pets.

CHAPTER EIGHT

Canine Infancy

Having a dog, even an adult dog, join your household is like adopting a child. Life changes, hopefully for the better. There are new routines and if you plan ahead unexpected surprises are kept to a minimum. All of us, from one side or the other, have experience in parenting, but caring for another species is slightly different. Your goal is to make integrating your new dog into your family as easy as possible.

Preparing for your new dog

When a dog joins your household, think of yourself as a pre-school teacher with a new child in class too young to reason with so you've got to think for them. Natural teachers understand how important it is to focus and direct a child's vitality and enthusiasm, and consider not just the new arrival but also the rest of the class – or in your case the rest of your family. You'll be most successful if you control your emotions (easier said than done), ensure that everyone is consistent, and find ways to channel your new dog's energy.

The only way to do this is by assuming calm, sure leadership. Yes, I know how thrilling it is to watch a naïve pup learn that it can carry a shoe in its mouth or climb onto a bed, but if you allow it now, all you're doing is giving yourself future problems. When Bean was eight weeks old, it was really cute that she would so carefully pick up my pyjama top, wrapping it in a neat bundle, and parade high-headed with it in her mouth, or carry a bundle as big as she was down stairs without tripping. Now, it's less cute that she compulsively takes my pyjamas and leaves them on the living room floor. Her routine is to take one half of them, have breakfast, remember the other half, go back upstairs and bring it down too. She does this for no more important reason than "This is what I did as a pup."

Fitting in This new addition to the family needs consideration and to be included in all your plans, but should not take precedence and run the schedule. Teach your new dog its place from the start.

Prepare your family

Before you pick up your pup, decide who will have primary responsibility for it (in a family, it's usually whoever takes care of the kids). They should take charge and ensure that everyone else has a consistent approach. Warning: men are invariably a weak link in this, letting pups roam rather than play in a pen, playing the wrong games, and feeding treats without having the pup do something in return. Second warning: women are also invariably a weak link, likely to up their voices an octave when talking to a pup, pick it up at the first sign of distress, and carry on extensive conversations with their pups, losing the key words in an unending flow of vowels and consonants.

In my family I'm the weakest link. My wife Julia is she who must be obeyed, as natural a dog trainer as she is a mother. "No" means "no", not "maybe", or "just this once", or "you're so cute I'll let you but don't tell anyone." Just like our kids, dogs thrive on consistency, so control yourself, control your partner, and control your kids. I know that's a tall order, but try posting written house rules on the fridge door as a constant reminder.

Learning curve Dogs can be great for kids, but there are some hurdles to get over. Younger children in particular can be inclined to view them as animated stuffed toys, and need to be reminded of their pet's physical and emotional needs from time to time.

This list includes both the house rules I did use for Bean, and the ones that I really should have.

- Bean is a natural retriever. She has her own retrieve toys; don't give her others. Don't let her retrieve socks, underwear, shoes, or pyjamas.
- Dogs walk on the floor, not on furniture. Bean is not allowed on chairs, sofas or beds. Repeat. Bean lives on the floor.
- When left alone, Bean stays in her crate or play pen.
- Watch Bean in the garden. No digging or chewing on plants.
- Don't make a fuss when you leave or return. Don't squeal a baby talk hello or reach down and stroke her.
- Bean gets nothing – food or play – for free. Only give treats after Bean does something for you.
- Always use Bean's name when you want her attention.
- Don't use Bean's name if she can hear and you're just talking about her.
- Take Bean to her toilet area and ensure she performs before playing with her. Take her back after you have played with her. Play with her indoors only immediately after she has used her toilet.
- Play with Bean on the floor or on the lawn, not on furniture.
- Make sure Bean has frequent quiet times.
- Bean is part of the family. Remember her when making your plans.

As part of your preparations, choose a short name with snappy consonants for your pup. In our family we have Bean, Inca, Maggi, and Bill. I've also lived with Angus, Macy, Lex, Sparkie, Duchess, Lib, Misty, and Bejo. A short name is easy for a dog to learn and recognize. If you already have a dog, pick a strikingly different name for your new dog so they don't get confused.

Prepare your home

Shopping is fun, and later you can indulge yourself in a variety of sensible and sophisticated items for your dog, but right now stick to the essentials: a lightweight nylon collar with identity tag, a short lead and a longline (*see p.186*), non-slipping food and water bowls, a crate large enough to grow into, with bedding and a cover, and possibly a playpen, the same food the breeder gave plus what you will be changing to, some treats (most pups find freeze-dried liver intensely attractive) to use as bribes, up to three toys, a grooming brush, comb, or glove, a personal towel. You'll also need to make some provision for a toileting area (*see pp.175–79*).

Before you pick up your pup, inspect the areas it will have access to. Chewing is as normal for dogs as eating and sleeping. It's the contented core of a dog's dogginess. A free-range dog will chew just about anything. I know a home where skirtings, doors, carpets, walls, and furniture all bear the signs of puppy chewing. That's my home, permanently marked by Bean's predecessor, Macy, who didn't have a crate and was the most destructive pup I ever had. Bean restricted her chewing to toys, and had a crate during her first months. Remove anything chewable, from dangling electric cords to rugs – they can come back later. Move all household cleaners out of reach, and make sure your waste and recycling are in proper bins with lids.

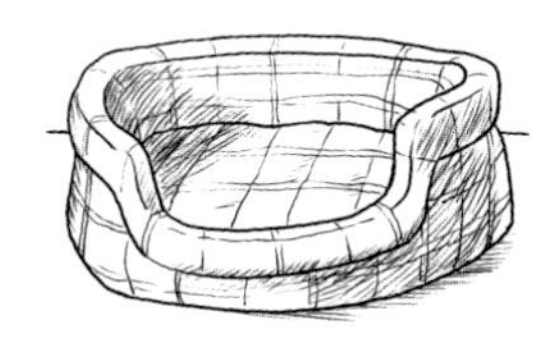

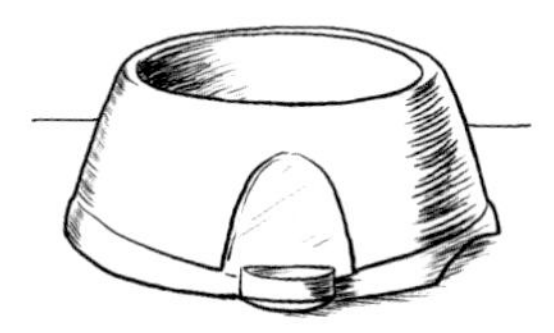

Basic needs A place to sleep, a place to eat, a collar with an identity tag, and a lead are the basics that any pup needs. Don't go overboard on other accessories; wait and learn what will really be worthwhile for your particular dog.

Watch your pup around chewable surfaces, such as wooden kitchen table legs. And never give an old shoe to chew on; a pup can't tell your old slippers from your new Jimmy Choos.

If you have a garden, yard, patio, or balcony, think dog thoughts. Check for poisonous plants and put all chemicals and equipment in a secure area your dog can't wander into, break into, or chew into. Plan where you want to place an outdoor water bowl and make sure there's a shaded area for your dog in hot weather. Make sure the hedge or fence will prevent puppy escape and withstand a mature dog, especially if you're acquiring a natural digger such as a terrier. A 1m (3ft) barrier is fine for small dogs, but you'll need up to a 2m (6½ft) fence for agile large breeds. Ensure that your gates have latches (the safest swing shut automatically) and no gaps underneath that a pup or small dog can wriggle through. Fence off the vegetable garden and compost: pups love to dig. If you don't mind earthy paws and nose, consider installing a fresh earth digging zone. If you have a fish pond, temporarily cover it with mesh, and if you have a swimming pool ensure that the safety fence around it is puppy- as well as childproof and that any cover is absolutely dog-proof. Avoid placing potted plants where they can be knocked over. Bins are fun to knock over, so keep them in a latched box.

Using a crate

There's no right or wrong about where your pup should sleep, other than it should be in its own den. It doesn't matter what it's called – crate, cage, or den – a dog's personal space is not a jail! It's a safe haven, a private place, a comfort zone. It's home. As soon as you get your pup to your home, introduce its own personal home. Place comfortable bedding in the crate. Synthetic lambswool or soft fleece with a tough backing are both excellent. A removable cover makes a crate den-like and comforting – I threw a blanket over Bean's. Position the crate and play pen in a place that is busy during the day; kitchens and living rooms are ideal.

A pup also needs a play space. Call it a play pen, playroom, or exercise pen, this can be a purpose-built mesh pen or a small room such as the kitchen with no carpets or chewable articles and stairgates on the doors. It should contain your pup's den in one corner, the toilet area in another, a bowl of fresh water in a third, and three hollow toys stuffed with yummies.

Whether you confine your dog to a small space for short periods or a larger space for longer periods, you're restricting it to an environment where it's difficult to make mistakes. And the fewer mistakes your pup makes early in life, the easier and more enjoyable both your lives will be. Restricting pups to crates or play pens allows them to teach themselves to use a toileting area, to teach themselves to chew on appropriate objects, to teach themselves to be comfortable in their own company. The crate protects your pup from harm, including accidental injuries from kids or adults. It is preparation for the inevitable truth of virtually all pet dogs' lives, that there will be frequent occasions when they will be left at home alone. And it gives you time to concentrate on other matters, rather than on your pup for 24 hours each day.

Bringing your pup home

It still amazes me how readily an eight-week-old pup leaves mother and litter and settles into its new home. Almost invariably it's simply a new adventure, but this may be the first time your pup has left the breeder's home, so be prepared for a little trepidation. Take someone responsible with you. Ask the breeder for a small towel with the litter's scent on it to put in your pup's crate. Before setting off, let your pup play vigorously. If you're lucky it will then sleep for part or all of the trip, but if not, keep activity to a minimum on the way. Be prepared for motion sickness: bring wet wipes and ask the breeder not to feed your pup for three hours before travel. Travel during a cool time of the day and break any journey longer than 90 minutes. Make sure that your pup has a collar with a tag and that you have total control if you let it out of the car.

Making introductions

Before your kids meet your new dog, make it clear that this isn't a new toy, but a living being with the same feelings and emotions as them. Meeting an existing family dog can be problematic, although demarcation disputes are amazingly infrequent. Even so, assume that initially your resident won't be too happy with either the effervescence of the new arrival or the invasion of its personal space. It's best for them to meet on neutral territory first, such as someone else's home or garden. Thoroughly exercise your number one dog before they meet. On neutral territory, your resident will be interested in the space, and your new pup is just one of the things there. Let

Settling in During the time I've been a practicing vet I've met almost 10,000 new dogs during their first weeks in new homes. Many of these have joined families that already had another dog, and the incidence of serious problems is close to zero.

Protective custody Stair gates across doorways can be useful for letting resident pets and newcomers get accustomed to each other's presence safely.

them investigate each other and don't interfere unless either looks stressed or agitated. Keep the puppy on a lead so you can control when you need to. Back at home, let them meet again, in the garden if you have one, having removed items the pup might find and play with that could provoke a jealous reaction from your resident. Expect your older resident to be irritated by any roadrunner antics. If you think there might be a snarl or snap from your resident, avoid the garden and take your new dog directly to the crate.

A cat accustomed to dogs will probably stand its ground when approached by your newcomer, and hiss, spit, or take a swipe with a paw if it gets too close or is too rambunctious. Of course, if you're bringing an older dog with an unknown history into your home, be very careful. Dogs that have learned to chase cats go onto autopilot whenever they see one; don't take that chance (*see pp.285–90*). Playful chasing is more likely when your pup has settled in and is more confident; don't let it happen, especially if you have two dogs. Pack mentality easily overwhelms familiarity, and a playful chase can instantly escalate into a lethal one. If your pup chases your cat or any other pet, keep it on a light longline so you can step on it at the first move. If your pup creeps up and playfully jumps on your cat as it would on a littermate, distract it with a toy or a food treat. If your cat creeps up and jumps on your dog, it simply emphasises to your dog that cats rule. During the first weeks never leave a resident cat and new pup together. When you can't supervise them, put your pup in a crate or pen.

Eating and emptying

You and your vet will have your own ideas about what to feed your new pup, but for the first few days stick to what the breeder gave. Once your pup is producing well-formed stools you can gradually, over a four day period, switch to the food you want to feed. Infant pups under 12 weeks of age need four meals each day. When feeding dry food, thoroughly moisten it until it softens. For the first few days give all meals inside the crate, with the door open so your pup can wander in, eat, then walk back out.

Immediately after any meal, take your pup to the area that you've chosen as the toilet. Infant pups usually need to empty one or both tanks within minutes or even seconds of eating, so don't delay (*see pp.175–79*).

Introducing the crate

Use the crate sensibly. Don't push your pup in, shut the door, and expect it to be happy. You need to train a pup to love a crate, and that's fast and simple when you use treat-filled toys. Offer your puppy a liver treat. Assuming it's dog-normal and wolfs it down, put more morsels just inside the crate (which is in the pen) with your pup outside the crate's closed door. Almost invariably, your pup wants to get in; let it in to eat the treat. Next, put the liver treat in a chew-toy and let your pup work to get at it – cheese spread and peanut butter are also both easy to put inside chew-toys. Once this new dog-job is established, repeat the closed door routine with the treat-filled chew-toy inside the crate, again letting your pup in to work on the chew-toy to get at the treat. Whenever you leave your puppy in the play pen, leave

The eye of the beholder Training your pup to see a crate as home is easier than you think. Training your partner, kids, parents, or whoever not to see a crate as a jail is the tough part.

treat-filled chew-toys with it. This gives the option of staying in the pen or entering the crate to find the delectable chew-toys.

Use the crate when you eat or sleep, when your pup eats or sleeps, when you go out, or when you need a break from puppy tailing. We're allegedly smarter than dogs, so use your grey matter. Remember that a pup needs regular toilet breaks: err on the side of many breaks, and if your puppy toilets in the crate, don't make a fuss. It's your fault for not anticipating its needs. Finally, never let a pup out of the crate when it's barking simply to get out. If you do, you're actually training your dog to bark, through the reward of your attention. Ignore barking and only open the door when all is quiet. Do determine whether your pup is barking to get out because you haven't let it out to toilet! That can be hard at first, but if you think the tanks are full, let your pup out immediately, opening the door during an episode of silence. Finally, never, ever, ever use either crate or pen as a punishment.

The night time routine

Here's a simple routine for your dog's first night in your home.

- Take gifts to neighbours, explaining you have a new pup and that there's a possibility it may cry because it's just left mother and littermates.
- Prepare the bed, crate, or play pen with bedding, newspaper, and a distracting toy. If you planned ahead and have bedding carrying the scent of your pup's mother and litermates, so much the better.
- Feed your pup a warm meal, visit the toileting area, and play awhile, so you're sure it's as sleepy as possible before putting it in the crate.
- Don't fuss. Don't kiss. Don't mutter words of affection. Simply and quietly leave your pup in the crate. Don't even look back – eye contact may trigger a mournful demand to be picked up.
- Stick earphones in your ears and disregard whimpering, crying, barking, or howling. If you respond, you're actively teaching your dog that these activities get attention.

First steps to maturity Like anything new, the first night in a new place, away from littermates and mother, is going to be daunting. But relaxing and sleeping alone or in a new place is a skill your adult dog will need to be happy and content. Make your pup comfortable, but don't hold it back by giving in to whining.

If your pup spends the night in a play pen, leave it in the crate in one corner of the pen. If you're not going to get up at night to let it outdoors, provide newspaper away from the bedding or crate for toileting and leave the crate door open. If you choose, as I did, to have the crate in your bedroom, keep the crate door shut. Set your alarm to wake you within four hours so you can take your pup to toilet. Stay mute, other than using your chosen toileting word, calmly return the pup to its crate and go back to sleep.

SMALL COMPROMISES DON'T HURT

We had decided to keep Bean's crate in our bedroom, by a window where her bed would be when she was older. We had told our neighbours we had a new pup, but after 15 minutes of her plaintive squealing we worried that she was awakening the entire street. Julia moved the crate to her side of the bed, close enough for her to lie with the fingers of one hand in it, and that was enough to stop Bean's yips. Bean needed either the smell or closeness of those fingers for around a week. After that she was content with her crate simply physically close to our bed, and after a few weeks we moved it back to where she would eventually sleep.

The first month

During these first weeks you get to know who your dog is, what type of personality it has, what its attitude to life will be. Just like kids, some pups are sparkier, more alert than others, some can be more jumpy than others. Some pups don't enjoy being held and wriggle to get away. There's nothing right or wrong about such natural inclinations, but even they can be modified at this impressionable stage. With kids we've got up to five years while the basics of their personalities and attributes develop. With pups we've got roughly a month from acquiring them at eight weeks of age. If we understand how our dogs think, how they interpret our tone of voice, our body language, our use of rewards and discipline, it's relatively easy to mould what they do. If we set up the wrong house rules or are inconsistent, we create problems that can be difficult to solve. That makes it vital to spend time up front learning why a dog does what a dog does and how we should interact with them, rather than forging ahead with ill-thought-out training.

Treats are powerful

If your pup doesn't like being handled, associate handling with rewards. Get your pup addicted to a certain treat, then give one if it's not struggling while your hand is under its chest. Eventually graduate to giving treats when your

Cats rule, OK? Most family cats already know that cats are naturally superior to dogs, and cats are terrific at teaching dogs to respect their personal space.

Ready for anything In the first months of its life, your pup is likely to visit the vet more than it will for the rest of its life until old age. It will undergo health checks and vaccinations, and ideally microchipping. The more you get it used to routine handling, the easier all this will be for both of you.

pup is on your lap. I do this with pups coming to the clinic for the first time. Rather than put a pup on an unfamiliar and possibly frightening table, I'll examine it on the floor or on my lap. I've also scattered tasty treats, which the pup almost invariably finds and eats. If I'm giving an inoculation, the stab in the back that accompanies most first visits to the vet, I keep the vial of vaccine in my pocket to warm it, and give the injection when the pup is concentrating on a food treat. Most pups don't mind returning to the clinic. Some actively pull their owners in because they only remember the food treats, not the unpleasant events of previous visits.

All dogs are trainable, but the younger they are the easier it is. Young dogs are unwritten books, and careful exposure to new situations can produce confident, "bombproof" dogs, ready for virtually any challenge. Dogs raised in a noisy, crowded urban environment are invariably better socialized than dogs from a sheltered rural setting. The more your dog takes in, the less likely it is to develop idiosyncratic fears or phobias, the more mellow and tolerant it will be as an adult, and the more enjoyable your relationship will be. Always be on the lookout for signs of stress and fear: panting, shivering, trepidation, and submissive urinating. If you don't recognize these signs, you may press your pup into a situation that it can't yet deal with and unwittingly create fear, aggression, or anxiety problems.

If your pup is shy or lacks confidence take extra care. Shy individuals need special attention. They benefit just as much from socializing as do gregarious ones, but introductions need to be monitored more closely. Overprotecting a shy dog, for example from visiting children, will only increase its apprehension when visitors arrive. Ask the kids to be less noisy. Tell them to avoid eye contact with your pup, and give them food or toy treats to leave in a trail and eventually to give to your pup. Do the same outdoors. Control your natural inclination to comfort when your pup is frightened by a noise or movement. Picking it up and murmuring soothing words simply rewards signs of fear. Your vet may recommend professional help to ensure that shyness does not develop into lifelong fearful behaviour.

Take a fresh look at safety before taking your pup outdoors. Use the best method of restraint and an ID tag and a microchip (*see p.217*). Then introduce as wide a variety of experiences as possible, presenting each new situation so it's attractive, interesting, and fun, not frightening. Visit new environments with varying surfaces to walk on, investigate water and woods, introduce other dogs, other animals, toddlers, kids, people with canes or walking frames, people in uniforms or wearing hats or motorcycle helmets, kids in buggies, and people of different colours. Accustom your pup to being touched not just by you but by strangers too. Take it in the car on short shopping trips, and on the daily walk to and from school.

Dealing with crying and whining

Until your pup joined your home it lived in a true pack, with mother and littermates. Crying when hungry, cold, or alone worked, because when a mother hears a cry she responds, and her touch was enough to make your pup feel better. That was suddenly lost with the move to your home. Your pup might strut around like some tough cookie, but is still an infant and will whine for attention. You have to cope with this natural behaviour.

Remember, how you respond to crying and whining now determines how your dog will use those sounds in the future. A soft touch and gentle words tell your pup these are successful ways to get what it wants. What takes some skill on your part is to learn to respond to a cry or a whine that means the bladder and bowels are full and need to be emptied, and ignore a cry or whine that means your pup doesn't want to be alone. If you want to have a sane life, where you and not your dog make your daily decisions, don't respond to this brilliant form of manipulation. If Bean whined or in any way pestered for attention I disregarded her. I didn't want her to think that whining was an effective way to train humans!

Of course your pup doesn't want to be alone, so provide mental or physical activities when you can't be there. Some people put an insulated hot water bottle or a ticking clock in the crate for their pup's first nights in the new home, to act as transitional objects for the pup to move away from life with mother. Certainly, give your pup a tasty chew toy to work on when alone. Make sure the bedding is soft and warm. Gundog breeds and many other pups seem to enjoy sleeping with soft toys, falling asleep with their heads on them. It may look silly, but there's no harm in giving your pup a teddy bear to sleep with. It may not be as comforting as curling up with littermates, but it's better than nothing at all.

Performance-related bonus Tasty treats are your greatest asset in these first few weeks. Measure out a daily ration and carry them around with you to reward your dog whenever necessary. Remember, that's whenever necessary, not whenever possible: don't hand them out for nothing.

Understand body language

From puppyhood, a dog communicates using the position of tail, body, and ears, combined with eye contact and facial expression. Voice is also used, in barks, howls, growls, and whines, but is much less important. Dogs are more acutely aware of body language than voice. This is why pups respond to hand signals so well. When communicating with your dog use sensible body language accompanied by voice signals. For example, standing over your dog and looking straight down at it will be interpreted at a threat, while squatting down at dog level and spreading your arms wide is an inviting gesture. Most dogs will naturally respond by approaching you, and if you couple your actions with calling, you've begun training.

Don't misinterpret your dog's body language. Staring at you may indicate interest but in certain circumstances it's also a sign of potential dominance. Showing the teeth – very rare in infant pups – is almost always a sign of dominance, although some dogs do show their teeth in a greeting "grin", really a submissive sign of appeasement (*see p.135*).

When using your voice consider the sounds a dog naturally responds to. "*Be-e-e-ean*", my personal howl, instantly catches Bean's attention. If a pup does something wrong, bites too hard for example, mother responds with a growl. A low-pitched, quick "Bean!" with a deep inflection, like her mother's growl, communicates a wholly different meaning. If during play Bean bit a littermate too hard, that puppy yipped in pain, called it quits, and stopped play. Do the same. Say "ouch!" in a sharp way and walk away. Your pup will understand your inflection and your body language.

Talk to the animals Dogs understand body language more readily than words, and read our gestures better than any other species – sometimes it seems they even do better than other humans.

Housetraining

Inevitably, everyone's greatest concern with a young dog is toilet training. We want our dogs to reliably empty where we choose. Housetraining isn't quantum science, it's common sense, but it is vital in your developing relationship with your dog. If it goes well, easy obedience training almost inevitably follows. If it doesn't, it's the first exasperating reality check.

Dogs are instinctively clean, a powerful reason why they are our favourite house pets. They are unwilling from puppyhood to soil their nest; it's up to us to take advantage of this and teach them that the entire home is the nest. This is why crates speed up housetraining enormously. A dog instinctively doesn't want to mess in its den, so if it is either in the crate, out toileting in your chosen area, or discovering the rest of the world as a reward after emptying both tanks where you want it to, housetraining is accelerated.

In essence you're training your dog to do a swap with you. In return for dumping urine and faeces, on command and in the right place, your dog receives tasty treats, invigorating play, and temporary access to more territory. Housetraining is simple, but it demands vigilance. Dogs naturally want to relieve themselves after eating, after play or exercise, after any excitement, such as greeting people or other animals, and after waking up. At eight weeks a pup needs to empty its bladder every two hours, by twelve weeks most can hold it for up to four hours, and a month later most have six-hour bladder control. Many can actually get through an entire night.

Watch your puppy's body language for clues that it needs to urinate or defecate. Look out for sniffing the floor, running with the nose to the floor, circling, and preparing to squat. When you see any of these activities, interrupt them and go to the toileting area. If you can, avoid picking up your pup; you want it to learn to walk there.

If you have a garden or back yard for housetraining, that's wonderful. It's easiest to housetrain a dog if you have immediate access to an outdoor area. Apartment dwellers and disabled people have a few more logistical problems, but wherever you live and whoever you are do the following. Always have scoops (such as biodegradable poop bags or surplus plastic bags) available, and get everyone in the family into the habit of cleaning up immediately. Puppy stools are occasionally soft; carry tissues to help.

TREAT EACH DOG SEPARATELY

- Take extra care with a new pup in another dog's home. Jealousy is as common between dogs as it is between children.
- Never give the new pup any of the resident dog's toys to play with or carry.
- Don't give your new pup any more privileges than your resident dog "because he's a puppy".
- Don't feed the two dogs close together. It's best if they are tail-to-tail, so they can't watch each other eat.
- If your pup gets too rambunctious and your resident dog tells it off, this is natural. Allow it to happen but supervise so that threat doesn't descend to violence.
- Keep to your established daily routines with your resident dog.
- Provide satisfying individual time for both dogs.
- Avoid training one dog when the other can hear. If it can hear, you may unwittingly be training it to disregard your commands.

Outdoor training

Select a toileting area away from activity and distractions. With Bean, this meant our paved back yard, where I put down a roll of turf so that she could get used to urinating and defecating on both hard and soft surfaces. Scooping is simpler from a hard surface than from grass, and nothing prevents acidic dog urine from burning grass. The best treatment is prevention, so train your dog to urinate in a specified area; ideally install a sand-pit toilet area.

At appropriate intervals, take your pup out; if you stay in, your pup may concentrate on wanting to get back to you rather than on toileting, and the excitement of returning to you can stimulate messing inside. Be prepared to be out for four or five minutes while your pup sniffs and wanders; take an umbrella if necessary. Don't play games. Be patient, silent and still as a statue. If after five minutes your pup hasn't produced, return indoors and keep an eagle eye on activity so you're prepared for a quick trip back out.

Have a special treat, such as a liver treat, in your pocket. As your pup dumps, say something you're happy to associate with this activity in the future, such as "hurry up". Then instantly give the treat. If you say the same thing each time, your dog will associate the phrase not just with toileting, but with the need to toilet. Hearing it will speed up the performance. Trainers called this conditioning: your pup develops a conditioned response to urinate or defecate on hearing certain "trigger words". This means that later you're assured all systems are emptied before leaving your dog alone for a while or embarking on a journey.

Paper training This is a lengthier process than outdoor training, but a practical way to train apartment pups. Protect the floor with plastic and lay down paper or, ideally, a sample of the surface your dog will later use.

After your pup has finished, give sufficient praise to make its tail wag. Overreact with joy. "That's amazing!" "You're wonderful!" "That's the most humungous turd a little dog ever passed!" Be a clown. Use a happy voice. You want you pup to think it's incredible for eliminating outside. If the weather permits, stay out a little longer. Give a treat, toss a ball, play chase, or walk around and explore. You want to show that first your pup urinates or defecates, then the fun begins. Most dogs love being outdoors, so play a game. Don't overdo the food treats: a really clever dog will learn to deposit just a thimbleful of urine for a food reward and keep a large reserve in the tank knowing that more rewards are possible.

Indoor training

Housetraining without immediate outdoor access is a bit more complicated. Indoor paper training to newspaper, a litter tray (fine for small dogs) or disposable pet pads is a pragmatic second choice. If not using a crate, the easiest way to paper train is to restrict your pup to one room or area of a room. Cover the floor in plastic sheeting with lots of newspaper on top, so your pup can only relieve itself on the newspaper. You'll see over a few days that your pup prefers some specific spots. When removing soiled newspaper, leave small bits in the areas where you want your dog to urinate. It takes less than a week for a pup to be trained to eliminate only in these areas. Day by day, reduce the paper-covered areas until only a few are needed. Take your dog out as frequently as possible so that it learns to use an outdoor toilet as well, for example the gutter of the road. As with any other housetraining, only let your pup investigate other parts of your home after eliminating.

This method does prolong training. You're training your pup to mess on paper, then retraining it to mess not on paper but outdoors. Some puppies trained to go on paper inside take time to switch to outside toileting. Don't just put your pup outside and expect it to perform. Put on collar and lead – not for corrections or pulling your dog, but to keep it close to you. Stay out until your pup performs, then do your rewarding clown routine. Some pups will hold on outside because the feeling underfoot is unfamiliar, or it's raining, or that leaf that just fell was really scary. They wait until they're inside, where they feel safe, to toilet on a familiar surface. If this happens, keep the pup confined to the crate and take it out more frequently, having already taken some soiled newspaper to the chosen outdoor toilet area.

You can shorten this transition if you think about where your dog will eventually use to relieve itself, and integrate that into training. If it will be grass, lay down part of a roll of turf in the pen on top of vinyl or plastic sheet. If it will be the gutter, it's heavy work, but get a paving slab. Your aim is to familiarize the feel under foot that your dog will experience later.

Accidents will happen

It's astonishing how fast something so young can learn to toilet the way we want, but remember, your dog remains emotionally immature until well after puberty. Expect lapses. Later, during canine childhood or adolescence, housetraining may temporarily be lost (*see p.213*). Don't punish your dog for

Caught short Any adult animal instinctively keeps its own home, its nest, clean. Young animals can fail through poor timing or an unclear idea of just how large the human "nest" is. Don't punish these mistakes, because that's all they are. Consistent correction will work in the end.

accidents. It won't understand, but will simply think that you're angry and act submissively, grovelling or hiding, to appease you. We mistake these cowering signs of appeasement for signs of guilt. They're not. They're just recognition that you're going to do something awful. I cannot emphasize this enough. Taking dogs to the mess, pushing their noses in it, and telling them they're bad is simply a dumb, pointless, idiotic, brainless thing to do. Where did the idea ever come from? It might satisfy someone's foolish need for retribution, but all it achieves is to make your dog frightened of you.

When you see your dog relieving itself in the house, say "No!" firmly, not to frighten or punish, but to get its attention. If your dog is frightened or thinks you're angry, it learns to sneak away to relieve itself, making housetraining harder. As soon as you have your pup's attention, call its name then briskly walk to your designated toileting area, encouraging it to follow you willingly. After the excitement has subsided, your pup will complete what it started earlier. When you return to the house, keep it in another room while you clean up the mess. If you find a mistake, forget about it. Dogs can't understand you're angry because of what they did, even if it's only minutes before. Punishing after the fact is counterproductive; you're just teaching your pup that you're irrational and unpredictable.

When cleaning up, remember that the sensitivity of a dog's nose is simply beyond our comprehension. Routine cleaning and disinfecting of accidents may work for us, but will not get rid of residual odours that draw your dog back to the site, so it's vitally important to break down odour molecules. Soiled carpet, underlay, even the floor beneath should be treated with an odour-eliminating product. Your veterinarian can supply you with enzyme-containing eliminators, and in my experience these work well. As an alternative, liberally soak the area with biological (enzyme-containing) washing powder mixed with hot water. Alcohol also breaks down odours, and diluted white vinegar can remove stains from carpets. Avoid any cleaner with ammonia; this is a natural body by-product and will attract a dog back.

The principles of training

There's one great difference between training children and training dogs: eventually it becomes possible to reason with kids. They come to understand fair and unfair, and how you make decisions. Kids understand "three strikes and you're out", but dogs never do. They can't think in the abstract or grasp conditional ideas. If I say "Do that again Bean and I'll be really cross", all Bean hears is "Blah blah blah blah Bean blah blah blah blah blah". Don't expect more from your dog than it's capable of giving.

The dog's most critical stage of development is from roughly three to twelve weeks of age, when a pup is almost desperate to please you. But it's also working out its position in this new pack, your family. If you give the right signals now, your dog learns that all family members are pack leaders; get it wrong and any dog will naturally try to rise to a higher position in the hierarchy. Yes, some dogs have an amazing generosity of spirit, but they are naturally possessive, naturally territorial, and sophisticated observers of hierarchies. They are opportunists and will take advantage when they can.

Good leaders and happy dogs mean fast results

In your relationship with your pup forget about consensus and democracy. Don't be a boss, but a natural leader. What's the difference? Here's my slightly sexist answer: men often find it easy to be bosses, while women are often better at leadership. Men are inclined to command from the front. Men say "Do this." "Follow me." Women are more likely to let someone believe they thought of doing something themselves. The clever woman gets what she wants done without being bossy, without threats. That's classic leadership, and that's the best way to induce your pup to do what you want.

Your relationship with your pup involves both leadership and friendship, and during those are the keys to a future happy relationship. No matter how much your pup amuses you or irritates you, remember that you're both leader and friend. A dog who sees you in both roles will want to please you, because it loves your praise. That is the attractiveness of dogs in a nutshell: their desire to please. Don't turn it into disdain through inconsistency, or

UNEVEN PROGRESS

We used our kitchen as Bean's playpen. Each morning we moved her crate from the bedroom to the kitchen, where we closed the internal doors and gave her free access to the newspaper-covered floor. We left the door to the back yard open when weather permitted. Having read the textbooks, she never soiled inside her crate, and because I took her to the back yard each night, she would wander out there whenever she needed to defecate. But at first she frequently urinated inside on the newspaper-covered floor. She was fairly typical in this pattern of learning one aspect of housetraining faster than another, reliably dumping solid waste outside well over a month before she would reliably do the same with liquid waste.

fear through punishment. A wonderful relationship depends upon your using calm understanding, a positive attitude, and consistency. Time devoted to good training pays dividends for years to come.

Dogs innately understand status and respond to confident leaders, so ensure that from the start your actions tell your pup that it should respect you all the time. Even when you're not training your dog, you often are. Handle your dog routinely. Groom it every day. Go through doors first. Make sure your family eats before your dog. To a dog, all of these are obvious signs of leadership. Above all, be consistent. Never underestimate your dog's ability to notice your lapses and to chisel away at them. Dogs thrive on consistency, more so as they become older; inconsistency is very confusing to them. Dogs want to know the rules, what's allowed and what's not. This is most important when giving rewards or meting out verbal discipline.

If formal training sessions are to be productive and fun, your pup should be relaxed and not apprehensive. Relaxed pups appreciate praise and learn faster. Some people still feel that old-fashioned dominance or punishment training, originally developed for military dogs, works. Yes, it can, but at the expense of creating needless fear. Motivation with rewards works better and faster. Rewards are obviously positive, but even when using discipline never leave your dog on a negative note. After a reprimand, let yourself cool down then do something positive with your pup.

Playtime Some people seem to think that a well-trained dog means a dog that walks to heel all the time as if on parade, with no fun. This coulnd't be further from the truth: if you know your dog will come when you call and stop when you tell it to, play can actually be more relaxed.

Choosing and using rewards

A reward or "reinforcer" is anything your dog likes. Food, toys, access to the outdoors or people a dog enjoys being with, petting, stroking, your tone of voice, certain words, your facial expressions, are all day-to-day reinforcers of your dog's behaviour. Some, such as tasty food treats, are more powerful than others, such as kind words. One powerful reinforcer that's easily forgotten is escaping from something unpleasant. If your dog is frightened of someone on a skateboard, for example, running away makes it feel better, which reinforces running-away behaviour. When training your dog, use powerful positive reinforcers, especially food and toys, and couple them with less powerful reinforcers, such as touch and voice. Once a behaviour is learned and entrenched you'll use voice alone. Be on the lookout for negative reinforcers; all of us unwittingly reinforce something in our dog's behaviour we later regret. Behaviours aren't forged in steel, and can be changed, but it's always easier to create a behaviour than eliminate one.

Use tiny treats during training sessions, part of the day's allotment of food. With many pups just a piece of kibble is a sufficient reward. For more particular dogs or difficult training, use liver treats. For Bean I used yeast-based, liver-flavoured vitamin and mineral tablets. They smell disgusting enough for dogs to love them, while not too disgusting to keep in your pocket. Keep food rewards with you whenever you go out with your pup.

Toys are almost as powerful as food, especially chewable or squeaky toys. Use them for pups that are not piggy by nature – as a breed, German Shepherds respond well to them. Remember, however, that the toys belong to you, not your pup, and are only given temporarily as rewards. An ideal toy is small enough for you to hide in your pocket, but big enough not to cause a danger from choking. Sometimes you have to build up interest in a toy to use it during training. Do silly things with it. Produce it from your pocket, sniff it, and put it back. Talk to it. Wave it at your pup then put it on a shelf. Your aim is to trigger your pup's interest and desire to possess it.

A soothing lick from mother was comforting to your pup, and now a gentle stroke from you does the same. Use contact comfort as an important reward when your pup responds well, and associate it with food rewards and words of praise. It's always good to start training a pup to be touched while it's eating. Later I'll explain training your dog to let you take its food away while it eats, which reduces the risk of it becoming possessive and guarding its food (*see p.284*).

At the same time you give a potent reward such as food, a toy or touch, give a verbal reward. Your pup will soon find just the words "Good girl" or "Good boy" satisfying, and you can graduate to the less powerful secondary reward of words alone. Use words precisely. Your dog understands black and white, not shades of grey. Think "yes" or "no", never "maybe" when speaking or interacting in any way with your pup. If your dog becomes too excited by food or a toy as a reward, ignore it and go away. Repeat what you were trying to do when your dog is calmer, using a less potent reward. If a pup is not responding to any of your rewards, schedule all activities just before feeding time, when dogs are most alert.

Using discipline

Dogs use discipline with each other to assert authority, and that's how you should use it. Use it as wisely as you use rewards. "No!" will become a truly powerful word, strong medicine. Use it only when you see your dog doing something wrong. Don't shriek it, mumble it, whine it, or use it so frequently that your pup disregards it. Growl it, deeply and sharply. You are not teaching your dog right from wrong, but acceptable from unacceptable. Vary your forms of discipline, so you can always surprise your dog. As I said, don't overuse "No!" A good alternative is a crisp "Bad dog". I also like "Arghhh!" because it's a bit like what a pup's mother used to say when really annoyed by her pups' antics. Pups also know the difference between being looked at and being given the eyeball. Dominant dogs stare down others, and you can do the same, especially with the advantage of your height.

Dogs are intensely social. They don't like being separated from family activity. Use symbolic isolation as another potent form of discipline. By symbolic I mean for its shock value, not as a form of retribution. If your pup bites you too hard during play, emit your well-practiced high-pitched shriek, get up, leave the room, and shut the door. Wait up to 30 seconds, no more, go back in, disregard your dog for another minute, then do what you want. If too many other people are in the room, take your dog to an empty room, the bathroom for example, shut the door, wait 30 seconds before letting it out, and then disregard it for another minute or so.

Use your dog's name wisely

The sights, sounds, and smells of life are intriguing and your pup wants to investigate them – now. You have to compete with these thrills and excitements for its attention. You've already chosen a crisp, short, distinctive name, so use it only to call your dog for fun, games, and rewards. Never call your pup to discipline it, and never call when you can't enforce the recall. If a dog learns during these most impressionable weeks that response is optional, you'll find it frustratingly difficult to get its attention for just about anything in the future. During these first days with your pup, get its attention only when you know you can. Dogs respond to happy voices, smiles, easy, non-threatening body language. For example, when calling your pup, squat down to dog level, throw your arms open wide and say enthusiastically "Bean! Come!" Women usually find it easier to be theatrical than men do, but guys, try it. It's fun. And women love it when you behave this way. Don't act like a dominant male with your pup: a harsh, low voice is threatening, looming over your dog is intimidating, grabbing triggers fear. Women, don't babble at your pup: keep commands brief and succinct. Use eye contact when needed but never force your pup to have intense eye contact with you. That can be frightening and counterproductive. If you're in a bad mood, skip that training session. Don't take it out on your pup.

Concentrate on good timing

Good timing is important. Actually, it's vital. Rewards and gentle discipline should be immediate, not even seconds after the fact. Give rewards as soon

Just like us At school, we all did the work we had to for the teacher who scared us. But I bet we all did our best work for the teacher who rewarded us with praise, approval and encouragement – and maybe prizes. Be that teacher.

as your pup tries to do the right thing, or even as soon as you see your dog *thinking* about doing the right thing. That may sound abstract but it's really quite simple. When I crouched down to say hello to Bean when she was a pup, I was already rewarding her with praise as soon as she got up to move towards me. Poor timing confuses pups in particular, getting the relationship off to a poor start. Rewards given too late, even seconds after the event,

cause confusion. Good timing is a skill that some people naturally have and an aptitude that others, including me, have to learn. Stay alert. Concentrate.

During these first weeks, take advantage of the guaranteed highlights in your pup's day. Discover what is most valued – food, toys, or games – and associate these and your dog's name with training to come to them. It's easiest to get your pup's attention in the quietest and dullest part of your home, often a hallway. Have a selection of rewards, so that when distractions do occur you can increase the value of the reward you can offer. Once you easily get your pup's attention there, graduate to more stimulating places with more distractions, such as a larger, quiet room, a room with more activity, the back garden, and eventually, exciting public spaces. Remember that the more you both practice, the more reliable you both become. Practice basic obedience for a minute at a time, but 15 to 20 times daily.

Learn body language

It's easy to make mistakes when training your dog if you misinterpret body language. Most of us recognize the overt signs of fear, worry, or submission: the desperate look in the eyes, turned-back the ears, tucked tail, rolling over showing the belly, or submissive urinating. But less overt signs, such as panting, yawning, or looking away, are just as important, and a wagging tail can mean happy alertness, but sometimes worry or trepidation.

It's easy to respond exactly the wrong way to a pup's signs of stress, because the right way is the opposite of how you respond to a child's distress. Every day at the veterinary clinic I see a few dogs that simply don't want to be there. Typically, a dog cowers behind its owner, who responds with petting. Occasionally a dog will growl at me, and the owner will speak

Quick studies At this young age, training even individuals not genetically endowed with an intense desire to please takes just a few weeks. It can take as little as a couple of days for a pup from a working line of gundogs – who will pick up bad habits equally fast, so be vigilant. This might not seem so cute next week.

I'm bigger than you Standing over your pup, saying "Bad dog," and maintaining your stare is a strikingly powerful form of discipline. Eventually, your stern look is enough.

in "motherese" – that soft, octave-higher voice – and stroke reassuringly to calm it. In both instances, the dogs' fearful behaviours are being unwittingly rewarded. To avoid this, it's sometimes necessary to act counter-intuitively. If your dog shows stressed body language signs, don't kiss and cuddle; stop training, do something else. Work out what caused the stress and avoid it.

Rules for formal training

During basic training you're teaching your dog a completely new concept – associating words with specific activities. Be patient and reasonable. It can be either amazingly easy or infuriatingly difficult. A pup will respond in just a few possible ways, and always for just a few possible reasons. Inevitably, we're the inconsistent ones, so remember to follow these guidelines.

- Don't bore your pup with overly frequent or long periods of training. Its attention span is extremely short. Set aside time each day for several one- or two-minute sessions.
- For more natural training, take advantage of feeding times, when dogs are most alert, and exercise times. Let a pup burn off over-the-top energy first, so it can concentrate more on what you're doing. Start in quiet places with few distractions, where you have most control.
- Be realistic. You're training a dog: a vibrant, sociable, and very trainable species, but not a human.
- Everyone should use the same specific words and hand or body signals. Write these down, post them for everyone to see and remember, and be consistent. For example, when training your dog to "come", always use the same word, not varying it with "here" and "c'mere".
- Make sure your dog comes right up to you, so you don't have to reach out to give the food reward.
- Use theatrical body language as well as words and combine these with immediate food rewards.
- Don't give your dog a command you know it's not listening to or you can't enforce. If you allow your pup to ignore a command at this age, you're actively teaching it that it doesn't have to pay attention to you.
- Train by increments. Avoid leaps from one level to a much higher one.
- If a session is going badly, forget that session and think about what you're doing. The problem is with you, not with your pupil. If your pup is distracted by something more exciting, temporarily stop the session. Avoid repeatedly shouting a command. It only confuses your dog.
- Never try to train several dogs at once. It's virtually impossible. If you have two pups, keep one out of earshot while you train, reward, or discipline the other.
- No matter how exasperated you are, finish with fun and games so your dog looks forward to the next session. But don't save the most powerful reward for the end; that trains your pup to look forward to the end of the session and the potent reward.
- Continue using the play pen when nobody's there to monitor your pup.
- Don't be bashful about asking for help. Front office staff at veterinary clinics are probably your best bet for sound advice.

GETTING STARTED WITH TRAINING AND COMMANDS

I'm going to use Bean as an example in all this. Your pup has a collar, an ID tag, and a lead. You have tasty food treats to use as inducers and rewards, or a toy for the rare pup not thrilled by food.

You should invest in a longline or houseline, a very long, light lead typically used to control a young dog in the house; if you have your foot on one end, you always have the dog under control. Don't use one to reel your dog in, but to ensure it doesn't run away or to get its attention. Then, no matter how long it takes, use praise and treats to bring it to you. Don't go to it.

Your dog needs a specific word that means a training exercise is over, especially when learning to stay, sit, or lie. I use "OK" with Bean, but a less often used word, like "Finished" or "Let's go" is better. After your dog obeys, give a release command, and give rewards only when it obeys you or after the release.

Your dog might misunderstand basic training, or think its a giggle and make it a game. I save "No!" for serious misdemeanours and use the more neutral "Wrong", spoken flatly, when a pup rolls over or tries to play during training, before simply starting again.

PRACTICAL TRAINING EXERCISE 1

SITTING

Dogs learn to sit just as quickly as they learn to come to you. Concentrate on the head: control the head, and the body does what you want it to do. Kneel beside her, not facing her, with a food treat in your hand. Move the hand holding the food treat over her head, making sure she has eye contact with it. As the head follows the food up, the rump will naturally go down. As you see the hind legs bend, give the command "Bean. Sit". Use your words carefully. "Sit" means sit. "Down" means lie down. Asking a dog to "Sit down" is confusing. As she assumes a sitting position say "Good sit" and give the food immediately.

Once she's obediently sitting with you sitting next to her, graduate to standing beside her while giving the command "Sit". At first give food rewards every time, but later give them intermittently. Eventually words of praise alone are sufficient.

Most dogs naturally assume a sitting position to keep an eye on something above them. Some don't. In this case, hold her collar or harness in one hand and use your other hand to tuck her hindquarters into a sitting position. Never push down on the back. Give the command "Sit" as you do this and instantly reward her with a food treat and a verbal "Good sit". Avoid over-excitement. If meals are too exciting, your dog can't concentrate on your commands. Train her on a fuller stomach, using less stimulating but still interesting rewards. Once more, never give a command without ensuring your pup complies; otherwise you're training her to disregard that command.

1 Dogs should obey all reliable members of the family, regardless of their size. With the treat in the right hand to get the pup's attention, the left hand holds the harness or collar to prevent any unwanted forward movement towards the powerful reward.

2 The food treat is slowly moved above the dog's head, making it easy for the pup to maintain eye contact. As the dog spontaneously sits, to keep an eye on it, give the command "Sit" and rewards compliance with the food treat and the praise "Good sit".

PRACTICAL TRAINING EXERCISE 2

COMING WHEN CALLED

Coming to you is one of the most important obedience commands your dog will ever learn, and the bedrock of a reliable recall is your positive relationship with your dog. You are at the very beginning of that relationship. Your pup is still not sure exactly how wonderful you are, so use your most powerful rewards or "reinforcers" for recall training – the tastiest treats and the best toys. After you've finished, give lots of cuddles and petting, even an exciting game of tug-of-war. You want your pup to think that coming back to you is more worthwhile than doing anything else, that being with you is better than being anywhere else. At first your pup has no idea what "Come" means, so start with the name and say "Come" when your pup is on the way towards you.

Mealtimes are ideal for teaching this command. With the longline attached, crouch down a short distance away, show her the food, and say "Bean". As she begins to move towards the meal, say "Come". Then as she approaches, say "Good come" enthusiastically, and give her the meal. Do the same frequently between meals, using kibbles from the daily food ration as the reward. Graduate to standing upright while calling Bean's name then saying "Come" as she starts to approach. Use stroking as an alternative reward. In a few days Bean will come to you willingly when she hears her name and the word "Come". If she doesn't respond, don't get frustrated or annoyed. Try a different reward. If Bean starts to wander off, put your foot on the longline and say nothing. When she looks at you, and she will, smile and show the treat. Use the longline until she comes on command every single time. If she's easily distracted and you have a helper, play hide-and-seek. Have your helper hold her while you hide. Then call "Beeean!" As she starts to respond, your helper drops the lead and you say "Bean. Come!" Reward her with her favourite treats when she finds you.

1 For most dogs, the great outdoors is intensely exciting and full of distractions, some of them dangerous. For the safety of your dog, it must learn to come when called outside. Get a friend to hold your dog while it watches you walk off.

2 Ensure compliance by attaching a lightweight longline to the dog's collar. At first, keep one end of the line secure so that your dog doesn't wander. Graduate to only wearing a shortened longline, then no longline.

3 Your dog is more likely to come to you when you are on the ground at its level with a food treat or a potential object of play as well as a treat. With a food treat in hand, enthusiastically encourage your dog to come and, as it does, give the "Come" command.

4 Once your dog reliably comes to you on command in a quiet location, graduate to an area with more distractions. At first, keep distractions minimal, such as other people present, before training where there are other dogs, which are perhaps the most powerful distraction.

PRACTICAL TRAINING EXERCISE 3

LYING DOWN AND STANDING UP

These require a little more work on your part and more understanding from your pup. Commands to come and sit anticipate willing, natural behaviour by your dog. Now, you're commanding her to do something a little more unusual.

With your pup in a "Sit" position, kneel to her right with her collar with your left hand and a food treat in your right. Hold the food treat in front of her nose, then move your treat-holding hand downward in a sweeping arc. As your pup lies down to keep in contact with the food treat, now at ground level, give the command "Down". Keep the treat clenched in your hand so she can't grab it, and move it along the floor towards her if necessary until she's in a complete down position. Praise her with "Good down" and give her the treat. Release her with your chosen release word.

If your pup creeps forward on her haunches rather than lying down, kneel beside her and while she's sitting put the palms of your hands under her forelegs, lift them gently into a begging position then lower into a lying position. Instantly reward her with praise and treats. If she refuses to stay down, using both hands apply gentle pressure to her withers, the area above her shoulders. Reward her for lying down then release her with your chosen release word.

When teaching "Stand" follow the same steps but instead of moving the food in an arc down to the floor, move it straight ahead in front of your pup's nose and as she stands up, give the command "Stand". At the same time, use the left hand on her collar to gently restrain her from walking forward – this is of course why she got up, to follow the treat.

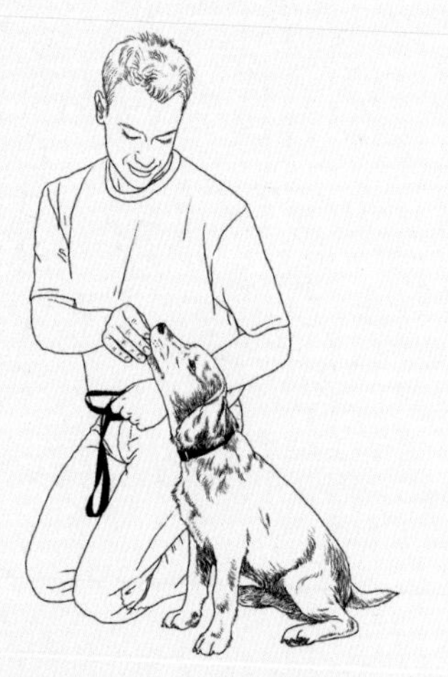

1 In the "sit" position by its owner's side, both the dog and the owner are facing in the same direction, ready to start the exercise.

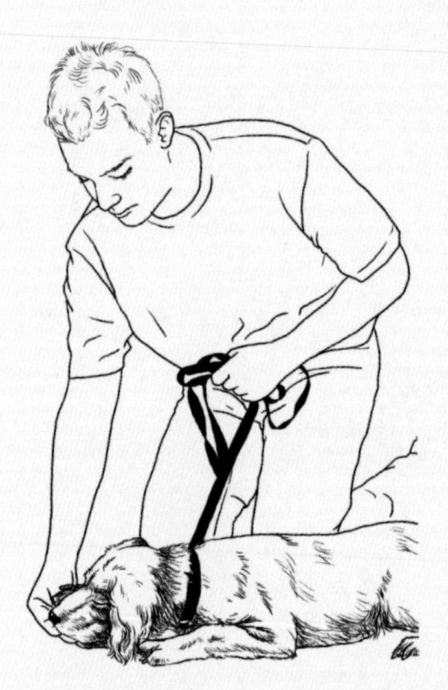

3 As the dog lies down, give the command "Lie down" and then reward your dog. If the pup's backside comes up, simply start again from sitting but keep the treat closer to the dog's nose.

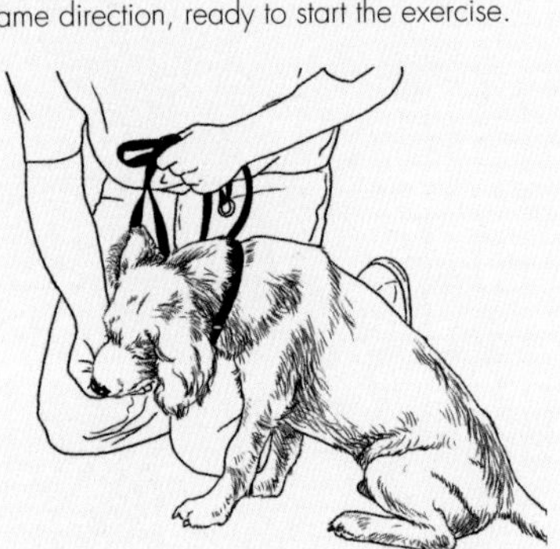

2 Move the right hand with the treat down near the pup's front paws. Don't slide the treat forward: if you do, the pup's butt end will come up to follow it.

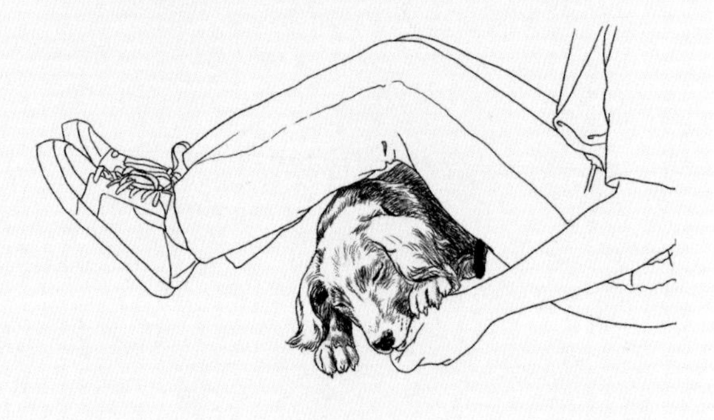

4 Another way to teach your dog to lie is sitting on the floor with your knees raised. Lure it under your legs with a treat until it is forced to lie down to fit through, while giving the command "Lie down", then reward it.

PRACTICAL TRAINING EXERCISE 4

STAYING PUT

"Stay" should eventually tell your pup that you will return to her, so there is no need for her to come to you. While she's learning, don't call her out of the stay, always go back to her. This is really a variation of "Sit", "Lie down", and "Stand", and subtly different from "Wait" (*see p.256*). Once your dog will sit for just verbal praise, graduate to "Stay", reinforcing the command with a hand signal. Teach this when she is full of food or tired, so she remains calm and contained, not when she's dying for a game. Too much praise also encourages exuberance, so keep praise muted, and never train where it is hard for your dog to concentrate. And don't rush this one. Dogs should become really steady before you significantly add distance between the two of you.

Ensure her head is up, looking at your face. Don't stand too close; you don't want her looking up vertically. After she sits, show her the palm of your hand while you command "Stay" and back away a step. Starting with your pup sitting at the base of a wall keeps her from sliding backwards. If she doesn't respond properly or moves, she has done nothing wrong. Use your neutral word, quietly replace her and start again. Save the word "No" for more serious misdemeanours. Shorten the distance between you until she gains the confidence that you will return to her. Initially keep the duration of the "Sit-Stay" short, and give a low-value food reward in a low-key manner. Gradually increase the duration and move to the command word alone without the treat. Repeat over a week or so, gradually backing away until you are giving the command at a distance. Always follow the "Stay" command with another command or a release word such as "Finished" or "OK".

1 Use an obvious hand signal when training your dog to stay on command. With the pup on its lead to ensure compliance, give your chosen signal and command the dog to "Stay".

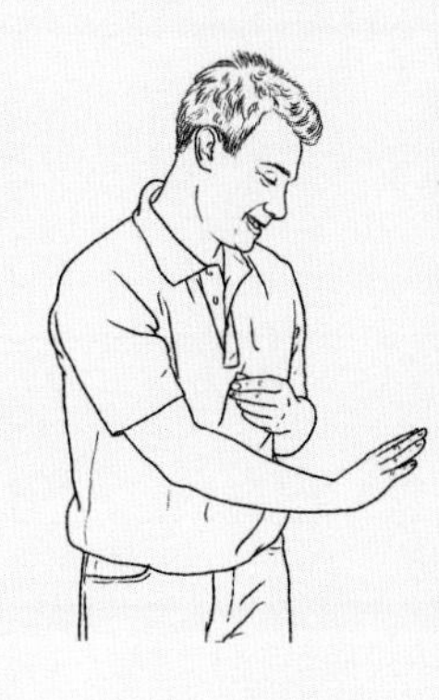

3 Having taken a first step away, maintain the verbal and hand signals for another second. If the pup moves, quietly replace it in the original position and start again with command and hand signal.

2 Maintaining the hand signal, verbal command, and eye contact with your pup, move your farthest leg away. Sometimes a reminder, such as holding the collar, is necessary.

4 Once the puppy has stayed, return to its side and give quiet words of praise. Release it with your chosen release command, but avoid excitement and give it no further praise.

Playing and toys

Just as children learn how to play by themselves and with others, your pup will learn how to do the same by playing with toys alone, playing with you, and playing with other family dogs. Later, playing with new people and new dogs are added in the local park and at puppy play school. By actively playing with your pup now you will quickly learn whether it is shy, fearful, bossy, or loud, or simply the perfect puppy. During those first days in your home, any new pup is the perfect pup but then inevitably reality sets in and you come to realize that having an infant pup can be very, very frustrating and unexpectedly time consuming – which is why this chapter, covering only a month of your dog's life, is one of the longest in the book.

Choose toys sensibly

The selection of toys for your dog has never been better. There are practical toys, educational toys, and downright witty toys you could leave around your home as if they were installation art. Whatever you choose, remember they belong to you, not your dog. That may sound harsh, but toys serve two fundamental purposes. They are distractions and they are rewards. If they are always just lying around, they have less value in your dog's eyes. You want your dog to look upon playing with toys as an exciting highlight of the day, as a reward for doing something or a stimulating distraction when you have to concentrate on the rest of your life or are absent and your pup is home alone. Your selection of toys depends on your dog's size, activity level, and personal predilections, and you won't know the latter until you offer a variety of toys and see which are preferred. With Bean I was really surprised that her favourite toy was a high-tech item from Germany, a hard rubber ball in the middle of a scented nylon bone. The ends of the nylon bone unscrewed to allow edible rings to be added at each end. At eight weeks of age her teeth were too small to eat the edible rings but this was the toy she always chose when offered a selection, so this was the one we withheld and only gave her when she was being left alone.

Hours of fun (from top) Bone shapes are naturally good for chewing, and rings are an excellent shape for throwing. Some dogs find toys that dangle satisfying to retrieve, and some squeak or jingle for added interest. Hollow Kong-types or hollow marrow bones can be filled with pasty or sticky food to reward chewing. At the very low-tech end of the spectrum, a sturdy knotted rope is still a favourite tug-of-war toy.

Throughout life a dog will get pleasure from playing with toys. Because this is one of their most natural behaviours, we can take advantage of it and use it to train a dog to behave as we wish. Some pups, however, don't seem to be particularly interested in toys. This can happen when too many are given, so remove all but one chew toy and let your dog see you hide it. Make that toy a real resource by showing that others – you, your kids, your partner – want it but your pup can't have it. Play piggy in the middle: two people throw the toy between them, encouraging the pup's interest. If you don't have a helper, tie a string or thin rope to the toy and throw it up in the air or swing it. Act excited but still ignore your pup. Just like us, pups like the forbidden and are interested in what you have and they don't. Eventually, let the toy come almost in reach of your pup – in the air or on the ground – then take it away. Finally, let your pup make contact and "win" it. With other dogs who have a more typical enjoyment of toys rotate them weekly by making only three or a maximum four available at a time.

Fetch! Sensible retrieve toys are soft enough to be thrown safely, but tough enough to withstand chewing. Good, solid plastic toys will bounce, float if they land on water, and most can even be put through a dishwasher once in a while.

Distraction toys provide food rewards when your dog plays with them alone. Some, such as activity balls, release food when they're pushed around by a nose or paw. Other distraction toys include Nylabone-type and solid Kong-type toys treated to have appealing odours, which are used for chewing or carrying. Small plastic water bottles are cheap, plentiful and can be carried by larger pups or used as distraction toys, for finding out how to manipulate them to get water out of the neck of the bottle.

Interactive toys are those you use when playing with your dog. These include Kongs on ropes, tug-of-war toys, Frisbees, and of course tennis balls. Dogs love tennis balls. All of my dogs have collected abandoned tennis balls from the park, which seems only natural as they've all been Golden and Labrador Retrievers. Tennis balls are lightweight, but potentially obstructive for giant breeds with wide throats. Because of this, manufacturers have produced giant tennis balls, dumbbells made from tennis ball material, and a variety of other toys with the same surface texture. Whichever interactive toys you choose, playing with it together is important for because it bonds your dog to you and teaches it what the limits of playing with people are.

Always remember when playing together that in evolutionary terms, a dog's teeth and jaws are adapted not just to capture, hold, kill, and consume prey but also for a dog to protect, defend, or assert itself. We expect our pet dogs to forget they have teeth, to inhibit their use, certainly never to use them as weapons, which is unnatural. Channelling the natural need to chew and bite into chew-toys makes it much simpler for pups to learn to be gentle

Easy does it Dogs need to use their teeth, and they only learn to inhibit hard biting through play, with other dogs and with us. Interactive play, complete with the occasional accident, is as essential for pups as it is for our kids.

and "soft-mouthed" with all other animals, including us, during these first weeks, while they still have their baby teeth. When your pup bites too hard when playing with you, be theatrical, scream "ouch", stop the game and walk away. Avoid eye contact for a minute, then continue play if you like, but if there is any more hard biting repeat your theatrics and leave further play for another occasion.

Comfort toys are soft toys suitable for carrying around, and particularly good for breeds with a heightened desire to carry, such as spaniels and retrievers. Because my extended family all own retrievers we have the sad habit of returning from holidays with soft toys for the dogs – moose from Canada, sharks from Florida, leprechauns from Ireland, cuddly Brad Pitts from Los Angeles. Soft toys should be machine washable, and ideally purpose-made for dogs. If not, they should be labelled safe for children under three, but that only means that the filling isn't toxic, not that the toy is indestructible. If your dog prefers a particular soft comfort toy, always leave that one out. Comfort should always be available, all day, every day.

Comfort toys aren't appropriate for all dogs. Terriers, for example, often want to shake and "kill" them, and tend to destroy them. Be particularly cautious with any toy that contains a "squeaker" buried in it. Some terriers have a compulsion to seek and destroy them, and some hormonally influenced bitches take to relentlessly squeaking them.

Nutrition

The dog is, like us, both a predator and an opportunist scavenger. A dog prefers meat and animal fat, but when these aren't available they'll eat what they can find – berries off bushes, even vegetable roots. They can also have their own idiosyncratic eating habits. Many dogs like to graze on fresh grass, not because they need roughage but simply because they enjoy occasional salads. Others seem to enjoy the taste of rabbit or deer droppings as much as they do their own dog food. A dog can survive on the most miserable of diets, but that's certainly not the fate of the dogs I see. The clinical nutritional problem I most commonly see is caused by canine gluttony – too much meat, too much fat, too many calories, and not enough chewing.

In northern Europe and North America one out of every three dogs is overweight. Many are clinically obese. An American study published in 2006 reported on 48 Labrador retrievers from seven litters, kept by the same people, and treated by the same vets. Half were kept lean by feeding them 25 per cent less than their brothers and sisters. The lean dogs lived on average 18 months longer than the free-fed brothers and sisters, and had x-ray evidence of hip joint osteoarthritis appear only at 12 years of age, while it appeared at half that age in the other group. Good nourishment is more than just tasty food. Balanced nutrition enhances the quality of a dog's life as well as extending it. Healthy dogs need extra calories when they're growing, pregnant, lactating, or recovering from illness, otherwise they need just enough daily calories to maintain slim, healthy bodies.

Feeding basics

Dogs need energy to live and because they, like us, are omnivores, they can get their energy from any good animal or vegetable source of protein, fat, or carbohydrate. Energy is measured in calories: a calorie is the amount of energy needed to warm 1g (4/100oz) of water by 1°C (2.7°F). A kilocalorie or "kcal" equals 1,000 calories, and is commonly called a Calorie with a capital "C". Food labels usually list energy as "kcals". Dogs also need a range of organic compounds loosely classified as vitamins and 12 different minerals. Some, for example sodium, are needed in relatively large quantities, and others, like iodine, in remarkably small amounts. Vitamin and mineral deficiencies in pet dogs are in my experience, extremely rare. Vitamin and mineral excesses are more likely, because owners feed well-balanced diets then sometimes add inordinate quantities of supplements, unwittingly creating nutritional problems by over-supplementing.

Stay in control The amount you feed your dog should be decided by its size, activity level, and state of health, not by how easily you give in to soulful brown eyes. If you want a healthy and long-lived companion, don't pander to a pup's natural inclination to become a glutton.

A pup needs food to maintain body functions but also to grow. At the breeders' home, pups started being weaned off their mother's milk at three weeks of age and were introduced to solid food in the form of a soupy gruel. Some breeders pulverize dry puppy food and add water or goat's milk to it, others feed tinned or other forms of wet puppy food or offer home cooking such as scrambled eggs, mince, and baby cereal. At six weeks of age the pups were weaned off their mother (allowing her milk to start to dry up) and fed up to six times daily. By the time your pup arrived in your home it was on four meals a day, which will decrease to three meals daily at three months of age, then to two daily meals at six months.

Puppies have high energy needs until they are physically mature, so commercial puppy food contains more energy, vitamins, and minerals than the same manufacturer's adult food. From birth until it is half its adult size, a pup needs about twice the amount of energy it will need as an adult. During the rest of its growth it will need around 50 per cent more than it will as an adult. As soon as your dog reaches full size, you will need to cut back on energy intake. That means reducing the quantity of food you offer or switching from higher energy puppy food to standard energy adult food. Serious illness can affect a dog's energy needs and higher energy food may be needed both during and after some illnesses.

Boundless energy It may seem that your pup never stops moving, and you might be tempted to fuel all that action with a little more food. But do stick to the recommended guidelines: the shape your pup is in now is a foundation for the rest of its life.

ADULT WEIGHT IN KILOGRAMS	DAILY KCAL REQUIREMENTS
2–5kg (4–11lb)	295–590
6–10kg (13–22lb)	675–990
11–20kg (24–44lb)	1065–1665
21–30kg (46–66lb)	1725–2255
31–40kg (68–88lb)	2310–2800
41–50kg (90–110lb)	2850–3310

Protein, fat, and carbohydrate

Protein is made up of units called amino acids. Dogs can synthesize some amino acids, but not others. They need these in their food, and they are called the essential amino acids. High-quality protein, especially meat protein, contains a good balance of all ten essential animo acids. While amino acids are needed for all the body's biologically vital compounds, to get technical for a moment, amino acids also "donate" carbon chains needed to make glucose, a sugar that provides the dog's body with energy. Give a dog a choice and it will pick foods high in protein. That usually means meat.

Dogs normally consume more fat than we do, either from animal fat or from seed oils, such as sunflower or rapeseed. Fats are made up of smaller units called fatty acids. Your dog's body can synthesize some of these, but not others, which are called essential fatty acids, sometimes abbreviated to EFAs. Essential fatty acids not only play a life-sustaining role in the structure and function of the cells in the body, they also carry the fat-soluble vitamins A, D, E, and K. The omega-3 essential fatty acids, such as DHA (docosahexaenoic acid) and EPA (eicosapentaenoic acid) act to reduce inflammation and might assist learning during puppyhood, while omega-6 essential fatty acids (such as linoleic and arachidonic acid) are needed for good coat condition, blood clotting, and heart function. Pet food manufacturers ensure that their foods have good quantities of fat because, apart from being necessary, fat smells and tastes good. Dogs love fat and are attracted to a food by the aroma of its fat.

A final source of energy is digestible carbohydrate, usually from cereal crops and legume vegetables. Some digestible carbohydrates contain sugars, usually glucose or fructose, that are absorbed by the intestines. Others are broken down into sugars by enzymes in the intestines. Undigestible carbohydrates don't break down, but pass undigested through the small intestine into the large intestine or colon where resident micro-organisms ferment the fibre, creating some fatty acids but also gases. If your puppy is bombing you out of your home, this is how and where puppy wind is manufactured. Undigestible (or fermentable) carbohydrate is good for dogs. It may lead to gas production but it also helps regulate blood glucose, and there's evidence it also plays a positive role in immune function.

Right time, right place You may have read that if your dog waits to eat until after you've eaten it understands you're the pack leader and it must wait its turn. That's true in a wolf pack but not in your dog's human family. A full stomach discourages begging at the table. So does giving meals away from where you eat yours.

Be consistent with your feeding plans

Train your dog to have food only from your hand or its food bowl, never from you at the table or off your plate. If you have two dogs, feed each from its own bowl, preferably tail to tail so they don't watch each other eating. The best treats are nutritious and tasty ones given as rewards because your dog has earned them. Dried liver is the caviar of all dog treats. Remember, food isn't there just to satisfy nutritional needs, or something you use to

tell your dog how much you love it. Food is your USP: it's what makes you different from all those other humans out there.

Eating is one of your pup's greatest pleasures, so harness that fact to help with training. You can do this in two ways, but in either case, measure out daily food intake and set it aside. Option one is to feed most, but not all of it in four equal portions during the day, inside the crate. Save the tastiest bits, for example spoonfuls of wet food, to stuff in hollow chew toys for sucking and chewing on between meals. A more powerful and in a curious way a more natural option is to make your pup work for all of its food by giving everything stuffed in chew-toys. Bury the most succulent bits, such as the liver treats, deepest in the hollow bones or Kongs, soften the meal itself into a porridge-like gruel and pack into the toys and then stick dry kibbles or biscuits – easy to pull out – into it.

Consistently feeding the same food maintains a stable balance of microflora in a pup's digestive tract, and that produces well-formed stools. It can, however, be boring. If your dog tells you your chosen food is tasteless, there's no harm in gradually switching to another food, as long as you don't unwittingly increase calories, and so weight. Cat food is not dangerous for dogs. It contains much more protein than a dog needs and as a consequence, is tastier, especially to picky eaters but, contrary to what you might be told is safe (just more expensive) for your dog to eat.

Breeders of large and giant breeds still occasionally tell new owners to add calcium to their pup's food. *Don't!* It's not only unnecessary, it can be damaging. And forget any breeder advice about not letting your large pup go up or down stairs or run until fully grown. Those are myths as well. All moderate exercise, including step exercise, is wonderful for all growing pups, even the fastest growing.

Commercial foods

Commercial dog food may be wet (75–80 per cent moisture), semi-moist (15–30 per cent moisture) or dry (6–10 per cent moisture). Dry and semi-moist foods usually contain more energy-laden carbohydrates, while moist foods (in cans and sachets) often contain higher levels of animal-derived protein and fat. The wetness of a food doesn't make it better or worse, it makes it more or less convenient for you and often more or less tasty for

RAW BONES ARE A NATURAL PART OF A DOG'S DIET

Eating raw bones is both natural and dangerous. Yes, of course raw bones are nutritionally good for pups. Dogs evolved from a species that captured, killed, and consumed other animals, including their bones. Bones are nutritious, and chewing on them keeps the teeth and gums healthy. On the other hand, I've had to operate on dogs, including young pups, to remove bones stuck in their stomachs or intestines. If you plan to feed your dog bones, start when it's a young pup and more likely to learn to eat and chew sensibly. Remember that in hot weather bacteria multiply quickly in raw bones, and dispose of the remains of them on the day they're given. Raw bones are messy, for your pup and for your home. They are also very valuable possessions. If you have two dogs, one will almost inevitably want the other's bone even if it has its own. If there are signs of aggression, don't give bones when two dogs are in the presence of each other.

Chewing it over If you do choose not to give your dog raw bones, remember that its teeth still need a regular workout. Soft dog food and small dry kibbles won't provide this, and besides, dogs just love to chew, so give commercial rawhide "bones" to do the job.

your dog. Dog food comes in a great range of prices, and as with most things in life, the more you pay the better the quality of the product. The cheapest foods are those with the cheapest ingredients and the smallest advertising budgets, and the most expensive are those with the highest quality ingredients and/or the largest advertising budgets. Ecologically well-sourced dog foods are now made not only by small manufacturers but also by the major manufacturers.

If you have ethical or religious concerns about feeding your dog meat, there are commercially produced vegetarian diets, but because I am not aware of any for which feeding trials have been carried out it is safest to supplement them with a general vitamin and mineral supplement containing a good quantity of vitamin D. In North America and Europe all dog foods must be fit for human consumption, although mistakes in manufacture can and do occasionally happen.

Complete dog foods have vitamins and minerals added to ensure that they contain all the dog's known nutritional requirements. Some of these substances, for example vitamin E, act as antioxidants. These prevent damage to nutrients in the food and, once consumed and in your dog's body, they are also called "free-radical scavengers". Diets for large-breed pups sometimes contain nutrients such as glucosamine that are thought to protect (or help make) cartilage and joint tissue. The science is not yet convincing, but there are no known problems with these supplements. Flavours are usually derived from animal and plant sources, although synthetic artificial smoke or bacon flavours are added to some dog treats because they appeal to our preferences. Herbs and botanicals are sometimes added either for their flavours or because of perceived or real medicinal effects, while synthetic colours are used in some foods, especially the cheaper ones, to make them look brighter or meatier. Natural colours, such as chlorophyll from green plants and carotene from carrots, are also used.

Home cooking

If you plan to cook for your pup, don't overdo the meat. Meat is low in vitamins A and D but particularly low in calcium. You can actually kill a pup by feeding it nothing but muscle meat. Avoid tofu and other bean products, especially for deep-chested pups such as sighthounds. These foods stimulate gas and increase the risk of life-threatening bloat.

Here's an example of a well-balanced home-made diet: this recipe produces around 880 kcal of energy, enough for a day for an active 10kg (22lb) dog, such as a 12 week old Labrador Retriever pup, and you can continue feeding it as your pup matures and through adulthood, adjusting the quantity as necessary to provide the right amount of energy.

Protein	70g (2½oz) chicken and 30g (1¼oz) chicken liver
Carbohydrate	140g (5oz) uncooked rice and 40g (1½oz) wheat bran
Fat	A teaspoon of sunflower, rapeseed, or corn oil
Minerals	pinch of iodised salt and 10g (0.35oz) sterilized bone meal

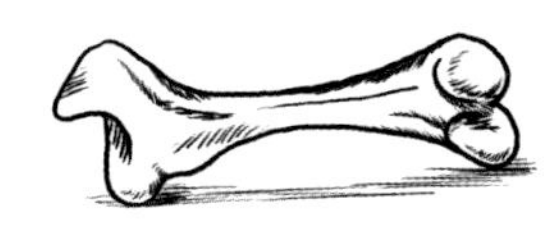

Diet decisions Commercial foods are standardized, safe, and convenient, homecooked foods feel more natural, and some owners aim for a diet as close to the fresh-kill-on-the-bone as possible. Your choice will depend on many factors, from what you can afford in money to what you can afford in time, but the more you choose to do yourself, the more you have to know about canine nutritional needs.

Prepare the chicken and liver as you would if you were cooking it for yourself and chop it up finely into small pieces. Boil the rice and cook the bran, then mix them together, add the oil, salt and bone meal, mix the meat in thoroughly and feed it to your dog. If you see any grain in your dog's stool that means it wasn't cooked long enough. Try soaking the grain in water overnight, cooking it longer, using more water or using flaked or cracked grain instead of whole grain.

Health during the first weeks

They can be daunting, these first weeks with an infant pup. Is she scratching too much? Is he urinating too frequently? Pups seem so small and fragile. Inevitably there are health problems, and the most common ones involve the stomach and the intestines.

Always visit your vet on acquiring a new pup, within 24 hours when possible. She or he will carry out a full health check. It's fortunately rare, but sometimes a hidden problem is discovered, for example a congenital heart murmur. Even though you have already made a substantial emotional investment in your pup, it may be better to return it to the breeder now than to undertake the emotional and financial costs of looking after an individual with an incurable health problem.

The people you meet at the veterinary clinic can be your best, unbiased resource for handling, health, and behaviour advice about your pup. They can advise you on different types of food (although some vets may have an interest in suggesting particular foods that may only be available through veterinarians), on local puppy classes, on how to carry out a simple, daily, head-to-tail physical examination of your pup, how to keep your pup clean, how often to bathe, and how to groom. If you don't get this advice from your vet, no problem, I'll cover it in the next chapter.

Stool consistency and urinating

Because of what they eat and how their brand-new digestive tracts work, most pups produce formed but slightly soft stools. The colour varies with what they eat, with chicken- or fish-based foods producing more yellow-brown stools and with lamb- or beef-based diets more plain brown. It's not unusual for pups to have soft-to-loose stools for a day or so after they leave their breeders and join your home, but this should return to formed-but-soft within two days. There should be no vomiting. If there is, withhold food and contact your veterinarian.

Once stools have settled, and are formed and relatively easy to clean up (this will be easier in a few weeks when they become drier), expect your new pup to excrete every three to four hours. Constipation is quite unusual in pups under three months old and warrants a call to your vet, but loose stools or actual diarrhoea are expected hazards of early life. Pups taste life – anything on the floor or on the ground will be tried, and many items irritate the stomach or bowels. So do some diets. That's why you changed your pup's diet gradually from what the breeder was feeding to what you want to feed, but even so, what you selected might not be exactly right for your pup's digestive tract. It may take a little trial and error to find the right diet, food that produces stools that are well formed and easy to clean up.

Urinating is more frequent than defecating, again, up to every three or four hours but more frequently when life is exciting. Expect it after any physical, physiological, or mental activity. Urine should be almost odourless and very light in colour, and the bladder emptied in a single squat. If a pup tries to urinate again immediately after emptying the bladder, it may have a burning sensation, a cystitis or urethritis; call your vet for advice.

Other discharges

A typical pup is sufficiently well designed to have no discharges from any body openings, but some pups have poorly designed eyelids and suffer from tear overflow even at this very young age. Tear overflow leaves a clear, colourless wet streak of tears from the corners of the eyes down the side of the nose. When tears are exposed to air they eventually turn a shade of mahogany, staining white hair in particular. This is commonly seen in breeds such as white poodles and Cavalier King Charles Spaniels. Tears also often overflow in other small breeds such as Yorkshire Terriers, but in these breeds tears are often mixed with mucus and harden into crusty mats of hair in the corners of the eyes. Tear overflow should be removed daily by cleansing with damp, tepid cotton wool.

Some pups produce an occasional drop of clear, colourless discharge from the nostrils but no more. Green or yellow discharge almost invariably means infection and warrants a visit to the vet. Young male pups rarely have prepuce discharge but some young females, particularly shorthaired breeds such as Boxers and Pugs with vulvas that are small and "lost" between the thigh muscles, may have a crusty yellow-green vaginal discharge. This can be difficult to resolve medically but almost invariably clears up spontaneously with the female's first oestrous or heat cycle.

Familiar face You're going to see quite a lot of your vet at first. Don't worry, and don't think it's always going to be like this. Just like doctors, vets inevitably see their patients most at the beginnings and ends of their lives.

Handling the first illness

Inevitably, there will be medical concerns during the first month. Your pup's behaviour changes. "She's not herself". When this happens, think practically. If you have had experience with children, use the same common sense that you'd apply when deciding what to do for them. If your pup vomits, for example, don't let it immediately drink its bowl dry. If there's blood appearing in anything or from anywhere – vomit, diarrhoea, urine, coughing – treat it just as seriously as you would if your child coughed up blood or passed blood in the stool. If your pup is shivering and it's not cold, assume that something hurts. If she limps or holds a leg up, assume something hurts. If he's upset when you touch him, assume something hurts. If your pup hides away and doesn't want to play, doesn't want to eat, or just seems morose, assume something is wrong.

Your vet expects you to make liberal use of the advice they can give you during these first critical weeks. At this time in your pup's life it's better for you to be over-cautious rather than let your questions go unanswered. Websites can offer superb information but right now, it's best to ask a human any questions you have about your pup's health and welfare.

A final few words about you

As you've seen, there's a lot to take in when settling a pup into its new home. You and your family are just as important a part of the equation as your pup is. During the first few weeks of living with a dog you are likely to feel frustrated, compromised, angry, helpless, and, if my clients are at all typical, guilty. Guilty that you're not doing enough for your dog, guilty that the dog is interfering with the rest of the family, guilty that the resident dog has to put up with the new canine cannonball, guilty that you've let the dog become ill or didn't go to the vet sooner, guilty that you've discovered it's not the fun you thought it would be and that you find your new dog irritating rather than enjoyable.

So let me say this. You shouldn't feel guilty about feeling guilty. The first months of living with a dog are inevitably more difficult than most people imagine they will be. Don't obsess about your dog's health and welfare. Don't fret about your dog being lonely if it's left alone. Don't agonize about whether it's fair for a dog to live without the constant company of other dogs. And don't think it has all gone pear-shaped and your dog will always be a nuisance and never be enjoyable to live with.

It's easy to get angry at yourself because it's not going as you planned, or angry at your dog because it's not living up to your expectations. Relax. This dog business takes time. Settling a dog into your life can be exasperating. And the worst isn't yet over. Almost invariably, all the pieces of the jigsaw will start to fall into place over the coming months, and by the time your dog is physically mature, life will be back to reliable routines – until your dog goes through adolescence and challenges what you have taught. It's only after adolescence that the powerful rewards of living with a dog are realized, and for most of us these will far outweigh the exasperations that we go through getting them there.

CHAPTER NINE

Canine Puppyhood

The period up to three months of age is sometimes called the "critical" period in dogs' development, when they are like modelling clay, easy to form into what you want them to be as adults. But the coming months, until your pup reaches puberty and begins adolescence, are just as critical. There's no sudden end to the early flexibility of their minds. If I can continue that clay analogy, as long as you continue to add a little moisture, and that means thinking about how your dog thinks, your material remains wonderfully workable. If you don't, just like clay, your material slowly hardens until habits have to be broken down instead.

How you and your pup navigate puppyhood depends in part on your pup's nature and in part on how well you work with what you've got. Most pups I see brim with brio. They strut their stuff from their first visit to the clinic, sparkle when they meet others, and have such unmitigated confidence their owners have to stop them from doing stupid things. These natural extroverts are instinctively inquisitive, confidently explore all new situations, fearlessly challenge other animals, and boldly confront danger. They find every new element of life invigorating and exciting. When denied physical or mental activity they have tantrums – barking, yelping, destroying, demanding attention. If you channel a bold, confident pup's energy you will have a dynamic and gratifying adult, but these OTT pups need firm and consistent handling during puppyhood, and even more during adolescence.

There are a significant number of pups, however, who lack confidence. We're inclined to protect shy dogs by comforting them, but this can let shyness develop into fear and fear into frustrating phobias, so don't be overprotective. It might sound anthropomorphic to call a dog shy, but researchers at Monash University in Australia compared owners' descriptions of their dogs with an established human personality model. They concluded that two of the five terms used to describe us – "energy and extroversion" and "nervousness and sensitivity" – were also regularly used by dog owners. They classified other factors as "amicability", "self-assuredness and motivation", and "responsiveness to training". I have a similar three categories, "extroversion" or "self-assurance", "neuroticism", and "amicability and training focus".

Shy pups need their confidence bolstered, but it's easy to do the opposite unwittingly. For example, a head pat tells a shy dog that you're all powerful and she's an insignificant worm. It's better to reward most pups with chest or back strokes. Watch your dog's body language: insecure pups avoid eye contact with what worries them, flatten their ears, tuck their tails between their legs and lie down, roll over, or even submissively urinate when confronted with dominance. They do, however, pay more attention to what you ask them to do. If your pup is insecure and hides behind your legs, invest in sensible one-to-one advice from an experienced dog trainer.

Ready to go The average pup is keen to seize the day and squeeze as much out of it as possible. At this age, your pup has energy, an open mind ready to learn, and eagerness to please: if you want more (like obedience, reliability, and good manners), this is the time to put it there through training and planned experience.

The typical pup is neither excessively dominant nor overwhelmingly needy. Typical pups enjoy your company, enjoy being petted, and respond readily to routine training. They thrive on consistency and leadership in your tone of voice and posture (*see pp.179–80*). Consistency also helps your pup to listen and to think, so be black and white with your words and actions. "No" means "No" not "Maybe". If you're not consistent, you end up either with a confused dog or (more likely) with one who realizes that you're not a natural leader and don't need to be listened to. Does that ring a bell? Does your dog treat you that way? If so, it hasn't learned to respect you as a natural leader.

Training and discipline

We'll revisit obedience training later in this chapter (*see pp.253–65*), but first a few words about discipline, which you may feel inclined to use as your pup grows up. Discipline works, if used intelligently. Used incorrectly, it risks creating a dog who's frightened of you rather than one who looks forward to your company. During puppyhood you'll get angry with your pup (though probably not as angry as you'll get once you have a rebellious adolescent), but never use discipline to get even. Use it only to help your dog understand what is or is not acceptable. Remember, that's not teaching *right* from *wrong*. Natural instincts tell a dog it's right or normal to pull on a lead, to howl when alone, to chew on hard objects, or to guard their food. Training teaches dogs that however normal these activities are, they're not acceptable to you, the leader.

Female clients routinely tell me that their dogs listen to their husbands but not to them. That's in part because guys have lower voices, but also because men are more inclined to give uncluttered commands. Remember to be succinct – dogs can get mixed up by lots of words. Be concise. "No!" is a perfect word, but don't overuse it. "Bad dog!" is almost as good, or my personal choice of "Arghhh!" Say that to your dog, with a raised lip, and it leaves no doubt that you're displeased. Just about the easiest body language for dogs to understand is a direct stare; combine this subtly effective form of discipline with your height advantage for guaranteed effect. Remember that dogs are intensely social, so symbolic isolation for short periods – still no more than 30 seconds, followed by a minute of ignoring – works when used for surprise, never for retribution.

I can't think of any circumstances where hitting a dog is acceptable, but occasionally a little theatricality is needed. A short scruff shake – holding the loose skin on both sides of the neck and giving a short, gentle shake – is what a mother does when a pup is too mouthy or physically rambunctious. Use it very sparingly and wisely, only on confident pups when they're being truly wayward, never on a shy or fearful pup. Another form of theatrical discipline is a water pistol. My previous dog, Macy, was a successful hunter, but I didn't want her chasing the neighbours' cats. Armed with my trusty high-velocity water pistol, I sat in the garden with her until a cat arrived. As Macy went into a stalk position, I shot her in the face with the water and said "No". Although she loved water, the completely unexpected water in

Quick spritz A mildly unpleasant surprise is far better than a painful shock, making your dog avoid the behaviour, rather than fear you. The water pistol is excellent for delivering your message suddenly, and from a distance.

Beauty sleep At three months of age all pups still sleep for most of the day. This is vital, because their bodies only produce growth hormone, which stimulates physical development, during sleep.

the face when looking at something to chase was enough to stop her chasing. More painful forms of discipline, for example shock collars (*see p.283*), belong in the hands of professionals.

Development continues

Month by month your pup will need less sleep, and you will need to be ever-more creative in devising mental and physical activities. Try to develop routines that will continue into adulthood. When Bean was young, we always left her unattended after her morning exercise. We gave her a favourite chew toy, but didn't talk to her and didn't respond when she tried to trigger us into playing with her. She learned that humans are busy in the morning, and set her biological clock for fun after lunchtime. Sleeping patterns also change. Early in puppyhood, your dog will show only a few outwards signs of dreaming, but by six months of age it has rough and ready dreams, often accompanied by paddling forelimbs and twitching lips, sometimes even yips or groans. No one really knows whether these dreams are bad or good. My wife Julia is inclined to awaken any dog having a dramatic dream, but I let the dogs pass through them.

During puppyhood a dog's comfort habits become fixed. Bean's habit of carrying my pyjamas around is one that retrievers are particularly prone to, which easily becomes a ritual unless you intervene to prevent it. With any unwanted activity, prevention is always, always, always easier than retraining, but if I really didn't want my dog carrying my pyjamas, I'd put them in a drawer or cupboard where she couldn't find them and give her an alternative soft carry toy. At my clinic we stock soft, squeaky vets, Canada geese, and "Jimmy Chew" shoes, all of which are perfect comfort toys for pups that like to carry something soft.

Other pups get equal comfort from masturbating. Long before they reach puberty and its surge of sex hormones, any pup, male or female, may hump your hand, elbow, or leg. If allowed they will continue, and what's silly and harmless in a pup can be threatening in an adult dog. Meeting an adult male Rottweiler who wants your knee for sex can be an intimidating experience. If your pup – male or female – tries to hump your arm or leg, just say "No!" get up, leave the room for ten seconds, then return. Command your pup to sit, then give a treat. Have everyone in the family do this, including the kids.

Shy and normal pups find cuddles comforting, while more dominant individuals are less inclined to want or enjoy them. Many Nordic breeds, Chinese breeds like the Chow Chow and Shar Pei, and virtually all the indigenous Japanese breeds are not natural cuddlers; virtually all gundogs and many working breeds, including Dobermanns and German Shepherd Dogs, openly are. Don't cuddle needlessly. If your dog enjoys cuddles, use them sparingly as rewards. If you go overboard, your dog will mature into an adult who needs constant physical contact just to get through the day.

Avoiding separation anxiety

Allowing a shy pup to stick to you like superglue is bound to create separation anxiety problems, but this can also become a problem for active dogs left at home alone with nothing to do. High-energy dogs, such as Labrador Retrievers and Border Collies, are particularly susceptible during puppyhood or adolescence. This is a learned behaviour, and it's learned through your inconsistency. It develops more often in males than in females and, contrary to popular belief, it's no more common in rescued dogs than in dogs acquired straight from their breeders. Pups that suffer from it might bark, urinate where they shouldn't, run from room to room, or just turn into statues staring at the door you left through. They might take your clothing into their beds, possibly even chew it. (Bored or over-excited pups do similar things.) Dogs don't feel "shame" at this, no matter what many owners think. If you come back to a messed-on floor, chewed shoes, or redesigned kitchen, and a sheepish pup, that look isn't shame. It means your pup was unhappy that it was at home alone. It means that you need to learn what to do so that your pup doesn't suffer when you're away.

The best way to prevent both separation anxiety and boredom is to raise your pup in a stimulating social environment, so it is used to contact with many different people, and accustom it early to being separated from you. From the very beginning of puppyhood, leave your pup at home alone for increasing periods. Occasionally, leave it for a short time with willing neighbours. And – this is very important – don't turn your departures into a song and dance routine. Just get up and go. No smooches. No prolonged goodbyes. No promises you'll be right back. These things may help you emotionally, but they make problems for your pup. Downplay your returns too. Don't pump your voice up an octave to greet your pup. Don't instantly play rough and tumbles or go directly to the cupboard and give a treat. I know it's tough, but just walk back into your home, avoid eye contact, do whatever else you need to do, and when your pup is assuredly calm, give

Comfort habits If your pup likes to carry around a comfort toy, that toy should always be available. Check where it is before leaving your pup alone: it's no use if it's abandoned in the sitting room and your pup is in the crate in the kitchen.

Where did everyone go? Give a pup a choice and, although we make terrific dog substitutes, there's nothing better than having another dog to do dog things with – neck chewing, bum sniffing, ear licking, speedway chasing. The reality for most dogs, mine included, is that they live their lives in human families, only meeting other dogs when they leave their homes. Dogs on their own do get lonely, and that leads some to howl and yowl, others to creatively deconstruct your home.

low-key praise. If you want to give a treat, make your pup "sit" for it. At some time during puppyhood, if you have a garden, you'll be able to leave your pup alone in it with suitable activity toys, water and a shady place to relax in. By the time she was six months old Bean was spending her evenings in ours, I'd like to say simply rolling on her back kicking her legs in the air, listening to birdsong, and contemplating nature. She did all that, but she was also on the alert, and if there was something exciting outside the garden, she'd have been out of it like a shot. Before you leave your pup alone in the garden for the first time, check the security of the garden perimeter to ensure a determined dog can't go over, under, or through it. And remove not just anything potentially edible but also inedibles, such as garden and pool chemicals.

Avoiding boredom

As I write this, Bean is snoozing on the floor beside me. Her only mental or physical activity today was for two hours early this morning when she ate and had her morning exercise in the fields. Later this morning, if she follows her regular pattern, she will go to her toy basket, bring a toy back into the room where I'm writing, settle down and chew on it. She may wander outside and lie down on the grass, seemingly contemplating nature, but she'll remain in a state of calm repose until noon. Then she will come, sit down beside me and stare at me. Her biological clock tells her that my biological clock will by then be telling me that my brain is about to shrivel up and die unless I take a break. She has learned that when I take a break, life becomes more exciting for her.

A dog's life Most of the loved and cared-for dogs I see lead surprisingly dull lives, and they don't seem to mind. Staying relaxed during extended periods of inactivity is a skill best learned early.

Bean is an easy pup because she's not an individual with overwhelming mental energy and she has learned to accommodate to the routines of her human family. When I'm not at home writing, which is most of the time, Bean knows that mornings are dull and has learned to just chill out and do zip. More energetic pups have more difficulty doing that. Even with us around, my previous dog Macy had high mental energy needs. When she was a pup, we knew that if she was out of sight she was doing something we didn't want her doing – usually chewing.

If you have a high-energy pup, start by being tidy. Leave nothing chewable available other than selected chew toys. Whether you are home or not, put your pup in the playpen when leaving it unsupervised, and use a toy that drops morsels of food when moved, both in and out of the playpen. Give meals before you leave, so that when you're away your pup is full and more inclined to sleep. Discover which are the favourite chew toys and give these only when your pup is left alone, hiding them away when you return.

Controlling excitable behaviour

The exuberance of an over-the-top pup needs to be channelled now, before it causes real problems in adolescence. Excitable behaviours include nipping your clothes or you, jumping up, barking, chasing anything that moves (including your ankles), and not coming when called because there is something else much more exciting, such as a buzzing bee. Life is exhilarating, so be prepared for the unexpected. Once your dog is obedient in one place, take it to another and do some training there; this teaches your pup to control its excitement everywhere, not just in one training location.

Excitable pups can go over-the-top when they see you pick up the lead. If this happens, stop doing whatever you're doing and just stand there, silent. Give no clues as to what will happen next, and avoid eye contact. This takes time and patience, but eventually your dog will calm down and sit. When it does, give praise and a food reward. Your pup is now learning what to do,

Busy body Left alone, pups with high energy levels excavate the garden, learn how to strip wallpaper, or chew corners off carpets.

and more importantly, what not to do. One footstep at a time, start moving towards the front door. This is as tedious for you as it is for your pup but after many repetitions your pup will sit very rapidly when it sees you doing nothing. Constantly repeat this exercise. Once your pup settles on its own, you can reintroduce active commands that it will listen and respond to.

Treat all excitable behaviour the same way. Virtually all pups naturally pull on their leads when excited; they want to do things *now*, not in five seconds or only when you have said "OK". This is the most common of all behaviour problems and is controlled in exactly the same way. With the lead attached, move outside into a quiet area and continue training, taking one step at a time. One step. Stop. Wait until your pup sits. "Good sit." Give a reward. Once your pup is obedient for a few steps, increase the number of steps, rewarding each sit both verbally and with a food treat. Now introduce a new command, "Walk", which means "Start walking again." No food rewards for this – moving on is its own reward. Always use a short lead and if you feel tension, surprise your pup by instantly turning in a different direction. Don't slacken the lead when it's pulled, or your pup, who works in a simple cause-and-effect manner, scents victory. If your pup is a born puller, you can also use a head halter such as the Gentle Leader or Halti. The lead attaches to a ring just under the chin, so if your dog pulls, it pulls its own head down and to the side, where it simply doesn't want to be. And invest some time in proper Walk or Heel training (*see pp.257–58*).

Housetraining is completed

The nuisance of indoor puddles and poops ends in puppyhood. The amount of waste pups produce becomes considerable as they grow, so it's vital to continue the routines you set up during infancy (*see pp.175–78*). Remember, you don't let your pup out, you take it out, on waking up, after meals, and after play. Be there outside, regardless of the weather.

Curb your enthusiasm
Controlling excessive bounce is a vital part of training a good canine citizen. If your dog jumps all over other dogs, or their owners, nobody will want to know either of you.

Continue to harness your pup's love of routine by associating toileting with powerful rewards. Now that you're spending more time outdoors, use an invigorating walk as an additional potent reward for your dog toileting when and where you want. That means adjusting your timetable to fit in with with your pup's bladder and bowel functions. In early puppyhood, take early walks, just after your pup awakens, goes outside, and toilets; later you'll be able to take later walks as your pup is able to control its body for longer.

Bean gives a single "woof" to us when she wants to go outside, but her predecessor Macy just sat staring at the door, willing it to open. If your pup does this, you can train it to ring a bell for attention. Hang a line of dangling bells from the door handle and hold a favourite treat such as dried liver in your closed hand right beside them. As your pup noses or paws your hand to get at the treat, ringing the bells, say "Good dog" and give the treat. Both

These things happen If your pup is not yet housetrained, it is usually because there hasn't yet been enough, or effective enough training. It may be because you forgot a trip out. It may be because something exciting or upsetting occurred. No matter how it looks, it is never because your pup knew there were people coming round and did it to annoy you.

of you then go outside. Gradually reward only nosing or pawing that actually touches the bells. Training for two minutes two or three times daily should have your pup reliably ringing to go out within three weeks.

There are still lapses

Almost inevitably, we expect too much from pups at this age. Owners frequently ask me, with great frustration, just how long it will take before their pup is fully housetrained. In most instances, their pup already knows the when and where of toilet training, but there are lapses. Think how long it takes children to be potty trained, then marvel at how fast dogs learn. Pups almost always become fully housetrained between three months of age and puberty, but some take longer than others. Labrador Retrievers, German Shepherd Dogs, Golden Retrievers, and Cocker Spaniels seem to be more "houseproud" than Yorkshire Terriers, Bichon Frises, and Pugs. This may reflect the fact that large breeds make bigger messes to clean up, so their owners concentrate more on housetraining, but there's no doubt that some dogs are reluctant to go outdoors in inclement weather and this creates housetraining lapses. Expect lapses under these circumstances:

- Inconsistency or unavoidable changes in household routines
- Changes in who is the primary leader/trainer
- Emotional turmoil at home
- Arrival of another animal
- Inclement weather
- Illness
- Sexual maturity

It's not uncommon for a dog to be fully housetrained during the day, with the control to get through six or more hours indoors, but mess at night. The pup has learned to mess at night and needs to unlearn it. Restrict the pup to a crate in your bedroom. When it needs to relieve itself, it will whine. Make the trip outside. The next night, when it whines, wait 10 minutes then go out. The next night wait 20 minutes. Yes, this may put shadows under your eyes, but it takes less than two weeks to train a pup to wait until morning, and then the crate is no longer needed for toilet training.

You can, if you wish, retire the crate entirely and continue with only the playpen when you can't monitor your pup. If your car is large enough to use the crate when travelling, keep using it both at home and on journeys.

HOW LONG CAN A PUP HOLD IT?

Age	How long	Minimum toilet breaks
13 weeks	3–4 hours	6–8
16 weeks	4–5 hours	5–6
20 weeks	5–6 hours	4–5
6 months	6–8 hours	3–4
7 months	8 hrs or more	3

Might is right – usually
Puppies submit to older dogs, and especially larger ones, but this is not necessarily true of adult dogs. Some small dogs seem to have a Napoleonic desire to box above their weight. Many small breeds were created as razor-sharp, nose-to-nose killers. They have short fuses and just react, rather than thinking. They are inclined to take on much larger dogs, and often actually get away with it.

Submissive urination

As a pup, Bean piddled when visitors touched her. She piddled when they merely looked at her. She sometimes piddled with excitement when she looked at them. Urinating through excitement or submission isn't a lapse in housetraining. As a mature pup, Bean had typically superb bladder control, choosing not to relieve herself when offered the opportunity last thing at night, choosing not to do so the following morning because she was more interested in breakfast, then waiting for another half hour until we got to the park for her morning exercise, rather than using the always-available back yard. In the park, she actively submitted to large dogs by running full speed to them, dropping down, avoiding eye contact, and urinating. She would then bounce back up, body bash the large dog, and induce it to play with her.

Bean never urinated submissively with little dogs, only with big ones. In her mind, people were the same as big dogs, which is why she behaved in this exasperating way with her family and with visitors. If your dog piddles because of excitement or submission, never reprimand or show anger. That only makes it worse. Reduce the excitement of seeing you by disregarding your pup when you return home. Tell visitors, "Don't touch. Don't look. Don't talk." When you can, manoeuvre your pup to and through your back door so that if it piddles that's where it does it. Fortunately, submissive urinating is almost always self limiting and gradually disappears, although often not until after sexual maturity.

Taking your pup outside

We've already covered the benefits of taking your pup out at an early age to experience the cacophony of sights, smells, and sounds that make up the world (*see p.173*). Extend the range as your pup matures. If you're one of the lucky few who can, take it to work with you to learn what life will be like, lying and chewing on a toy while you do what you do.

There are things to remember. Dogs bark. Dogs bite. Dogs urinate and defecate. Dogs intimidate. Dogs can be real problems, but only if you let them. Although the majority of people either like dogs or are dog-neutral, there is always an active minority who are anti-dog. Don't give them ammunition. Clean up after your dog, using surplus plastic shopping bags or purpose-designed biodegradable poop bags (available from vets, pet shops, or some municipal authorities). If your community has dog waste bins, use them. If not, take your bags home. Don't let your dog bark at people or frighten animals. A dog can only act irresponsibly if you allow it, and even the law says you're responsible for your dog's actions. Your liability is usually covered in pet care or property insurance, but double check.

Most people go soft and gooey when they see pups, so capitalize on this. Take treats with you for strangers to give to your pup. Pups may be scared by obvious threats, such as growling big dogs, or even innocuous events, such as an unexpected rustling of leaves. A frightened pup may try to run, cower, shiver, or hide, or it may defensively snap, growl, or bite. Don't encourage this by offering soothing words and hugs; instead, go all theatrical. Use your funny voice and offer toys, food treats, or games to get your pup's mind back on the positives. If that's not enough, back away from whatever frightened your pup until it calms down. From your new position, start rebuilding confidence with treats, games, and activity. On future walks, if possible, gradually get closer to whatever was frightening, praising and rewarding more relaxed behaviour, but never rewarding fear.

Let me say a few words about stealing from other dogs, because this is common when many dogs meet and some have either toys or treasures found in the park. Stealing from other dogs is harmless but if it happens in puppyhood, it can become threatening in adolescence or adulthood. If your pup is a thief, train it to drop on command (*see p.259*) so that you can return stolen items – by hand – to their rightful owners.

Your dog, your mess If your dog messes in a public place, pick it up: no arguments. And do take the bags home to your own bin if there aren't bins available. Dump them by park gates and there will probably soon be a campaign to exclude dogs from that park.

Invisible fencing is shocking

Invisible fencing is electrical wiring buried around the perimeter of your property, which sends a signal to a special collar that your dog wears. As your dog approaches the wiring, the collar buzzes ever louder, and at the wiring it delivers a painful electric shock. Because of the pain, your dog learns not to continue moving in the direction of an increasing buzzing sound. In most circumstances I cannot see a justification for this training by using pain – but that doesn't mean invisible fencing should never be used. There are instances when the only way to ensure a pup's safety is through the use of invisible fencing. If you need to install an invisible electrical fence,

Taking liberties Dogs may play with other dogs, and with other dogs' toys. That fine – just make sure the toy ends up with the right dog when the game is over.

get veterinary advice on how to introduce your dog to its dangers and be aware that some extrovert dogs find the thrill of escape so rewarding – for example, to chase wildlife – that they will knowingly endure the shock.

Buy sensible accessories

Almost invariably there are more risks outside than there are inside, so ensure you have reliable control over your pup before developing outdoor routines. Use two forms of ID, a name tag on the collar and an implanted microchip. It's a good idea to have your vet's telephone number on the name tag, as well as yours, and make sure you've got the right information on the tag when you travel. Microchips are tiny transponders the size of a rice grain, injected under the skin. When scanned, for example at a lost dog centre, they reveal a number, and a central database will provide the rescue centre with the most recent contact information you've given your vet.

You already have an inexpensive puppy collar and lead, but pups grow extraordinarily quickly, so check frequently to ensure that the collar doesn't get too tight. It should be loose enough to get two fingers under, but not so loose it can slip over your dog's head. When your dog graduates to an adult-sized collar, it's your choice whether to provide just one or a range of collars for different occasions; on dark evenings, I use a Velcro backed, reflective, flashing-light collar on Bean, so I can let her off her lead in the park and still see her. If you swap collars, always transfer any tags. Head harnesses, such as the Gentle Leader or Halti, are excellent for controlling powerful dogs, while body harnesses are essential for dogs with necks as big as their heads (Bull Terriers), those with small heads (Affenpinschers and Pugs), or those with soft windpipes (Maltese and Yorkshire terriers).

Use a lead with a bolt-snap of appropriate weight for your dog. Leads can match collars, and you can add a small container that holds a supply of poop bags. A 1m (39in) lead is fine for walking your pup, but use a longer one, up to 10m (33ft) if you live where dogs are never allowed off their leads. Right now, your pup wears a lead for security. Lead training has yet to come (*see p.258*), but when your pup meets other dogs keep the lead loose and make sure it doesn't get tangled in the other dog's. I don't like extendable leads, not because they aren't practical, but because people seem to use them mostly for tying themselves and their dogs in knots. Some people like chain leads because they can't be chewed through. I don't: they are certainly much too heavy for young pups. Train your dog not to chew by spraying the lead with bitter spray so that chewing brings no reward. (Do the same with your shoelaces.) Practical dog owners wear a waist bag when dog walking with all their dog's essentials in it: treats, a chew toy, poop bags, and the lead when you take it off.

And please don't dress your pup in silly clothes. Yes, there are eye goggles, visors, sports-branded sweatshirts, faux-fur coats, and unending designer paraphernalia – but who are these things for, you or your pup? Your pup has no say. Do you think any dog would really choose to wear antlers and sunglasses? There certainly are circumstances where clothing is necessary – rainwear for pups with poor waterproofing, reflective coats for

Kids together Of course the kids want to walk "their" dog, but until training and recall are rock steady, there should always be an adult hand on the end of the lead, even if the child thinks they're in charge.

We know everything
A microchip contains a unique number recorded in a central registry with your contact telephone numbers and address. At my clinic we use microchips that also house built-in thermometers. When asked, ten out of ten of my patients tell me they prefer to have their temperature taken by my waving a magic wand over their shoulders rather than the old-fashioned bum method.

night-time walks or for hunting companions, cold-weather coats for poorly insulated dogs in cold climates, boots for dogs susceptible to paw damage from sharp or very hot or cold surfaces. I do stock a small range of thin but insulating t-shirts for dogs, clothing that states "I am ill" or "Please don't feed me. Vet's orders". Have fun when buying accessories for your new dog, but bear in mind canine dignity as well as human fashion sense.

Raise a confident canine

Hundreds of thousands of dogs endure lives of disregard or abuse but the very fact that you're reading this book means that your dog isn't one of them. You probably do your utmost to give your dog as enjoyable a life as possible. That's laudable, but I must say that it's also at the root of some of the problems I see. Because owners value their dogs so highly, I often see pups that aren't allowed to behave in simple and safe ways that should be allowed. The fact is this: if you raise your pup as a helpless dependent, then through adolescence, adulthood, and old age, it will remain a needy individual who suffers emotionally, even physically in your absence.

If you want your pup to mature into a confident adult, don't hover, at home or outside. Don't constantly intervene. You might be worried your pup will contract a disease from another dog, or be bitten by a tough-looking or bigger dog, but your pup learns how to handle life through interactions with other dogs and other people. Don't obsess about possible injury. Yes, pups occasionally cut their pads, break their nails, or scratch their skin, but these are minor and inevitable aspects of growing up. Don't let your worries turn your pup into a basket case, carried wherever you go. Let it live a natural dog's life. Your dog won't die if it sniffs another dog's bum or recently dumped droppings. Don't feel guilty when the natural accidents of puppyhood occur and it gets under your feet or is hurt when it tries something silly. It's a wonderful world out there, inevitably more exciting than being in your home, and there's really no limit to how long your pup can stay outdoors, as long as the weather is safe and comfortable.

All pups do need careful supervision outdoors, of course, and extrovert pups need more. They act impulsively, so it's up to you to think ahead, to anticipate risks from local vegetation such as stinging nettles or poison ivy, from poisonous snakes or insects, from difficult terrain. Don't expect your pup to have any common sense whatsoever. If you're near any danger it's your total responsibility to think for both of you. Many dogs, especially gundog breeds like Labradors, are attracted to water. Of course, they are great natural dog paddlers, but they don't understand currents, cold, or contamination. If water is too cold for you, don't let your pup into it, because even thick hair gives only partial insulation. Working dogs often wear insulating neoprene vests for retrieving game from cold water. If you want your pup to swim and it doesn't know what to do, get in the water alongside, holding your pup firmly against your body, then gently release it, saying how wonderful it is as it swims to you, while you back towards the shore. A pup may splash frantically, forelimbs breaking the water's surface, but almost instantly, the strokes will become more effective.

Play it safe Always ensure *you* are properly lead trained before visiting exciting or possibly frightening places. But on a lead with all four feet on the ground is safe enough: don't breed anxiety by pulling your pup behind you or picking it up at the approach of every new dog or person.

The hunter unleashed

Outdoors, a pup is revealed as a hunter looking for things to chase, capture, kill, and consume. In your garden there may be insects and occasional birds, but beyond your boundaries your pup has the real McCoy: squirrels, rabbits, whatever wild mammals live where you live. Watch carefully, and you'll see that that "play" has real meaning.

During puppyhood a young dog learns to identify and follow first ground scents and later airborne smells. All pups are scent searchers, and some instinctively stalk from their first day outdoors. Hunting dogs tend to have more patience than terriers, which are initially more inclined to look and chase. Pointers and some others will break their stalk with a point, freezing like statues rather than chasing. Herding is another normal behaviour used by wolf packs when hunting large game. It is most extravagantly displayed by Border Collies from working lines; with nothing else to round up, they commonly go into their classic drop, eye other dogs, and try to herd them.

The "capture and kill" behaviours – stalking, throwing, and catching – are play activities for many dogs. Most pups shake toys, some throw them in the air, and others – Border Collies and Springer Spaniels are perfect examples – obsessively enjoy catching. Terriers in particular shake and throw small mammals when they capture them. All pups are hardwired to dig out prey that has gone to ground, but terriers are professionals. My previous dog Macy learned to follow rabbit scent to ground as a pup and dug like a terrier if I ever let her. The classic behaviour of bringing a catch back to the den is modified in Labrador and Golden Retrievers to include retrieving, food carrying, or gift giving (which is why Bean gives my pyjamas to visitors). If your pup is an enthusiastic carrier, take a carry toy to the park.

Sneaky snacking The best way to cure scavenging is to lay a "bait" marinaded in a taste your dog really won't like. Commercial products are available, but chilli sauce works well. This is technically called aversion therapy.

Eating al fresco

Many dogs eat grass because they like it, not because they have stomach aches. Don't be surprised if your pup does this. It's a natural dog behaviour, and some eat so much that they vomit it back up. If a pup that is not a natural grazer unexpectedly eats grass, it may have indigestion. Later in puppyhood your dog may develop more food-related activities. Some bury bones, but few remember to go back and dig them up. Occasionally pups take their food from the bowl and go somewhere else to eat it. This harks back to their evolution as pack animals. More commonly and worryingly, some develop the habit of guarding either real food or their pretend food, their toys. I'll discuss this habit in detail when we get to adolescence (*see p.284*).

Once upon a time dogs chewed and gnawed to eat. This evolved into a comfort behaviour, and your dog will probably want to chew on sticks. There are pros and cons to this. Sticks can get stuck in the roof of the mouth – an uncomfortable but relatively minor problem – or pierce the back of the throat, leading to painful infections and sometimes extremely complicated surgery. They can be chewed up and swallowed and lead to gastrointestinal pain, or worse, to surgery to remove bits. Pups need to chew, and as a vet I say they should be given chew toys, such as Kongs or hollow sterilized bones. As a dog owner, however, I let Bean chew sticks. I do so because the greatest thrill in life for all the retrievers I've lived with is to find a stick that weighs as much as they do and parade it past any human or dog they see, head and tail high. When Bean's neck is about to break she puts it down and chews on the end of it – under my supervision, just as she chews on bones under my supervision. Others will disagree, but there are risks in all aspects of life and this is one where I find the value to Bean outweighs the risks.

Opposite top All dogs are hardwired to hunt, but some are wired harder than others. Spend time training your pup not to chase, but if you have a hound or a terrier you may just have to spend a lot more time with the lead on.

Opposite left You might have made your garden escape-proof, but stay vigilant if you let a pup out in a new garden or off the lead in a park.

Opposite right Tag is as natural for dogs as for kids (though the rules are a bit fuzzier). As long as both dogs are having fun, let them play.

Dogs and cars

If you plan to travel with your dog, even if only on short journeys, accustom your pup to it now. Condition it to travelling in a crate, or if your car is not large enough, buy a pet harness that attaches to the rear seatbelt system. You'll need a seat cover to protect the back seat and a car towel. Take your pup on visits to petrol stations and to the car wash if you use one frequently.

Car sickness is common in young pups. You can condition yours to not be sick by inviting it into the car, giving a food treat then letting it jump out. Progress to putting it in the car, turning the engine on for a minute, then off, and rewarding for not being sick. Next, turn on the engine, drive out of your parking space and back in, and reward the absence of sickness. Gradually increase the length of the journey until your pup is reliably conditioned. If you have an unavoidable journey before this, don't give a large meal before the trip – but curiously, a very small meal is helpful for some dogs. Ask your vet to supply you with anti-nausea medication and of course, take a towel and cleansing wipes with you.

If you're travelling from one climate to another, remember that your dog needs to adjust to changes just as much as you do. We sweat over our entire bodies; dogs sweat only through the pads of their feet, so they rely on panting, which is a very inefficient way to prevent overheating. In a car in

Safely stowed If your dog is used to a crate, this is the best way for it to travel. It is less likely to distract the driver by moving around, and in a smaller space will be thrown around less on corners. Make sure the crate is secured: your dog can move to keep its own balance, but can do nothing about a shifting crate.

Play school Young dogs learn their social position and make friends through play. Don't be too quick to intervene, unless something is clearly wrong: your pup may lose one round, but be top dog in the next, and both dogs learn from this. Only when play is obviously unbalanced or escalating into a fight is it time to call it quits.

direct sunshine, with the air-conditioning off and the windows closed, a dog can suffer from heatstroke within minutes. This happens fastest in hot weather, but I've seen it even in winter when dogs are left in airtight cars on brilliantly sunny days. Never leave your dog alone in a car in sunshine, even with the windows partly open. Find someone to look after it.

Socializing with other dogs

You begin to really understand your dog's mental abilities once it routinely goes outdoors. Initially pups try to make friends with all dogs they meet, but through trial and error they narrow their choice to others on the same physical and emotional wavelength, which often means other pups. This is good for socializing, because in most instances all that other pups want to do is play; an older dog uses what was once simple play to assert dominance, and play can quickly explode from harmless to intimidating.

As I've mentioned, humans and dogs are neotenized species, retaining juvenile characteristics into adulthood. Both of us thrive on playful activity throughout life. Sports, mental games, whatever it is we enjoy, we both flourish when we do it. Playful activity satisfies the senses, but behind the obvious there is more. Konrad Lorenz wrote that playful animals such as dogs are "specialists in non-specialization". Play helps dogs to be generalists, with the plastic ability to adapt to circumstances. The more a pup plays, the more inventive it becomes and the better it will be at solving problems.

As the months go by, and your dog plays more and more with other dogs and people, it not only improves physical coordination and dexterity but also develops greater mental flexibility. Play allows safe exploration and experimentation, improving balance, timing, and the ability to intercept or intervene. Interactive play helps high-energy pups sort out appropriate and inappropriate behaviour. Watching your pup play also gives you clues about subtleties you can employ in training; play both moulds and predicts adult behaviour, especially whether a pup will want to become a dominant adult, giving you vital forewarning of a troublesome adolescence. Your pup is learning to carry out sequences of actions, such as retrieving, vital for any moderately advanced training, so use games in training (*see pp. 262–65*).

I think play is also an end in itself. Pups in particular play with each other simply because it's so much fun to chew on another dog's neck or have your own neck chewed. Watch carefully and you'll see role-reversal is common during puppy play. "OK, I'll hit the deck so you can shoulder slam me and chew my neck." says one dog. Then the other says, "OK, watch this. At top speed I'm going to do a somersault, land on my back, and you can pin my shoulders to the ground until the referee blows the whistle". Participants intentionally slow down so they can be caught more readily, or tease the other dog with a toy or stick if it seems to be thinking about giving up.

The nuances of body language

In puppyhood, dogs develop greeting rituals, learn how to use an inhibited bite, and establish social relationships. All sociable species use body language, and dogs use it brilliantly with each other. They also use it with you, your family, and other people, so learning to understand and mimic these signals makes further training a whole lot easier. Concentrate on one or two at a time, watching how your pup uses them, then use them for similar reasons. You'll be amazed how soon you and your pup will be reading each other much more acutely and accurately.

As I mentioned, Bean submitted to other dogs as a pup by running up to them, averting her eyes, cowering, and urinating. This evolved into a more extensive repertoire, which Norwegian dog trainer Turid Rugaas has called "calming signals", gestures that appease other dogs and cut off potential conflict. A pup will use many of these with other dogs. Shivering, chattering the teeth, and urinating are uncontrollable physiological signs of anxiety or fear, and all act as calming signals, appeasing potential aggressors, but many are more subtle. Have you seen your pup lick its nose for no apparent reason, yawn when it's not tired, turn its face away from you? If so, you've seen calming signals. Some of these are apparent as submissive behaviours during infancy (*see pp. 134–5*), but as your pup interacts more with other dogs outside, you will see more. Some are so obvious that even humans understand them without thinking. A play bow with front legs extended, butt high in the air, and tail wagging signals "No aggro. Just wanna play." Lifting a paw or "shaking hands" is more than a party trick. It is often seen in play, and broadcasts a lack of dominance and a willingness to comply.

Licking the nose is something I see many times each day. Some dogs hate visiting the clinic and calm themselves by licking their noses. There may be a good physiological reason for this, because a wet nose picks up more scent.

New dog, old trick When we teach our dogs to "shake hands" we're not really teaching them anything they don't know. Dogs often lift a paw as a friendly signal in play – we just turn it into a gesture that we recognize.

Very interesting Sniffing the ground might be seen as a conversational opener in the scent-driven world of dogs. Natural curiosity will almost always overcome anything from shyness to pomposity or aggressive intentions in the other dog.

Licking the face of another dog or human is a puppy behaviour perpetuated into adulthood. A wolf pup licks its mother's mouth to stimulate her to regurgitate food, and dog pups have inherited it as a vestige behaviour. That's why they aim at our mouths – often hitting bulls-eye. Pups use this on other dogs but also on us, especially when greeting us.

Slowing down or standing still is a very effective way for one dog to reassure another. Use this when approaching a worried dog or an individual you don't know. Jerking, jumping movements are of course the antithesis. If you call your dog and it returns slowly with head down, it's worried about what you might do. And if you've been foolish enough to get into the habit of calling your dog back for discipline, don't be surprised if it freezes: it is trying to calm you down – although it may have exactly the opposite effect. Turning the whole body is another calming signal that can have the opposite effect on us. It is often seen when when play gets too rough, and older dogs do it when a pup pesters them. It calms activity, protects the head, and partly inhibits jumping, so try this if your pup is an excitable jumper.

Walking in an arc rather than walking directly towards another dog is a visual calming signal that says "No aggro – just interested in meeting and sniffing you". If you ever approach a fearful or apprehensive dog, do so on the curve, avoiding eye contact. Walking past normally rather than reacting to another dog's body language can also be a powerful calming signal, to both the potentially aggressive dog and the timid and fearful one.

Sniffing the ground or air is an effective signal used by confident individuals. When an overtly aggressive dog enters our reception and tries to impress the resident Pug, Beatrice, she just turns and sniffs the floor as

Keep calm and carry on When we yawn, we often find everyone else in the room follows suit: something similar happens in dogs, where a wide yawn (top left) acts as a calming signal to others. Sitting down (top right) gives a pup time to think, and also tells any other dogs it's not about to make any sudden moves. Panting (bottom left) is a more overt sign of worry, while sniffing around (bottom right) shifts attention to something new that might be interesting.

if checking for food. This invariably deflates the dominant dog and often leads to nose-to-nose sniffing. I don't know if it works by acting as a distraction – "What on earth is that flat-faced thing sniffing the ground for?" – but it does work.

A dog that feels uncertain and needs time to think naturally sits down. Dogs do this frequently to calm both other dogs and themselves. If your pup is fretful or nervous, sit down. Bean's ability as a pup to sit and calm herself and other dogs was of Olympic standards. Some dogs sit down and scratch as an appeasing signal. (We do this too, scratching our heads when we need time to pause and think.) Top dogs also often lie down – sphinx-like – when underdogs appear frightened of them and they want to signal "Calm down, dear. I'm only a big dog." Dogs often lie down when meeting other dogs as a signal that they have no aggressive intent; this is different from the overtly submissive signal of lying on the side.

Worried or apprehensive dogs yawn, so if your pup gets overexcited outdoors, something terriers are prone to, stop all play and yawn. It's amazing how this calms down even goofballs. I see yawning at the veterinary clinic, and dogs that are hugged too hard yawn, but clients tell me they also do it when family members are quarrelling. If a dog sees the emotional barometer between you and another person (or dog) rise, it's also likely to try to calm down that emotion by getting between you two. Successfully getting between you eliminates the need to use aggression to intervene, but jealousy is also a powerful component of this behaviour.

Tails are great visual signals. A high-wagging tail is an active greeting, but a low-wagging tail is a sign of appeasement. Fearful dogs wag their tails at people or other dogs. More fearful ones lie down and roll over, constantly wagging. Tucking the tail between the legs is a classic sign of submission, and a great use of the tail. The degree of tuck varies considerably, by breed and individual, and is easiest to read in long, lean breeds such as Whippets.

Hunkering down to an insignificant size is a classic signal used to deflect aggression, signalling "I'm no challenge. I'm not worth the trouble." If your pup is fearful or apprehensive, make yourself smaller when interacting. The active grovel or crawl is a signal we also use for extinguishing aggression – this is not one you as a leader should imitate!

Dominant signals

Give and take A pup that always has to win in wrestling games, tugs of war, or any other play, may develop an overly dominant personality.

Dominant behaviours – the opposite of calming signals – are usually self-evident. Many are used in the give and take of routine play by all dogs, but if your pup uses most of them most of the time you have a potential troublemaker, who will certainly be a challenge come adolescence. If your pup consistently shows a wide range of dominant behaviours now, get personal advice from a trainer who uses positive reinforcement training techniques. Some dominance signals are already apparent in early infancy (*see p.134*), but keep looking out for these as your pup meets more new dogs. In addition to those early signals, you may also see some new ones.

Play fighting may be taken beyond play into aggression innocently, when one participant fails to inhibit its bite. It's less innocent when a dominant

In the detail It's usually fairly easy to tell a play-fight that's all in fun from seriously dominant behaviour once you know what to look for. Even if the actions are broadly the same, pay attention to the details: are the teeth bared? How are the ears held? Is the body pinned down, or the head? You'll soon learn to tell what's what.

dog decides to use play to enforce its position. Genuine attacking and biting, especially around the neck, is usually a dominant behaviour, but it can also be the defence of a submissive dog that attacks pre-emptively out of fear.

Body language is as important as actions. Ears that are held completely forward signal excitement and dominance; they are completely flattened to avoid damage during a fight. Standing on another dog with the forepaws on its neck is a powerful indicator of dominance, and worrying if it's done by male pups from breeds naturally inclined to be dominant. Placing the head on another dog's neck, usually standing at right angles and stiff necked, is a more subtle sign, occurring in early puppyhood, and a signal that you will need to develop firm control.

Feeding your growing pup

A typical dog thinks its job title is "living vacuum cleaner". But some, often very small dogs, are the opposite – picky eaters that nibble at their food half-heartedly. They start out as picky eaters and, given a willing owner, they will play poker with your emotions, telling you that they will die – and rapidly – unless given the tastiest of foods. That's why manufacturers produce ranges of especially tasty foods for small dogs, but surprisingly, some large individuals, including many German Shepherd Dogs, will also behave in this exasperating way.

I promise you, as long as you offer nourishing food, your pup will not die of starvation. Remember that a dog's gastrointestinal system is like a wolf's: a large holding-tank stomach and relatively short intestines. They can go without food for much longer than we can. If you blink first, your dog will treat your home like a five-star restaurant. Whether you have a gorger or a picker, good-quality food in proper quantities – not too little, and more importantly, not too much – is essential for your pup to grow to maturity.

The digestive system matures

Until birth all your pup's nutritional requirements were met via the umbilical cord from its mother. At birth, its own digestive system took over, and was populated with "good bacteria" from the mother's milk that enable her pups to digest that milk. When weaned onto solid foods, your pup's intestinal tract received more new bacteria. Most of these died off within a few days, but some stayed, creating a stable environment for digesting food. Inside your pup's intestines is a dynamic, living ecosystem, with bacteria ultimately achieving the balanced state needed for optimum digestion.

When your pup arrived in your home there might have been a short episode of loose stools but after that, if you feed a consistent diet, the digestive bacteria should stabilize and your pup should produce consistently well-formed stools. As your dog grows, your aim is to maintain this balance, providing nourishment and avoiding digestive upsets that lead to diarrhoea. That's easier said than done, because pups "taste" life, investigating with their mouths. During puppyhood there are inevitable episodes of diarrhoea, sometimes accompanied by vomiting. While many of these are self-limiting, some are life-threatening.

Changing your pup's food

If you want to change your pup's diet as it matures, do so gradually. Changes affect the living environment of microorganisms in your pup's intestines and the demands on digestive enzymes, which need time to adjust. This is why sudden changes can cause diarrhoea. Change diets or switch from one source of nutrients to another over five to ten days. Begin by adding a little of the new food to the existing diet, and gradually increase the proportion of new food over the following days. Any bowel problems or signs of going on hunger-strike because of smell, taste, or texture become obvious before they become serious. Remember that all pups, especially the little ones, have their own particular preferences for odours, textures, and flavours, just like us. Finicky eaters are made, not born, so don't turn your kitchen into a canine restaurant with your customer choosing from a varied menu. Simply offer a fresh, tasty, and nutritious diet. As time moves on, modify it according to your pup's unique needs. Provide more nutrients when they're obviously needed, for example in cold weather. Weigh your pup routinely. It should gain weight quickly at first, tapering off as adolescence approaches.

Food intolerances may appear in any dog at any age, but are often first seen during puppyhood. A food intolerance is a reaction that doesn't involve the immune system but may cause vomiting, diarrhoea, or other clinical signs. A food allergy occurs when a dog's immune system reacts to a component of its food, and often causes an itchy skin reaction, vomiting, or diarrhoea, alone or together. Food allergies are rare during puppyhood; they occur more commonly in older dogs, and I'll discuss them in detail in the chapter on Adulthood (*see p.319*).

Complete diet A nursing pup gets all the nutrients they need from their mother automatically. After this, it's up to you to provide a diet at least as good as nature would.

Winning team Both the components of the food you give and the vitamins that are manufactured by your dog's own gut bacteria are needed for your pup to grow and build an efficient immune system.

Most dogs never learn when to stop

Dogs are attracted to food by scent (*see p.117*), while the need to eat is controlled by the hypothalamus. After a meal, sugar in the blood travels to the brain and turns off the need to eat, but dogs are competitive feeders, and most pups are competitive gorgers. Eat first. Eat fast. Eat most. This is an excellent gambit when food is scarce, but is at the root of the most common nutritional problems today: over-nourishment and obesity. Don't assume a pup knows when it's had enough; chances are it won't. Be accurate with the amount of food you give, in three meals each day until six months of age, then reducing to two. The competitive urge also means that dogs eat quickly if fed together, the pushiest dog eating its own food first then trying to eat another's. Feed pups out of sight, hearing, and smell of each other.

Pups don't need snacks. If you give them pointlessly, your pup will follow you to the kitchen, just because this once resulted in a snack. Occasional rewards or "intermittent reinforcement" are a powerful form of training. If you have a compulsion to make your pup happy, use snacks in training. At the very least have your pup sit – but I bet your clever pup already sits without your asking. If that's the case, have it give a paw, roll over, speak.

Feeding a dog is similar to feeding a baby, in that both depend on us to make the right decisions. Decision-making for a dog can be more difficult than for a baby, because you can't apply what is nutritionally good for us directly to dogs. We're omnivores, able to digest almost any food, but dogs are primarily carnivores, preferring meat. If it isn't available, they are fairly good omnivores, but this isn't where their basic abilities lie. Choose food for your growing pup's needs, and understand what you are choosing.

Count the calories

Early in puppyhood your growing pup's energy requirements are enormous, both for developing the body and for maintaining it. As your pup gets closer to full size, the rate of growth and the need for extra energy both decrease, so cut back on how much you feed. Finally, when your dog is physically mature, cut back once more.

The energy needed is difficult to calculate accurately, both because dogs vary in size and because their growth phases vary according to size. Below are average requirements during puppyhood for dogs of different sizes, giving double the adult requirement for the first half of a puppy's growing

DAILY KCAL REQUIREMENTS AFTER 12 WEEKS

Adult weight	To half size	Half to full size	Full size inactive	Full size active
2–5kg (4–11lb)	370–740	270–555	185–370	210–420
6–10kg (13–22lb)	840–1240	630–930	420–620	480–705
11–20kg (24–44lb)	1330–2080	1000–1530	665–1040	775–1180
21–30kg (46–66lb)	2160–2820	1620–2110	1080–1410	1225–1600
31–40kg (68–88lb)	2890–3600	2170–2620	1445–1750	1640–1990
41–50kg (90–110lb)	3560–4140	2630–3100	1780–2070	2025–2350

period, and one-and-a-half times the adult ration from then until maturity. Small dogs finish growing much earlier than giant breeds do. For simplicity, assume that dogs of an adult weight up to 12kg (27lb) finish growing by six months, those up to 20kg (44lb) finish by nine months, those up to 45kg (100lb) by fifteen months, and dogs larger than this by two years. Feed according to your pup's activity levels within these given ranges, and remember that dogs in cooler climates will need slightly increased kcal intake according to the amount of time they spend outside.

Highly digestible diets

A healthy diet provides well-balanced nutrition, but we also want it to produce well-formed, small faeces. You can feed any of the high-quality commercial foods, or cook for your dog. If you cook, make sure you understand canine nutrition: you can continue using the recipe on p.198.

As dogs progress through the stages of life, their energy needs change. During growth, a pup's diet should contain around 22 per cent protein and 5 per cent fat on a dry-matter basis (*see p.236*). The protein requirement will drop to around 18 per cent dry matter once your pup is mature. The exact amount of protein required depends upon the quality of protein used: animal protein is higher-quality than vegetable sources, and the higher the quality, the less is needed. Take care! If pups eat too much when they're young they may be heading for life-long obesity. And just as we're the fattest people that ever lived, the same, unfortunately, is true of our dogs. I know I'm hammering this one, but overfeeding early in life creates a larger number of fat cells, and it's harder to reduce the number of fat cells than to reduce their size. Avoid over-plumpness during puppyhood; it looks cute but it's not healthy. Thin is good – even very thin is good, as long as the muscles are bulking up well. The medical evidence is as clear as spring water: lean dogs are healthier and live longer.

Sources of protein, fat, carbs, and fibre

All dogs need protein to provide essential amino acids (*see p.194*). The most natural source of protein for dogs is meat, but like us, they can get all the protein they need from vegetables. Some people are emotionally blackmailed by picky pups into feeding them meat-only diets. Don't! Plain meat lacks a healthy balance of calcium and phosphorus, and will eventually cause serious, even life-threatening illness.

Dogs also need fat for energy, palatability, and fat-soluble vitamins. The most energy-dense nutrient, with more than twice as many calories weight-for-weight as protein or carbohydrate, it consists of fatty acids, and some of these, called essential fatty acids (EFAs), play vital roles in health. Pups need a good supply of linoleic acid (almost entirely found in vegetable oil), which is an omega-6 EFA, and any of evening primrose, fish, or linseed oil all of which are naturally high in omega-3 EFAs.

Carbohydrates are not a natural source of energy for pups, as they are for us, but with the right digestive microorganisms pups can convert them to the sugar glucose, stored in muscle as glycogen for later use. (Greyhounds

Making choices When you buy a commercial food, you buy years of research and testing. If you think you can do better, or your dog has special dietary needs, be prepared to do your nutritional homework.

Water balance Fresh water should always be available for your dog, even if you are giving wet food. It's a good idea to work out roughly how much your dog drinks daily, so you will know for sure if it changes significantly. Rinse and refill the water bowl daily.

are particularly good at storing glycogen.) Starch is the most common source of carbohydrate for dogs, and cooked starch is easily digested.

Until recently the role of soluble and insoluble fibre in a dog's diet was under appreciated, but both are potentially beneficial for preventing or treating constipation, sugar diabetes, obesity, inflammatory bowel disease, and excess fat in the blood stream. Fibre is found in a feral dog's diet as the fur or viscera contents of other mammals, and stimulates saliva and gastric juice production. Water-soluble fibre increases the stickiness of food, keeping it in the stomach longer and slowing digestion in the small intestine; psyllium is an excellent form of soluble fibre. Insoluble fibre stimulates "intestinal hurry", and is found mainly in whole grains. In people it may help to prevent the build-up of carcinogens that cause cancer of the colon, but there's no evidence that it plays a similar role in the dog's gut, and whole grains have never been important in the dog's diet. The fermentability of fibre is important, because fermentable fibre creates substances in the intestines that may inhibit harmful bacteria. Beet pulp, chicory, rice bran, unprocessed bran, and bran breakfast cereals like All-bran are common sources of both fermentable and non-fermentable fibre.

Vitamins, antioxidants, minerals, and supplements

Vitamins help your pup grow properly, acting as catalysts for the metabolism. The fat-soluble vitamins (A,D,E, and K) come from dietary fat and are stored in the liver. Some Cocker Spaniels may have a problem manufacturing enough vitamin A, leading to oily skin conditions, and may benefit from supplementary fish oil. Vitamin D deficiency (causing rickets) is now rare; excess vitamin D, leading to calcium deposits in soft tissue and skeletal deformities, is more common. Dachshunds may benefit from extra vitamin E, and there's some evidence that pups that develop clinical skin problems associated with the skin parasite *Demodex* may have a deficiency in this vitamin. Stressed and hard-working dogs also have a higher requirement for vitamin E. Vitamin K is manufactured by bacteria in the dog's intestines, and pups on prolonged antibiotic therapy could have reduced levels.

There is virtually no risk of overdosing with the water-soluble vitamins, B and C. Many of the B vitamins are synthesized by bacteria in the pup's

BEWARE OF NUTRITIONAL MYTHS

I hear more hocus pocus about nutrition than just about anything else to do with dogs. Some ideas, such as the bones and raw food (BARF) diet, have logical origins but are co-opted by single-issue fanatics. Others are downright loopy. Be wary of those who write or tell you any of the following:

"Dogs that eat commercial food live shorter lives or are not as healthy as dogs fed table food." There's not an iota of evidence for that.

"Vitamin and mineral supplements are good for dogs." Amazingly, there is no evidence that healthy dogs benefit from extra vitamins and minerals.

"Canine malnutrition is common." True, in feral dogs – but it's over-nutrition that's common in owned dogs.

"Dog food makers conspire to hush up food dangers to dogs." Impossible. There are too many conscientious people in the industry. There would be a whistle-blower. But there are occasional unexpected contaminations.

intestines. Because antibiotics interfere with the bacteria that manufacture these vitamins, your pup might benefit from yeast tablets during prolonged antibiotic treatment. Unlike us, dogs also manufacture their own vitamin C and they can probably increase production during stress, as rats do.

An antioxidant is a substance that destroys free radicals, molecules and atoms in the body that damage cell membranes. Vitamins C and E and carotinoids such as lutein or beta-carotene are antioxidants. Eating food with these free-radical scavengers may boost the body's defences, and pet-food makers add antioxidants to food to help pups get through the stresses of growing, and to preserve dried foods.

About 4 per cent of your pup's body is made up of minerals, which play vital roles at the cellular level. Calcium and phosphorus are found mostly in bone, but also in the blood. They are necessary for growth and maintenance of the skeleton, and for cell membrane and neuromuscular function. Marginally more calcium is ideal, in the ratio of 1.3 to 1. A meat-only diet is low in calcium and can lead to deformed, weak bones, and swollen, painful joints especially in young dogs. Magnesium helps maintain normal mineral balance. It also helps with muscle contraction and nerve impulses, and low magnesium levels are implicated in heart arrhythmias in giant breeds, especially those on heart medication.

Other minerals are used in smaller amounts. Selenium is an essential part of the enzyme systems that maintain healthy body tissue such as heart

Minimizing mess Some pups seem to want to eat their food off the floor rather than from a bowl, but even normal eating can be messy. Buy heavy bowls, and if an enthusiastic eater still pushes them all around the floor, try putting them on a rubber mat – the kind sold as table mats or sink liners – for added grip.

Too much of a good thing? It is a very rare pup that ever needs a vitamin or mineral supplement. Take care and professional advice before making additions to a basic balanced diet.

muscle. As a free-radical scavenger, it may also be involved in reproduction and play a role in the immune system by helping to neutralize carcinogens. Copper is stored in the liver and, with iron, is associated with the transport of oxygen around the body in red blood cells. Bedlington Terriers may have an inherited copper-storage disease that can lead to copper poisoning, and Dobermanns, West Highland White Terriers, and Cocker Spaniels may suffer from a copper build up in the liver, which is secondary to other liver disease. Zinc is vital for healthy skin, an efficient immune system, and competent taste buds. It's also essential for the effective function of many enzymes and is involved with detoxifying ammonia waste. Some Alaskan Malamutes and Siberian Huskies have an inherited zinc-metabolism disorder where zinc absorption is poor, so need an optimum level of zinc in their food; zinc is sometimes low in low-quality dry foods. Iodine is vital for efficient thyroid gland functioning. Although hypothyroidism, an underactivity of the thyroid gland, is probably the most common hormonal imbalance seen in dogs, it's rarely associated with an iodine-deficient diet.

In my experience, supplements are only needed for specific medical problems that produce deficiencies or that respond to specific supplements, such as zinc-responsive skin conditions. Take care if you supplement your pup's diet: higher levels of one vitamin or mineral can reduce the absorption of others, and it is potentially dangerous to give large amounts of any single mineral. If a higher dose of a single nutrient is needed, use a broad-spectrum vitamin and mineral supplement formulated especially for dogs. This helps to maintain a proper balance by raising the nutritional levels of other nutrients as well. And don't be too impressed by food substances with possible therapeutic activity called "neutraceuticals". There's very little control of the use of that word, and while certain vitamins, minerals, or fatty acids can be extremely useful for controlling some medical conditions, a neutraceutical is not a guaranteed solution to a medical condition.

Choosing foods and reading labels

By law, dog food must be fit for human consumption. Premium foods, usually available from specialist pet shops and vets, are made to fixed formulas, so the ingredients are always the same – important if you have a pup with a tricky tummy or fixed taste preferences. At the next price level down, supermarket foods are manufactured to fixed nutritional and quality standards from varying ingredients. Much of the world's commercial dog food is manufactured by four companies: Nestle (Purina, Friskies), Pedigree Masterfoods (Pedigree, Whiskas, Royal Canin, Waltham), Proctor & Gamble (Iams, Eukanuba), and Colgate-Palmolive (Hill's). If you want to know about any brand, visit the manufacturer's website. Post questions there or telephone the consumer services department. Reliable producers will tell you everything you want to know; unreliable ones will not.

Manufacturing often exposes foods to a range of stresses, such as heat pasteurization, which make them safe but can destroy micro-nutrients such as vitamins, so all good manufacturers add vitamin and mineral supplements to their foods. The processes may also change foods in unknown ways: an allergic dog may respond well to a fresh diet of lamb and rice, only to have problems return on a commercially made lamb-and-rice diet. And in any manufacturing process mistakes can and sometimes do happen. In Britain, garlic was mistakenly added to a vitamin combination used by a variety of manufacturers; more seriously, a product from China tainted with melamine found its way into a variety of canned dog foods in North America.

What's in a food is listed on the label, but labelling laws often prevent manufacturers from being explicit. Following EC directives, European foods carry a "typical analysis" and a "best before" date that usually corresponds to the shelf life of the fat-soluble vitamins, and state what preservatives have been added. In the United States, label information under the Association of American Feed Control Officials (AAFCO) is more extensive, giving minimum protein and fat levels and maximum fibre and moisture, but not the actual amount in the package. In Canada, the Canadian Veterinary Medical Association monitors a voluntary scheme in which manufacturers provide more information about ingredients and must substantiate any claims. Wherever you are, the information on the label often needs interpretation or even an explanation direct from the manufacturer.

A typical or guaranteed analysis usually lists typical or minimum protein and fat and typical or maximum fibre and moisture. On its own, this says little about quality. The ingredients list gives you more information, but is not usually specific. Constituents are given in descending order of weight. "Meat" means muscle, while "meat by-products" or "derivatives" mean viscera, bone, and marrow, all natural components of a dog's diet. "Meat meal" means dry products rendered from animal tissues. If you want to know what the "permitted colourings, flavours, and preservatives" are, the manufacturer's consumer services will tell you.

The recommendations given in feeding guidelines on packaging are suggestions based upon an average dog, in average weather, and assuming ideal body composition. Your pup is an individual who may need more – but usually less – than this, so feed just enough to maintain slow, steady, expected growth. On North-American manufactured foods, look for the phrase "animal feeding tests" in the nutritional adequacy statement. If the statement says "formulated to meet the nutritional profiles" instead, the manufacturer is relying upon laboratory analysis, not real-life feeding trials, to determine the food's nutritional content.

Comparing the levels of protein, fat, or fibre on labels is pointless, because they vary according to the food's moisture. The only way you can accurately compare one food with another is to convert the information to a "dry-matter" basis: what remains once all moisture has been removed. All pet food manufacturers will gladly give you this information, or you can work it out. The dry-matter nutrient content is the nutrient percentage on the label multiplied by 100, then divided by the dry-matter content percentage. For example, a typical canned food label might say:

Protein	6.5%	**Oil**	3.5%
Fibre	0.5%	**Moisture**	81%

Personal preferences Wet foods are more smelly than dry ones, but remember smell is what attracts dogs to a food. They also keep for longer than dry foods – but you will need to provide exercise for teeth in some other way.

This tells you the food is 81 per cent moisture, so it's 19 per cent dry matter. Therefore, the crude protein percentage is $6.5 \times 100 \div 19 = 34.2$ per cent.

Can I have some more?
Most animals, including us and our dogs, eat more when given a variety of food – novelty is interesting. Finding one type of tasty and nutritious food and sticking to it helps ensure stable digestion. If your dog gets bored with it gradually switch to another equally nutritious variety

Dry food or wet food?

The convenience of all-in-one dry foods has made them popular. These foods are cooked under pressure, dried, and sprayed with fat for palatability. The potentially greatest problem occurs after they leave the factory, and that's spoilage. Heat, humidity, light, even oxygen can spoil dry foods, starting with the fat, so they need preservatives. Antioxidants such as Vitamin E (tocopherols) and Vitamin C (ascorbic acid) are usually added. To avoid feeding your pup old dry food, buy from retailers with a rapid turnover. Whenever possible, use the products within six months of their manufacture date, and always store them in a sealed container in a cool, dry location. Curiously, natural antioxidants don't last as long as synthetic ones. If you choose a "naturally" preserved dry food, be particularly careful.

Canned or sachet foods, mixed with kibbles, remain popular. They are almost invariably nutritionally complete and highly palatable, but provide no exercise for the teeth and gums. Heat sterilization and vacuum sealing prevent spoilage, so no preservatives are needed. Manufacturers rarely state how many kilocalories (kcals) there are in their foods, but as a rough guideline, assume 1 kcal per gram (28 kcal per oz) of wet food. A call to the manufacturer's helpline will give you an exact answer for each product.

Alternative choices and extras

Dogs are natural carnivores and prefer meat in their diets but they are able to survive on a well-balanced vegetarian diet. If your beliefs compel you to follow this course, begin early. Commercially produced vegetarian diets are available, or you can create a balanced home-cooked diet. Get nutritional advice from a specialist, but as a general rule, what's balanced for us is also balanced for pups, although they need more protein, most readily available from beans and peas. Avoid tofu and other processed bean products as food sources, especially if you have a deep-chested pup (*see p. 198*).

If you have a cat and a pup, the chances are that your pup has already told you it prefers the cat's food to its own. Cats need more protein than dogs do, so while dog food does not meet a cat's nutritional requirements, a dog's nutritional requirements are almost always met by tasty, high-protein cat food. A pup simply converts the additional protein into available energy.

TEETHING SCHEDULE

Your dog starts puppyhood with 28 temporary or deciduous incisors, canines, and premolars; pups have no molars. Between 10 and 22 weeks, the incisors are shed and replaced. The baby canines and premolars are shed from as early as 16 weeks, with adult premolars appearing at 18–26 weeks and canines by 22–30 weeks. Molars emerge at 22–30 weeks, giving 42 adult teeth, 20 in the upper jaw and 22 in the lower jaw, which has two extra molars. New teeth are the whitest Hollywood white.

HUMAN FOODS CAN BE LETHAL TO DOGS

Dogs taste life and some tastes, especially of our little pleasures, affect dogs much more seriously than they affect us. Chocolate is the most common cause of severe food poisoning. The smaller your dog, the greater the risk from these foods, but regardless of your dog's size, avoid any of the following.

Chocolate: This contains theobromine which gravely affects the heart and nervous system. The darker the chocolate the higher the concentration. "Chocolate-flavoured" confectionary is not chocolate so, other than being high in sugar and therefore calories, is generally safe for dogs.

Peach and nectarine stones: These are easy to swallow and difficult to see on x-rays. A peach stone can come to a halt in the intestines, causing a life-threatening obstruction. Don't leave these fruit or their stones where a dog can find them.

Tofu and legumes: These can stimulate gas production, particularly dangerous in deep-chested breeds susceptible to life-threatening bloat.

Bread dough: Made with yeast, unbaked dough can expand in the stomach and lead to life-threatening bloat.

Caffeine drinks: Coffee and tea – but in my experience more frequently the "energy drinks" – can adversely, even dangerously affect the heart and nervous system of dogs.

Raisins and grapes: Although safe in small portions for some dogs these cause kidney failure in others. Just a single portion of grapes or raisins can be toxic, although the effect is usually cumulative.

Avocados: While safe for some dogs, in others these lead to fluid accumulating in the chest and associated breathing difficulties.

Onions, chives, and garlic: These are safe in occasional small quantities, but large amounts (or frequent small amounts) can cause serious anaemia.

Artificial sweetener xylitol: Commonly used in chewing gum, this can induce a sudden drop in blood sugar and associated neurological consequences.

Human vitamin supplements: Supplements are unnecessary for healthy dogs. Excess human supplements, depending on the formulation, can cause varying problems involving the digestive tract. Regular iron supplementation, for example, can cause serious constipation.

Alcohol: Even small amounts affect the brain, whether it comes from a bottle or naturally fermented fallen apples. I've treated one dog that endured a day-long coma from martinis fed to it by its owner.

Marijuana: This can cause extreme neurological and behavioural consequences in dogs. What you do with drugs is your business, but don't feed them to your dog and don't leave them where they can be found and eaten.

Too much of a good thing
Keep a supply of dog treat in your house, your coat pocket, your glove box. It reduces the temptation to reward with morself of human foods which aren't so good for your dog and can be dangerous.

Cat food is safe for healthy dogs, but it should be avoided if your dog needs a protein-restricted diet for medical reasons.

Other foods can be more troublesome. Take care with dairy products; pups produce an enzyme that digests milk, but by adulthood some dogs produce little of it. If cow's milk causes diarrhoea in your pup, and you still want to feed milk, try the lactose-free milk sold for lactose-sensitive people. Chocolate in excess is dangerous to dogs. The darker the chocolate, the higher the levels of theobromine, its poisonous constituent. Baking chocolate is most dangerous, while white chocolate is least. Just 100g (4oz) of baking chocolate can kill a dog under 4kg (9lb). Dog "chocolate" is low in theobromine or is not chocolate at all but chocolate-flavoured candy.

Know your food If your dog seems intolerant of some foodstuffs, or upset by small dietary changes, it's worth checking labels and often worth buying foods with a fixed formula.

Our own earliest natural diet was raw meats, fruits, and roots. Then we found that cooked food is not only often tastier, but safer, because cooking (or preserving with salt) kills bacteria. Cooked food also delivers more nutrition to our bodies than raw food, weight-for-weight, a definite evolutionary bonus. It's the same for dogs: their natural diet is raw body parts, including meat, fur, bones, and gut contents, but raw meat is no more necessary for them than it is for us. And it carries risks – to us as well as them. Around two per cent of dogs fed home-cooked or commercial food have the food poisoning bacteria *Salmonella typhimurium* in their faeces, but well over 30 per cent of dogs fed raw meat carry it. Because of the risks of bacterial contamination and (in some regions) parasites, raw meat for your dog is, generally speaking, more dangerous than cooked meat.

Scavenging and chew toys

Dogs are natural scavengers. Expect a pup that goes outdoors to find its own delicacies, from discarded junk food to animal faeces. These activities are normal in the biological sense, but they also dramatically increase the amount of bacteria, and sometimes parasites, in the intestines. Your dog needs to be trained to drop dangerous items (*see p.259*) but may need to be trained not to scavenge in the first place. The most effective way to cure coprophagia, or eating faeces, is by lacing them with an unpleasant taste. Inject a little of an offputting substance into a turd, and leave it for the pup to find and eat. It will naturally avoid repeating the unpleasant (but not harmful) experience. This also works for scavenging and unwanted chewing.

Ask your vet about which rawhide toys are safe and which aren't. Unless you're told otherwise, "chewies" like hooves, pig's ears, and rawhides should be supervision-only goodies. Dogs with powerful jaws (or stomachs where they should have brains) are inclined to eat them, and end up at the vet's with nasty stomach aches. Very hard rubber toys are safer and last longer.

Grooming your pup

All dogs may roll on smelly things like dead fish or fox droppings, so even if you have a smooth-coated pup, get it used to being brushed or bathed. Expect the first heavy moult in these months: many pups grow their adult hair during puppyhood, but some don't until adolescence or adulthood.

Smooth coats such as those of Dobermanns, Boxers, and Whippets are the easiest to maintain. Use a chamois, hound glove, or soft bristle brush, rubbing first against the lie of the coat and then with it to loosen and remove dead hair. Dense coats such as the Labrador's have an insulating undercoat and moult massive amounts. Use a bristle brush and finish by combing, especially through the thickest hair on the tail and neck. Treat wiry coats, such as the wire-haired Dachshund or Fox Terrier, in the same way, but also "strip" the longest fly-away hair monthly with a stripping comb. Three or four times a year have the coat reduced by a professional groomer.

Long, silky coats, such as those of the Yorkshire Terrier and Maltese, require careful daily brushing and combing. These breeds have little or no protective undercoat, so be particularly gentle. Long, dense coats, such as the Collie's, require twice-weekly brushing with a pin brush and combing with a wide-toothed comb. Excess hair needs monthly trimming. Shorter and less dense coats, such as the Golden Retriever's, need less attention: weekly brushing and combing plus twice yearly trimming of excess hair on their legs and between their toes should do. Some coats, such as the Poodle, Bichon Frise, and Miniature Schnauzer, need regular clipping. Unless you have a passion for topiary, leave this to professional groomers, and accustom your pup to this monthly or bi-monthly event now.

Like kids, pups love to muck around in sand, mud, and water, and the hairier your pup, the messier it will get. Remove dry mud with a bristle brush, comb, and chamois. Your dog needs its own towel for removing rain and snow; shower off sea salt. A water-filled washing up bowl is useful for cleaning feet. Dog hair is naturally self-cleaning, but not so self-cleaning that it never needs washing. If your dog rolls in fox droppings (the most alluring perfume to Bean), shampoo and rinse, not just to remove the stink. You dog has been where foxes are, and foxes are a common source of scabies mites. If you live where there are lots of burrs, keep either talcum powder or vegetable oil handy to help with removing them.

Bathing pups

Forget myths about never washing a dog. If your pup is smelly, wash it. If the smell returns within a week, see your vet. There's probably a skin problem. Washing cleans hair and skin but too much, especially with the wrong type of shampoo, can dry them and interfere with the skin's natural defences. There's rarely a need to wash your pup more than twice a month, but if someone in the house is allergic weekly washing with a mild shampoo helps. If it's warm enough, bathe outdoors using a spray attachment on the garden hose. If that water is too cold, bath large pups in your shower or bathtub, smaller ones in your sink. Baby shampoo or unscented shampoo is almost always safe. In a pinch, if your pup rolled in something foul and there's no shampoo around, mild washing-up liquid will do. If you plan to dry your pup using the low setting on a hair dryer, let it hear the dryer and give a food reward for calmness, then aim the dryer at the body and reward with a food treat before using it to dry. In warm weather, outdoor drying is fine; in cold weather, make sure your pup is absolutely dry before letting it go outdoors.

Daily routine Grooming keeps the coat tidy, reinforces your role as pack leader, and provides a once over check for any incipient health problems.

Pups need manicures

Pet pedicures Routine nail clipping is most likely to be necessary for lightweight dogs which don't naturally wear their claws down.

A young pup's nails are pin sharp for a good reason. Pups stimulate milk release by using their heads as battering rams and kneading with their forepaws. As they grow, kneading with sharp claws becomes uncomfortable, a trigger for the mother to start weaning her pups. Those needle-sharp, tights-tearing nails need blunting. Your vet will do this, but you can do it at home, especially if you plan to routinely cut your dog's nails. The first time, your pup will not resent what you're doing, although it may squirm. Turn nail cutting into a positive experience by liberally giving food treats while you trim. Start by holding the paw and giving a food treat, then hold the paw, cut the nail and give a food treat, and always finish with a game, so that your pup enjoys the experience.

Cut nails when they're softest, after bathing, or soften them for a minute in warm water. Use a sharp guillotine-type clipper and replace it twice yearly. If the nail is white, cut in front of the visible pink "quick" which is filled with sensitive nerves. If the nail is brown or black and you can't see the quick, cut only the thin, talon-like tip, not the wide part of the nail. Have a blood-stopping powder or pencil, available from pet shops or vets, handy in case you cut the quick. If you have a large or giant breed and plan to keep the nails especially tidy, use an emery board or file on rough edges.

Teething and dental care

During puppyhood the milk teeth are replaced by adult teeth. More often than not you never see the shed milk teeth (they are usually swallowed), but you may notice a fetid smell to the breath due to gum damage when the larger ones are lost. Teething is usually uneventful, but in many small breeds the milk teeth fall out late, or never do. The large eye teeth or canines often remain, and the adult canines, unable to grow into their normal positions, are pushed either forwards or inwards. Check your pup's teeth at around 24 weeks. If you see new, large teeth together with solidly rooted, smaller milk teeth, contact your vet; in some circumstances it is best to carefully remove the milk teeth. In larger breeds such as retrievers, the growth of the upper and lower jaw can temporarily get out of synch, and the erupting adult teeth are not in ideal positions. This usually corrects itself before adolescence.

If you are willing and able to care for your pup's teeth, start brushing now. Use a soft, child's toothbrush and an up-and-down action, giving a food treat each time you brush initially, and later intermittently. Concentrate on the side teeth, the molars, premolars, and canines; these are where plaque is most likely to build up, leading to gum disease and eventual loss of teeth. Gum disease is perhaps the most common reason why I anaesthetize adult dogs. And while typical pet health insurance covers most conditions, many policies exclude dental problems.

Tooth wisdom Training your pup to allow you to brush its teeth not only improves its general health, it will save you visits to the vet.

Emptying the anal sacs

Some pups, especially spaniels, retrievers, and Dachshunds, start dragging their butts when they're a few months old. Most people assume their pup has worms, but this is rarely the problem. The anal glands (*see p.118*) may fill excessively during puppyhood, especially if there has been a prolonged episode of diarrhoea early in life. The fullness irritates the dog, who responds by dragging the butt or intensely licking the anus. Both can be successful; you'll know by the disgusting fishy smell that envelops your dog. While most dogs never have anal gland problems, some need routine help. Your vet can empty them routinely every few months, or show you how to do it, which is easier on lean dogs than on those with massive thigh muscles.

Wear rubber gloves and place your pup on some newspaper. Lift the tail straight up and place your fingers at four o'clock and eight o'clock on either side of the anus. The region will feel like a small grape. Give a food treat, remove your hand and let the tail drop. Repeat, but this time give a firm squeeze, with your fingers finishing at three o'clock and nine o'clock. Immediately give another food treat. A watery, smelly discharge will drip onto the newspaper. Let your pup smell it. Once you are adept at squeezing the sacs, do so through a few pieces of kitchen roll to catch the discharge.

Slippery customer Warning: no matter how much of a water lover it is, you should assume that your pup will not placidly submit to being bathed. Second warning: your pup will almost invariably want to roll on the ground or carpet once washed!

Your growing pup's health

In their prime Your dog is a marvellous collection of self-regulating systems, and most of the time they keep it healthy without intervention. But even when you have a young, vital dog, you are likely to see quite bit of your vet to deal with inoculations, infestations, injuries, and upsets.

When choosing your vet, it's worthwhile considering factors other than convenience and cost. You're at the beginning of what will hopefully be a long relationship that will last from puppyhood to old age and inevitable death. Make sure there is genuine 24-hour coverage. Visit clinics and ask questions, get advice from dog-owning friends. If you have certain ethics, you may feel more comfortable at a clinic whose staff share your feelings. If you had niggles on your initial visit for vaccinations, make an appointment to discuss them. If you're not happy with their response, try another recommended clinic. Concerning costs, the more time-consuming or detailed the diagnostics or treatments, the greater the costs. Think about either getting insurance or finding out what it would cost and putting that amount yearly into savings you can call upon if unexpected costs arise.

Once upon a time, your local vet did everything – that time included my first decade in practice, and I loved it. Being omnicompetent wasn't just a boost to the ego, it was mentally stimulating to surgically repair a cow's twisted stomach, work out why a cat was peeing in suitcases, mend a dog's bones after a road traffic accident, reconstruct the urinary tract on a blocked tomcat, determine why a dog was losing its hair, find the reason a pond of Koi carp were egg-bound, diagnose the cause of stone-like deposits in a parrot's nose, and deliver spring lambs, all in the same week. Vets loved this Dr. Doolittle fantasy just as much as pet owners did. Today, I make my diagnoses based on book knowledge and previous experience, but I've also got a constellation of "ologists" I can call upon, people a lot more knowledgeable in their specialities that I'll ever be.

I see pups and their owners frequently at this time, because pups have not yet built up the energy reserves needed to overcome relatively minor problems, or developed the sense to rest after injury. Their owners are also learning or re-learning the difference between what can be handled at home and what needs veterinary intervention. Regardless of the primary reason a pup is brought in to me, I'm always asked routine puppy care questions, and almost always I'm asked about how to know when a pup is in pain.

The body's defensive fronts

Any part of your pup's body that's in direct contact with the outside world has a superb ability to repair and regenerate itself. I don't mean just the skin. The entire gastrointestinal tract, from the opening at one end to the opening at the other, has similar powers of recovery, as do the respiratory and urinary systems. The skin acts as a physical barrier, while in the gastrointestinal tract microbes are killed by saliva and stomach acid, and toxic substances are either denatured in the stomach or intestines or detoxified by the liver. Both the skin and the gastrointestinal tract are also populated by troops of cells belonging to the immune system, which identify, attack, and destroy invaders. This is a brilliant system, and what I do as a vet is try to maintain it so that it works as efficiently as possible. During puppyhood it usually works exceedingly well, and repair is swift.

Vomiting and diarrhoea are the most common reasons pups are taken to the vet, scratching the second most common, and limping or hurting the third. Coughing and sneezing are a distant fourth. I'm inevitably asked to do something to stop these things happening, to overcome diarrhoea, stop scratching or coughing, get a temperature down, but that's not always in a pup's interest. To get technical, none of these are illnesses: they're natural defensive mechanisms to rid the pup's body of potential dangers or protect it from further damage. Vomiting and diarrhoea expel undigestible matter or bacteria from the gastrointestinal tract. Scratching and licking remove parasites and potential pathogens. Coughing or sneezing expel foreign or unwanted material from the respiratory tract (although they also spread the pathogens). Even fever creates an environment in which it is easier for the immune system to kill pathogens.

Itchy and scratchy Every dog itches from time to time, but serious scratching can be cause by many things from fleas to a contact allergy or even a food allergy.

The immune system

If a pathogen (a bacteria, virus, fungus, or yeast) gets past these natural barriers, it's confronted by the second line of defence, the white blood cells. Even after 40 years as a vet I'm still awestruck by how adept this system is. It is challenged every second of every day, yet seldom fails until a dog is old. Cells called macrophages (literally "big eaters") circulate around the body and engulf bacteria and dirt that got through broken skin, assisted by aptly named "natural killer cells" and "armed helper T cells". Macrophages also identify pathogens to other white cells that paint chemical labels on them, targeting them for attack. To prevent this system from attacking a pup's own body, the surface of every cell in your pup's body carries a sort of cellular photo ID, called its "major histocompatability complex" (MHC).

Sometimes – very rarely – even this system is overwhelmed, but there's another back-up line of defence. White blood cells called "memory T cells" also patrol the body. When these cells meet a pathogen they've met before, they instantly remember and stimulate the production of antibodies, killing the pathogens before they cause infection. This is how vaccination works. Primary inoculations with modified pathogens that don't cause illness exposed your pup's immune system to such threats as rabies, distemper, and parvovirus. It took only two weeks after an inoculation for the body to produce memory T cells that recognize the pathogen. Now, if one of those viruses tries to invade, the defences respond instantly.

These defences work almost faultlessly in most, but not all pups. For reasons that are still poorly understood, some breeds have systems that over-react. They produce an inflammatory response to environmental stuff that is of no threat at all, such as flea saliva, birch pollen, grass sap, or meat protein. If the skin is involved the dog gets itchy; if the gastrointestinal tract is involved the dog develops diarrhoea. Later in life, once a pup is mature, some cells can seem to "lose" their photo ID and the immune system turns on them. For example, in some lines of Cocker spaniels, the immune system can attack and destroy the red blood cells, leading to a life-threatening anaemia. The immune system can also target the thyroid glands, in Cocker Spaniels, Golden Retrievers and many other breeds and crossbreeds.

Pain is not an illness

Pups hurt themselves, and when they do it's distressing and frustrating, because you can't explain that the pain will pass. Pups usually hurt because of physical injuries, such as running into something, jumping where they shouldn't have jumped or, as frequently happens, being accidentally stepped on by us. As a boy I accidentally stepped on the paw of my 12-week-old Yorkshire Terrier, Sparkie. The local farm vet examined her, pulled the toothpick from between his teeth and splinted the broken toe bone with it. That's when I had my first inkling that veterinary medicine might be fun.

Pain is a defence. Pain protects. Pain ensures your pup will stop doing what it's doing, and probably acts as a reminder not to do the same thing again. Continuing pain leads to resting the damaged tissue and buys time for repair. Curiously, the amount of pain your pup feels is not in proportion to the amount of damage done. Damaged cells release chemicals called prostaglandins, which stimulate nerve receptors throughout the body. According to the "gate control" theory, information travelling to the brain has to pass through nerve "gates" controlled by a number of factors from other stimuli to emotion. These can raise the levels of endorphins, the body's natural pain killers. This is why in the emotional intensity of a dog fight, the combatants fight on despite obvious injuries. Your pup's brain interprets and sets a biological priority to incoming information, which is partly learned and partly inherited and so varies from pup to pup and breed to breed. Cavalier King Charles Spaniels are particularly pain-sensitive: a simple inoculation, even if the vaccine has been warmed to body temperature, may cause a Cavalier pup to squeal. At the opposite end of the spectrum, most bull-type terriers are pain-insensitive. They rarely give any indication they have felt an injection, even if the vial is taken directly from the fridge.

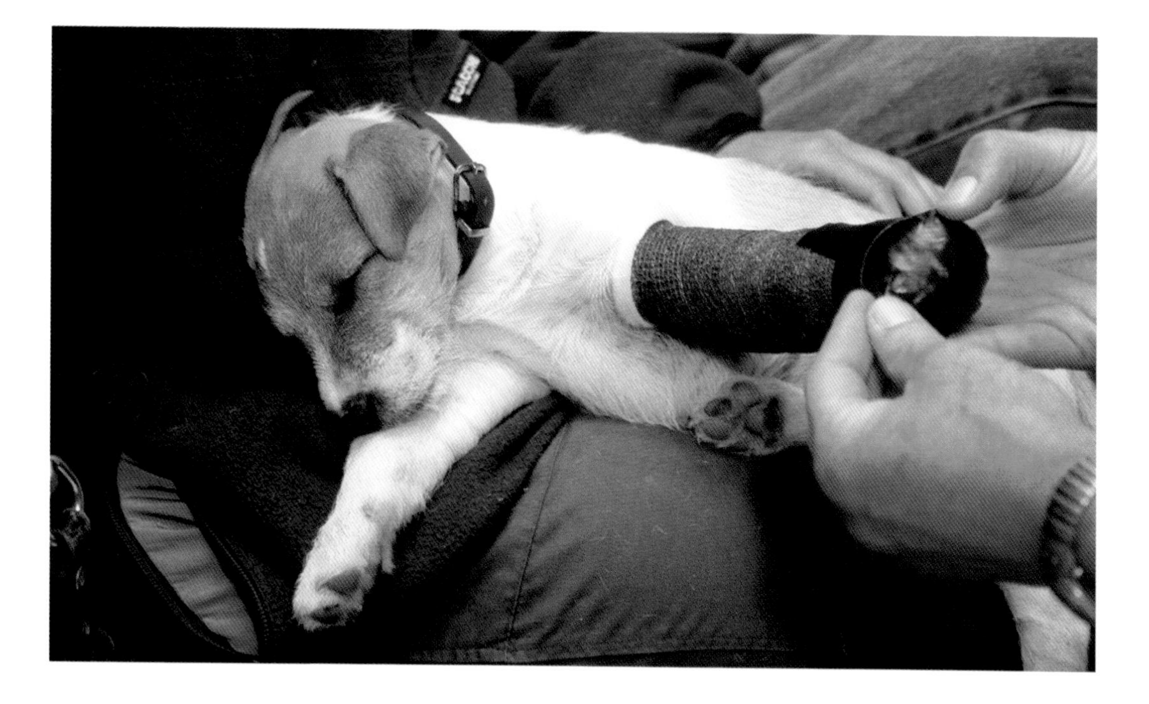

Out for the count Some pups get themselves into serious trouble. Remember even the most sweet-natured dog may snap if it is injured and you touch where it hurts. Handle with care and take an injured dogs to the vet; at a clinic it can be sedated if necessary for treatment.

Assessing pain

"She doesn't cry so how do I know if she's in pain?" I'm routinely asked variations of this question. We need to watch how dogs are behaving to determine how much pain they're experiencing. Crying, or screaming or shrieking, only occurs when pain is sudden and intense. When you bring your pup to me I learn as much about its state of health from what you tell me as I do from physical examination. I depend on you to notice unusual behaviour. Watch for personality changes including unexpected aggression, apparent depression, fear, anxiety or timidness, unexpected quietness or indifference. Any of these changes may mean your pup is uncomfortable or ill: increased sleeping or resting, increased irritability, reduced interest in playing, reduced interest in you, reduced alertness or responsiveness, tiring more easily, clinging to you, hiding, apprehension, resentment at being touched, unusual odours, overexcitement, disorientation, changed breathing rhythms, or changed eating, drinking or toilet habits.

At my clinic we developed a scale to help us both during routine physical examinations and after surgical procedures to determine how much pain a dog is in. Most of their categories can be used by you at home.

Symptom and treatment
Limping tells you a limb is injured, but its real purpose is to rests an injured muscle or joint or keep weight off a paw with a thorn in it.

DEMEANOUR	
Happy and content	No pain
Quiet or indifferent	Possible pain
Nervous, anxious or fearful	Possible pain
Depressed or unexpectedly aggressive	Probable pain
Completely uninterested in us	Probable pain

VOCALIZING	
Using voice normally	No pain
Unexpectedly quiet	Pain
Groan, cry, shriek or scream	Severe pain

MOBILITY	
Normal gait and movement	No pain
Walking slower	Significant pain
Lame, stiff or limping	Significant pain
Reluctant to jump up or down	Significant pain
Reluctant to move	Significant pain
Refuses to move	Severe pain
Shaking or trembling	Severe pain

POSTURE	
Normal	No pain
Tucked abdomen or hanging tail	Significant pain
Sitting or lying in a tense position	Significant pain
Hunched	Significant pain
Rigid	Severe pain

RESPONSE TO TOUCH

Behaves normally	No pain
Flinches	Significant pain
Guards, growls	Significant pain
Snaps, cries, screams or moans	Severe pain

The University of Glasgow Veterinary School developed a different system for hospitalized dogs. Most of it applies to our own dogs in our own homes. A pup with signs of mild pain should be seen by a vet within 24 hours, with moderate pain within 4 hours, and those in severe pain immediately.

NO PAIN – Happy and bouncy, eating, sitting, lying, sleeping, and walking normally.

MILD PAIN – Generally quiet, still eating and sleeping, wagging the tail when approached but may limp during walking, tend to guard the tender area (such as the surgical site), and react to being physically examined.

MODERATE PAIN – Depressed (keeping the head down), may tremble, uncomfortable, sitting or lying in a tense position (standing with abdomen tucked and tail hanging down or lying with all four legs stretched out), lying but not sleeping. May or may not eat, may cry, be slow to interact with caretaker, may pay attention to the wound and react to wound pressure (by looking back, licking or trying to bite).

SEVERE PAIN – Continuous vocalizing, not interested in surroundings but may respond to direct voice (may stop crying, may turn head or eyes). May be restless, changing its position continuously or may refuse to move (urinates and defecates without moving). Sometimes may be quiet or may be shaking, refuses to eat.

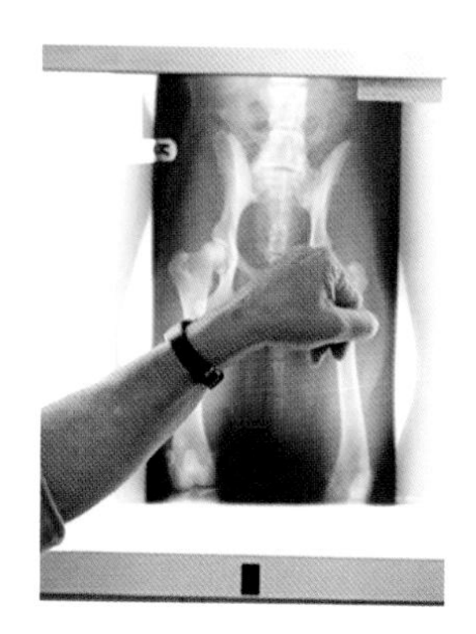

See through If you suspect a serious injury, the best way to be sure is to take a good look. The range of diagnostic tools for animals is a little more limited than it is for us, but it's improving all the time.

Train yourself to carry out head-to-tail inspections

Regular physical examinations reinforce that you're the genuine top dog, but also help me. A pup already familiar with someone flexing its joints, examining its paws and tail, or opening its mouth is more likely to let me do these things. At first quickly inspect only one part, then reward with a food treat. Each day, repeat the initial inspection and add another part of the body to your examination, always rewarding your pup for being obedient and staying still. It may take several weeks before your pup fully accepts all of these inspections, especially of the feet and anogenital regions.

When you examine your pup, run your hands over the head, cheeks, jaws, and throat. Check the eyes for redness, tear overflow, discharge, cloudiness or obvious injuries. Look inside the ears for redness, odour, discharge, excess wax, or changes to the ear flap. Check the nose for discharge. It's usually cool and wet but a hot, dry nose does not necessarily mean there is a problem. Noses often go dry when pups sleep. Examine the lips for inflammation, dryness or odour, especially the folds on "lippy"

breeds such as hounds and spaniels. Lift them and check the teeth and gums on both sides for inflammation or unpleasant odour. If your pup has facial skin folds, gently lift them to check for redness, discharge, or odour.

Once you've completed the head, move on to the torso and limbs. Check for sensitivity, injuries, or stuff that simply shouldn't be there. Gently turn the head up, down, left, and right; resistance could mean pain. Run your hands over the neck, chest, and back, feeling for stickiness, bumps, or dry matts of hair. Frequently part the hair and check the skin for redness, damage, or signs of parasites (such as shiny black flea droppings). Run your hands over the hips and groin and down each leg, checking that everything feels symmetrical. Flex each limb; there should be no resentment. Examine the feet and pads – pups often don't like this, so have extra treats ready – and check for damage or debris and the state of the nails. Feel along the tail then lift it up to check the anus, and on females the vulva. Some female pups, especially those from muscular, short-haired breeds such as Pugs, Dobermanns, and Bull-type terriers, develop a dry, crusty, vaginal discharge called juvenile vaginitis. This is often resistant to treatment by cleansing with antiseptic or systemic antibiotics, but almost invariably resolves when

Know your breed If you've picked a breed with prominent eyes, expect to spend a bit more time looking after them and dealing with problems: regular checks will find these early when they can be dealt with most easily.

a pup has her first season. On males check the prepuce for redness or discharge; after puberty, a discharge called smegma is normal.

Keep an eye on toilet habits. By mid-puppyhood your pup will have developed rituals for urination and defecation, and you'll have an excellent idea of both the frequency and the quantities, which vary and can sometimes be Olympian. Bean produces several poops in quick succession in the morning, but my daughter's Labrador Lola (and Lola's mother Inca) produce single poops so large they don't fit in commercial dog poop bags.

Parasite control

Many pups inherit worms from their mothers, just before birth or in the first milk they take. Your pup's breeder will have started a course of worming and your vet will have continued it during primary inoculations. The risks from internal and external parasites vary not only according to location but also according to lifestyle. Pups that travel from Starbucks to Starbucks in shoulder bags have a lower risk than my pup, who regularly visits wooded areas where deer ticks abound. You and your vet will be able to tailor a parasite control for your pup according to risk.

Fleas need blood meals before they can reproduce, so love thin-skinned pups even more than thicker-skinned adult dogs. Dog fleas (*Ctenocephalides canis*) are rare; most dogs suffer from cat fleas (*C. felis*). They can complete their life cycle in just over two weeks but stretch it to an amazing 21 months when food is scarce. In other words, a house occupied by a cat almost two years ago may still have eggs or larvae capable of producing adult fleas. Fleas thrive wherever the humidity is above 50 per cent and the temperature above 20°C (68°F), but don't like altitude over around 1,500m (5,000ft), or Alaska; so if you want to avoid them move to where its high or cold, otherwise expect them to cause problems. Flea saliva can trigger intense skin irritation and is, in my experience, the cause of more skin problems than anything else, perhaps even everything else.

Garlic, brewer's yeast, tea tree oil, ultrasonic collars – I'm afraid none of these deter fleas. You will only control them by using insect growth regulators, insect development inhibitors, or insect killers. If your pup has fleas, your home needs treatment too. Use an insect growth regulator such as methoprene or pyriproxyfen in your home and an insect killer such as fipronil, selamectin, or imidacloprid on your pup. Take special care if you use a permethrin insect killer; these are safe on dogs but very toxic to cats. Vacuum your home thoroughly (and immediately dispose of the vacuum cleaner contents) before any treatments; this removes fleas and raises the pile on carpets, making penetration by spray easier. Spray insect growth regulator on your carpets, especially under furniture, and in crevises on hard floors. Apply a spot-on or spray flea killer to your pup, and if you have a cat treat it too, because that's the source of your pup's fleas.

Cohabiting pests Only one quarter of a flea's life is spent on a host animal, when it is an adult. If your dog has fleas, your home has fleas.

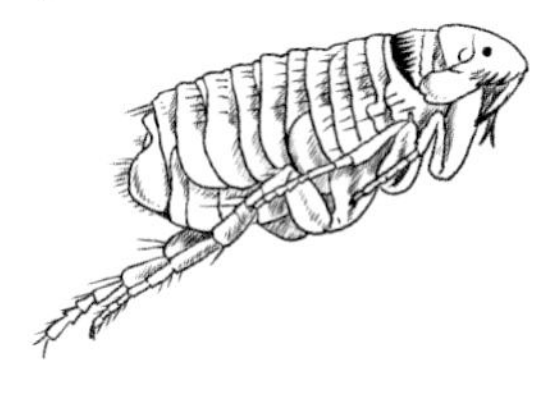

Ticks are tiny blood-suckers that lie in wait in grass or low vegetation, hop on your passing pup or your own legs, embed themselves in the skin, gorge until they swell like balloons, and finally drop off. In temperate climates they are most active from spring until autumn, in warm climates they suck all year. The danger lies not in the bites themselves but in the diseases they can transmit, some of which produce life-long illnesses or are life threatening. If your pup visits places where ticks exist, use a preventative spray, spot-on, or collar recommended by your vet. And if you go with your pup, tuck your trousers into your socks.

Consider neutering now

This is a topic I'll cover in Adolescence, but I want to touch on it now because in many instances puppyhood is the right time to neuter a dog. Neutering – spaying females or castrating male pups – is an emotional subject, influenced by our gender, religion, culture, traditions, even what our neighbours think. Neutering has two functions. By removing the organs that produce eggs or sperm, it prevents unwanted pups. By removing the source of most sex hormones, it eliminates many behaviours associated with sex hormones, for example mounting or territorial urine-marking in males.

Castrating involves a single, small incision just in front of the scrotum, through which both testicles are removed. A vasectomy, cutting the spermatic cords but leaving the testicles, is very uncommon in dogs because it doesn't alter behaviour, which is the reason people have dogs castrated.

Spaying a female is more invasive. In most instances an incision is made in the abdomen through which both ovaries and the uterus are removed. Tying the fallopian tubes to prevent conception is rarely if ever done in dogs. Increasingly, females are spayed by removing only the ovaries via keyhole surgery. This is much less invasive, but the long term consequences of leaving the womb are not yet known; the worry is that it may become a site of infection (a pyometra), requiring further surgery.

Spaying a female before her first season eliminates a variety of life-threatening risks, such as pyometra and cancers of the breast or reproductive system, raising life-expectancy by an average of 18 months compared with unspayed dogs. That sounds great, but unfortunately very little in medicine is black and white: there is some statistical evidence that early spaying is also associated with increased risk of developing an under-active thyroid later in life. Spaying before puberty perpetuates the hormonally neutral personality of females, and I usually recommend it unless there are medical reasons (such as juvenile vaginitis or an infantile vulva) why a pup should have one season.

Castrating males at any age does not affect life expectancy, because malignant testicular or prostate cancer is uncommon, so the decision is based entirely on their behaviour. Sort of. An excellent study of older dogs in Spain revealed that older females were more likely to develop senile dementia than older males, and older neutered males were more likely to develop senile dementia than intact males. The researchers concluded that testosterone – male hormone – may have some protective qualities, helping to preserve brain function. If a dog's owners have decided they prefer to have a neutered male I usually wait until the pup starts lifting his leg to pee before neutering. This happens earlier in male pups living with other males than it does with male pups raised in all-female dog households.

Build on the basics As your pup grows up, its ability to concentate should increase. This means you can extend your training sessions a little and do some more advanced work as time goes on.

Continuing basic training

Strangely, there was a time when experts recommended that active obedience training not begin until the end of the period that I'm calling true puppyhood, but that's utterly wrong. At the end of the socialization period and the very beginning of puppyhood, or canine childhood, your pup still overwhelmingly depends on you and is eager to please you. Simple obedience training is easiest now, and should gradually become more extensive during puppyhood. At the start of this period, a typical pup can only concentrate for one or two minutes. By the end of puppyhood, sessions can be as long as ten minutes for thoughtful, listening pups, and up to five minutes for more reactive individuals with wandering minds.

During your first visits outdoors, most pups will also run back to you when you call them, simply for security, but by the end of puppyhood they become much more independent. Between now and then, your puppy needs to be taught to return to you when you give either a verbal or a hand signal command. A pup who routinely goes outdoors can get into a whole lot more trouble, and you need to reduce the risks. That means training to wait, to leave, drop, or trade items, and to walk beside you on or off the lead. This is a lot of training, but a natural continuation of the basic training you did before three months of age. Don't attempt any new basic training until a pup reliably comes to you, sits, stays, and stands or lies on command.

A pup's intrinsic personality influences not just willingness to listen and learn but also speed of learning. Bold pups can take longer to train than insecure ones, simply because their minds wander. Some pups instinctively question, challenge, or just disregard you. In the wild, these "go-alone" or assertive pups would eventually either make stupid mistakes and die or become command-givers rather than command-receivers. The littermates who learned by watching and listening were more likely to survive, and to continue to be content responding to instruction and direction as adults.

Now that you have a better understanding of your pup's personality and body language, you should also be better at anticipating what it's thinking about doing. This means you can intervene with your commands at the thinking stage, before your pup acts. Gradually increase the length of your sessions. Actively train when both of you are mentally alert, and start new ideas in quiet places, only moving to more distracting locations once you've succeeded there. Take rewards with you when you go out. You may need a small container for smelly rewards if you don't want all the dogs in the vicinity pushing their noses into you. As your pup matures and becomes more confident you may find being consistent with rewards and discipline more challenging. Use your pup's name carefully to get attention, and follow this with a command. Concentrate on your timing; your accuracy should be pretty good by now.

You'll get frustrated. I promise. But remember, you're the one with the bigger cortex. Don't get flustered. Don't get angry. Overcome your need to get even when your dog does something irritating. When training is going belly-up, just end the session there and then, on a positive note.

The vocabulary of dog training

Academics prefer the word "conditioning" to "learning", but both mean the same thing. Humans have a greater capacity to learn by watching and observing than any other species, because 30 per cent of the white matter in our brains is the pyramidal system, the complex of cells needed for skilled voluntary movement. This complex is poorly developed in the dog, so they are nowhere near as good as us at learning by observing; but they are still most open to it in puppyhood.

CLASSICAL CONDITIONING trains the dog's body to respond to some sight, sound, or smell. Pavlov trained dogs to salivate at the sound of a bell by ringing it when they were fed; I give liver-flavoured vitamin tablets to all pups when they visit my clinic. We classically condition dogs actively, but they also classically condition themselves.

OPERANT CONDITIONING is giving a reward for an action, and routine dog training. When you say "Sit", your dog sits, and you reward, that is operant conditioning. Unfortunately, when the postman arrives, your dog barks, and the postman leaves, that is also operant conditioning. Your role is to control operant conditioning, both by training and by intervening if you see your dog is training itself in unwanted ways.

REINFORCER is the word academics use for reward.

AVERSIVES do things your dog doesn't like. One excellent aversive is a marker disc, a ring of discs you toss on the floor to get your dog's attention. Trainers will show you how to time it. Choke collars are aversives for incompetents who don't know how to train their dogs; they damage windpipes. A half-check collar, which is wide-meshed fabric on the windpipe side, is acceptable for some rambunctious pups. Shock collars are painful aversives. Believe me: I've tested them on myself. Don't use them. They belong in the hands of professional trainers when the only alternative is that the dog will be put down. Ultrasonic or aerosol collars should also only be used under the instructions of a competent trainer.

EXTINCTION means losing a behaviour. If you stop rewarding your dog for coming on command, that behaviour is lost, or becomes extinct.

SHAPING means refining a natural behaviour into a highly specific one. For example, a dog naturally follows a scent. This behaviour is shaped by giving rewards for following only specific scents, such as game or drugs.

CHAINING means learning to carry out a sequence of events in a specific order. Learning to retrieve really means learning to chain together a sequence of commands – go to, pick up, bring back, drop.

HABITUATION means getting used to something that might otherwise be either distracting or frightening. Bean sits calmly while noisy traffic thunders past because during puppyhood she was habituated through exposure. Constant exposure is technically called "flooding".

SYSTEMATIC DESENSITIZATION is a form of gradual habituation used when retraining. If Bean had been fearful of traffic noise, I would have found the distance at which she wasn't frightened and rewarded her for not showing fear. Day by day I would have gradually reduced that distance, always rewarding her lack of fear, systematically desensitizing her.

Extend your spoken commands and hand signals

Like most pups, Bean understood a variety of spoken words by three months. She knew the name we used, Lucca Bean, (her formal given name is LL Bean). She understood the words *Come*, *Sit*, *Stay*, *Stand*, *Down*, and *Hurry up* as well as *Good girl*, *Eat*, and *Out*. She understood our release word *OK*, and our neutral word *Wrong*, as well as our more negative *No*, which we use only for serious misdemeanours. During the coming months your dog will learn just as many new words: *Wait*, *Walk*, *Steady*, *Off*, *Leave*, *Drop*, *Find*, *Fetch*, *Trade*, and *Go to bed*. Any pup can easily understand an extensive vocabulary, as long as you use words in the right circumstances.

Inside your home or your back garden it's been easy to get your pup's attention by calling its name and then giving a verbal command. Out in a large park, hand signals are wonderful, if only to save your voice when your pup is a long distance from you. With your family, decide the exact words and signals you want to use then write them down, copy them for everyone, and make sure everyone sings from the same songsheet all the time: one of the problems we had with Bean was that I said "Down" when I trained Bean to lie down, and Julia said it when Bean jumped up to greet her.

Clicker training needs a teacher

Clicker training accelerates classical conditioning. Your pup learns to associate a meaningless sound – a click – with something rewarding, usually a tasty food treat. To associate the click sound with the pleasant reward, you repeatedly sound the clicker then give a food treat a few seconds after the click sound. The clicker is concealed in your hand: you're using it for its noise, not as a visible prop. Timing the click is critical, because it must underline the behaviour that you want to reinforce, emphasize to your pup that it has done well and will be rewarded, and indicate that whatever you're doing has just ended. After a click and a reward you'll be starting something new. Don't pet your pup during sessions, because touch is distracting, or give verbal praise, because the clicker does the talking.

Once your pup understands that the click is associated with a reward you have two alternative ways of using it. The first is to wait for your dog to do what you want, such as sitting, then click and give the food treat. The second is to lure your dog into doing what you want, then click and give the food treat. Don't wait for a perfect sit: if your pup's bum is moving into a sit position, click and reward. You'll be able to refine or "shape" the action. Think of the click as the equivalent of saying "YES!" and punching the air; it should have that emphasis to your pup. If your pup is frightened of the click sound, stop using it; if your pup gets on with the clicker, stop a training session while your pup is still deeply interested.

If this sounds complicated it isn't. A clicker is essentially more accurate than spoken words as a reinforcer of behaviour. Clicker training, when done accurately, is less stressful both for you and your dog, but I believe it's a training method that must be started under the supervision of someone experienced in its use. A book can explain why and how it works, but only hands-on training teaches exactly when to use the clicker. If you want to use clicker training, employ an experienced clicker trainer for an hour of one-

Clicker It's a simple gadget, but it has a powerful effect. Clicker training needs live help to get started, but the principle is simple and sound.

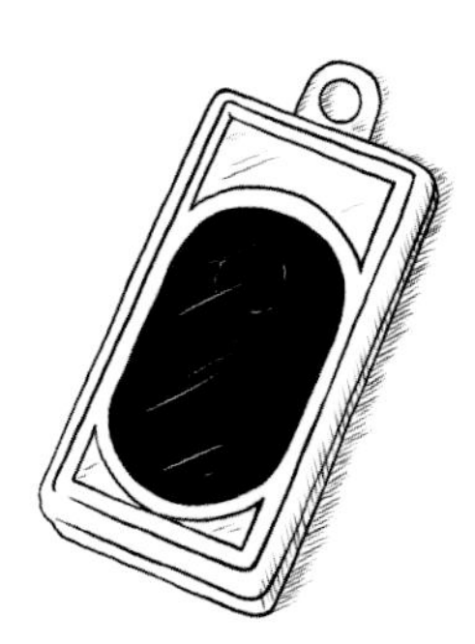

to-one training. Clickers are used only during the training stage of learning: once a pup does what you want, use of the clicker fades away and you replace it with a simple verbal command.

Enrol in a puppy class

Puppy play school, also called puppy classes, puppy parties, or puppy kindergarten, are pre-school for pups, an opportunity to develop social skills with other pups and with other people. As far as I'm concerned there's no better investment of your time or money than in joining well-run weekly puppy classes. These are usually restricted to fully vaccinated pups over 12 weeks old; some are for pups from 12 to 20 weeks of age, others are for any pre-pubertal pups. The trainers give you and your pup professional help with continuing basic training. At well-run classes there's one trainer for every six dogs. The shyest, gentlest pups are initially placed together in a smaller group (usually with a "perfect" pup who helps ginger them into a little activity) and if any pup is genuinely frightened, that one initially sits on the sidelines and just watches until it's confident enough to join in. Sometimes there's a very forceful and dominant pup that always plays to win, and at well-run classes the trainers will take that pup's owner aside and arrange special training so that the bossy pup doesn't disrupt the class. Noisy barkers also get remedial attention. Poorly run classes can be chaotic, but in well-run classes you're being trained in how to train your dog.

Look for instructors who are members of a recognized and respected association such as the Association of Professional Dog Trainers (APDT) or the Association of Professional Behaviour Counsellors (APBC). Ask your vet or the owner of a well-behaved dog to recommend a class. Good classes are restricted to pups within a specific age group, and cover a set curriculum over six to eight weeks, with classes lasting around an hour and "homework" for you and your pup between sessions. A pup's entire human family is encouraged to attend, and there is free play among small groups of pups.

Using play for training

Playing creates long-lasting, trusting bonds, and the better your dog trusts you, the easier further training will be. Games mix the business of training with the pleasure of playing. Your pup doesn't differentiate between them, but simply focuses on you because there's always the possibility that, out of nowhere, a chance to play may happen. Use games to reinforce standard obedience and reward good behaviour, to learn how your dog thinks and how willing it is to interact with you. When focused on a specific task, like repeatedly returning a tennis ball, or playing hide-and-seek with treats or toys, your pup is also safely releasing pent-up mental and physical energy. That makes the times when you can't interact with your dog – because you've got your own life – much less stressful. Think about what rules and regulations you want to apply to games with your pup. Remember that you're in charge, at least in theory, so you write the rulebook. My suggestions are listed over the page.

Call of the wide Only take your training practice out into open spaces once your commands are consistently obeyed at home. And if your pup is distracted away from home, get enthusiastic, get excited, get theatrical, but get its attention back to you, your voice and your hand signals.

- You decide when to play, where to play, what to play with, and when play ends. Start with short play periods and stop while your pup is still interested. If your pup tries to instigate play and you're happy to oblige, give an obedience command first.
- Think theatrically, and make your body language and voice exciting and appealing, but always keep it in proportion to your dog's excitement. Don't wind it up too much.
- Choose toys carefully, because pups in particular find the weight, texture, and smell of some toys much more attractive than others.
- Maximise natural preferences, integrating what your dog enjoys – fetching, digging, rolling, following a scent – into games.
- Toys belong to you. Keep all game toys out of your pup's reach. Bring them out only at game times, keeping them out of sight (and if possible out of scenting range) until play time.
- Keep toys low to the ground. This removes the incentive for your pup to jump up to them.
- Stop play immediately if your pup jumps up, mouths you, or refuses to drop once that command is learned. Game over until the next time.
- Know your pup's physical and mental limits and avoid physical dangers. Don't play jumping-in-the-air games while your pup is still growing.

Work or play? You might think of it as retrieve training, but your dog probably sees it as a fun game where you obligingly throw toys for it. Don't be too obliging though: you should decide what to throw, and if it isn't a toy you brought with you it should preferably be a stick that you find, not one suggested by your dog. You're in charge.

There for the making A dog that finds, retrieves, and gives isn't the exclusive preserve of those involved in field sports or showing; it's available to anyone willing to put in some time and effort. Of course, it helps if you have an amenable breed, like a gundog.

Start with hide-and-seek

This game satisfies your pup's need to investigate or hunt. With your pup out of sight, place a few dog treats around the room. Let your pup in, tap your finger on the floor by a treat and as it is found, say "Find it". Repeat this with each of the treats. Once your pup reliably responds to "Find it" by searching and finding easy-to-find treats, make the treats more difficult to find, for example behind furniture, in open paper bags, or in food-dropping toys. Your pup can even be trained to search for you, hiding behind a tree.

Keep quiet and let your dog use its nose to to find the treats on its own. Don't show it where treats are once it has the idea it should look for them. If it naturally brings back a food-dropping toy to show you, give praise: your pup is now well on the way to retrieve training (*see pp. 260*). For nose work games, start your pup using its nose by encouraging it to find its dinner. If you're the hidden object, keep quiet and let your pup work out where you are: finding you is a huge reward. Play this game often and you'll find that more and more your pup will keep checking to locate you on your walks.

Introducing a dog walker, minder, or sitter

Puppyhood and adolescence can be fraught times, and your pup needs consistent indoor and outdoor training during these months. Inconsistency creeps in when other people are responsible for raising your dog. You can only rely on others when your pup is properly trained to walk on the lead.

Professional dog walkers are available virtually anywhere with both dogs and busy owners willing to pay someone to exercise their canine buddies. They typically have several dogs to walk, and although conscientious walkers exercise only a small number of dogs at a time, usually no more than four, they still don't always have the time for the one-to-one attention that a pup demands. Only let a dog walker exercise your pup if that person is a responsible dog handler, understands positive reinforcement dog training, and is willing to walk your pup alone or with a maximum of one other dog. A walker will want to meet your dog, play with it, and see how it responds to commands before taking it on. You may be asked for proof of vaccination not only against the most common canine infections but also against kennel cough, a name for a variety of infections that cause a transmissible cough.

For even busier people there are doggy day care centres, and these too can be used once your pup obediently walks on the lead. If you choose to use a one, investigate the service. Play should be supervised, and there should be rest periods. There should be parasite- and disease-control policies. There should be a policy to prevent barking problems, as well as on-site remedial attention for any behaviour problems that may develop because your dog has 'joined a pack'.

When considering either of these options, choose who you use based upon the recommendation of either someone who uses the service or of your veterinarian. If you think about taking a short holiday, you can either send your pup to a kennels or employ a dog sitter – most veterinary practices also know of reliable and insured individuals who will move into your home and care for your pup in your absence.

Helping hands If you or an obliging neighbour can't take your dog out during the day, a dog walker can be a real boon for a working owner.

PRACTICAL TRAINING EXERCISE 5

WAIT TRAINING

This is arguably the most vital of all commands: it's a real life saver. I use it several times every day when I'm out walking Bean. Wait tells her to stop regardless of what she's doing or where she is. It allows me to go down stairs first. It makes it simple and fast to put the her lead on before going out for exercise. A dog trained to wait doesn't just wait to go through a door or jump out of the car. It waits before diving into food, or charging through mud or across a road. Food treats may be just too powerful to use as rewards in this training. They're likely to motivate your pup to come to you for the treat rather than wait where you want. Instead, use other reinforcers that your dog values less, such as toys.

The Wait command is always followed by either another obedience command, such as Come, Sit, Stand, Down, or Stay, or the release word OK, which tells Bean that she can continue doing what she was doing before I told her to wait. In essence, this is beginning to teach a chain of commands, to do one thing, then another. This is the basis of the enjoyable games you'll play when your pup is a little older, stringing together learned behaviours such as waiting until you throw a toy, then running after it, picking it up, carrying it back and dropping it at your feet.

To take Bean as an example, first get her attention by using her name. Now use a hand signal – try the flat of your hand in front of her face – and say "Wait", then immediately give the chosen release command. Repeat this many times a day, gradually increasing the length of the wait. Don't rush this. Expect it to take several weeks, during which you reduce the frequency of training and increase the length of the wait, until she is able to wait for a full minute. How she's waiting – sitting, standing, lying , twiddling her dewclaws – doesn't matter. What does matter is that all four feet are on the ground, waiting for you to give your release command.

TRAINING STEP-BY-STEPS

1 The command "Wait" means "stop what you're doing now." Put slight pressure on the dog's collar as you are approaching the "wait" moment.

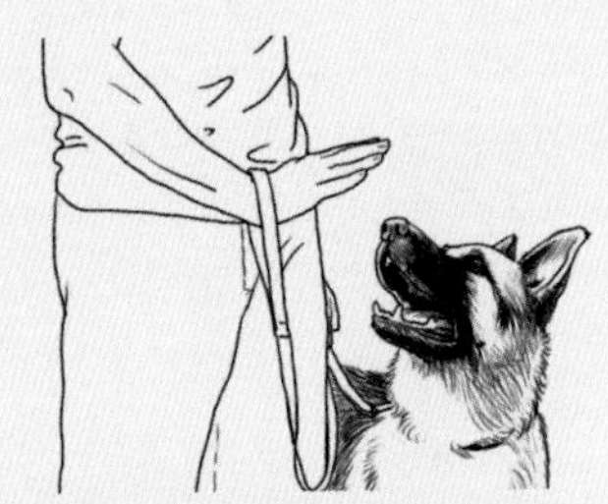

2 Having gained the dog's attention, use a hand signal to tell it to wait, issuing the command "Wait".

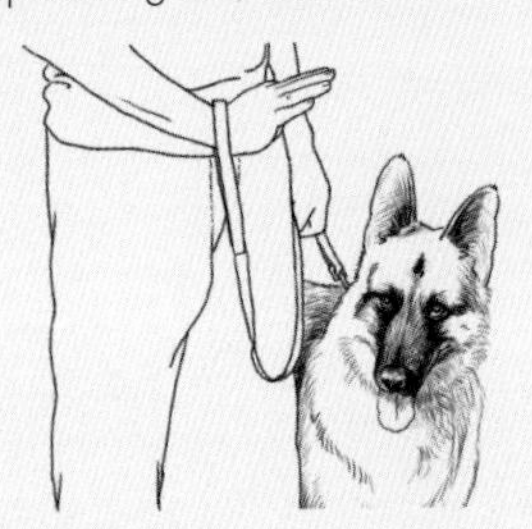

3 Maintain the hand signal with the right hand and place no tension on the lead, held in the left hand.

4 When ready to proceed, withdraw the hand signal and give either a release command or another command. Dogs must wait for the release command.

5 Once released from the Wait, the dog walks with you. Calm breeds are easily trained to wait on command, but start training in a quiet location.

PRACTICAL TRAINING EXERCISE 6

WALKING WITHOUT A LEAD

If you plan to participate in training classes, have your pup walk on your left (a relic of gundog training, where the handler carries a shotgun on the right); otherwise, a pup should be on the side you lead from. I naturally lead with my left foot, so I keep Bean to my left, as described here, and her cue to start to walk is my left leg starting to move. Start training in your home, after vigorous play, and once your dog is relaxed when wearing a collar and lead. Begin with a few seconds and a few feet walked, twice a day, and gradually increase both the time and the distance. While training to walk on a lead is most practical, it doesn't matter whether you start training on or off the lead.

Start with your pup by your left side. Say "Bean" to get her attention, and let her scent the food treat. As your step forward, she will automatically follow that treat, and incidentally the "Walk" command. After only a few steps at first, give the command "Wait", get down to her level and give the food reward.

If your pup is distracted during training, use your hand on her collar to bring her back to the correct position by your side, get her attention again with the food treat, and continue. If the distraction is overwhelming, give a command for something you know she'll do, such as a sit, then reward her with verbal praise. Continue later, after meals or play, or elsewhere, without distraction. Repeat the exercise but don't overdo it, each time extending the distance.

When your pup is consistently walking and waiting in a straight line, introduce left, right, and about turns. Walk forward with your pup at your left. Keeping your right hand with the food treat low in front of her nose, give the command "Walk" as you turn to the right. Your pup speeds up because she has farther to go when turning right. After a few steps in the new direction, give the command "Wait", stop, and reward her with the food treat and kind words. Left turns are more awkward at first. With your pup walking forward at your left give the command "Steady" and move your right hand with the food treat in front of you and to the left. Your pup slows (and learns that 'steady' means 'slow down') as her nose leads her body to the left. You may need to guide her with your hand on her collar. After a few steps give the command "Wait", stop, and reward her.

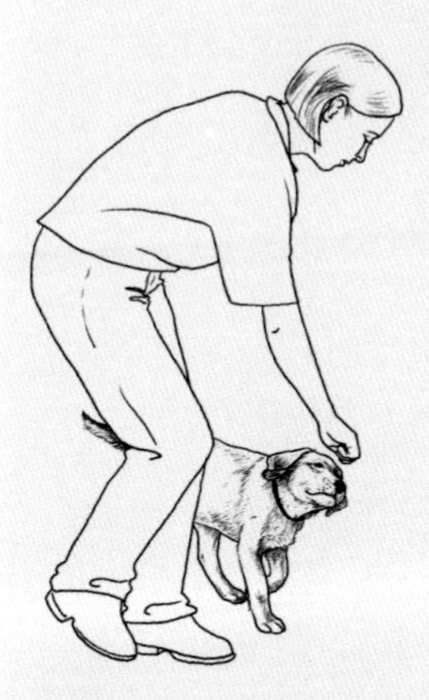

1 Start with your pup on the same side every time. Use its name to get its attention, and then let it scent the food treat held in your closed hand. Keep the treat at your pup's nose level to prevent jumping up.

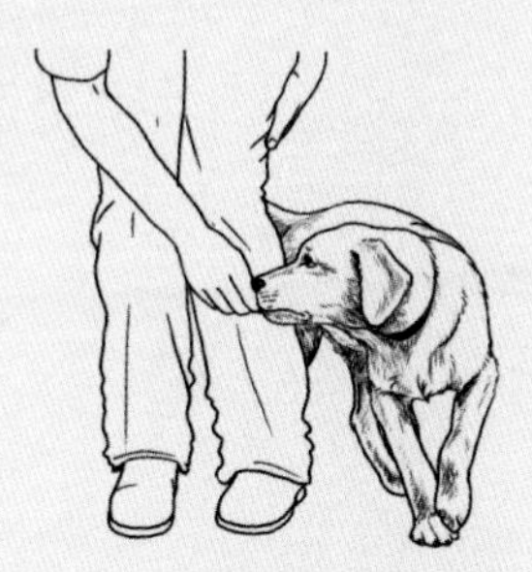

2 As you step forward with the foot nearest your dog, and it follows the scent of the treat, say "Walk" – or "Heel" if you prefer, but be consistent.

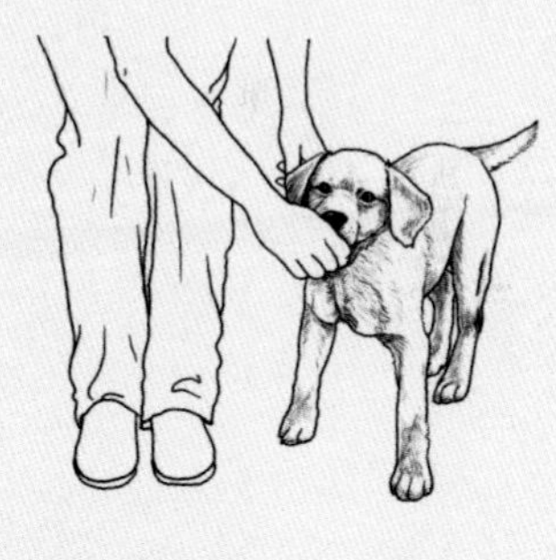

3 After a few steps, give the command "Wait". When your pup stops walking, give it the food treat. Don't hold it so high that your pup is inclined to jump.

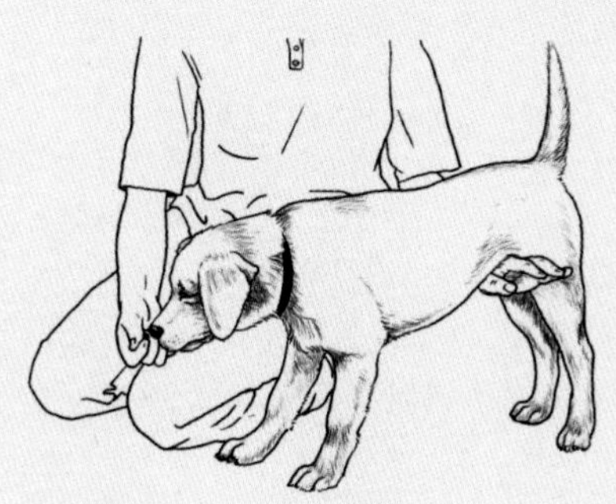

4 If it's necessary use your free right arm, extended under her belly to prevent her from moving forward out of the 'wait' position. If your pup is an obsessive foodie who concentrates too hard on the treat, try training for a few minutes after meals.

PRACTICAL TRAINING EXERCISE 7

WALKING TO HEEL

When your pup willingly follows you off lead, it's easy to graduate to walking on a lead. Pulling on the lead is the most common behavioural problem that dog owners have with their dogs, but a trained dog is always at its handler's heel, which is why Walk training is also known as Heel training.

1 Start with your pup in a sit on your chosen side, holding the lead loosely. Hold its end and the treat in your right hand, leaving the left free to slide along the lead.

As before, start with your pup (I'll use Bean) in a sit to your left and, holding the collar with your left hand, say "Bean" to get her attention. Attach the lead, and hold its end and the food treat in your right hand. Let her scent the food treat in your fist. Start walking as before, saying "Walk" (or "Heel" if you prefer, as long as you are consistent) as your pup follows, and let her feel only the slightest tension on the lead. If she surges forward, slide your hand down the lead, give a slight jerk and say "Steady". After a few steps say "Wait", get down to her level to prevent jumping up, and reward her.

Again, once walking in a straight line is established, graduate to turns, much as you did off the lead (*see p.265*). Teach left turns by increasing your speed at first rather than having your pup decrease hers. When she has learned to turn left at her regular speed, repeat the manoeuvre with your walking at your regular speed and her slowing down. As she slows down, say "Steady".

If she tries to climb her lead, say "No!", move away, say "Sit", and start again. If she thinks it's more fun to chew the lead, spray it with a safe deterrent, such as bitter apple spray. Some pups collapse because they're overly submissive, others because it's a giggle. Use a favourite squeaky toy and plenty of praise to encourage submissive pups; make gigglers sit and give you their full concentration before proceeding with lead training.

Graduate to walking on streets and in the park only once your pup walks to heel in your home and garden, and knows that the commands mean "walk close and pay constant attention to me". Vary the speed of your walk to give your pup the stimulation of the unexpected.

2 Set off, leading with the leg nearest to your pup. As you step fowards and your dog gets up and follows, say "Walk".

3 Guide your pup to the right with the scent of the treat; your pup will speed up to turn right.

4 When turning to the left, again lead with the treat, and move to the left around your dog.

PRACTICAL TRAINING EXERCISE 8

LEAVING, DROPPING, AND TRADING

It's only when you go out and about with a dog that you fully appreciate just how much dangerous stuff there is lying around on the streets and in parks – or along country roads and in woods and fields. Mouthing, tasting, or swallowing things they shouldn't leads to vomiting, diarrhoea, poisoning, or obstructions, amongst the most common reasons why dogs are brought to see me at the veterinary clinic.

This is why learning the command "Leave it" was vital for Bean and is just as important for any pup, urban or rural. "It" may be anything from a discarded pizza box to a decomposing squirrel carcass: your aim is for your pup to leave it alone.

Have your pup sit and stay, and get down on your haunches with a treat visible in your open hand. Move the treat right in front of your pup's eyes, and as she reaches for it close your hand. Your pup will soon quizzically back off. She has temporarily left it. Repeat this, and as your pup leaves it again, say "Leave it". Reward her good behaviour with praise.

Repeat this sequence frequently, gradually lowering your open hand from your pup's eye level until it's down at floor level, the location of most items you'll want her to leave alone. Each time your pup leaves it, reward with verbal praise, but of course don't give the food reward. Most dogs learn very quickly.

There's an added bonus to this command: male dogs always sniff first before urine marking, and "Leave it" works just as well to stop leg lifting where you don't want legs lifted as it does to prevent scavenging.

Like leaving, dropping and trading are potentially lifesaving, but they are also core activities for retrieving. Gain your pup's interest in an attractive toy by waving it around in front of her nose or dragging it along the ground. Wiping your hands on it adds the satisfaction of your scent. Your pup will inevitably take hold of the toy in her mouth when given a chance. When she takes hold of it, say "Drop it" and as you speak, place a food treat right by your pup's nose. As she scents the food, your pup should naturally let go of the toy; immediately after she does so, say "Sit". As your pup sits, give her both praise and the food treat. Sitting prevents your pup from jumping up to grab either the toy or the treat. Eventually fade out the food treat.

Trading is an important extension of dropping, used when you want your pup not to eat something that's extremely interesting but also potentially dangerous if chewed or swallowed, such as discarded takeaway chicken bones or dead (possibly poisoned) rodents.

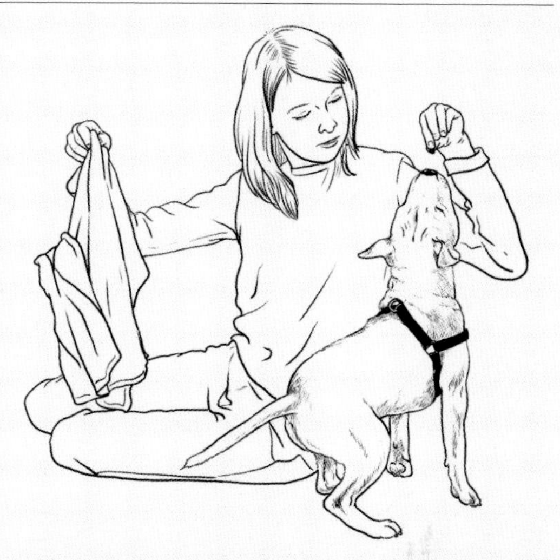

All of these training exercises rely on you teaching your dog that whatever it is interested in, you can offer something more valuable. For low-value items, your praise should eventually be enough to induce your pup to leave or drop an item, but there will always be some things (usually food) that arouse almost overwhelming interest. Teach your pup to trade these for praise plus a valued treat, and always keep a few treats in your pocket on walks.

Practice trading routinely, both indoors and outdoors, from the time you get your pup. Start by giving your pup a chew-toy but with no food in it, then offer her a liver treat. As your pup drops the toy in favour of the more powerful food treat, say "Drop". Repeat this exercise several times in a row, several times a day, until your pup responds well, then graduate to trading a more valued item, for example the chew-toy with a biscuit in it. Once your pup willingly and consistently trades familiar toys you, graduate to other, less familiar, items you don't want her to eat, such as sticks in the park or rubbish on the street.

When your pup does pick up some undesirable item, regardless of what she has in her mouth, even if it's another dog's turd, stay calm. Don't wind her up by chasing or shrieking. If you do, the activity immediately turns into a game and she holds the trump card, which is a quick swallow. Find something at hand you know your pup will value highly – a piece of fresh meat, a treat, whatever – and play trading.

These exercises with your pup should be practiced by everyone in the family, including responsible children, so your pup will trade anything with anyone. If you don't have any kids, rent some.

PRACTICAL TRAINING EXERCISE 9

RETRIEVING GAMES

Retrieving is a great game, satisfying natural desires to find, to carry, and to work as a team. It lets your pup chase, but in circumstances that you control. I live with a retriever, hardwired to play this game, but other dogs find stringing together a chain or sequence – send out, find, pick up, hold, bring back, drop – a complicated game. Many will pick the item up, but lose interest in bringing it back. If you're no good at throwing, arm yourself with a tennis racket or a ball thrower.

Before trying this game, make sure you and your pup understand your house rules. I carry a tennis ball to the park in one of the lemon-scented poop bags I take with me, masking its scent. I stick to my toys: if Bean were to find an item and persuade me to throw it, it's just as likely she would decide when the game should end.

Problems can occur in any link in the retrieve "chain". Concentrate on that link until it is rectified before going on with the full retrieve. Never correct your pup when the retrieve item is in her mouth; that's confusing. Never take the retrieve toy from her; that only leads to tug-of-war. Offer a tickle or a food treat, accompanying the release with the words "Drop it". And don't let your pup turn this into "catch-me-if-you-can". Never, ever chase a pup who refuses to bring back or drop the toy. I walk off in the opposite direction, let her be proprietorial and proud for a few minutes, then quietly return to "Drop it".

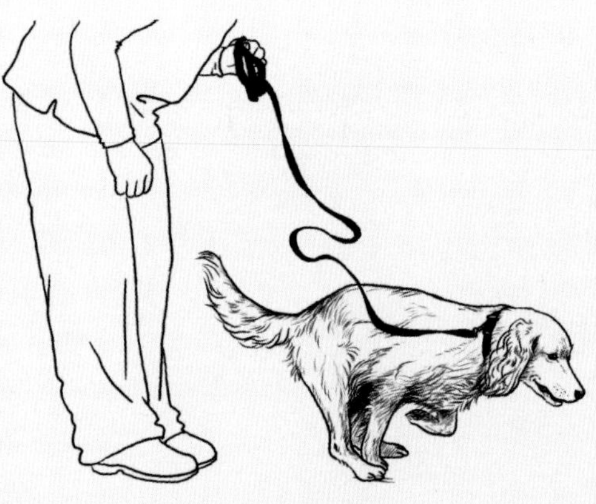

1 Develop your dog's interest in the retrieve item by sitting indoors playing with it, enticing your pup to show interest. Roll it on the floor if it's a ball, or toss it a short distance if it's a beanbag or odd-shaped toy – avoid using sticks.

2 If you've succeeded in getting your pup interested, it will race to pick the retrieve item up. Encourage it to come the short distance to you, praising it for carrying the toy with the words "Good hold".

3 Once your pup has returned to you, give the command "Drop it" and exchange the retrieve toy for a food reward. Repeat this sequence, gradually increasing the distance you ask your pup to come back from.

4 Once the routine of fetching and dropping is established, have your pup sit before you say "Drop it". Always reward your pup verbally then give your release word to release it from the sit at the end of the exercise.

PRACTICAL TRAINING EXERCISE 10

"GO TO BED"

There will be times when you want your dog to simply disappear. "Go to bed" is really just an extension of down and stay (*see pp. 188–89*), and it's a great command for when you're busy or when you have guests who aren't quite the dog lovers that you and your family are. Here's what we do.

• Standing near your pup's bed, call "Bean" to bring your pup to you. When she comes to you, say "Go to bed" as you lead her to her bed.
• At her bed, put her into a Down and Stay, and reward her for staying put. This will take a little practice, and you must be consistent.

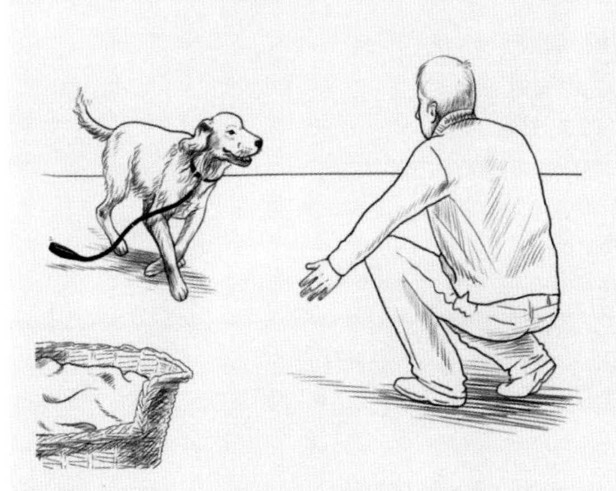

PRACTICAL TRAINING EXERCISE 11

"OFF"

This is a vital command if you don't want your dog on the furniture. In our home, we let Bean on the furniture – after all, we're classic empty-nesters – but she still understands when she's told "Off" that she has to get off to make way for humans. It's quite easy to achieve this.
• If your pup gets on the sofa, couch or bed without your permission, take her by the collar, say, "Off" lead her down to the floor then praise her.

• If your pup is a persistent offender or if there's even a hint of aggression from her, leave her lead (or a houseline) attached to her collar while she's indoors. Whenever you see her on something that she shouldn't be on, give a slight jerk on the lead, aiming the tug in the direction that you want her to follow off the furniture. When your pup's feet hit the ground, command her to sit, and praise her when she does.

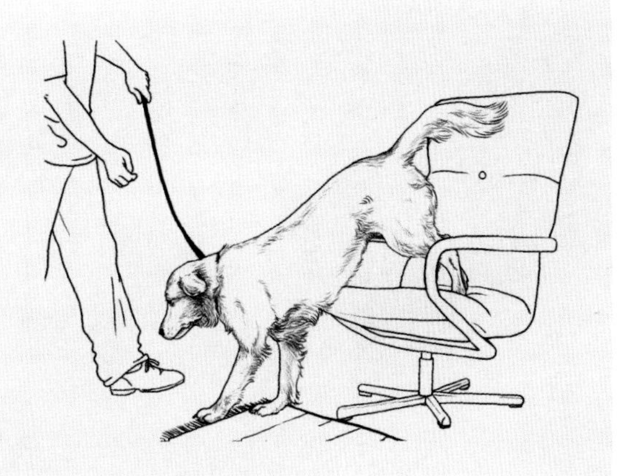

CHAPTER TEN

Canine Adolescence

Canine adolescence begins at a precise moment, and that's puberty. Your dog has gained adult length and height, but the body still needs time to muscle-up; this point may be reached any time between five and fifteen months of age. At puberty, your dog's behaviour is modified by the onset of hormonal activity. Pups neutered before they reach puberty don't experience the same changes in their behaviour as intact dogs, but puberty remains a pivotal point in their development.

As with us, sexual maturity arrives long before emotional maturity. Although intact adolescent dogs are sexually adult and quite capable of successfully breeding, true adulthood – when a dog becomes emotionally as well as physically mature – is still months, maybe even years away. It is usually reached between eighteen months and three years of age. And yes, it's absolutely true, some dogs (including some individuals neutered before puberty) never emotionally mature, retaining throughout adulthood and even old age the joyous behaviour of puppyhood.

Adolescence in dogs is the equivalent of our teenage years and, just as with us, can be amusing, irritating, or downright exasperating. Relatively obedient until now, a typical adolescent dog will start to experiment with exactly what it can get away with. Disobedience often creeps in, often simply because there's something more interesting to do than obeying a command but also, sometimes as true rebelliousness. Most dogs continue to build on their early learning, but some challenge what they've been taught. "Sit," you command "Why should I?" your dog shoots back. Many, especially males, will challenge the authority both of other older dogs in the home and of you and your family. Some truly dominant individuals will work out where your inconsistencies are and then exploit them. This isn't deviousness, it's simply normal dog behaviour. Territorial behaviour will develop in both males and females. Adolescence is a time of testing for dogs, but it can also be a testing time for us: more dogs are abandoned or given away to dog shelters during adolescence than at any other time in their lives. This is the most problematic passage of a dog's life. But it does end.

As an example, let me tell you a cautionary tale that has a happy ending. A few years ago one of my clients, an elegant, intelligent Greek woman, got two Bulldog pups. The brothers snuffled and waddled into her life as adorable "babies". Their puppyhood was complicated because, as she quickly found, it's very difficult to efficiently train two dogs at the same time, but they developed well. Then wham, the dogs hit adolescence and the proverbial hit the fan. They became the bane of her life.

She wasn't too surprised when they began to fight viciously with each other. They had always gone a bit over the top when playing, but now they were biting each other hard, holding on, penetrating the skin. These were damaging fights, with neither dog backing down. On my advice, one of them was castrated and a professional trainer showed the owner how to

Boys will be boys It would be wonderful if our dogs made a smooth transition from the goofiness of infancy to the calm maturity of adulthood – it would be great if our kids did too. The truth is, however, that adolescence is always a time of uncertain and even turbulent change, and males are usually the most trouble.

treat the unneutered dog as the dominant one and the neutered dog as the subservient one. This stopped their fighting – but now they started acting as a team and picking fights with other male dogs in the park.

My client was now figuratively pulling her shiny dark hair out. Her Bulldogs each weighed almost 30kg (66lb). We couldn't find muzzles to fit their enormous heads and thick necks, and she had physical difficulty controlling them on their harnesses. "Is this what I have to live with for the next ten years?" she asked. She had got a pair because she thought it was good for dogs to have dog company, but all they did was act like dogs! We decided to castrate the unneutered brother too and hope than his aggression towards other male dogs would diminish, although the brothers might start fighting again once they were hormonally more equal. I didn't hear any more until six months later when the two dogs, now 27 months old, were brought in for their annual health checks.

The owner looked more relaxed than I'd seen her for some time and when I asked how the dogs were she beamed and said, "Wonderful". They played tag with each other but their games never escalated into aggression. They exercised in the park, usually off their leads, and she had learned to read their body language so that when she suspected they might gang up on another dog, she put their leads on and walked away. "They are so calm now. They finally grew up" she said. She hit the nail on the head: a particularly turbulent adolescence was over, and the dogs had become adults. They had emotionally matured, and she had learned how to adapt to their particular temperaments and found a simple way to avoid problems. In the home of someone less willing to work through their problems, these dogs could

Keep busy This is where the training you did (you did do it, didn't you?) comes into its own. As well as having a pack leader's control of your adolescent, you can build on their ability to obey you to teach them to do tricks and play energetic games that will burn off some of that energy.

easily have been abandoned, given to a rescue centre, or at the very least split up. She was so pleased with them I didn't have the heart to mention their loud, difficult, snorty, grunty breathing, an anatomical problem that is only resolved through surgical correction.

Anticipating problems

We keep dogs for our benefit. We want them to adapt to our standards rather than live as their feral relatives do. And then we get annoyed when our dogs, denied their natural outlets for social interactions with other dogs, denied their need to burn up energy, denied the need to use their brains, howl or bark for companionship, jump on us with excitement or try to dig their way to China. These aren't dog problems. They're our problems.

You provide yourself with mental, physical and social activity, so do the same for your adolescent dog. Routine training when you are around provides daily mental stimulation. Play more games with your dog at home, especially hide and seek, searching for food and, as long as you don't have an overtly dominant adolescent, tug-of-war. Train your dog to do some tricks, for example "roll over" or "high five". "Fetch" is terrific for athletic adolescents living with sedentary owners. Give your adolescent plenty of exercise. Jogging, cycling, and swimming all are excellent for you. Take your dog along and set a pace that means your dog trots rather than runs. Swimming is a great exercise for spaniels and retrievers, although places to

Out of their depth Swimming is excellent for exercise, but adolescents can be foolhardy risk takers. Make sure that you know the place your dog is swimming is safe, and check that it can get out easily before you let it plunge in.

swim are of course limited in urban areas. Only let your dog in a swimming pool that has steps for easy entering and leaving. Before starting any activity program, check with your veterinarian about its suitability for your dog, especially if it's small. And remember, dogs don't sweat the way we do. Never exercise your dog vigorously in hot sunny weather, and always carry water, for your dog as well as for you. Finally, visit a local dog park at least twice daily to provide your dog with off-lead social interactions with other dogs. Its amusing, fascinating, and socially fulfilling. Make sure your dog has something to keep it occupied when you're absent by providing stimulating toys. Peanut butter or soft cheese in the hollow of a sterilized bone is excellent, as are the plastic balls or cubes that drop food rewards as they're nosed around the floor.

Every dog, every single dog, will develop unwanted habits. You can anticipate whether serious problems are likely to develop in adolescence by answering the following questions. If your answers are mostly in the left column, the chances of serious problems are much lower than if they are mostly in the right column.

ASSESSING POTENTIAL PROBLEMS

From the following questions make a note of which answers are most appropriate to you and from which of the two columns they come

Questions to consider	Less trouble	More trouble
Where did you get your dog?	Breeder or friend	Ad, shelter, or pet shop
How old was it then?	Under 12 weeks	Over 18 weeks
Has your dog been or will it be neutered?	Yes	No
Have you previously owned a dog?	Yes	No
When is your dog fed?	At set times	On demand
When does your dog relieve itself?	At set times	No set times
Where does your dog sleep?	Its own bed	On a human's bed
How often is your dog groomed?	Frequently	Infrequently
How does your dog react to grooming?	Willingly	Unwillingly
When is your dog exercised?	Set times	On demand
How long is the exercise time?	Over an hour a day	Under an hour a day
Do you have off-lead control?	Yes	No
Where are the dog's toys kept?	In a toy box	On the floor
How often does your dog have special playtime with you?	Frequently	Infrequently
How often does it play with other dogs?	Frequently	Infrequently
How often does it meet other people?	Frequently	Infrequently
How long is your dog left at home alone?	Less than 4 hours	More than 4 hours

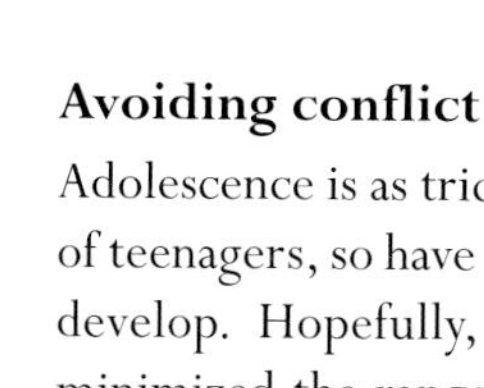

Bad habits Don't get wound up by your dog doing things you dislike – you may just be telling it which of your buttons to push for the best effect. Just shut the lid, shut the door, do whatever works fastest to make that behaviour impossible.

Avoiding conflict

Adolescence is as tricky for some "parents" of dogs as it is for some parents of teenagers, so have a plan. Know what you're going to do when problems develop. Hopefully, what you did during your dog's puppyhood has minimized the range of problem behaviours that might develop. During adolescence, ensure that there are no grey areas in your relationship with your dog: everything your dog is told should be in black and white, clear and consistent. A dog is not allowed on furniture *ever*, not given tidbits from the table *ever*, not allowed to jump up on people *ever*, and doesn't growl at anyone *ever*. And nothing in life is free: ensure that your dog knows it always has to do something for you before you do something in return.

When problems appear, it's better to create circumstances that simply avoid the problems if you can, rather than going through the whole rigmarole of retraining. For example, if your adolescent raids the rubbish, move the rubbish where it can't be raided. If it's drinking from the toilet, keep the lid closed. If shoes are chewed, train your family not to leave their shoes about, but leave a chew toy accessible. If your dog successfully begs at the table the reward is obvious: banish the tidbit-giver from the kitchen, and begging will stop. If your dog jumps up to say hello, rather than disciplining it, train it to sit when you come home and reward it for that. If barking at noise is a problem, train your dog to fetch and carry, because it's tough to bark effectively with a mouth full of soft toy. Sometimes it's best to compromise, especially with behaviours that are hardwired into your breed. For example, terriers are naturally inclined to dig. You can try to stop this completely, but it's much easier to put in an approved digging area and train your dog to dig only there.

Your dog is taught by you, but just as efficiently it teaches itself. Create circumstances where your adolescent learns to stop doing something by itself, without your obvious involvement. Use bitter apple spray, chilli sauce, or other safe but disagreeable tastes to prevent chewing where you do not want chewing. Use noise in the same way. Inexpensive and widely available vibration-sensitive windows alarms are ideal for putting on beds or sofas if you don't want your teenager sleeping on your furniture in your absence. If you're at home and see your dog doing something you don't want, a squirt from an ever-ready water pistol or a clunk on the floor from a drinks can filled with a few coins, combined with a verbal 'No!' from you, will work wonders. Be creative and (as always) a little flamboyant.

Actively breaking bad habits

Although bad habits vary, almost all of them can be diminished or corrected. Go back to basic obedience and make sure firstly that your adolescent understands all the basic commands, and secondly that you can enforce them. Make sure your dog does something for you, such as sitting or lying down, before receiving any kind of reward, even a verbal greeting. Satisfy your dog's natural needs by creating acceptable outlets for natural behaviour, while eliminating the satisfaction your dog gets from unacceptable behaviour. Sometimes this will involve mild punishment.

Distraction therapy Your dog may look grown-up now, but that doesn't mean you can forget all the toys and games. They are still the most potent way of rewarding good behaviour and distracting from bad behaviour (such as destructivenesss) before it has a chance to happen.

When I've got dog visitors actively playing outdoors and hear Julia tell them to "Stop that right now!" I know there's humping going on. All our family dogs are female, and their humping is rather innocuous and usually occurs during hormonal activity. They usually take turns at being humper and humpee. With adolescent male dogs, humping cushions, legs, or the kids can be an easily learned nuisance behaviour but it's simple to overcome. Leave a light lead or houseline attached to your dog's collar, and when he starts to clasp on to hump something, simply grab the lead, pull the dog away, march him through a door then close it, waiting 30 seconds before letting him back in the room. Avoid touching the dog, because that in itself can be a reward. Repeat each time: you may have to do this 30 times or more on the first day, but the frequency will drop quickly and the problem is almost invariably overcome within three weeks.

Dogs and cats usually get along fine, but during adolescence a feisty or boisterous dog might decide to create its own amusement by ambushing the family cat. If this happens, attach a houseline to your dog's collar and step on it if it looks like a chase is starting. You want your dog to learn that it plays games only with people or other dogs.

Whatever you do, don't give up. Persevere. Don't expect overnight miracles, but all dogs eventually emerge from adolescence into the quieter waters of adulthood. Typically, it takes about three weeks of re-training to overcome most common behaviour problems. If you're uncertain, or if aggression is involved, get professional help. Don't think that professionals will view you as a failure if you ask for advice and help. Asking for advice is the surest sign of your commitment to your dog, your family, and your neighbours. Obedience classes for adolescent dogs are marvellously useful. Ask your veterinary receptionist who the best trainers are, or contact one of the recognized training groups (*see p.262*). While reinforcement of basic training is all that's needed to overcome most adolescent dog problems, advanced training in areas such as agility, games, tracking or canine sports provides an outlet for the natural energy of individuals from breeds originally used in these activities. There's nothing better than one-to-one training. If you can afford it, a personal trainer for you and your dog is ideal, and should be available in almost any urban area. Ask your vet for advice.

A bored dog is a neglected dog

Some degree of boredom in life is perfectly natural. It's only when your dog's boredom is neglected that it develops into behaviour problems, which can be particularly troublesome during adolescence. Don't punish your dog for destructive behaviour. It won't know why you're angry. If your dog is destructive in your absence, work out why and correct the cause: the problem is yours, not your dog's. If your male dog is barking, digging, destroying or escaping because he's looking for sex, consider neutering. Chewing, howling or barking when alone, pacing, and jumping fences are all signs of boredom. So is digging, but don't mistake digging a cool pit to lie in or digging to bury something for boredom digging. Labradors and Dobermanns are particularly prone to excessively licking their forelegs when bored, leading to skin problems that need veterinary attention.

Prevent boredom by leaving your dog full, exercised, calm, and with a favourite toy (*see pp.190–92*). If you have the time, increase the frequency or length of outdoor physical activities when you are around. Even if you haven't got the time, never leave your dog at home alone all day. If you have a reliable dog-loving neighbour, discuss their taking care of your dog in your absence. I have found that recently retired men are often a wonderful source of conscientious dog minders. Alternatively, employ a dog walker, preferably someone recommended by your vet, or if you can afford one, consider a dog drop-in centre (*see p.265*).

If your dog is chewing, apply taste deterrents to objects you don't want chewed. Use the dog crate constructively if your young dog is simply going through an irritating chew-everything phase (which can last until a year of age or longer), but always provide exciting chew toys, because dogs need to chew something.

Some teenage canines compensate for boredom by creatively discovering how to escape from the garden or how to make excavations worthy of a civil engineer. Tin cans strung on a rope a little way out from the fence and 1m (39in) from the ground make a noisy and natural deterrent for fence jumpers. Chicken wire on the ground at take-off distance from the fence works well, but make sure the gauge of the wire is too small for your dog's foot to slip through. Chicken wire is also an excellent deterrent to digging. If you have an instinctive digger, redirect that energy away from the flower beds or lawn to an acceptable area, such as a sand pit.

Digging machine Digging is not always a bad habit; it is a normal part of dog behaviour, and if your dog loves to dig you're best advised to give it an outlet. After all, you'd throw balls to amuse a retriever.

Control barking by training your dog to "speak" on command. Attach your dog's lead to a fence, stand a few feet away and tease it with a toy. When it barks from frustration, give her a food treat. Give the command "Speak" the moment your dog barks, then give the toy as a reward. Once your dog consistently barks on commend for the toy or food, switch to verbal rewards. Now give the command "Quiet" when your dog is barking and reward with the toy or treat as soon as it stops. Be patient. This takes time. Once it consistently stops barking when commanded, move a short distance away and repeat the exercise, initially returning with a food or toy reward. Eventually switch to verbal rewards at a distance when your dog responds to your "Quiet" command. When this is completed, set up mock departures, giving the "Quiet" command before you leave. Stand outside the door. If your dog barks, make a noise, for example by dropping a drinks can, to startle your dog into stopping barking. Return and give praise for being quiet. This exercise takes time and patience. I've never had either the staying power or fortitude to undertake it with my dogs but (don't tell this to professional dog trainers) they have learned to stop barking when I shout, and I mean really shout, "No barking!"

If separation anxiety problems such as barking, messing, or destroying have developed, desensitize your dog to your departure by occasionally picking up your keys or putting on your coat and not going out but continuing with chores in your home. Practice mock exits, leaving calmly then instantly returning, gradually increasing the length of your time away. Avoid both goodbyes and hellos, ignoring your dog for at least 20 minutes before leaving (that means no voice, eye, or physical contact) and giving low-key praise on your return only once your dog is calm. Ensure your dog is well-exercised and fed before you depart and has something to do while you're gone, such as working on a favourite chew toy that you keep set aside for occasions such as these, and calmly limit access to the whole house so your dog can't run from room to room while you are gone.

Welcome home When you come back to the house and your dog quietly wags its tail, thats the time to dole out treats and contact. Not before. And always after a "sit".

Nip it in the bud Don't panic if your dog shows signs of aggression, but do take it seriously. Aggression against other dogs is more common and less difficult to deal with than that directed at humans, but it all needs prompt action.

Dealing with teenage aggression

Hunger, sex, aggression, and territory marking are all normal behaviours shared by all animals. Yet some of us are still surprised when some of our dogs scavenge, mount visitors' legs, bark and bite, or urinate on curtains. We want our dogs to be ideal canine citizens, and it is possible to get close to that ideal, but getting there involves our understanding why adolescent dogs behave the way they do.

The vast majority of dogs don't want to ever be pack leaders. They don't want confrontation, they don't want to dictate to others, they simply want to have a safe and secure territory, water and nourishment, and social companionship. But there are also dog owners who don't want to be leaders, and if this type of owner is paired with a naturally dominant dog, the greatest problems of rebellious canine adolescence develop. Of all the problems that adolescents can develop, the most serious for both them and us is aggression. There's always a reason why a dog bites, although it's not always obvious to us. Once aggressive behaviour has developed, it never disappears on its own. We have to do something to contain it, reduce it, then eliminate it. Our problem is we often fail to see the warning signs, or we do nothing about them. Ask yourself whether your own adolescent dog does these things:

- Growls at you, other people, or other animals
- Shows its teeth to you or your family
- Snaps when you try to take away a toy, bones, or food
- Cringes and hides behind you when visitors approach
- Barks and runs to the door when delivery people arrive
- Nips at your ankles when playing exuberantly
- Chases after moving objects
- Chases, stands over, or nips other dogs
- Gives you a glassy-eyed, hard stare that lasts for minutes
- Makes you find excuses for its aggressive behaviour, telling your friends that "It's just a phase"
- Gets away with these things because it is a Yorkie, not a Pit Bull, and its pushy behaviour is "cute" rather than threatening

If you answered "Yes" to any one of these questions, your dog either has real potential to become aggressive or already is.

All dogs, like all people, have some potential to become aggressive, but selective breeding has enhanced forms of aggression in certain breeds. Rather surprisingly, these include Chihuahuas, Miniature Smooth-haired Dachshunds, and a variety of small terriers alongside the more obvious bull-type terriers, Rottweilers, and German Shepherd Dogs. Problems only occur in homes that wittingly or unwittingly encourage aggression: early socialization to the family, strangers, other animals and a range of experiences (*see p.173*) dramatically reduces the likelihood that a dog will become a problem. For example, the Pit Bull is a worrying breed because of its genetic tendency towards aggression and the extreme power of its jaw muscles. Yet in my practice I see many well-mannered Pit Bull-type

No doubt It looks scary, but what these German Shepherds are doing may just forestall a full blown fight. At the very least it gives you time to react.

dogs, properly socialized to friends and strangers. Personally, I'd never recommend getting a breed like a Pit Bull, because their instinct to chase and kill anything small is too great, but early learning is the most powerful tool for reducing the risk of aggression in your dog.

Aggression takes many forms

Pups rarely bite with aggressive intent until they're over seven months old, unless they're really frightened or really bold. Until that age they cope with problems by hiding, running away or appeasing other dogs with the classic "I'm not worthy" routine. But during adolescence confidence grows. A dog will use body language: hackles up, an intent stare, tail raised. If this doesn't work, a growl or teeth-baring follows. And if that isn't successful, aggression ensues to sort out the situation. Most breeds – the German Shepherd Dog is a classic example – are superb at body language. This makes it easy for us to read what they're thinking. Other breeds – the Rottweiler comes to mind – have a truncated form of body language, skipping several stages and going from play to aggression very quickly. This makes it more difficult to read them, and makes that breed more dangerous to non-doggy people. Dogs become skilled very quickly at using aggression in stressful or other situations.

It's important to understand exactly what's going on when your dog shows aggression. For example, at any time in life, not just during adolescence, a dog's response to pain, even to anticipated pain, is to bite. This is a perfectly natural form of aggression. Be careful when touching or moving an ill or injured dog. Certain medical conditions are also known to be associated with aggression, most famously rabies, but some dogs with underactive thyroid glands develop behaviour changes including aggression.

While biting you because you touched where it hurts is perfectly justifiable aggression on your dog's part, biting you because you tried to push your dog off the sofa is a crime. There's a whole variety of different forms of aggression, each with its own cause and treatment, and one type often occurs in synchrony with another. This is serious business. Unless the cause and cure are obvious you should not rely simply on a book to overcome an aggression problem. If your adolescent dog is behaving badly, get help from your veterinary clinic or local dog training club.

Statistics leave no doubt that aggression is more likely to be a problem in adolescent male dogs. You and your family are prime targets. The reason is the pecking order. During adolescence some dogs aim for higher rank in the pack, and challenge people they sense have lower rank, often children. At the same time, sex hormone induces rivalry with other males. Most of the fight injuries I treat result from two male dogs fighting each other. Good socialization is the best way to avoid this; I'll also discuss hormone control.

Dominance aggression

This is often directed against you and your family, and is the most common reason why dogs growl at or bite their owners. You might think the growl or bite was sudden, but it wasn't. Your dog will have assessed your position for some time before deciding to challenge you.

Avoid physical punishment for dominance aggression. It's too provocative, and may make matters worse. Instead, make sure that you always use your own body posture, facial expression, and tone of voice to leave your dog in no doubt that you're always in charge of them. Keep a lead or houseline attached to your dog's collar, and move to temporary isolation from the family, for about one minute, to reassert your authority over a pushy dog. Don't hold a grudge, but review your relationship with your dog to determine why it thought it could challenge you.

Dominance aggression between two dogs is more likely to occur when both of them are relatively equal – the same sex, same age, same size. Some breeds, such as the Dobermann, are more prone to aggression between equals. Overcoming this problem depends upon you determining, or sometimes even deciding which is the higher-ranking dog, then treating him or her as such. An instinct to comfort the underdog only increases the problem. The dog that has the highest rank eats first, is petted by you first, and goes out the door first. If aggression is severe and this doesn't work, ask for your veterinarian's help. Neutering one dog lowers its rank and will often cure the problem. It may seem heartless, but it is usually enough to put a stop to dominance fighting.

Play favourites Dogs don't think like us. They are happy with hierarchies, and a dog that knows its place is not a downtrodden, sad creature, but a dog that can get on with the rest of its life in peace. It's your job to make sure they know their place in relation to you, but also to each other.

Sex-related aggression and neutering

Sex-related aggression can occur all year round in males, and male-to-male aggression is the most common form of sex-related aggression. If you have a male dog, expect an occasional aggressive incident. If you sense a problem from another male dog, the best policy is avoidance. Play with your dog so that he concentrates on you, not the provocateur. There's never any harm in your carrying a water pistol for squirting another dog that comes too close. If a fight breaks out, keep your arms and legs out of the melée to avoid heat-of-the-moment bites.

In female dogs, sex-related aggression triggered by female hormone occurs during and after each heat cycle. While in season, a bitch urine-marks more and wanders more under the influence of oestrogen, the hormone that stimulates egg release. The hormone of pregnancy, progesterone, always follows and has a calming effect on behaviour, but it also stimulates a possessive or protective attitude, which can be displayed towards either real pups or puppy substitutes such as toys. Maternal hormonal aggression is probably the most fearsome type of aggression that exists. Mothers don't mess about: they mean it when they say that they'll do anything to protect their litter. And there's a curiosity to canines: unlike all other domestic animals, regardless of whether she's pregnant or not, after ovulating any bitch goes through a two month "phantom" hormonal pregnancy. During the latter part of this she may become possessive over shoes, soft toys, and socks, perhaps hoarding them under the bed or table. This problem can be avoided through early neutering, and early socialization also reduces the likelihood of maternal aggression.

Neutering either males or females means removing the apparatus that produces the sex hormones: in males this means the testicles, in females the ovaries (*see p.252*). It is still the procedure of choice for preventing unwanted puppies, but it also has effects on behaviour. Eliminating (or to be more accurate, dramatically reducing) male hormone is likely to reduce a male dog's need to frequently mark territory with urine, to be aggressive with other male dogs, and to wander over a large territory, preoccupied with sexual scents left by other dogs. If your male dog is aggressive towards other male dogs and you want to find out whether neutering will solve this problem, you can ask your vet to use hormones to "chemically castrate" your dog temporarily. This is a safe procedure when used short term, but these drugs may produce unwanted side effects if used over a prolonged period of time, so it is just a test. Neutering females eliminates the behaviour changes resulting from ovulation and phantom pregnancies. In very rare circumstances however, the absence of the twice yearly calming effect of progesterone can exaggerate the dominance of naturally dominant females.

Neutering has no effect on house guarding, on fear biting, on predatory aggression, or on territorial aggression. It has no effect on other aspects of a dog's personality, except that neutered dogs pay more attention to people because they're paying less attention to sex-related activity. Whatever the reason for neutering, just before puberty is an excellent time to carry out this procedure, because early neutering perpetuates the personality as it is. If you like your pup's personality at six months of age, then, subject to your veterinarian agreeing there's no reason why it shouldn't be done, this is when he or she should be neutered.

Fearful aggression

Fear is the most common reason for dogs to bite strangers, and is most acute in breeds prone to emotional stress, such as Border Collies. Fear biting is most likely to occur in under-socialized dogs that didn't have the opportunity to meet lots of people as pups. It occurs most frequently in shy or fearful dogs that started off life by hiding behind you or running away from what they saw as threats. Submissive wetters can turn into fear biters. In stressful situations these dogs learn to use aggression to make the perceived threat go away. Watch your adolescent for signs of fear – body postures, growling, baring teeth – and eliminate problems before they develop into fear biting. Allow the fearful dog time to make its own decisions, to be brave enough to come forward on its own to a suitable reward. This means you need to protect your dog from well-meaning people who reach down to stroke it or pick it up.

Predatory aggression

Your almost-adult dog may look like an angel, but it's closer to its roots than you imagine. Dogs evolved to chase moving things. They chase squirrels and rabbits, cats and other dogs, and livestock. They chase joggers, they chase bicycles, and they chase cars. All dogs chase, but terriers, herders, and sight and scent hounds in particular are genetically super-primed for chasing. For many the chase itself is the fun; others enjoy the pounce at the end of the chase, holding down the small dog that has been caught, grabbing the ankle of the jogger. Still others bite after pouncing, killing cats or savaging livestock. This is a primitive and very basic form of aggression, and

CHILDPROOFING YOUR DOG

Some dogs are timid and fearful or are unsure of themselves in new surroundings and prone to act defensively, while others get overexcited with rough and tumble play. In all these situations, a dog might bite. Whether it is a fearful or a playful bite, you don't want it to happen to your kids or to others, so reduce the risk by conditioning your dog to accept childlike behaviour. Gently prod your dog, then instantly give a food reward. Poke and prod some more, instantly rewarding again with treats. Once your dog considers poking and prodding as positive experiences, gently grab it and reward calm acceptance with more food rewards. Never permit this, but now if your dog is unexpectedly poked, prodded, or grabbed by a child, it is much less likely to be frightened or annoyed by it.

Fast and furious A dog that watches pedestrians walk past without a murmur may seem to think that cyclists are dinner. Things that move at speed tend to trigger dogs to chase, unless they are trained not to, and things that move away at speed (like an alarmed cyclist) are rewarding and naturally reinforce the behaviour.

it's potentially there within all dogs. Bean's predecessor was as soft-mouthed and as gentle a Golden Retriever as you'd ever meet, but our neighbouring farmer rightly credited her with controlling the local rabbit population. Channel your dog's natural desire to chase and kill by teaching chase-and retrieve-games (*see p.260*). If your dog chases joggers and bicycles, get friends armed with water pistols involved in these activities. When your dog chases, the jogger or vehicle stops and the dog gets an unexpected shot of water in the face; this is aversion therapy.

Some dogs' predatory instinct is so strong, the thrill of chasing and killing so overwhelming, that this mild aversion training doesn't work. This is why farmers have the right to kill dogs that worry livestock. In my experience, predatory aggression needs dramatic intervention, and that intervention is a shock collar used under the instructions of an experienced dog trainer. Don't *ever* do this yourself. Shock collars cause pain, and the timing of their use must be absolutely perfect. I'll be much happier when they can only be used by people licensed to use them, but when the only other alternative is to put down a livestock worrier or killer, I don't have objections to this form of extreme aversion therapy.

Territorial aggression

Chase aggression often blends with the desire to protect territory. As a dog matures through adolescence it becomes increasingly confident on its own territory, in your home, yard, or car. A dog well socialized to visitors to these areas will not see strangers as possible threats, but without this early learning any visitor means a potential threat. Barking gives the stranger a warning, and a show of aggression may follow. The evolution of territorial aggression may already have been taking place during puppyhood, and you may have seen it without recognizing it. The post arrives, making a noise at the letter box, the dog barks, and the stranger outside leaves. The recycling truck comes, making noise, the dog barks, and the strangers outside leave again. Guarding and barking work!

To prevent (or overcome) this problem, introduce your pup to delivery people, even if it means altering your early morning habits for a while. If you can't do that, talk to whoever delivers your post and leave some food treats for him or her to put through the letter box with the mail. If your dog is in the garden when delivery people call, leave a favourite toy or food in a weatherproof box at your gate, with instructions to give it to your dog when the gate is opened. Your dog will still alert you when someone comes to your house, but will not be compulsively protective of your shared territory. Use the same principle in your car. A car is a delightfully small territory, easy to protect. It's your choice how you want you dog to behave in your car. If you don't want it to be aggressive, nip any potential problems in the bud by avoiding rewards for delinquent behaviour.

Even stevens There is a sort of urban myth that if you ever let your dog win at tug of war games, you will turn it into a possessive, challenging biter. Top dogs have to let the underdogs win sometimes, or a game is no fun, but do keep the balance on your side, and avoid this game with dogs that show signs of aggression.

Possessive aggression

You may have noticed a degree of possessiveness in your dog when it was a pup, a tendency to guard treasured items such as toys or food. This is surprisingly common in both Golden Retrievers and Cocker Spaniels, and during adolescence it can evolve into possessive aggression. It's easy to prevent this from becoming a serious problem; harder to deal with once the behaviour has been learned.

Accustom your dog to taking food gently from your hand. This focuses its attention on you. Sit where you plan to feed it and offer small amounts of kibble in the palm of your hand while you stroke with your other hand. Offer only a few pieces at a time. This trains your dog to accept and enjoy your presence when eating. Train your dog to accept you both touching and removing the food bowl while it's eating. Do this by staying next to your dog while it's eating from the bowl and dropping a tasty treat into it. Use your hand to mix the treat into the food, or hide the treat in your hand, put your hand in the food bowl and as your dog noses your hand open it up and give the treat. Then let it finish the meal. Graduate to offering a liver treat by hand and as you do so, lifting the food bowl, adding the treat, then giving it back. Your dog quickly learns to enjoy your presence rather than feel threatened. Use the same procedure with bones or chew toys. Do this daily at first and intermittently later in life, and your dog will learn to accept the temporary "loss" of its food or toys.

Are you part of the problem?

We can be too ready to point at problem breeds, or talk of problem individuals, when there are problem owners too. Cambridge University scientists made a fascinating observation when they studied a form of dominance aggression that is not uncommon in red or blond Cocker Spaniels, less common in black Cockers, and almost unheard of in parti-coloured Cockers. The scientists had owners fill in self-assessment questionnaires about their own personalities and found that there was a direct relationship between dominance-aggression problems in Cockers and "pushover" personalities in Cocker owners. The more of a pushover you are, the more likely it is that your dog will develop its potential to become dominantly aggressive. It may be difficult to alter your personality, but you can certainly make sure your dog learns about life and learns how to accept its place by having as full and as stimulating an early life as possible.

Natural aggression cannot be "cured"; the aim of training is to control it. This needs a willingness on the part of the owner to accept that there's a problem and to do something about it. Danish research into dominance aggression between dogs revealed that this is a greater problem in dogs owned by young people, especially young males, than it is amongst other dog owners. Without the owner's willingness to acknowledge a problem, it can be almost impossible to eliminate aggression. Just as we need to pass a test to drive a car, or meet legal requirements to own a gun, I see no reason why there should not be parallel requirements to own a dog.

Some people even teach perfectly decent dogs to be aggressive. I think that the guys who want their dogs to be aggressive do so because they think their own willies are too small, but that's my personal view. As far as I'm concerned, training dogs to be aggressive should be left solely to police and other security forces – and the best police don't train their dogs to attack, they train them to "retrieve" targets. If you seriously want home protection, train your dog to bark fiercely and invest in a good burglar alarm.

Rehoming a troubled teen

Canine adolescence is too difficult for some dog owners. That means dog shelters contain more adolescent dogs, especially males, than any other age group (elderly dogs make up another large portion). A harder-than-average adolescence, combined with being abandoned or given to a shelter, results in dogs that have "issues". These issues are no different from those of other adolescents – lack of house training, over-excitability, barking, destruction, separation anxiety, or various forms of aggression – but they are less predictable in rescued or recycled dogs from an uncertain background than in a dog you've raised through puppyhood yourself.

Before you even look at a potential rescue dog, check out the rescue centre itself. If you have kids, don't take them with you on the first visit. The

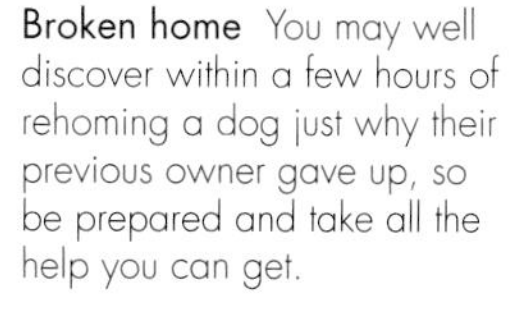

Broken home You may well discover within a few hours of rehoming a dog just why their previous owner gave up, so be prepared and take all the help you can get.

centre and the staff should be clean, organized, and efficient. Resourceful rescue centres measure both the health and the behaviour of their canine guests and should have written records of these assessments. Don't be too distracted by barking: traditional kennels, with rows of units, actually promote barking while more modern ones, built "in the round" so that dogs can easily see each other, reduce barking. Barking can be a behaviour problem that is unintentionally created during a stay at an old fashioned kennel. When adopting a dog, ask about the centre's adoption procedures. I don't just mean warranties on good health and a sale-or-return policy. The best canine rescue centres want to continue rehoming new dogs, not just recycling the same dogs. They will give you written instructions on training, feeding, and preventative health care. The best provide continuing advice on both basic obedience training and overcoming behaviour problems, while some offer continuing help with veterinary problems. If they haven't already neutered the strays and rescues they've taken in, they will often stipulate that you do so within a specified time. All dogs at rescue centres should be microchip identified (*see pp.217*).

Check that all dogs at the centre have been fully vaccinated against diseases common in your locality, and treated for external and internal parasites. Find out what the centre does to prevent the introduction of infectious disease. In the best kennels, new arrivals are housed separately, usually for a week, to ensure that they aren't bringing infections into the kennels. When you see a dog that appeals to you, ask whether it's a stray or has been handed in. If it has been handed in, a medical and behavioural history might be available.

Forewarned is forearmed

The dogs in dog shelters reflect both the dogs that people acquire either on a whim or because they're fashionable, as well as the types of dogs that are valued least by society. Mixed-breed dogs, regrettably, are deemed to have less value than purebred individuals, so often make up the majority of dogs needing new homes. Throughout North America and Europe, aggressive-looking dogs – bull terrier-types, Rottweilers, German Shepherd Dogs, or fighting breeds – are fashionable, especially amongst male new dog owners who were not raised with dogs as children. All are perfectly trainable, but they grow fast, they grow big, and many of them are rambunctiously active during adolescence, testing their owners' skills, finding out exactly what they can get away with. That's when inexperienced or irresponsible owners give up and either abandon their dogs or give them to shelters.

The result is that while there is always a variety of well-mannered, well-trained dogs needing new homes, the adolescents you're likely to meet at a dog shelter, however vibrant or beautiful, will have a selection of behaviour quirks that are unseen at first. If you're willing to select a dog carefully rather than on impulse, and if the people at the rescue centre are willing to help with their knowledge about a dog's behaviour, you can test a dog to determine not just its personality but what behaviour problems you may be inheriting.

ADOLESCENT BEHAVIOUR TESTS

Testing the behaviour of adolescents is much more accurate and reliable than testing young pups. In the following tests, give a score from 1 (least apparent) to 5 (highly apparent) for each of the symptoms. A low score means there is a low likelihood of the dog having or developing that particular behaviour, and a high score a high likelihood.

ATTACHMENT AND ATTACHMENT-SEEKING BEHAVIOUR indicate dogs are more likely than average to be trainable, but also either to suffer from separation anxiety or to develop it in the future. These are signs of attachment to particular members of the household or kennel:

- Displays a strong attachment to them ☐
- Tends to follow them from room to room around the home ☐
- Tends to sit close to or in contact when they sit down ☐
- Tend to nudge, nuzzle or paw them for attention when they are sitting ☐
- Becomes agitated when they show affection towards another person ☐
- Becomes agitated when they show affection towards another dog or other animal ☐

SEPARATION-RELATED BEHAVIOUR indicates significant separation anxiety problems. If a dog shows any of these behaviours when left or about to be left on its own, only take it on the basis either that the rescue centre will continue to provide one-to-one help to overcome the problem or that you will get hands-on help from an experienced dog handler:

- Shaking, shivering, or trembling ☐
- Excessive salivation ☐
- Restlessness, agitation or pacing ☐
- Whining, barking, or howling ☐
- Chewing or scratching doors, windows, walls or curtains ☐
- Loss of appetite ☐

TRAINABILITY indicates not only whether dogs are well trained, but whether they are suitable for and open to advanced training. Look for the following:

- Returns immediately when off the lead and called to do so ☐
- Immediately obeys a sit or stay command ☐
- Appears to attend to or listen closely to everything that the owner says or does ☐
- Is fast in responding to correction or discipline ☐
- Is fast at learning new tricks, tasks, or activities ☐
- Is not easily distracted by interesting sights, sounds, or smells ☐

EXCITABILITY can be a clue about future separation anxiety problems. Excitable dogs are more prone to barking or destructiveness when bored. Most dogs will be less excitable as adults than they are as adolescents. Judge how reactive and excited a dog is in these circumstances:

- When a member of the household returns home after a brief absence ☐
- When playing with a member of the household ☐
- When there is a knock on the door or the doorbell rings ☐

Where are you? Relatively few dogs actually howl, but this vestige of wolf behaviour is the canine way of asking where everyone has gone, and could they come back *right now*, please.

- Just before being taken for a walk ☐
- Just before being taken on a car trip ☐
- When visitors arrive at the home ☐

CHASING is common to all dogs, but some chase more than others. Moderate scores are typical, but if a dog has an overall high score on these it indicates potential re-call problems:

- Behaves aggressively towards other animals, such as cats or squirrels, while outdoors ☐
- Chases cats if given the opportunity ☐
- Chases birds if given the opportunity ☐
- Chases squirrels, rabbits, or other animals if given the opportunity ☐

DOG-DIRECTED FEAR AND AGGRESSION can be difficult to differentiate, because fearful dogs may use aggression to make the fear go away. Look for signs of fear when the dog is directly approached by any unfamiliar dog, whether it is larger, smaller, or of the same size. Check for signs of aggression in the following situations:

- When directly approached by an unfamiliar male dog while being walked on the lead ☐
- When directly approached by an unfamiliar female dog while being walked on the lead ☐

FEARFULNESS AND ANXIETY are common problems, not just in rescued dogs, and can be social or non-social. Fear of strangers develops during puppyhood but becomes firmly set during adolescence. Non-social fears can be completely idiosyncratic. A dog can develop a fear of almost anything, these are only a few examples:

- Unfamiliar men, women, or children while away from the home ☐
- Unfamiliar people visiting the home ☐
- Sudden or loud noises ☐
- Cyclists or skaters ☐
- Heavy traffic ☐
- Strange or unexpected objects ☐
- Thunderstorms ☐
- Unfamiliar situations ☐
- Wind or wind-blown articles ☐

AGGRESSION TOWARDS STRANGERS can occur for a variety of reasons discussed in more detail elsewhere (*see pp.283–84*). Regardless of the cause, signs of any form of aggression in these circumstances are a strong indicator that you will need professional help:

- When directly approached by an unfamiliar man, woman, or child while being walked or exercised on a leash ☐
- When approached by unfamiliar people while in the owner's car ☐
- When an unfamiliar person approaches the owner or a member of the owner's family either at home or away from home ☐

- When postal or other delivery workers approach the home ☐
- When strangers walk past the home or joggers, cyclists, rollerbladers, or skateboarders pass the home while the dog is outdoors ☐
- When unfamiliar people visit the home ☐

AGGRESSION towards owners is observed in only the most dominant or possessive individuals. Possessive aggression – over toys, bones, food or other articles – can be overcome through retraining (*see p.284*). Dominance aggression is more serious and difficult to overcome, and any dogs that show this form of aggression are best homed only with highly experienced handlers. Look for signs of aggression when a member of the household does any of the following:

- Verbally corrects or punishes the dog ☐
- Takes away toys, bones, or other objects ☐
- Bathes or grooms the dog ☐
- Directly approaches the dog while it is eating ☐
- Takes away food ☐
- Stares at the dog directly ☐
- Steps over the dog ☐
- Retrieves food or articles "stolen" by the dog ☐
- When an unfamiliar dog visits the home ☐

SENSITIVITY to pain or anticipation of pain is a test I'm particularly interested in. Dogs with low scores are easy to examine, meaning I can make a diagnosis about what is happening more efficiently. Judge whether the dog shows agitation during these activities:

- When examined or treated by the veterinarian ☐
- When having its nails clipped by a household member ☐
- When groomed or bathed by a household member ☐

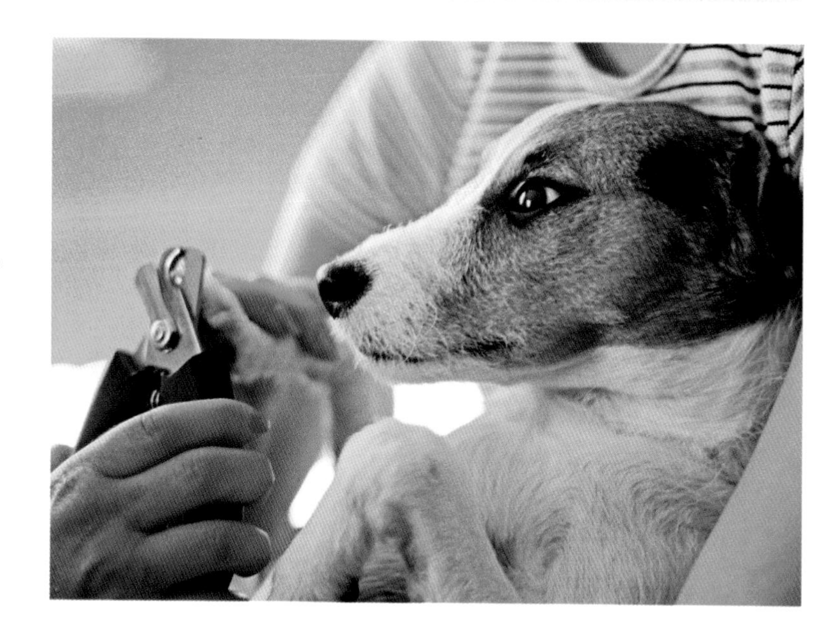

Trust in me It takes only one painful nail clipping to make even the least sensitive dog fear the procedure. Use a sharp clipper and replace it at least yearly. Nails are softest and easiest to clip after bathing. Ask your vet to show you exactly how to avoid the sensitive living tissue in the nail.

RECYCLED DOGS HAVE SPECIAL NEEDS

A rescued stray abruptly moves into a new cultural climate when it joins your family. After fending for itself, after making its own decisions, after doing for all of its life, it's now expected to do nothing. That's tough, really tough, especially for a dog with "street smarts". Compelling statistics from dog trainers show that overwhelmingly the most common problems in rescued adolescent dogs are those related to not being given enough activities to do. Whenever possible, condition a new adolescent to an indoor kennel, to its own personal space. Under a table can be a good location for a crate. When your dog considers this as its secure place or personal home, it becomes much easier to maintain an equilibrium at home, to quietly remove your dog from stimuli such as the doorbell until it's calm and controlled. This is especially vital for Border Collie types with exaggerated herding drive, for German Shepherd types with intense guarding instinct, and terrier types with powerful prey drives.

Reinforcing housetraining

All the principles of toilet training a pup apply equally to adolescent or older dogs (*see pp.175–79*). The important difference is that rescued older dogs have to unlearn their existing toileting habits before learning new ones. Crate training is ideal for housetraining adolescents, although a dog not used to a crate will first need to be conditioned to using it. In these circumstances I'd suggest a sturdy plastic crate that comes apart in the middle, leaving the bottom much like a typical dog's bed. Get the adolescent used to this bed and after several days, replace the top, keep the door open, and toss a little food or favourite toys in. Serve meals in it if you like, but don't close the door. Get your dog used to spending time in it with the door open. This works fastest when the crate is in your own bedroom at night.

Adolescent dogs can control their bowels and bladder far longer than pups can – eight hours or more – so they can be crated for longer periods of time. Make sure the dog has amusements in the crate, for example a hollow chew toy with soft cheese spread in the middle. Take a dog out as you would a pup, at least eight times a day and always give a "Do it!" command during toileting, followed by praise. Realistically most of you won't use a crate, because it's difficult to quickly train an adolescent who has never used a crate to accept it. Instead, tether your adolescent to you and don't let it roam freely in your home until after it has relieved itself outdoors. Of course, spend as much time as possible outdoors together so that your dog learns you are pleased when it toilets there. If at the first sign of toileting inside, correct with a sharp "No!" then immediately take your dog outside. Praise lavishly when it performs where you want. The key to success is to limit the chances of messes where you don't want them. Be consistent. Accidents will happen, but keep your cool. If accidents are happening frequently, it's your fault for not keeping close enough tabs. Be patient. An adolescent dog will learn the essence of house training within two weeks. If training is taking you longer, contact your veterinarian to ensure there are no medical problems and ask for advice from a professional trainer.

Health and first aid

Dogs have great biological clocks, which work best when you create daily routines. Feeding times are important: what goes in at a certain time comes out at a certain time. Many adolescent dogs are fed twice daily, but with their large stomachs and relatively short intestines, once a day feeding is perfectly acceptable. If you choose to reduce to once a day feeding, the evening meal may be the one to eliminate. This reduces the load of food in the gastrointestinal tract over night. A physically mature dog no longer needs nourishment for the body to grow, only needs to maintain itself. That means that most adolescents need less food than they needed during the growth stages of puppyhood. Now is the time to switch from a higher energy commercial puppy food to an adult formulation, which almost invariably contains fewer calories.

Adolescence is usually a time of good health for dogs. The variety of conditions associated with puppyhood are no longer problems, especially the gastrointestinal upsets and conditions such as juvenile vaginitis or juvenile pyoderma (a skin infection usually of the chin which is not uncommon in Dobermanns, Pugs, and other shorthaired breeds). Accidents can happen at any time of life, and in my experience adolescence is the time of life when dogs are most likely to injure themselves. In their excitement, adolescent dogs don't think, they just do. They get into trouble, sometimes potentially lethal trouble. Unfortunately the most common emergencies, road traffic accidents and penetrating wounds, are caused by us. The best approach to accidents is prevention. Keep sharp, toxic, or otherwise dangerous items out of your dog's reach. This is particularly important when events such as birthday parties might distract you.

Shock and vital signs

If your dog is injured, your help may be vital if it is to survive long enough to get to the vet. The priorities of first aid for your dog are simple: save your dog's life; prevent further damage or injuries; reduce pain and distress; get your dog safely to the vet. Always look first for shock, the silent killer.

Shock occurs when blood fails to get transported throughout the body. Advanced shock is life-threatening, and treating it takes precedence over all else. Signs of clinical shock are faster than normal breathing and heart rate, persistently pale gums or colour taking more than two seconds to return to the gums after finger pressure is applied and released, anxiety and restlessness or alternatively lethargy and weakness, and a normal or subnormal body temperature. The signs of advanced shock are shallow breathing and an irregular heart rate, very pale or blue gums or colour taking more than four seconds to return to gums after finger pressure applied, extreme weakness or unconsciousness, and a body temperature below 36.7°C (98°F). Shock requires immediate treatment. If your dog is conscious, don't let it wander and give nothing to eat or drink. Stop any bleeding and give heart massage and artificial respiration as necessary. Wrap your dog in a blanket to prevent further heat loss. Elevate the hindquarters and keep the neck extended to enable more blood to flow to the brain, and immediately transport it to the nearest vet.

Pain, shock, heart, or lung problems all increase a dog's breathing rate. Breathing fast is different from panting, which increases when a dog is hot or stressed. Calculate breathing, not panting, by timing chest movements. Large dogs normally breathe in and out around ten times a minute while the smallest may normally breath up to three times faster. Faster or shallow, irregular breathing are signs of life-threatening shock.

The heart rate also increases with pain, fever, and in the early stages of shock. A large dog may have a pulse rate as low as 50 beats per minute, while a small dog's heart might normally beat three times faster. Monitor your dog's pulse by feeling it through the femoral artery on the inner thigh. Alternatively, monitor the pulse of a lean dog by placing your hand over the heart, just behind the left elbow. On smaller dogs, you can feel the heart rate by grasping the chest just behind the elbows on both sides with your thumb and forefinger, then gently squeezing until you feel the contractions. This is difficult to do on fat dogs.

The ABC of first aid

The airway, breathing, and circulation are sometimes called the "ABC" of first aid. Your dog may stop breathing due to choking, near-drowning, smoke inhalation, electrocution, concussion, poisoning, diabetic coma, shock or blood loss. Heart failure is rare, but can be caused by electrocution if your dog chews through live electrical cables. If this happens, pull the plug from the mains and move the wire away from your dog with a wooden handle before even touching it.

First, ensure the airway is open. With the unconscious dog lying on its right side, extend the head forward, open the jaw and using your fingers sweep away any debris in the mouth or nose. Immediately close the mouth, keeping the neck aligned with the body. Next, check breathing. If the gums are a healthy pink colour, your dog may be unconscious but oxygen is probably still being carried around the body. If they are blue or white artificial respiration is necessary. If a dog's small size makes it difficult to determine if it's breathing, hold a small piece of tissue in front of a nostril and see if it moves.

Give artificial respiration only if you know that your dog has stopped breathing. Close the mouth and either place your mouth either directly over both nose and mouth or use your hand to form an airtight funnel over them, and blow in. You will see the chest rise. Take your mouth away, letting the lungs naturally deflate and the chest fall. Repeat this procedure 10 to 20 times per minute until your dog starts to breathe on its own. Check the pulse every 15 seconds while giving artificial respiration to make sure the heart is still beating. If it's not, add heart massage.

Heart massage is given when the heart has stopped and always takes priority over artificial respiration. When combined with artificial respiration it's called CPR or cardiopulmonary resuscitation. Add heart massage only if the heart is not beating. When the heart stops, the pupils dilate and the gums don't refill with blood. Place your dog on its right side, with the head lower than the rest of the body. On large dogs, place the heel of one hand on the chest just behind the elbow and the heel of the other hand on top, then vigorously compress the chest 100 times per minute, pressing down and towards the neck. On small dogs, grasp the chest behind the elbows with your thumb and forefinger and squeeze firmly up towards the neck, compressing the rib cage with 120 pumps per minute. Every 30 seconds, stop heart massage and give a breath of artificial respiration. Continue until the pulse returns, then give artificial respiration only until spontaneous breathing returns, and transport as soon as possible for veterinary attention.

Keep calm Everyone's first instinct is to rush and help, but until you know what the damage is, be cautious in handling an injured dog. You can make matters worse, or earn a bite if you touch a painful injury.

Trauma and bleeding

Trauma, the most common cause of physical injuries, occurs most frequently outdoors and in fair weather. A wound may not produce much blood but it can still be life-threatening. Don't waste time treating minor

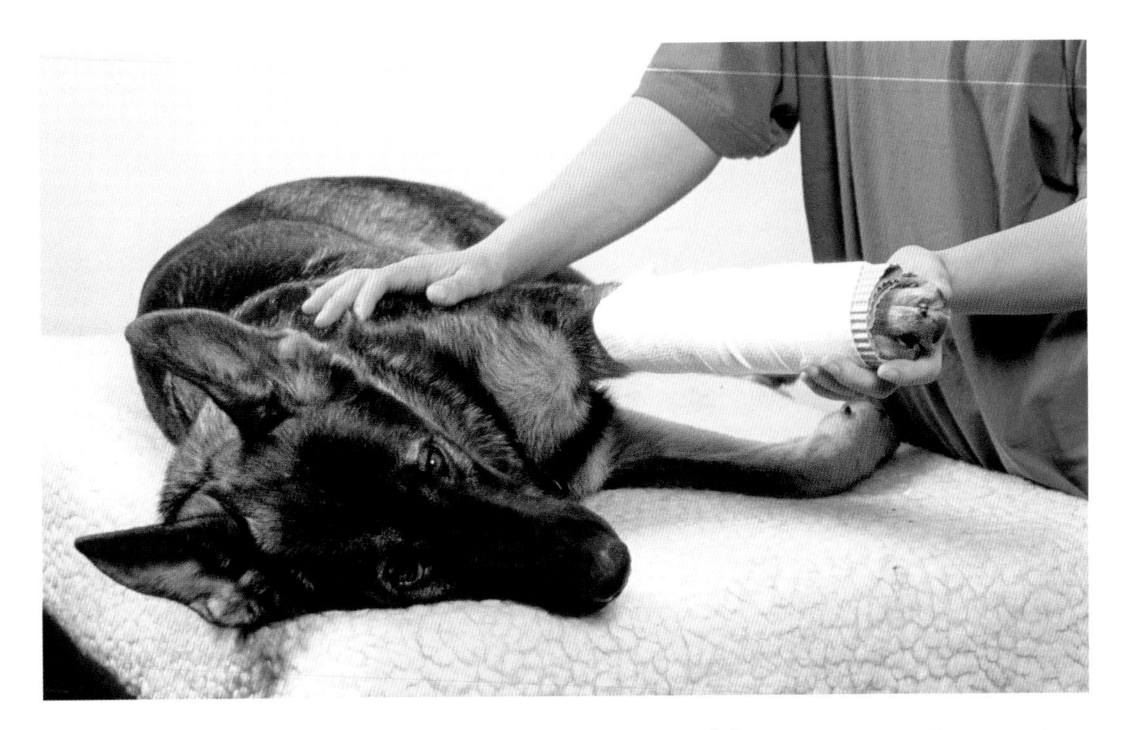

Prevent further injuries If a leg is obviously broken prevent further damage, without putting yourself at risk, by wrapping the limb. A bath towel is excellent but if you're good at first aid use something firmer such as corrugated cardboard. Get immediate veterinary attention.

problems if your dog has any penetrating wound to the chest or abdomen (with or without bleeding), a wound that spurts blood (indicating a bleeding artery), profuse bleeding from any body opening, or any bleeding that doesn't stop after five minutes pressure. These injuries need immediate emergency veterinary attention. Bright red blood in vomit or diarrhoea also requires immediate veterinary attention.

Bleeding injuries, cut paws, or crushed tail tips are amongst the most common injuries that need your immediate attention. Pads cut by glass, metal, or sharp ice are perhaps the most common foot injuries. Ice injuries are usually clean, but others get contaminated by debris. Dog bite wounds may appear small and clean, but invariably a variety of nasty bacteria are injected under the skin by the penetrating tooth. These wounds are often around the neck or on the thigh, and usually need veterinary attention. Before dealing with any wound, put a lead on your dog and command it either to stand or to sit.

Wash the area in clean tepid water; a sports drink bottle is excellent for squirting water over an injury. If bleeding has been minimal, apply disinfectant or antiseptic, ideally one of the spray disinfectants for use on our skin. Bite wounds are much more difficult to cleanse: try to get disinfectant into the wound, to kill bacteria under the skin. Apply non-stick gauze, wrap with absorbent material followed by an adhering bandage. Seek veterinary attention even for minor penetrating bite wounds. I've seen dogs become desperately ill and even die a week after a minor bite because bacteria entered the blood stream and caused a devastating cascade of events. Don't use Vaseline or other oily substances to stop bleeding or prevent a bandage from sticking to the wound. If you apply anything around a wound only use water-soluble products such as K-Y jelly that can be easily removed.

Minor bleeding from cut pads or crushed tail tips can be considerable, but seldom life-threatening. To stop bleeding, apply pressure at the site of bleeding for several minutes. Ideally use absorbent material such as medical gauze, but in a pinch use anything at hand including kitchen towel or facial or toilet tissue. When bleeding stops, don't remove the blood-soaked pad, because the clot is controlling the bleeding. Wrap it in place to maintain gentle pressure and keep it there until the wound is seen by your vet, at the latest on the same day. Take care that the bandage is not so tight that it restricts circulation: improper bandaging can cause more damage than the original injury. If bleeding is profuse, keep the bleeding area higher than the heart, but don't elevate a bleeding limb if there is a possible fracture. Keep the bleeding area immobile. Prevent ear flapping or tail wagging by holding or gently binding these regions against your dog's body, and pull a sock over a temporary bandage on a bleeding paw.

Tourniquets cut off the blood supply, and used incorrectly they're extremely dangerous. Only use one when there is profuse and devastating bleeding. Wrap a tie or similar piece of material above the bleeding wound and tie it with a releasable knot. Slip a stick or pen into the knot and twist until bleeding stops. A tourniquet should be applied for no more than ten minutes; if it takes longer to get to a vet, loosen intermittently. Don't use a tourniquet if your dog has been bitten by a venomous snake, because it will only increase inflammation. Immobilise the bitten area and get immediate veterinary help.

Moving an injured dog

Take care when lifting or moving an injured dog, because even the gentlest may bite because of fear or pain. Approach with care, always speaking quietly and reassuringly. If your dog is large, wrap one arm around the neck and support the dog against your body. Hold smaller dogs gently but firmly by the muzzle, using the elbow of your free arm to press their body against yours. Always use a muzzle unless the dog is vomiting, convulsing, has obvious mouth or jaw injuries or is unconscious. Any long material such as a tie can be used. Make a loop and gently tighten it around the muzzle, with the knot on top. Drop both ends down, cross them under the jaw, and tie them behind the dog's neck. You can improvise a stretcher using any flat item such as an ironing board, or hold a strong blanket as taut as possible. Gently pull the dog onto the stretcher by its chest and rump with its back towards you. If there is no one to help during transport, lightly bind the body, but not the neck, to the board.

It's almost always better for you to get to the vet than for the vet to come to you. If your dog can walk to the car let it do so, otherwise carry it. If the chest is injured, lay the the dog injured side down. Gravity keeps blood in the damaged lung. If a limb is injured, keep it up so that weight is borne on the other limbs instead. If the head is injured, keep it higher than the heart to reduce pressure in the skull. Make sure the dog is restrained and supported during your journey. Heavy blankets packed around the body offer both support and warmth.

CHAPTER ELEVEN

Adulthood

Physical and sexual maturity are eventually followed by emotional maturity. Dogs finally become what most of us want them to be: sensible, undemanding, but active participants in the lives of our families. This happy stage arrives at different times in different dogs and varies considerably by breed. One of the reasons I enjoy living with Golden Retrievers is that their emotional maturity arrives early, almost always by 18 months of age. Bean, one year old as I write this, is already a sensible and obedient adult. My daughter Tamara's Labrador Retriever is almost five years old and still in denial that she must ever grow up – an attitude that many people enjoy in dogs, which is why Labs are such popular family dogs. Emotional maturity may not develop in some breeds or in some individuals until well over two or even three years of age. The most humanized dogs never become emotionally mature.

Lifelong dependant or free spirit?

It sounds a bit harsh to say it, but what many of us want in our adult dogs is a form of arrested emotional development, perpetual, dependent pups in adult bodies. One of my previous Golden Retrievers, Liberty, when I was reading in the garden, would pick an apple off one of my trees, carry it over to me, drop it in my lap then stare into my eyes. She'd look at the apple, look back at me and as eloquently as words could ever say, ask me to stop what I was doing and spend a little time playing catch with her. That's what most of us want from our adult dogs: dependence on us, an emotional affiliation.

And that's what many of us get. We create lifelong pups in adult bodies by selectively breeding for juvenile behaviour and then by training dogs from puppyhood to depend on us. Adult pets rely on us to feed them (although most still follow their hard-wired biological impulses and scavenge). They see our personal spaces, our homes and the perimeter hedges and fences we use to mark out our territories, as the limits of their territories. Their desire for sex is diminished because so many dogs, especially in North America and northern Europe, are neutered while young. And, of course, they look upon us as "family", as care-givers. Our dogs come to us when they're hungry or thirsty, when they're frightened or worried, or when they just want to have fun. Adult pet dogs behave dramatically differently from adult feral dogs. Adult ferals use their early experience to satisfy their hunger and thirst, need for territory, desire for sex, and requirements for stable social structures to their lives. The most dominant strive for leadership within their social structure.

The charity I'm involved with, Hearing Dogs for Deaf People, trains dogs to alert their deaf owner to everyday sounds such as the doorbell or a smoke alarm. We have a high rate of success training dogs if we get hold of them while they're still pups; we're much less successful training adults that

All grown up Some owners might miss the playful bounce their dog had as a puppy when it grows up. But when you have a fair-sized and energetic breed, such as the Dalmation or many of the gundog breeds, the arrival of a little maturity can come as quite a relief.

spent their adolescence thinking for themselves. These dogs understand what they're being trained to do, but are more inclined to ask why, or to do something else they find more interesting – guarding their territory, chasing small furry things, interacting with other dogs, searching for sex.

Adopting an adult dog will be less problematic than adopting an adolescent, but all the principles of training a young dog also apply to an adult. Remember, when a rescued dog abruptly moves into a new cultural climate, when it joins your family after fending for itself, it can find it illogical to do what you want it to do. Adults may need continuing housetraining if their initial training was never completed, but don't mistake other normal behaviours – such as sex-related urine marking, fear, stress or anxiety, or submissive urinating – for a lack of normal housetraining.

Travelling with your adult dog

Some of you know I took Bean's predecessor Macy on travels around the United States, up through Scandinavia, and down the eastern border of the European Union, staying in campgrounds and motorhome and caravan parks. So I can confidently say that dogs are terrific travel companions, but if you plan to travel with your dog, even if only on short journeys, accustom it to what you expect. Condition your dog to travel in a crate if that's how you want it to travel, or purchase a pet harness that attaches to your car's back seat belt system. You'll need a seat cover and, of course a car towel.

When travelling with your dog you'll need most of its accessories: lead, food and water bowls, food and food treats, a large bottle of water for use during the journey, bedding, a comfort toy, a brush or comb, towel, poop bags, and a vaccination certificate (which you might have to show at campsites). For security, ensure that your dog is microchipped and its name tag has your mobile telephone number on it. Of course, check ahead that the places you plan to stay (including with your friends) accommodate dogs.

Dog holiday homes

If you can't or don't want to take your dog on holiday, and there's no one at home, consider using a well-run, clean, recommended boarding kennel or a professional and insured pet-sitting service. For boarding kennels, visit and ask questions, such as what possessions your dog is allowed to bring. The most conscientious "dog camp" or "dog hotel" owners provide comfortable accommodation and should question you as much as you question them. While in kennels, dogs should have frequent contact with the kennel staff, who should be understanding, caring, and creative. They should provide supervised activities with other dogs and when circumstances allow, two dogs should be housed together so that they always have company. Of course, good kennels require that preventative inoculations are up to date. Staff should ask you about your dog's diet needs and possible sensitivities. You should ask them about veterinary cover and always give them your vet's telephone number. The best kennels are booked up months before busy seasons, especially Christmas and New Year.

Perfect passenger As long as they don't get car sick, dogs make great companions on a road trip: they rarely disagree with your choice of driving music and never criticize your sense of direction.

Holiday camp It can be jarring to see your dog, which usually has the run of your house, behind a mesh door – it doesn't look like the holiday accommodation we'd choose. But as long as they spend a decent amount of time out and about, most dogs don't mind. This is where crate training at home is useful for you both.

Your vet should know the most efficient home- and pet-sitting services. Always interview a prospective sitter with your dog present. If you or your dog don't feel comfortable with them, ask the agency for someone else.

Travel safely

Car sickness is common in adults that were not accustomed to the motion of cars as pups. If yours suffers from it, condition it in exactly the same way that you would a younger dog, with gradually increased exposure and plenty of treats (*see pp.222–23*). If you're travelling from one climate to another, remember that your dog needs time to adjust to the climate changes just as much as you do and plan your journey accordingly. Before setting off on any international travel, make sure all vaccinations and preventative treatments are up to date, and that you have insurance that covers your dog while it is away from home.

At home you know what and where risks are, the areas to avoid, where there are traffic hazards, where there are dangers from other mammals, insects or reptiles. Travel takes your dog into the unknown, where dangers lurk. While hiking with Macy through the Mohave Desert I almost stepped on a rattlesnake in a shady wash, and avoided doing so only because I heard maracas being played nearby. If it hadn't rattled, Macy would have scented its presence and would surely have nosed it. I picked her up before she could, stepped out of the wash, put her on her lead and stuck to terrain where it was less likely that snakes could hide. On another occasion I lost Macy in deep woods in a state park on the shores of Lake Michigan. It was only through the good fortune of her arriving at a campsite a few miles away and the campers reporting a lost dog to the Park Rangers that, with deep embarrassment but even deeper gratitude, I got her back.

Macy encountered different risks in Scandinavia and Central Europe. Even with weekly prevention treatment she picked up countless disease-carrying ticks, especially in the forests on the Russian border of Finland.

In the Baltic States and particularly near the Belarus border of Lithuania, she was routinely threatened or attacked by Caucasian ovtcharkas, intimidating guard dogs. Travel is fun, but it's often safer at home!

Dealing with heatstroke

Always remember how inefficient dogs are at getting rid of excess heat, because they only sweat through the pads of their feet and rely on panting. That means a dog's core body temperature rises rapidly, and if it is not immediately reduced death follows quickly. Lethal heatstroke can occur within minutes in a car in direct sunshine. As I've mentioned, never leave your dog in a car in sunshine, even with the windows partly open. Find someone to look after it. Heatstroke doesn't just happen in cars, of course.

When core temperature rises, a dog pants and may have a glazed look to the face; it may be disorientated or even collapse. There may be excessive salivation and either bright red or pale gums. The heart rate can be increased, and there may be vomiting and/or diarrhoea. If your dog has been in a warm or hot environment and you see any of these signs, remove it from the hot environment immediately.

Ideally put it in a sink or bath and run a shower over it, especially over the head, and allow water to fill the sink or tub, surrounding the body. Alternatively use a garden hose or place your dog in a pool of water; don't put the head under water, and if your dog is unconscious make sure no water enters the mouth or nose. A package of frozen vegetables on the head reduces heat to the brain; this can swell, causing further serious problems. Give a drink of cool water with a pinch of salt to replace salt lost in panting. Massage the legs vigorously to help circulation and reduce the risk of shock. If possible, take the rectal temperature every five minutes. Continue cold water immersion until the temperature has fallen below 39.4°C (103°F). Don't worry if it drops to 37.8°C (100°F) or a little less; slightly low is less dangerous than extremely high. Get immediate veterinary attention.

Greenhouse effect Don't ever assume that because the air outside is cold, your dog won't overheat. A small, glassy box heats up extremely efficiently given any direct sunshine.

Wasp and bees You might think a fur coat would be some protection against stings, but dogs suffer these just as much as we do. If the swelling is small and hidden, you just never quite know what made your dog yelp like that.

Treating frostbite and hypothermia

Outdoor activity, either at home during the winter or when travelling in high or cold regions, can lead to frostbite or a more serious reduction in core body temperature, called hypothermia. The extremities – the tips of the ears and tail – have least protection and can suffer from local freezing, or frostbite. If core temperature drops catastrophically, life is threatened. Many dogs look as if they are amply protected from extremes of cold by their dense hair, but even well-insulated dogs can develop hypothermia. Those with short, smooth hair or little body fat are most susceptible. Hypothermia can develop when air temperature is moderate but a dog has been in cold water. Remember, even adult dogs are likely to do stupid things like dive into freezing water.

When core temperature drops a dog shivers and may be disoriented. It can appear exhausted, even drowsy. Frostbite, especially to the tips of the ears, the paws, and the tip of the tail, can occur in dogs exposed to icy wind, snow, or low temperatures. The extremities may be either pale, red, or puffy and painful when touched. The skin remains cold even when the dog is removed from exposure.

For hypothermia, immediately wrap the dog in warm blankets, warming them quickly in a tumble dryer if you can. Place a hot water bottle wrapped in a towel against the dog's abdomen – an unwrapped one will burn the skin. If the dog is conscious, give warmed fluids to drink. Take the temperature every ten minutes. If it's below 36.7°C (98°F), get immediate veterinary help. Once it is above 37.8°C (100°F) remove the hot water bottle but keep the dog in a warm room. Avoid overheating: warming up too fast can cause a painful tingling sensation, especially to the paws. Your dog may chew them, sometimes with devastating consequences, unless you prevent it from doing so.

If you see signs of frostbite, massage the area gently with a warm towel. Don't rub hard or squeeze, because this can further damage the area. Warm the frozen parts with cool to tepid water; if warmed too quickly they become very painful. As thawing occurs the skin becomes reddened; if it turns dark, get immediate veterinary help.

Snake bites and insect stings

You may not know there are snakes in the region you're visiting, but a curious dog will surely find them. Most bites involve the feet or head. Non-venomous bites rarely cause problems, but venomous snakes (including cottonmouths or water moccasins, rattlesnakes, copperheads, and coral snakes in the United States, Mississauga rattlesnakes in Canada, and adders in Europe and Scandinavia) can kill. There's no relationship between the size of the snake and the amount of venom it leaves when it bites, but more often than not, you don't see the snake anyway. After being bitten, your dog may become restless or pant more than expected, drool saliva, develop vomiting and diarrhoea, lose coordination, appear depressed, or go into clinical shock. Coral snake venom contains a nerve poison that causes weakness, pinpoint pupils, difficulty swallowing, and respiratory paralysis.

There are many misconceptions about what you should do if a snake bites your dog (or you). Don't wash the wound; that only increases the absorption of venom. Don't cut the wound or attempt to suck out the venom; this myth from Western films only makes matters worse and may even poison you. Don't apply an ice pack; it doesn't slow down absorption of venom. If there's any chance your dog has suffered a venomous bite, keep it quiet and get immediate veterinary attention. Local vets, familiar with the snakes in their area, often stock antivenin specific to those snakes. The earlier antivenin is given the better the results. Intravenous fluids, antihistamines, and other medications may also be used.

You should also become familiar with the biting insects where you live or where you travel with your dog, and if a bite or sting occurs, whenever possible try to identify the insect. Venomous spider bites cause pain at the site of the bite. Bitten dogs become excitable, weak, and feverish and have apparent muscle and joint pain. Without antivenin, they may suffer seizures, leading to shock and death. Scorpion bites cause intense local pain and inflammation, and healing is slow. Wasp and bee stings and ant bites are most likely to occur around the mouth or on the feet. Bees leave their stingers behind; look for small black sacs and scrape them out with a fingernail or edge of a credit card, and apply a paste of baking soda to the area (stings are slightly acidic). An ice pack diminishes swelling, while both calamine lotion or hydrocortisone cream relieve itching. If you have an antihistamine that's used by you or one of your family for your own hay fever, give it to your dog, regardless of its size. When hiking out of reach of vets in regions with poisonous insects, discuss with your vet the value of taking antivenin with you.

Snacks that sting You might not think my dog is as beautiful as I know she is, but trust me, Bean doesn't usually have a lop-sided, swollen cartoon muzzle: this was the day she swallowed a wasp. The effects were not too long-lived or serious, but painful enough to make her more careful.

Things still change Don't assume that just because your dog has stopped growing and changing, you can simply feed it the same amount every day for the rest of its life. Pay some attention to its circumstances and lifestyle, and adjust what you give accordingly.

Diet and health

Many adult dogs reach a healthy nutritional balance, consuming the same number of calories each day that they use up, so their weight remains stable. Having established an ideal balance of digestive micro-organisms in their intestines, the frequency and consistency of their stools are regular. Many adult dogs, but not all. I routinely see dogs that almost surreptitiously gain weight. Sometimes the gain is so slow it goes unnoticed for several years. In other cases it is so rapid a dog becomes truly obese within ten months.

Each dog has its own individual energy needs, depending on age, activity level, and the time of the year. As with us, a dog's parents also predetermine its metabolic rate, and some individuals or breeds are born with a tendency to be lean or to go to fat. Below are some average daily kilocalorie (kcal) requirements for different body weights, lifestyles, and ages.

Active adults

Working dogs that herd, guard, search, participate in sports or agility, or act as assistants for disabled people need approximately one-and-a-half to two-and-a-half times the food energy that pet dogs do. If the weather is cold energy demands can go up another 50 per cent. In the most extreme circumstances of winter sled-dog races, a working sled dog may need 10,000 calories per day – the same amount my son Ben consumed when he raced to the South Pole in 2009! Human athletes increase their stamina by consuming carbohydrates, but this is not a natural source of stamina food for all dogs. Greyhounds and other dogs working in short sprints do benefit from increased carbohydrates, but endurance dogs (or men racing to the South Pole) need increased fat in their diet. If your dog is working hard, for example spending the day doing trail work or hunting, feed a high-fat, energy-dense, highly digestible diet in two or more portions daily. Provide a small meal about one hour before working and the largest meal an hour after hard work. During endurance work, provide small amounts of high-fat, high-protein food. There are special commercially produced high-energy diets for working dogs, which are sometimes called "performance" foods.

Sex burns calories

Sex takes up energy, and not just the act of sex. For male dogs in particular, just looking for sex is pretty energy consuming. It means more wandering,

DAILY KCAL REQUIREMENTS OF AN ADULT DOG

Weight kg	Weight lb	INACTIVE	ACTIVE	WORKING	PREGNANT	SENIOR
2–5	4–11	185–370	210–420	295–590	220–440	150–300
6–10	13–22	420–620	480–705	675–990	505–740	345–505
11–20	24–44	665–1040	775–1180	1065–1665	800–1250	545–850
21–30	46–66	1080–1410	1225–1600	1725–2255	1295–1690	885–1155
31–40	68–88	1445–1750	1640–1990	2310–2800	1735–2100	1180–1430
41–50	90–110	1780–2070	2025–2350	2850–3310	2140–2480	1460–1690

more leg cocking, more territory creation and defence, and more fighting. But while this increases energy demands, some dogs, especially males, go off food while out looking for sex. Male and female sex hormones also affect metabolism: when they are reduced, either through neutering or as a result of advancing years, about one third of all dogs have a tendency to go to fat. Preventing weight gain after neutering is simple: record your dog's exact weight when it is neutered, and reduce food consumption by 20 per cent. The chances are that your dog will retain its pre-surgical weight. If it loses weight, return to the former meal size.

Pregnant dogs require very little increase in food until late in pregnancy. During the last three weeks of her nine-week pregnancy, increase the food you give a mother-to-be by 10 per cent per week. Her energy requirements explode when she is producing milk for her pups, in part because bitch's milk contains about 40 per cent more energy than cow's milk. At the height of lactation she will need three times her normal daily food intake, and even after her pups reduce their consumption she will continue to need 50 per cent more than her normal intake just to get back into standard condition. A puppy or performance food is ideal at this time.

Fat genes?

As with us, the tendency to become overweight runs in canine families. A dog's body condition is influenced not only by what you feed but also by genetic factors. Surveys carried out at veterinary schools show that some breeds are more prone to obesity than others. If you have one of these breeds, you will need to be extra vigilant about the amount you feed and the number of treats and snacks offered.

- American Cocker Spaniel
- Basset Hound
- Beagle
- Cairn Terrier
- Cavalier King Charles Spaniel
- Dachshund
- Labrador Retriever
- Norwegian Elkhound
- Rough Collie
- Shetland Sheepdog

Obesity in dogs

In theory, no species in nature (including dogs and us) should ever get fat. Most animals maintain a normal body weight without apparently working at it. This is because hormones released in the intestines, together with glucose and various amino acids in the bloodstream, act on receptors in the brain to give the feeling of a full stomach. But sometimes this feedback system fails. North American and northern European pet statistics all sing the same song. Over one-third of our pet dogs are overweight, and a good (or bad) percentage of these are clinically obese – which technically means they are so fat that their health is seriously compromised and their lives are shortened.

The life less lived It might be that you can put off thoughts about future health problems your dog may have due to obesity. But every day that a dog is obese is a day that it can't do normal doggy things – chase small moving objects and actually catch up with them, hold its own in a game with other dogs, or run for the sheer joy of running.

There's evidence that natural brain opiates called endorphins, chemicals that make you feel good, are higher in fat dogs than in lean ones. The brain produces endorphins as a response to stress, and some scientists argue that because we don't let our pet dogs behave the way dogs would naturally behave – stalking, chasing, exploring, investigating – they're stressed, even if they don't look it. Another theory is that the body "defends" the number of fat cells that were created in puppyhood. Metabolically speaking, the dog's body wants to be the way it was during infancy, so a diet may lead to a temporary loss of weight, but the body will strive to regain what was lost. Regardless of the specific causes, most instances of obesity in dogs are inspired by and perpetuated by us. We control what our dogs eat, so it's only us who are to blame for fat dogs.

Some people say that fatness is just an aesthetic concern, that society has a social fixation about weight. But there are biological grounds for equating leanness with attractiveness. The dog food manufacturer Purina carries out feeding trials on their various brands of food, and it was one of their trials in Labradors in the 1980s that showed that dogs who were deliberately kept skinny lived on average 18 months longer than their more rounded siblings and developed signs of osteoarthritis much later (*see p. 193*).

I'm sure one of the reasons we allow our dogs to go to fat is because we feel good when we feed them. We just love feeding living things – birds in our gardens, squirrels in the park, animals at the zoo. We get our own rush of brain endorphins when we personally give food to animals. This is a running theme in my own home: I'm keeping Bean lean, so I can easily feel her ribs, but The Chief comments at least once a week on how skinny Bean looks. The mother in Julia is satisfied when she sees a well-rounded dog – not fat, but with a little more insulation.

Understand normal body shape

Our modern urban lifestyle is not what dogs were made for. Let's be honest with ourselves. For most of our dogs, life is tedious and dull. For many of them, just about the most exciting event each day is feeding time. Deep down most of us know this. We know we aren't providing our dogs with the type of physical exercise they really need. But while many owners of obese dogs know they're living with unhealthy companions, some people don't recognize when a dog is simply overweight.

All of us take pictures of our dogs. To help you to assess your dog's body condition, regularly take side and top photos in the same location and compare your dog's size with previous images. This is not as accurate as routine weighing, but it's useful to have an image of the condition you want your dog to return to. Here are the clinical descriptions of body conditions:

- Emaciated: ribs showing, no fat cover; severe abdominal tuck, bones at base of tail obvious with nothing between skin and bone; no fat palpable in the abdomen.
- Thin: ribs easily felt with minimal fat cover; waist very obvious behind ribs; bones at base of tail raised with only minimal tissue between skin and bone; minimal abdominal fat.
- Ideal: ribs palpable through slight fat cover; waist visible behind ribs; bones at base of tail covered in a thin layer of fat; minimal abdominal fat.
- Overweight: ribs not found easily because of moderate fat cover; waist hardly discernible; bones at base of tail covered by moderate fat; moderate abdominal fat.
- Obese: ribs disappeared under thick fat cover; no waist, distended abdomen; bones at base of tail difficult to feel through fat; extensive abdominal fat.

Tackling canine obesity

Keep a record of exactly what your dog eats – including all the little extras. This makes you more conscious of all the add-ons. Ideally cut out the extras but if this isn't possible (especially if there's a weak link in your home) replace them with bits of fruit and vegetable. Feed low-fat foods containing good-quality carbohydrates: barley and sorghum give a more gradual energy release into the bloodstream than rice, and the sugar in the bloodstream affects the "satiety" centre in the brain, damping down the desire to eat. Non-fermentable fibres like wheat bran or cellulose contribute virtually no calories and are added to light diets for overweight or inactive dogs and to breed-specific diets for those prone to obesity, such as Labrador Retrievers. Manufacturers seldom state the calorie content of their food, even if it is promoted as "lite" or "lean" – in some countries, the energy content is not permitted on most dog foods. As a rule of thumb, assume that such a food has 15–25 percent fewer calories than the average from that manufacturer. If a label doesn't explain the calorie content, reputable manufacturers will provide you with this important information, so visit their website and ask. Veterinary low calorie diets are also available, as dry or wet foods.

Naturally lean (top left) Greyhounds and related breeds don't just move fast, they look fast. Their high belly tuck and minimal fat cover might be alarming if we saw them in another dog.

Heavy bones (top right) Mastiff breeds have a heavy-set look that starts with a sturdy skeleton, on top of which they have a natural tendency to build bulky muscle. That's muscle, not fat.

In trouble (bottom left) This is not a natural, or healthy, look for any dog. The prescription is pretty simple: more fun and games, and either less food or a different food.

Sausage dog (bottom right) With some breeds, including Dachshunds, short limbs make it more difficult to see weight gain. You should always be able to feel the ribs.

ENCOURAGE HEALTHY EATING DURING ILLNESS

All dogs are occasionally ill, and energy requirements increase during convalescence after any prolonged illness. But a dog's desire to eat may be impaired by the illness, so when feeding a convalescing dog stimulate interest by warming up energy-dense food to just below body temperature. This enhances the food's taste and all-important aroma, and is easy to do in a microwave. If your dog normally has dry food, add a small amount of animal fat to it, to enhance the smell and make the food more appealing, or add water at body temperature. Unless your veterinarian advises you not to, increase dietary fat as well as protein. Feed small amounts frequently. If part of the veterinary treatment involves changing diets, make the switch gradually, mixing the new into the old in 25 per cent increments over several days.

The advantages of high quality, commercially produced dog foods are consistency and convenience: it's easy to exactly measure how much energy you are feeding your dog. But that doesn't mean you can't or shouldn't cook for your dog. Adults can lose weight on home-made diets as long as you stick to a consistent recipe: the one given on (*see p.198*) provides 880 kcal of energy, enough for a day for an active 10kg (22lb) dog.

Of course, increase your dog's exercise. This might accelerate the basic metabolic rate, and it's a guaranteed way for your dog not just to lose weight but also to become more fit. And avoid crash diets: they upset a dog and only drive the metabolism to be more efficient and fat-storing in the future. You may need help sticking to a healthy dog's diet just as much as your dog does: if you're being troubled by mournfully melting brown eyes, discuss the problem with your veterinary staff. In these circumstances they make fine, understanding, and tough counsellors.

Adult dog training

I'll say it again, because it needs saying: life with us is pretty dull for some dogs, especially for those that descend from ancestors selectively bred to work. The Border Collie is the prime example. Even Borders selectively bred for companionship rather than working still have an overpowering need to think and to do. The same is true for gundogs from lines selectively bred for their working ability rather than simply for conformation to an arbitrary breed standard based on looks. If you have the time and the inclination, you and your dog can participate in a variety of physical activites. All involve advanced training and are based on your dog having acquired reliable, basic obedience during youth.

In obedience trials, you and your dog will work through a series of competitive obedience exercises such as heeling, scenting, and retrieving. For some dog owners, this has evolved into top-hat-and-tails dancing with dogs. Personally, I die a thousand deaths when I see dogs being put through these routines – to my eyes it's like dressing your dog in a peach satin baby-doll outfit – but there's no doubt that from a trainer's perspective it's challenging and satisfying to train your dog to walk 30 paces backwards in a straight line to the beat of 'Jailhouse Rock'. Dogs enjoy the challenges, but especially the hugs they get when they perform well. All major kennel clubs sanction their own obedience trials.

In working trials, dogs do what they were originally bred to do: point, set, retrieve, herd, chase lures, follow scent trails, go to ground. One of the most popular forms is field work: scenthounds follow ground or air scent, pointers search, find a bird, then hold a classic "point", and retrievers retrieve objects in a variety of circumstances. In sheepdog trials, dogs and their handlers compete against each other to perform a set of herding manoeuvres, and there are even working trials for Newfoundlands to rescue people from water or to pull boats. For sled dogs, sled racing over set courses originated in North America and spread to Scandinavia. It's now popular even in countries with little or no snow, where dogs compete by pulling a wheeled sled called a gig.

In agility games, dogs complete with each other and against the clock over a set course of jumps, balances, and weaves. Thoughtful obedience is integral in classic agility, because the trainer is always near the dog, encouraging or instructing. That means both you and your dog should be physically fit. Border Collies are so outstanding at classic agility that there is often one competition for Borders and another for all other dogs. Borders also dominate activity sports such as flyball, in which dogs race down a short course over sets of hurdles, step on a board that launches a tennis ball, catch the ball, and race back over the hurdles to the start line, allowing the next canine member of the team to do the same.

High flyer This is where work counts, rather than looks or breed (except for Border Collies). Handlers have to direct their dog by voice and gesture alone around courses that can cross over themselves and involve complex turns and tricky choices. Both dog and trainer need to be fit, alert, and utterly in tune.

Miss Afghan Conformation shows essentially judge how well individual dogs conform to a written description of the breed. That's all. Originally the descriptions were derived from and related to the breed's role and abilities, but these days they are purely cosmetic in almost all cases.

Dog shows, or conformation shows, are the equivalent of Miss World for canines. I don't know if the women who participate in Miss World have any wryness or wit, but there isn't a whole lot of humour when you're competing at the top of official dog shows. It's a serious business. Ask a show-Poodle owner whether he or she also does hedges, and you're likely to be killed on the spot (at least with a look). Official dog shows are sanctioned by the organization your dog is registered with. Local clubs affiliated to the registration body hold competitions to select dogs that most conform to breed standards. These may then compete in regional shows and the best make it to national shows. I have reservations about dog shows, because in the worst of circumstances they promote unhealthy extremes – the flattest faces, shortest legs, largest heads – but the dogs that win do so because they genuinely enjoy being shown. They thrive in the show ring. So do their owners or handlers. It's all quite innocent – usually. Unofficial shows are much more relaxed affairs where dogs compete for "Face most like Madonna" or "Waggiest Tail" or "Best-preserved golden oldie".

Adult health

Adult dogs are typically healthy. More sensible than adolescents, they are less prone to injuries. Properly vaccinated and wormed, they are also less likely to have infections and internal infestations by parasites. Efficient immune systems keep potential cancers under control. Pet health insurance statistics reinforce this: dog owners make many insurance claims for dogs under the age of 18 months, then claims quickly and dramatically drop off and don't start to increase again until dogs are roughly over eight years old. That's pretty much what I see in practice. I see my patients frequently when they're pups or adolescents, usually once a year when they're adults, then increasingly frequently when they become "senior dogs".

But that doesn't mean that adult dogs have few medical problems. Moving dogs out of their natural outdoor environment into our own preferred indoor lifestyle has presented their immune systems with new problems that they often have difficulty coping with. As a very general rule the various forms of allergy – itchy skin, diarrhoea, raspy breathing – show themselves during early adulthood. A variety of hormonal upsets may also develop in middle adulthood, and bone, joint, circulation and reproductive system problems become evident by late adulthood. Other medical conditions can of course develop at any time during adulthood. Today, in my urban clinic, most of the problems I see in adult dogs are related to who the dog's parents were – to problems associated with selective breeding.

Sharpen up Weave-poles that just spike into your lawn (or a quiet corner of a park) can be bought or made, and even if you never enter a trial, they make a fun addition to your daily routine. Interesting walks are a necessity for dogs, but they can get a lot of physical and mental exercise in even the smallest garden too. As a bonus, your dog might knock things over a bit less inside.

Allergies are a modern affliction

Technically, allergy is an exaggerated, inappropriate, and unnecessary response of the immune system to non-infectious things. The word is little more than 100 years old, coined in 1906 by a Viennese paediatrician, Baron Clemens von Pirquet, and for both people and dogs this is largely a condition of modern, Western living. A dog's environment today is radically different from that it evolved to live in. In North America and western

Coughs are complex This can be one of the most difficult symptoms to assess. Coughing could be caused by anything from bonfire smoke or stuck food to an infection, a heart problem, or an an allergy. Visit your vet with any dog that coughs persistently.

Europe the majority of us spend 95 per cent of our time either indoors or in public or private transport. So do our dogs, and some of them suffer itchiness because of that. Allergic reaction often occurs on a dog's skin, causing itchiness, but it can also happen on the lining of the air passages, causing sneezing, coughing or difficulty breathing, or to the lining of the gastrointestinal system, causing vomiting or diarrhoea.

Allergy is caused by an antibody triggering extreme activation of specialized immune cells called mast cells. Antibodies are markers that "tag" foreign material for other immune cells to attack. Also called immunoglobulins or "Ig", they are proteins and they have different forms, given acronyms such as IgA, IgE, IgG, and IgM. In allergic individuals, IgE binds to receptor sites on the surface of mast cells in the skin and the lining of the stomach, lungs, and upper airways. Mast cells probably evolved to attack internal parasites such as intestinal or lung worms, and they are like mines primed with ten different chemicals. When an allergic dog is exposed to the allergen that the IgE recognizes, it causes the mast cells to either release some of their chemicals or quite literally explode, releasing inflammatory substances such as histamine and prostaglandins. If the chemical reaction occurs on the skin, the result is itchiness and the dog scratches. If it occurs in the air passages it causes coughing, and if it occurs in the digestive tract it causes diarrhoea.

Just as allergy runs in human families, there's a breed predisposition to it in dogs such as Akitas and Shar Peis and breeds with predominantly white coats, such as West Highland White terriers, Bull Terriers, and English Setters. Vets usually recommend avoidance as the best treatment for allergies. They try to determine specific causes through a detailed history-taking that usually extends through all the seasons of the year, by performing allergy tests, by feeding altered-protein or novel-protein diets, and sometimes by temporarily removing a dog from its normal environment.

Maintenance checks Daily grooming is a necessity for dogs with long coats prone to tangling, but on any kind of coat it gives an opportunity to spot anything amiss before it becomes a major issue.

This can be exasperatingly prolonged, so for immediate relief from allergy veterinarians try to "turn off" the allergic reaction at its source. Many different chemicals are released when mast cells explode, but only histamine can be moderately controlled, by using anti-histamines. An anti-leukotriene is licensed for use in people, but doesn't appear to be effective in dogs. A short course of a topical or even oral corticosteroid may be needed. High-dose essential fatty acid (EFA) supplements are thought to help by either affecting prostaglandin synthesis, and so diminishing the intensity of mast cell explosions, or locking into receptor sites on cell walls, preventing inflammatory chemicals such as histamine from taking hold.

Skin maintenance and itches

Statistics vary, but most agree that around 40 per cent of visits to the vet are to do with skin disease. The reasons are obvious: it's easy for us to see if something wrong is happening to the skin and quite simply, dogs get itchy and their scratching bothers us almost as much as it soothes them.

Dogs keep their hair and skin in a healthy condition by licking, nibbling, chewing and scratching, by rolling, especially on sand, grass, or dry earth, or simply by getting intentionally or unavoidably wet. Licking and scratching are perfectly normal activities. Adult dogs often develop grooming rituals, especially when they awaken in the morning. They often give a whole body shake to loosen up hair compressed during sleep then have a good old scratch. Bum maintenance – a few licks of the anal region – is often carried out at the same time. Rolling and rubbing are ways dogs massage their skin. These activities stimulate the oil-producing sebaceous glands that add sheen and water-proofing to the coat, and remove debris from parts of the body

Natural system Rolling is a great way for a dog to groom itself. Traditional cleaning for fur coats even copied rolling in earth or sand, and involved working in bran, starch, or fine clay and then shaking it out. Of course it's a different matter when your dog chooses to roll in something foul-smelling, an activity in which dogs (and Macy here was no exception) take peculiar delight.

Rinse cycle A bath or shower cleans more thoroughly than your dog can manage itself – but do rinse out any shampoo very thoroughly.

Dry cleaning Brushing does more than just untangle the coat. It removes a fair amount of debris and old skin cells at the same time.

that neither tongue nor paws can reach. Many skin conditions, including infections and parasites, accelerate wear and tear to the outer layer of the skin, the epidermis, leading to dander or scaling. Flaky skin, with or without itchiness, is a sign that something is going wrong. During adulthood, parts of the skin that are chronically irritated, such as the elbows on large dogs, thicken. The elbow calluses visible on virtually all heavy dogs by the time they are five years old are defensive, reducing the likelihood of skin breaking and pathogens getting through.

Selective breeding has enhanced the coats on many breeds, and these dogs need our help to keep their hair and skin healthy. Some breeds, including all the Spaniels, grow an abundance of hair between their toes, which acts like a magnet for dirt and debris, but also for grass seeds that once caught in the hair easily penetrate the skin causing abscesses. Grass seeds also get trapped by hair in the ears. Use blunt-tipped scissors to routinely trim out surplus toe hair, especially during dry summer weather. Even the moderately long hair of breeds such as the Golden Retriever collects burrs and other vegetation. Cooking oil is ideal for loosening these up for removal. Matted or tangled hair is more difficult. Some can be loosened up by applying cornflour as a dry lubricant and brushing out with a slicker brush or a wide-toothed comb, but it's often necessary to cut matted areas out. In warm weather, consider giving your dog a short haircut, regardless of what breed standards say. Thick-coated breeds such as Chow Chows, Pekingese, and St Bernards are so much more comfortable in short coats during hot, humid weather.

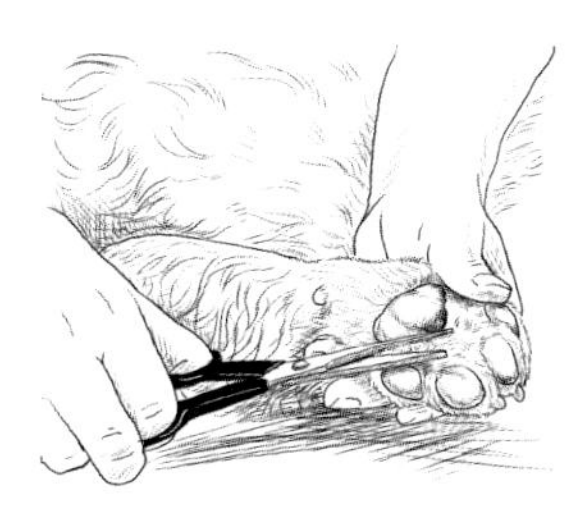

Safe snips If you're nervous about trimming paws, using round-tipped hairdressers' scissors avoids sharp pokes.

That hits the spot Scratching doesn't always mean there's a problem. It pulls out loose, tickly hair, dead skin cells, and debris that accumulate in the coat. A good scratch and a shake are natural – and clearly satisfying – grooming methods. But if your dog is scratching more than usual, think of other causes such as fleas or an allergic itch.

More dogs scratch because of fleas than perhaps for all other reasons combined. You probably won't see the fleas, you may not even see any flea dirt on your dog's skin, evidence that a flea has been on the premises, but flea saliva is intensely irritating to many dogs. Next most common is atopy, an allergic reaction to irritants such as dust mites, pollens, mould spores, even human dander. Further down the list of causes of itchiness are allergy to foods, to skin bacteria or yeast, and to materials such as grass sap.

Itchy skin inflammation can be triggered by allergens that are absorbed through the skin, but more frequently by allergens that are inhaled into the respiratory system. Only some dogs have respiratory signs; many others exhibit their allergic response to inhaled antigens through itchy skin inflammation, especially to the face, feet, and ears. In allergic contact dermatitis, the allergic reaction occurs only on parts of the body in direct physical contact with the allergen. Frequent shampoos are recommended for these: a rough coat is ideal for capturing mould spores and pollen. Liberty, one of my previous Golden Retrievers, was allergic to grass sap, which caused a dermatitis on the relatively hairless parts of her torso. Diagnosing contact dermatitis sounds simple, but it wasn't until Lib's third spring that I realized she got itchy immediately after the grass was cut for the first time after the end of winter.

Food allergies

Pups and adolescents may not be able to process some foods, and suffer from "dietary-intolerance diarrhoea" when fed certain items. True allergy to food only occurs in dogs over roughly a year of age, in adults. All purebreds, crossbreds, and randombreds are susceptible, but some breeds have an increased risk. These include the following:

- Cocker Spaniel
- Dalmatian
- English Springer Spaniel
- Golden Retriever
- Labrador Retriever
- Lhasa Apso
- Miniature Schnauzer
- Shar Pei
- Soft-coated Wheaten Terrier
- West Highland White Terrier

Surprisingly, food allergies may cause no gastrointestinal problems at all but trigger an allergic response in the skin, sometimes localized to the face or the ears. The most common antigens that cause canine food allergy are proteins. Some textbooks say beef and dairy proteins are the most likely to cause allergy, but allergy is most likely to develop to proteins a dog has previously been eating. Where beef is the most common protein in dog food, it accounts for about 60 per cent of diagnosed cases. Where protein sources such as lamb and chicken are more commonly used in dog food, beef and dairy are relatively minor causes of food allergy. Some vets feel that early weaning or early gastrointestinal infection may both be contributing factors to the development of food allergy later in life.

Food allergy is diagnosed by feeding a novel and unique diet that the dog has not eaten before for at least six weeks. Because the dogs I see seldom eat either fish or potato, that's the diet I usually recommend to see if anything in the former diet is provoking an allergic response. If skin disease or bowel problems resolve but return when the former food is fed again, this confirms true food allergy, and we usually stick to fish and potato as the new routine diet. The processing procedures used to produce commercial dog food may somehow increase the antigenicity of some foods, so processed food may trigger an allergic response while fresh food with identical ingredients doesn't. Some dog food manufacturers produce hypoallergenic foods, in which the protein has been "hydrolyzed" or broken down into its constituent amino acids. These diets are readily available through veterinarians.

Hormonal upsets

Hormones are chemical messengers that influence the activity of cells, and there is some evidence that hormonal upsets are occurring more frequently in adult dogs than they once did. Thyroid hormone regulates the body's metabolic activity. Excessive thyroid production is very rare in dogs, but underproduction of thyroid hormone may be the most common hormonal condition, and in four out of five sufferers of hypothyroidism, the thyroids have been attacked and destroyed by their own immune systems. Cocker Spaniels, Golden Retrievers, and Dobermanns are frequently affected breeds. An affected dog typically insidiously gains weight, acts older than expected, has reduced interest in exercise, develops skin and hair problems, and might have personality changes. The prognosis is excellent once replacement therapy starts. In sugar diabetes the insulin-producing cells in the pancreas are similarly attacked and destroyed by the immune system. Diabetic dogs, often overweight to begin with, eat well but lose weight and drink more than expected. They usually respond well to insulin. Another hormonal condition of middle-aged adult dogs that causes increased thirst and appetite but usually an associated weight gain is an excessive production of cortisone by the adrenal glands. This condition, usually called Cushing's Disease, occurs most frequently in Dachshunds and a variety of terriers and schnauzers. They usually respond to medication that suppresses overproduction of cortisone.

Lameness in older adults

In the excitement of the moment even adult dogs do dumb things. They turn too sharply, jump from heights, slam into stuff. Happy, healthy adult dogs inevitably hurt themselves. But as the years go by natural wear and tear also occurs, especially to joints. This leads to chronic pain although, stoics that most of them are, dogs seldom complain about their discomfort. If your dog is limping, something hurts. How you treat that hurt depends upon whether the lameness is caused by an accident (traumatic), and will repair with time and rest, or whether it's caused by wear and tear (degenerative) and will get worse over time.

Invisible problems Licking an area obsessively can be a result of any number of problems. It might be a minor injury, frostbite in winter, or something caught in the hair. Equally it might be an itchy allergy. Start by looking for the obvious, and ask for your vet's help if you draw a blank.

THE DIFFERENCE BETWEEN A SPRAIN AND A STRAIN

The terms your vet may use for a joint injury have quite specific meanings:

Strains means damage to muscle fibres and tendons. There can be accompanying bruising.

Sprains cause a similar lameness to strains, but they don't involve muscle. They are caused by overstretching a ligament, the fibrous tissue that connects bones to other bones. Knee ligaments are susceptible to sprains.

Dislocation or luxation is when a bone separates from its adjoining bone, while a subluxation is a partial separation. Both are caused by trauma or inherited joint faults.

Slack or lax joints feel loose when examined. Hip dysplasia can cause slack hip joints, especially in young adults. When a ligament tears or ruptures, the joint becomes loose, and a ruptured anterior cruciate knee ligament results in a slack knee joint.

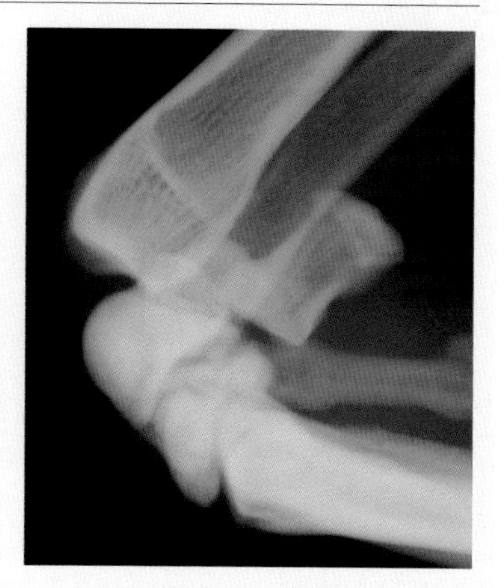

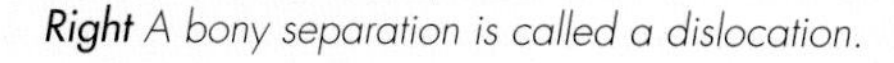

***Right** A bony separation is called a dislocation.*

If your dog is limping or favouring a leg, it's avoiding bearing full weight either because something hurts or because something has torn and the leg no longer works properly. In either instance, see your vet. If your dog is lame and licking a paw or part of a leg, it probably has a penetrating injury, from a cut, a bite, or even a piercing grass seed. Licking often means the skin has been penetrated, although some dogs also lick areas that hurt.

Arthritis – or more correctly degenerative joint disease or DJD – frequently develops during adulthood. The first signs of DJD are subtle. At first, all you notice is that your dog has a reduced ability to do things it used to be able to do, like jump a fence or bound up the stairs. Eventually DJD causes stiffness or lameness after robust activity, then eventually the same stiffness or lameness after only moderate activity. To begin with dogs "work out" their stiffness with a little exercise, but sooner or later the stiffness can't be worked out and the dog is permanently lame. That means permanently uncomfortable. Don't expect your dog to complain about discomfort from DJD. It won't. It's up to you to notice what's happening and help before the problem becomes overwhelming. Lameness is more apparent when DJD affects a joint or joints on one side of the body more than on the other side; if a dog has symmetrical DJD you may not see limping, only a reduced ability.

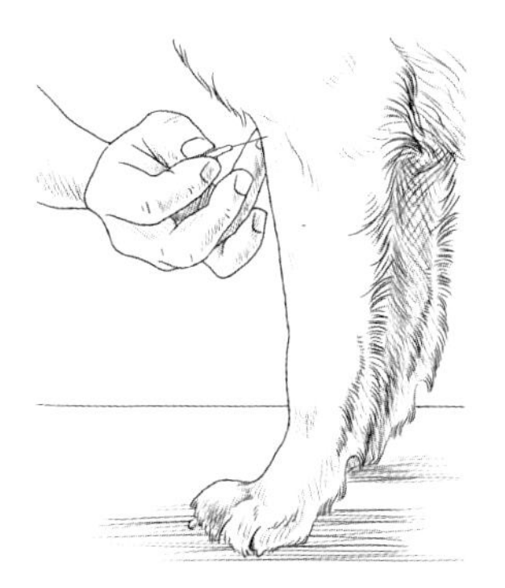

Suck it and see With chronic pain, you might try anything that may do more good than harm. Any therapy that enlists the body's natural painkilling endorphins can help with DJD.

Regardless of the cause of DJD, there is a standard treatment. First, control weight. If your dog is overweight, alter the diet to bring weight back to normal. If your dog's weight is normal, discuss with your vet a diet to make it lean. Second, control exercise. Avoid running and retrieve games, but keep your dog's muscles in good tone through sensible levels of walking. Swimming is ideal, either in safe, not-too-cold water or in hydrotherapy pools. Curiously, step exercises – walking up steps – can be useful for many dogs with DJD. Third, control the pain. Non-steroid anti-inflammatory drugs (NSAIDs) are effective and safe for DJD pain. They're used intermittently at first, but eventually may be needed chronically. Many owners report that acupuncture is beneficial for their dogs, that their dogs

Hydrotherapy Swimming is the ultimate non-weight-bearing exercise, recommended for human and canine senior citizens alike. A properly designed pool, with easy access and warm water, lets a dog strengthen the muscles and ligaments around a damaged joint without the discomfort of walking on it.

move with greater ease for days after an acupuncture session. Lastly, support joint health. There is reasonably good evidence that joint nutrients such as glucosamine improve joint health and that certain fatty acids such as EPA and DHA (found in high concentrations in both fish and linseed oil) act as anti-inflammatories. Adding a fish oil supplement may reduce the quantity of NSAIDs needed to control pain.

Knees and hips

Being only slightly overweight dramatically increases a dog's risk of tearing a knee ligament called the anterior cruciate. This is a remarkably common problem in dogs over seven years old (although it also occurs in lean young adult Boxer dogs). I was with my Golden Retriever Liberty when one of her anterior cruciates tore at nine years of age. She was trotting in the park when she abruptly stopped putting her right hind down but continued trotting. It was as if she had got a thorn embedded in her paw. No complaints, just lameness. I examined her pad – no thorns or penetrations – then felt her knee and the joint was slack. Large dogs such as Liberty need surgery to replace the torn ligament; in very small dogs natural fibrous repair over the following three months can produce a very acceptable mend.

Toy breeds, particularly Yorkshire Terriers, often inherit slipping kneecaps or patellar luxation. Being born with typically slightly rotated tibias (shin bones) leads to a slackness of the knee ligaments. The knee cap spontaneously slips out of place, to the inner side of the knee, and the leg is no longer able to support weight and is often held up. This rarely causes pain. An affected dog simply hops along on the affected side. More often than not the kneecap spontaneously slips back into its natural position and in these circumstances, in my experience no treatment is necessary.

Hip dysplasia (HD) is a condition in which the ball of the femur doesn't sit snugly in its deep socket in the hip. It's one of the most common causes of hind leg lameness in mature, large, adult dogs. While genetics plays a strong part in hip dysplasia, so too does overfeeding during puppyhood. If your retriever or giant breed dog was fat as a pup, your adult dog is prone to develop lameness caused by HD. Decades ago, breeders and vets recognized that HD is a serious breeding problem and developed x-ray screening where the quality of the hips is "scored" or "graded". Breeders use these scores to decide whether to use a dog in their breeding programme. This improved the quality of hips, but in some breeds, for example the Labrador Retriever, elbow dysplasia (ED) increased in frequency even as hip scores improved. ED is not uncommon in young adult Labrador and Golden Retrievers, Bernese Mountain Dogs, and Rottweilers. ED is really a constellation of different problems of which osteochondrosis (OC), a disturbance in bone formation at the ends of the long bones, is the most common. If your young, large adult dog is lame on one or both forelimbs your vet should examine it for signs of ED.

Coughing and heart problems

Coughing is often triggered by inflammation or damage to the lining of the air passages. Routine inoculations ensure that once-common infections such as rabies, distemper, and parvovirus are rare in adults today, but canine cough remains common in adults who spend time with other dogs. There are several microbes that transmit in aerosol form from dog to dog, causing temporary damage to the airways. Canine cough is a nuisance to a dog and its owners and is highly infectious so it spreads easily; because kennels are a natural location for transmission, it is also called kennel cough. Unlike many other inoculations that give three years or more protection, vaccines for canine cough protect for a maximum of one year. Dogs may cough for a variety of other reasons – allergy, pollution, foreign material in the air passages, worms, chest diseases or injuries, or a collapsed windpipe – but heart conditions are a common cause, especially in susceptible breeds.

The most common form of canine heart problem is valvular heart disease, which damages the heart valves. This occurs mostly in small adult dogs of middle age or older, and Cavalier King Charles Spaniels are particularly prone to valvular heart disease. The second most common problem, dilated cardiomyopathy, causes a dilation of the heart and thinning of the heart muscle. This occurs mostly in medium to large breeds, young to middle-aged. Dobermanns are particularly prone to it. Early stages of both of these conditions can be discovered during a routine annual health check-up, and this is as good a reason as any why perfectly healthy adult dogs should have full health checks once a year.

Certain varieties of mosquitoes, such as those on the Gulf coast and eastern seaboard of North America extending up into Ontario and Quebec, and in Europe throughout the Mediterranean and especially in the Po river valley of Italy, can carry the larvae of heartworms and transmit them to dogs through their bites. These larvae mature into worms the size of

No needles The inoculation against the bacterium that causes canine cough or kennel cough is normally given by a simple squirt up the nose, with no needles involved. This is just as well, because it has to be given every year.

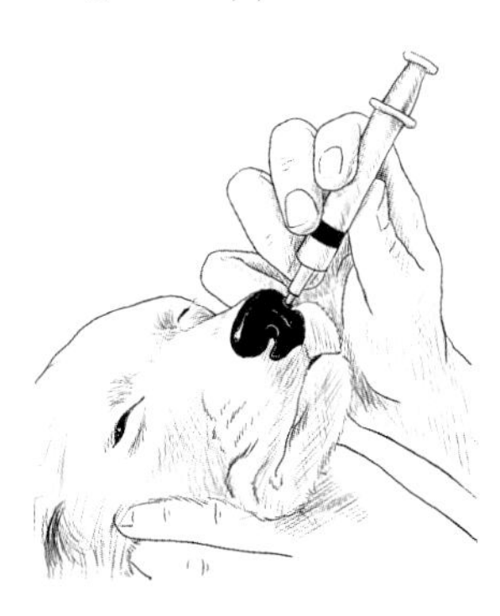

earthworms that live in the right chamber of the heart. There are effective prevention medications, and in areas where mosquitoes live year round, newborn pups should be housed indoors or in a screened outdoor area until they are old enough for preventative treatment.

Intact adults have common conditions

An unneutered male dog's prostate gland naturally increases in size, and by six years of age an enlarged prostate can interfere with his ability to freely urinate. Drugs similar to those used to shrink prostate glands in men are also used in dogs. Unneutered females, especially those that have never given birth, have an increasing risk of womb infection in the weeks following each oestrous cycle as the years go by. Bacteria move through the cervix and multiply in the womb, causing a pyometra. An affected female typically drinks more, eats less, and has less energy. If the cervix is still open there may be an unpleasant, pus-like vaginal discharge. A pyometra can be life-threatening and requires immediate veterinary attention.

Gum disease causes bad breath

Whether you call it "dog breath" or "death breath", if a dog's breath knocks you out there's something wrong. Smelly breath can be caused by gum infection or decomposing foreign material in the mouth, but it also occurs in what looks like a perfectly healthy mouth, with no gum inflammation and healthy, white teeth. This form of bad breath is caused by a specific microbe that thrives in some dog's mouths, which is easily eradicated with an inexpensive drug called metronidazole, but is often a recurring problem. Gum disease is prevented by routine brushing, which I'll admit is much easier to advise than to do.

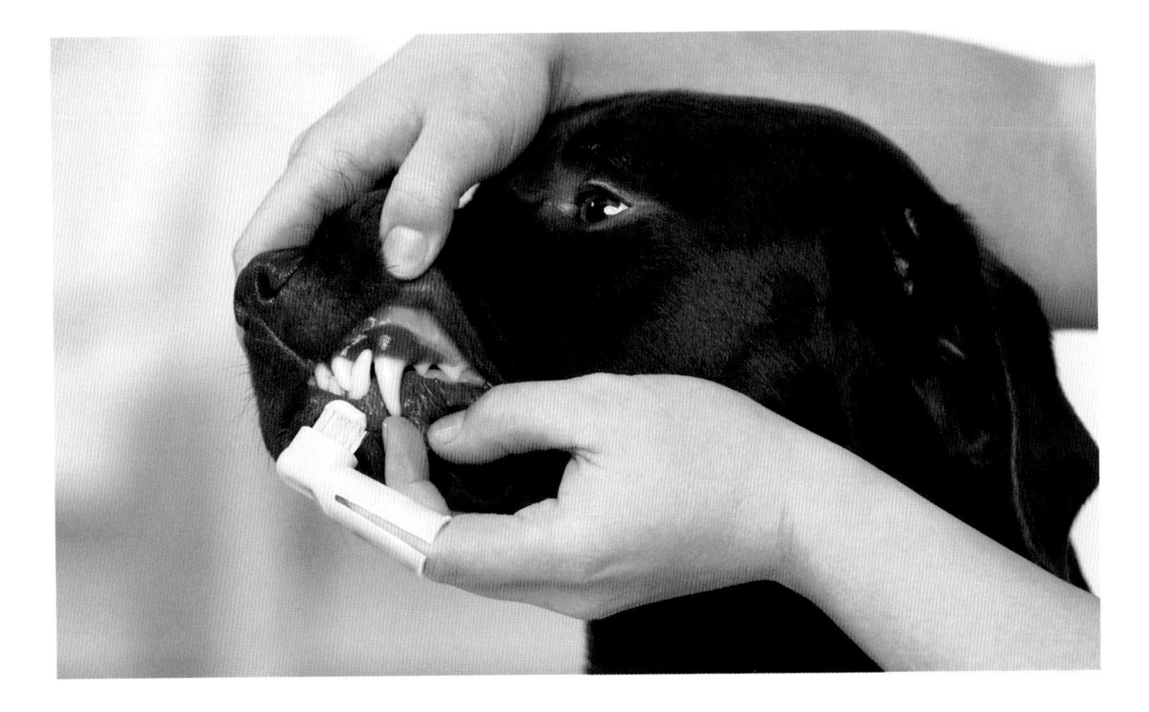

Tool for the job Brushing a dog's teeth with a standard toothbrush can be very awkward. Using a brush that slips onto one finger is much easier, although this is still often a slobbery business.

Seizures are not uncommon

Epilepsy, or fits or seizures, is much more common in adult dogs than many people are aware of. One study has found that 3 per cent of all Labrador Retrievers in Denmark have epilepsy. Other breeds, including Beagles and Hamiltonstövares, have a higher than average incidence. While seizures may begin during adolescence or earlier, they often begin in adulthood and affect otherwise perfectly healthy individuals. At first they can be equally disturbing to both the dog and the owner, but with time most dogs adjust well, sometimes better than their owners. Brain scans and cerebrospinal fluid analysis are used to identify specific causes, but in most instances the cause can't easily be determined. Anti-convulsants are used when fits occur above a certain frequency. This sounds vague because it is: the decision to treat varies with factors including the severity of the fits, their frequency, and the efficiency of the dog's liver. One of the dogs in my extended family, Inca, a black Labrador, has epilepsy and treatment has been problematic because her first fit permanently damaged three different areas of her brain. She is permanently spastic, a condition that is only dramatically apparent when she swims, but her fits have been reduced to an acceptable level of once or twice a month by a variety of medications, and she remains as gormless and funny and goofy as ever.

Swallowed items and poisons

Socks and pantyhose are favourite items for some dogs not just to carry but to chew and swallow. I've treated dogs that have swallowed packets of birth control pills, a rubber Donald Duck (whole), tennis balls, plastic bread bags, lead curtain weights, cat litter, tampons, bottles of aspirin, bars of soap, chocolate, and fruit stones. Some of these are just foreign bodies but others, such as lead, medicines, or chocolate (especially dark chocolate) are poisons.

When poisoning is suspected, always see your vet immediately. Your vet will need as much information as possible, including the product name, its manufacturer, and the list of ingredients. Other useful information includes what type of exposure to the poison has occurred – skin contact, air contact, or swallowing – how much was involved, when and for how long, how your dog is behaving and what you've already done.

If your dog has swallowed something it shouldn't have, don't panic. If shock has developed or the dog is unconscious keep the airway open, maintain breathing and circulation (*see pp.292–93*) and see your veterinarian immediately. If convulsions have developed, prevent the dog from damaging itself or from biting you or others, and get immediate veterinary help. For most swallowed items, it's best to immediately induce vomiting, but not if your dog has swallowed acid, alkali, or petroleum products.

If poison has been swallowed in the last two hours, induce vomiting by giving 3 per cent hydrogen peroxide solution or a crystal of washing soda. Don't induce vomiting if what was swallowed was an acid, alkali, or petroleum product. Don't induce vomiting with salt. And don't induce vomiting if your dog shows neurological signs such as disorientation or loss of balance; vomit may enter the windpipe causing an aspiration pneumonia.

Don't be a killjoy Sticks, bones, balls – the list of things you are warned against seems to get longer all the time. Occasionally an enthusiastic dog will swallow a tennis ball, but they swallow all sorts of other things too. You can't guard against all problems: just use a bit of commonsense and supervision.

If the poison is unknown do not throw out the vomit; keep a sample to take to your veterinarian, and see them immediately. If the poison is known, telephone your veterinarian for specific advice.

Give a washing soda crystal (*not* caustic soda!) as you would a pill. Lift the upper jaw with one hand, squeezing the upper lips over the teeth. The other hand drops the crystal to the back of the throat. Hold the dog's mouth shut and stroke the neck. When the dog licks its lips it has swallowed the emetic, and vomiting occurs within several minutes. Give 5–10ml (1–2tsp) of a slurry of activated charcoal in water to absorb the remaining poison.

HYDROGEN PEROXIDE DOSAGE PER DOGS WEIGHT

Hydrogen peroxide, available from a pharmacy, can be used to induce vomiting. Only give this if you know the poison swallowed was not an acid, alkali, or petroleum-based substance, or you could do more harm than good. The easiest way to weigh your dog may be to stand on your bathroom scales with and without it in your arms.

Weight	Dose	Weight	Dose
under 2kg (5lb))	2.5ml (0.5tsp)	15–20kg (35–45lb)	25ml (5tsp)
2–5kg (5–10lb)	5ml (1tsp)	20–35kg (45–55lb)	30ml (6tsp)
5–7 kg (10–15lb)	10ml (2tsp)	25–30kg (55–65lb)	35ml (7tsp)
7–11kg (15–25lb)	15ml (3tsp)	30–35kg (65–75lb)	40ml (8tsp)
11–15kg (25–35lb)	20ml (4tsp)	over 35kg (75lb)	45ml (9tsp)

Dealing with acid, alkali, and petroleum-based poisons

Vomiting these substances back up will only cause even more damage. The aim of treatment is to neutralize them instead and seek immediate veterinary help.

- Cleaners such as bleach, carbolic acid, dishwasher granules, laundry detergents, oven, toilet, or drain cleaners, furniture or floor polish, caustic soda (lye), phenol (carbolic acid), or chlorine for swimming pools or sterilizing units.
- Household substances such as glues, nail varnish, or nail varnish remover.
- Toolshed and garage substances such as paint thinner or stripper, turpentine, white spirit, or paintbrush cleaners, wood preservatives, plaster or putty, fertilizer, paraffin, petrol, or diesel, battery acid, motor oil, or salt for pavements and roads.

If you know the poison is an acid, give egg white, bicarbonate of soda, charcoal powder, or olive oil by mouth. If the skin has been burned, flush it for at least 15 minutes with clean running water and apply a paste of bicarbonate of soda to any burns in the mouth. If you know the poison is alkali give egg white or small amounts of citrus fruit juice or dilute vinegar. Apply dilute vinegar on skin and mouth burns. Epiotic ear wash, a salicylic acid solution, is excellent for treating alkali skin burns. For petroleum products or if you are uncertain of the nature of the poison, give a 50:50 mix of milk (or egg white) and vegetable oil solution. Depending upon how much has been consumed, give around 100ml (3½ floz) for each 5kg (11lb) of your dogs' body weight.

Changing lives

Life moves on. Our circumstances and priorities change. We marry, move home, have kids, get divorced. Sometimes we do all of these things during the adult life of a single dog! And most adult dogs just go with the flow, adapting smoothly to the changes in our lives that affect theirs. After the intensity of getting through a dog's puppyhood and adolescence, it's good to ease up and just coast along with an adult dog. I meet some people who can't do that, or simply don't want to. They obsess about their dogs, worrying that they aren't feeding them correctly or giving them enough exercise or letting them do what dogs want to do. It's great that people are so thoughtful, but it's also good to remember that life is never absolutely perfect for us and from time to time dogs too have to put up with second best – missing their routine exercise, not getting the normal amount of attention – because another priority has arisen.

I also see the opposite. The dog matures. It's reliable. It doesn't make demands. And it's virtually forgotten about. The owners of these dogs got them for specific reasons, and once the original need is no longer there the dog is redundant. It gets fed, and let out twice a day, and that's about it. These dogs aren't abused in the accepted sense, but they lead truly dull lives. Fortunately, most of the adult dogs I meet are owned by people who have a pragmatic attitude towards their pets. Yes, their dogs become part of the background noise of life but they're still properly exercised twice a day, fed sensibly, and played with. These dogs are true and reliable members of the family. Their owners know how they think and only when there are significant events or disruptions does the status quo get altered.

So what of those significant events? Well, every vet has heard this story. Woman has a dog. Woman acquires a boyfriend. Woman and new boyfriend make love. Dog stands on boyfriend's back and shouts threats and insults. Boyfriend says it's me or the dog. Woman consults vet. Adult dogs certainly become proprietorial over their owners, especially when the owner is of the opposite sex to the dog. It's an irritating behaviour, although most of the people I know who have protective dogs admit that they admire that characteristic in their canine, much as they want to alter it. Altering it is not particularly difficult; it just takes a little time. As with all behaviour problems, the best treatment is avoidance. If you want to get intimate with someone and your dog is a nuisance, keep your dog in another room. If you plan to have the new person become a more permanent fixture, have him or her do a few things your dog enjoys, such as putting the food bowl down or dropping a few treats or playing a game. Dogs are guilelessly fickle: anyone who provides tasty treats, affection, security, and mental and physical activity is easy to love.

Couples are having children later than ever before, and it's now common for a mother to have her first child in her thirties. Very often, in the absence of a human baby, people already have a "dog baby". That means that more babies are being born into homes where a dog has been the focus of

Love me, love my partner
Involve a new partner in things your dog enjoys doing right from the start. You want your dog to see your partner as a additional source of good things, not competition.

Good as gold Remember that children are the most common victims of dog bites. No matter how sweet your dog, this small, squealing, odd-smelling, prodding thing might not even register as human in its mind. Don't assume, don't take risks: essentially, don't give your dog a chance to make a mistake.

attention. Dogs don't like disruption to their routines; many worry about the unfamiliar, and babies can certainly be unfamiliar. If you don't have kids, do have a dog, and plan to have children one day, introduce your dog to children as early in life as possible: let it hear crying, let it smell baby smells. If (like some of my clients) you've got a dog while you're pregnant because you urgently needed something to mother, when you get back home with your baby, let your dog investigate the nursery sights, sounds, and smells, praising it for acting normally in your baby's presence. Let it sniff a soiled nappy, because that's something that really interests dogs. And, impossible as it will often be, try to continue spending time with your dog. Of course, never leave a dog of any age alone and unsupervised with a baby or crawling infant. If your dog has even a remote tendency to snap (and most dogs do), train yours to wear a muzzle in the presence of your baby by giving a treat and putting the muzzle on while the dog is away from your baby.

Some dog owners find it almost too painful to believe how very easily adult dogs accept new people. Every vet has been asked to put down a perfectly healthy dog because, for whatever reason, the owner can no longer care for a dog that they believe "can't live without me". That simply isn't true. A very few dogs do become worryingly dependent on one individual, and their anxiety when separated from that person can develop into a full panic attack (I'll discuss this further in the next chapter) but as long as that dog still retains the ability to learn, it can learn to accept and enjoy the presence of new people with a speed that can be quite galling.

The duration of adulthood varies considerably. In some breeds, such as small Poodles, Whippets and small Dachshunds, it lasts for over a decade. In others, such as the Bernese Mountain Dog and the Bulldog, adulthood lasts only half as long. Inevitably, old age arrives, often suddenly, and the cycle of life becomes starkly apparent.

CHAPTER TWELVE

The Older Dog

Dogs, even the Peter Pans, inevitably experience physical and mental wear and tear. For many of us this happens far too soon. It seems only yesterday that our dogs were pups when out of the blue they are, well, there's no other word for it – old. Maybe your dog decides it's time to stop playing before you do. Perhaps it just doesn't hear as well. Over the following months and years, your dog inexorably ages, right before your eyes, usually with grace and dignity. Our geriatric-adolescent housemates become tired and worn.

The speed of decline varies. Two dogs may be exactly the same age but behave in radically different ways, partly because of genes, but also partly because of their food and environment. All older dogs become less tolerant of any type of change. Physically they become less tolerant of weather changes, and mentally they become rigid in their wants and routines. Old dogs thrive on ritual and a constant environment.

With time, natural balances within the body start to falter. Every cell in your dog's body contains a biological clock that determines how long it will live. Some cells, for example those that line the intestines, live for less than a week and are constantly and efficiently replaced by new cells. This ability to create new cells eventually falters. New cell production is not as fast, as accurate, or as efficient as it once was. Other cells, for example brain cells, can't replace themselves. A dog has its maximum allocation when it is young, and then it's up to the body to hold on to them as long as possible.

Both inefficient replacement and no replacement create many of the conditions associated with ageing. With those intestinal cells, for example, this inefficiency may lead to less efficient absorption of nourishment and consequent weight loss, or poor movement in the bowels leading to constipation. If a dog "loses" its toilet training there may be a physical cause, such as sphincter muscle weakening, that leads to urinary incontinence, or the brain cells may no longer be overseeing body functions as they once did. Brain changes occur faster in some dogs than in others; just as with us, senile behaviour changes vary considerably from one dog to another.

In a culture obsessed with health, it can be difficult to remember that ageing isn't an illness. Although many illnesses occur most frequently during the last third of a dog's life, old age is natural and inevitable. Only when inevitable age-related changes happen faster than average can they be called illnesses or diseases. While ageing is inevitable, there is ample evidence that dietary modifications, weight management, changes in exercise routines, maintenance of good health, and routine mental stimulation can dramatically prolong a dog's active years.

Life expectancy varies

Some breeds of dogs live over twice as long as others. The old adage that one dog year equals seven human years was never entirely accurate, but it's certainly wrong today. Life expectancy could only be guessed at until pet

Silver threads Many dogs remain active and alert to the end, showing their age only in a greying muzzle and misty eyes. Don't slow your dog down before it's ready, but equally watch out for signs of age and don't push it past what it can do if health and abilities do decline.

insurance became sufficiently popular for statistics to be compiled. These statistics from the world's largest pet health insurer are for the United Kingdom, and reflect the national bloodlines of breeds in the late 1990s. Although over 10 years old, they are still the most accurate actuarial statistics available.

- OVER 14 YEARS: Miniature Poodle (14.8), Toy Poodle (14.4), Miniature Dachshund (14.4), Tibetan Terrier (14.3), Whippet (14.3), Bedlington Terrier (14.3)
- OVER 13 YEARS: Border Terrier (13.8), Jack Russell Terrier (13.6), Chow Chow (13.5), Shih Tzu (13.4), Pekingese (13.3), Shetland Sheepdog (13.3), Beagle (13.3), Random-bred/Mongrel (13.2), Cairn Terrier (13.2), Greyhound (13.2), Dalmatian (13.0), Chihuahua (13.0), English Springer Spaniel (13.0), Border Collie (13.0), Wire Fox Terrier (13.0)
- OVER 12 YEARS: Bull Terrier (12.9), Irish Red and White Setter (12.9), Basset Hound (12.8), West Highland White Terrier (12.8), Yorkshire Terrier (12.8), Labrador Retriever (12.6), Lurcher (12.6), Viszla (12.5), Cocker Spaniel (12.5), Bearded Collie (12.3), German Shorthaired Pointer (12.3), Dachshund (12.2), Rough Collie (12.2), Afghan Hound (12.0), Golden Retriever (12.0), Scottish Terrier (12.0), Standard Poodle (12.0)
- OVER 11 YEARS: English Cocker Spaniel (11.8), Irish Setter (11.8), Old English Sheepdog (11.8), Welsh Springer Spaniel (11.5), Corgi (11.3), Gordon Setter (11.3), Airedale Terrier (11.2), English Setter (11.2), Samoyed (11.0)
- OVER 10 YEARS: Cavalier King Charles Spaniel (10.7), Boxer (10.4), German Shepherd (10.3), English Toy Spaniel (10.1), Staffordshire Bull Terrier (10.0), Norfolk Terrier (10.0), Weimaraner (10.0)
- UNDER 10 YEARS: Dobermann Pinscher (9.8), Rottweiler (9.8), Flat-Coated Retriever (9.5), Scottish Deerhound (9.5), Rhodesian Ridgeback (9.1), Bullmastiff (8.6), Great Dane (8.4), Bernese Mountain Dog (7.0), Bulldog (6.7), Irish Wolfhound (6.2)

Culture influences life expectancy

Just as the average American doesn't live as long as the average European, the same is true of dogs: the median life expectancy of all British dogs is 12.2 years, but that of all American dogs is 9.8. Health problems within a breed vary from region to region according to genetic problems in the founder stock, but I'm sure this difference in life expectancy does not indicate dramatically different American and European life expectancies within breeds. It is a consequence of disparities in rates of infection, the frequency of physical accidents, and regional preferences for specific breeds with different life expectancies.

Even within Europe there are profound regional differences. For example, around 28 per cent of the dog population is over ten years old in both Germany and the United Kingdom, but only 17 per cent in Sweden and a scant 2 per cent in Greece. Veterinary care in Sweden is of the same high standard as in the United Kingdom and Germany, but national ethical

Small is beautiful There is a general rule that the smaller the breed, the longer the dog will live: most Toy Poodles and Miniature Poodles can hope to live past 14 years and the Yorkshire Terrier past 12 years. Less weight on the joints and less strain on the organs contribute to this lifespan.

values question the use of medical treatments such as radiation therapy or chemotherapy, or surgical procedures such as leg amputations. So older dogs in Sweden are more likely to be euthanized, while in Germany and the United Kingdom they are likely to receive more invasive interventions and live longer. In Greece, potentially lethal infectious diseases such as leishmaniasis are more common, fewer dogs are vaccinated, and the culture of the indoor pet dog is more recent, so dogs die young from infections or accidents. It's almost impossible to compare life expectancies between countries, but in most regions dogs are living longer, so there are more around and more that are likely to develop the changes and conditions associated with old age.

When is a dog an old dog?

There's no specific age when a dog becomes old. Signs of ageing are almost always obvious by the time a dog enters the last third of its expected life span, so large breeds with shorter lives age earlier than small breeds with longer expectancies. In my veterinary practice, I recommend a detailed preventative health check-up as early as six years of age in breeds such as Bernese Mountain Dogs, but not until nine for Labradors and Golden Retrievers, and ten for most of the smaller breeds including small Poodles and Dachshunds.

If a dog appears perfectly healthy on examination, I find no hidden problems in 98 per cent of these inspections, but in the rest blood tests reveal something amiss, such as inefficient kidney function or intestinal absorption. These age-related changes can be discovered long before a dog starts to show clinical signs: by the time a dog is drinking more because of failing kidney filtration, it has permanently lost three-quarters of its kidney function. The earlier a problem is discovered, the earlier treatment can begin and the longer your dog will live.

Exercise and diet for the older dog

Exercise is as beneficial for your older dog as it is for you, but it should be constant and routine. If your dog walks for half an hour a day and you plan a four hour hike on the weekend, leave your golden oldie at home. Walking and occasional trotting is best for ageing joints and weakening muscles. Avoid vigorous exercise and leave ball-catching to youthful canines, unless it's a simple toss to the mouth. Contrary to what you might read, walking up stairs is very good exercise and safe for all but overweight dogs, who are prone to tearing knee ligaments.

What your dog eats becomes ever more important. We all know the link between what we eat and how healthy we are at any age, but it becomes most important with the elderly – people or dogs. I know that a bag of potato crisps is not a healthy meal, but I might still eat them because they're tasty, they're available, I haven't got time to get something better, and I've got no will power. Dogs can't use those excuses. They depend on you for their food so – no joke – it's your fault if they aren't eating what's best.

Virtually all medical conditions associated with ageing respond to diet changes. In fact, all older dogs benefit from diet changes, even those with no specific medical conditions. When changing your dog's food, remember to avoid sudden changes. Start by adding a little of the new food to the existing diet and gradually increase the proportion over four or five days. Old dogs have also often developed their own fixed preferences for certain textures of food, or odours or flavours.

Controlling weight

Many dogs gain weight as they age; over 40 per cent of ten-year-old dogs are overweight or obese. Often, the gain is so slow it isn't noticed until the annual health check. Sometimes it is caused by a medical condition, for instance an underactive thyroid gland in susceptible breeds such as Cocker Spaniels, but for the overwhelming majority it is the result of eating more calories each day than are used. Once medical causes have been controlled or eliminated, control calories to control weight and reduce strain on old joints, the most common site of age-related pain. Generally speaking, an older dog needs around 20 per cent fewer calories than it needed in its prime, but with more digestible protein, vitamins, and minerals. Older dogs may benefit from diets that provide a minimum of 25 per cent of calories from protein – even overweight older dogs need more protein.

Reducing the quantity of whatever you're feeding and at the same time adding a vitamin and mineral supplement is a simple way to reduce calories, especially if you're already feeding a "senior" diet; these are usually fortified with vitamins and minerals and made from higher-quality protein. Make sure your elderly dog has a clean bill of health before adjusting the diet. Aim to slim down very gradually, over four to eight months.

Unless a dog is being dieted, it shouldn't lose weight. If it does, or if it is picky with its food, see your vet. There's almost certainly a medical problem: it may be as simple as gum disease, tooth pain, or diminished taste

Stay active Exercise is just as vital for older dogs as it is for young ones. They may not jump so much or gallop about, but keep up a reasonable amount of walking. Slowing down too much will speed up the ageing process. Reserve joint-straining jumps, however, for extra special occasions.

or smell, but it is just as likely to be caused by more serious medical conditions. If your oldie has lost weight because of illness and now needs to regain weight and strength, one of the variety of commercial high-energy foods may be beneficial.

Supplements and special diets

Free radicals, byproducts of normal body processes, destroy cell membranes, increasing the risk of illness and disease. The older you are, the more you have, and the more your body is damaged. That damage is the primary suspect in the ageing process of humans as well as dogs and as I'm pretty much an old dog myself I should pay extra attention to what I'm writing! Vitamins and minerals such as selenium, zinc, vitamin A, and vitamin E, and other substances such as the carotenoids lutein and beta-carotene act as antioxidants and "scavenge" free radicals from the body. Carotenoids are thought to improve skin and mucus membrane defences, while vitamin E is thought to protect internal organs such as the heart. Dogs have their own natural free-radical-scavenging systems, but these come under increasing pressure with age. All older dogs benefit from diets high in antioxidants and all conscientious dog food makers produce premium diets for older dogs that are in essence the canine equivalents of the "Mediterranean diet" that's good for us.

Some of my clients don't like the idea of feeding products made by multinational food conglomerates. They tell me they've read that the ingredients or the processes used are questionable, but I've never seen any evidence that this is so, although there have been incidents of accidental contamination. You still have the option of preparing fresh meals, but if an older dog needs a specific diet due to a medical condition, veterinary nutritionists have created a variety of appropriate commercially produced foods. There are reduced-calorie diets for reducing weight, balanced-fibre diets for constipation, extra-nutrient diets for joint disease, diets with balanced essential fatty acids and selected protein for itchy skin problems, ranges for kidney, bladder, heart, liver, or bowel conditions, high-energy convalescing diets for debilitated dogs or those who have had surgery, high-fat, low-carbohydrate diets to slow cancers, high-fibre diets for diabetics, pre-digested foods for allergy sufferers, and increased-digestibility diets for elderly dogs or those with digestive disorders.

WARMING FOOD

If your dog is less interested in a new food, warm it up to room or body temperature. Wet foods can be put in the microwave for a few seconds, but be very careful! You want to release the odours from the food by slightly warming it, not make it dangerously hot inside. Always thoroughly stir warmed food, especially if using a microwave, so that there are no hot-spots that will burn your dog's mouth. If the best food for your dog is only available in a dry form, you can add water and let it soak long enough to become soft. It can then be warmed just like wet food, releasing its odours, which hopefully your dog will find appealing. If this doesn't work, ask your vet whether it's alright to add some tasty and smelly fat to the food. A little tinned or bottled goose fat or duck fat can turn even the blandest diet into a gourmet dinner for a dog.

The spirit is willing One of the sadder symptoms of old age is when your dog gets up with a show of enthusiasm for a walk, then peters out a short way down the road and wants to turn back. If your dog's body seems to give out before its spirit, have it checked out: it may not be anything specific, but lung or heart problems and joint pain are also possibilities.

Pain in old age

Older dogs can suffer declines and changes in any of their body systems. People with older dogs ask me a whole variety of questions about these, but almost everyone asks about pain at some time. I've suggested ways to "guesstimate" your dog's pain (*see pp. 248–49*) but because this is so central to the comfort and quality of an older dog's life, I'd like add a little more. A degree of pain is an inevitable outrider of a dog's final years, but fortunately there are ways to prevent or at least to control it for what is often a remarkably long time, through a combination of medicines, nutrition and complementary therapies. Here are some guidelines for assessing pain, with the older dog in mind.

- MILD PAIN: More quiet or indifferent than usual; eating on one side of the mouth or dropping out food; changing position somewhat tentatively; initially stiff or lame when walking; reluctant to jump up or down; folding back ears and wagging tail more submissively that you'd expect when approached; guarding part of the body, and doesn't like being touched there.
- SIGNIFICANT PAIN: Unexpectedly quiet or seemingly depressed; less interested in interacting with you; tentative or very careful with eating; not chewing toys as it usually would; uncomfortable when sitting, lies in a tense position; reluctant to move or walking very slowly; standing with a tucked

belly and hanging tail; lies down but doesn't sleep as you would expect; flinching when touched; showing unexpected aggression.

• SEVERE PAIN: Continuous or frequent crying, yelping, groaning, shrieking or screaming; completely uninterested in you; refusing all food; can't get up or down or refuses to move or constantly changing position; rigid or shaking; urinates or defecates without getting up.

Natural, medicinal, and complementary painkillers

I've explained how pain is caused, perceived, and influenced by many factors (*see p.247*). Here's a typical example. An arthritic golden oldie hobbles into the clinic. He wobbles and limps because the chronically damaged cells in his arthritic joints are constantly pouring out chemical signals that stimulate the sensation of pain, and his painkiller medicine is neutralizing some, but not all. He finds it difficult to lie down and even more difficult to get up. I get out a tub of food treats and his ears perk up. Now, he quickly gets to his feet, walks straight over to me, and eats the treat. It may appear that all I've done is give him a tiny snack of dried liver, but in fact I've actually dulled his pain because I've influenced his emotions. Instead of concentrating on

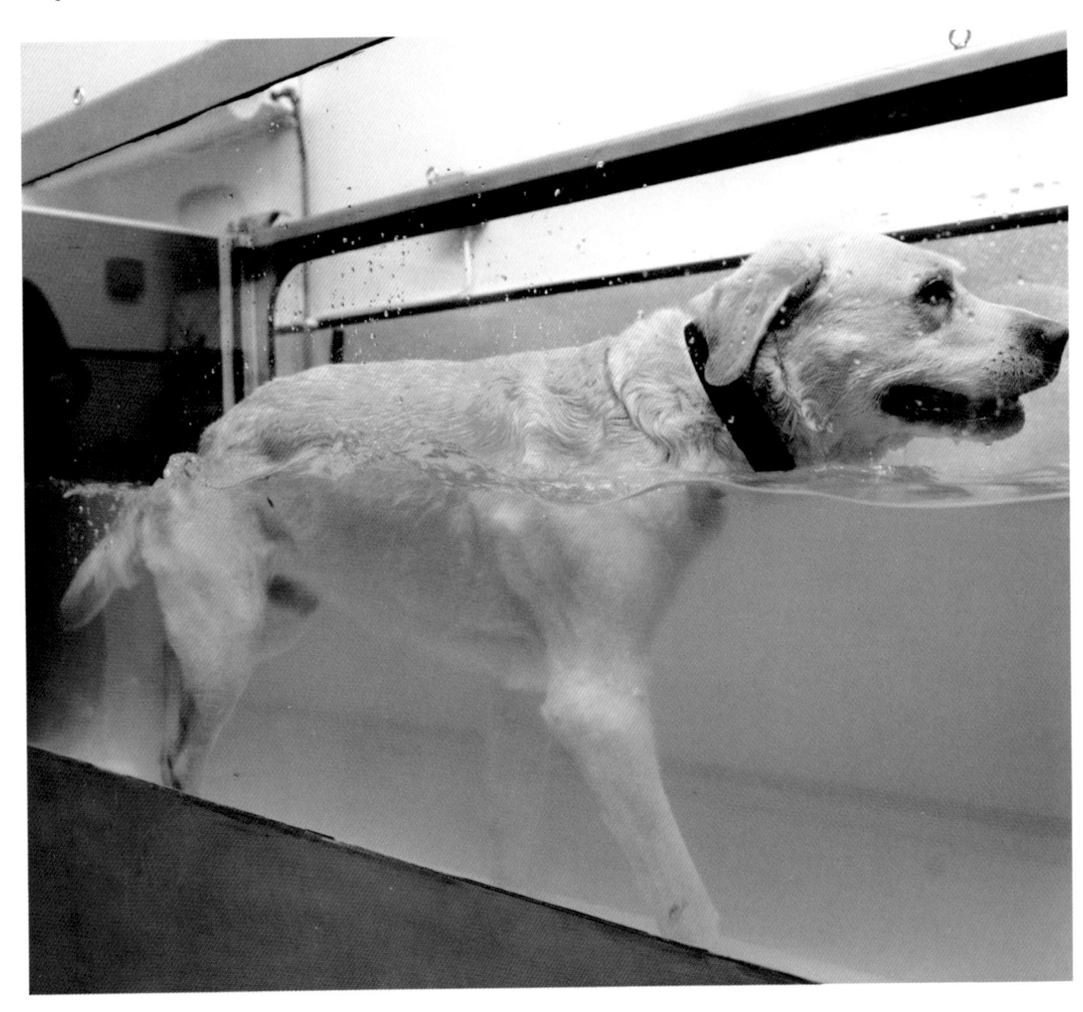

Faith healing To some extent, if you believe that a therapy will help your dog, it will. Your dog watches you, knows when you are making a fuss, knows when you expect something good to happen, and will respond accordingly. Don't abuse that trust by continuing therapies that your dog finds unpleasant, but if you are both happy with a treatment, whether it works for you and your dog is what's most important.

the pain, his brain is saying *Food! Good! Happy! Eat! More! Food!* I've just triggered his body's natural and powerful painkillers, his endorphins.

Non-steroidal anti-inflammatory drugs (NSAIDs) are the most commonly used medicines. Aspirin, ibuprofen, carprofen, and meloxicam work by preventing the release of prostaglandins, which trigger local inflammation and stimulate signals in local nerves, from damaged tissue. Paracetemol blocks pain impulses in the brain itself, so sometimes reduces pain when other NSAIDs don't. NSAIDs are very effective, but can be dangerous to dogs. They do not increase the risk of stroke, as the newer NSAIDs can in us, but have other dangers, especially when used chronically – that is, for months or years. All can cause gastrointestinal damage, even deep ulcers in the stomach. Some can also damage the kidneys or liver, although these problems are restricted to a very small, genetically susceptible populations and to seriously ill, dehydrated individuals. NSAIDs should always be given with food and in some instances combined with other drugs that protect the lining of the stomach, such as ranitidine.

When NSAIDs don't relieve pain, vets sometimes use steroid anti-inflammatories or narcotic drugs, including narcotic patches stuck on a shaved area on a leg bandaged over so that they aren't eaten. Just like endorphins, narcotics block receptor sites in the spinal cord or the brain, preventing pain signals from being transmitted. Steroidal anti-inflammatories such as prednisone often reduce pain, but have many other side effects. Like narcotics, they are very useful in the short to medium term but not for chronic treatment.

The pains of old age are almost inevitably chronic and don't respond well to conventional therapies. Fortunately, a variety of complementary therapies such as acupuncture, massage, manipulations, and hydrotherapy are beneficial if a dog has the right temperament. Acupuncture probably stimulates an older dog's body to release not just its own natural pain-killing endorphins but also prostaglandin-suppressing cortisone. Swimming therapy in a heated pool probably improves circulation to the muscles and so reduces the severity of both muscle and joint pain. For dogs that love swimming, it can have a beneficial psychological effect, but for dogs that hate water the opposite may be true. Transcutaneous electrical nerve stimulation (TENS) and pulsating electromagnetic field therapy (PEMP) are used to treat chronic joint pain in people, but there has been minimal success applying these treatments to dogs.

Dogs are comforted by touch just as much as we are, and "kissing it better" works just as well on our dogs as it does on our kids. The various touch therapies – massage, shiatsu, Tellington Touch, chiropractic, osteopathy, acupressure, even acupuncture – use touch to generate physical and psychological well being. Touch therapies can improve circulation and help old muscles, or calm dogs, lowering blood pressure and providing a pleasant distraction. To me, good medicine is anything that works. If your old dog has chronic pain, try a variety of treatments but remember, your aim is to reduce stress as well as pain. Don't increase stress by forcing your dog to endure something it doesn't like.

Aquacise If it's available to you, exercise in a heated pool is wonderful for older dogs with joint pain, just as it is for older people. Water supports the body and takes the weight off the joints, allowing a freedom of movement that exercises the muscles better than on land.

Physical problems

With time, all of the body's systems decline. Older dogs have decreased total body water, decreased cell mass, a frequent increase in body fat, and a tendency towards obesity. They are less able to compensate for changes in their acid-to-base balance and their hydration, which is why it is best for any older dog having an anaesthetic to be given intravenous fluids. Kidney function eventually decreases. The immune systems become less effective. A decline in the efficiency of the heart and lungs and decreased brain blood vessel elasticity mean that less nourishing oxygen reaches the brain. A decrease in both the gray and white matter volume in their brains is accompanied by a deterioration of the senses, a thickening of the meninges that enclose the brain, and chemical changes inside brain cells.

Grooming and oral hygiene

With age the skin loses elasticity, becoming thinner and more sensitive. Skin problems become more obvious in some older dogs, especially those who groom less because of arthritis, or because they're too fat, or have mouth pain caused by gum and tooth disease, or simply forget. Hair often thins, or moulting hair accumulates in the coat. Many older dogs resent being groomed, probably because it causes discomfort, but at the same time produce more flaky dander sebaceous secretions, so many old dogs smell like old dogs. Old dogs need more grooming and bathing than they did in their prime. This is a tough one, because you need to strike a balance of keeping your crochety old dog's skin healthy and not bothering it too much. Grooming not only keeps the skin and coat in condition, it enhances circulation and massages the muscles. If you don't need to groom daily, give your dog a gentle all-over massage.

While "dog breath" is common in adult dogs, broken teeth and gum disease are almost inevitable in the elderly. Toy breeds suffer from these problems earlier than large breeds. Gums recede, bone is lost around tooth roots, and teeth fall out or cause pain and need to be removed. Gum disease and dental calculus are real medical conditions requiring attention: if your dog has bad breath and you can see plaque on the teeth, I guarantee that bacteria are entering your dog's bloodstream each time it chews its food. The immune system usually kills off these invaders within 30 minutes, but occasionally bacteria will survive, circulate, and cause septicaemia. An affected dog is usually off its food and has a slight fever. The immediate problem is controlled with antibiotics, but the only way to eliminate the condition in the longer term is by scaling the teeth, draining the infection, and removing any rotten roots. In my experience, slowing down in older dogs is far too often attributed to "ageing" when in fact it's caused by treatable mouth infections. After treatment, dogs seemingly gain years in strength and vigour.

Prevention is always better than cure. Old dogs usually hate having their teeth brushed, but many enjoy chewing on rawhide, and some rawhide chews are enzyme treated to help keep the gums healthy.

Chewing it over With no ability to indulge in plaque-building sugars – and indeed little inclination to do so – there's no reason why our dogs shouldn't keep all their own teeth in good shape all their lives. Sensibly chosen chews and regular brushing both help dental health.

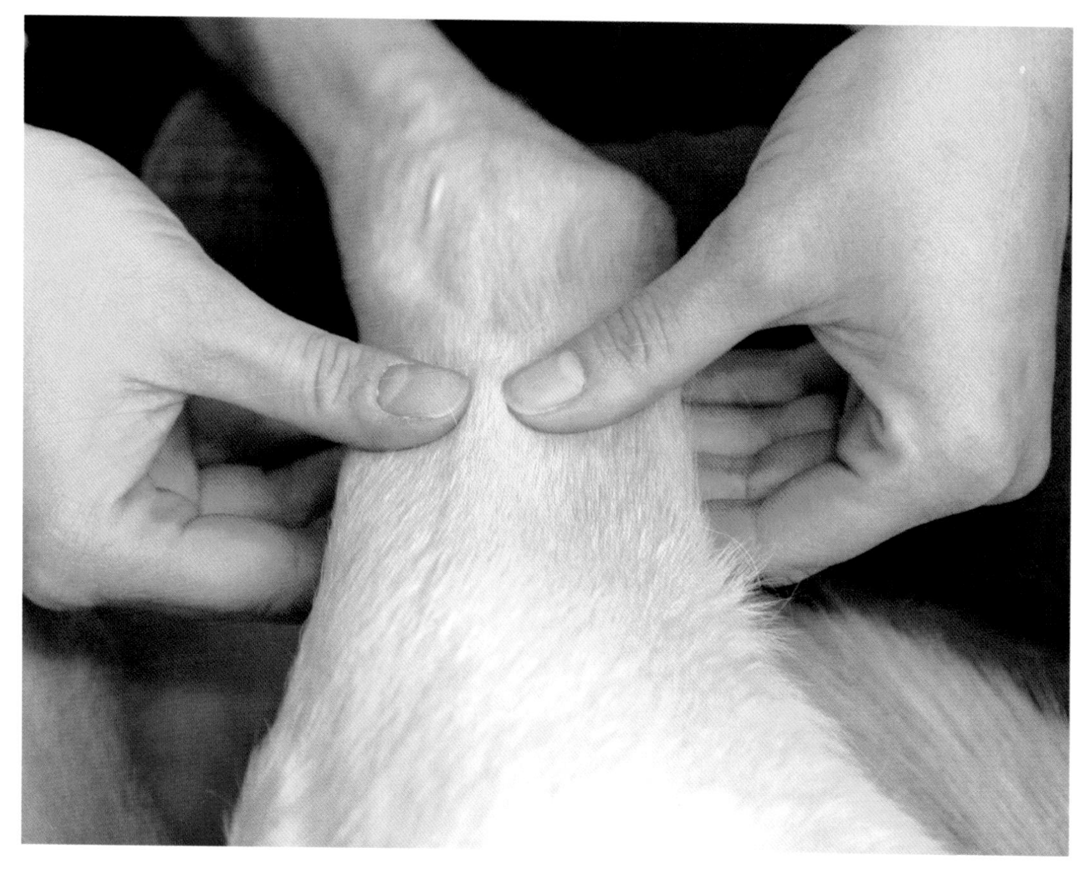

Rub it better The aches and pains of old age can respond well to touch therapies like acupressure and massage. These stimulate endorphins and also provide a physical distraction, triggering different nerves and sensations.

Muscles and joints weaken

Joint wear and tear that starts during adulthood (*see pp.320–22*) becomes serious in old age. Age-related joint disease can't be cured but the discomfort or pain can be controlled, often for years. DJD is joined by loss of muscle tone and eventually muscle mass. There are many causes for this – less efficient digestion, circulation, or filtration, reduced lung capacity, less exercise – so an accurate diagnosis is needed before it's possible to reverse, arrest, or slow muscle loss.

Don't delude yourself when you see an old dog getting up gingerly, walking slowly, or limping. It may not complain but it's certainly in pain. Osteoarthritis is virtually inevitable if a dog lives long enough. Weight and pain control are at the core of improving quality of life. Reduce weight, avoid running or jumping, but keep the muscles toned. Treat pain with non-steroid anti-inflammatory drugs and supplements of the essential fatty acids EPA and DHA. Make sure the diet contains high levels of joint nutrients such as glucosamine.

Once over Those regular all-over checks become more important as your dog grows older. Lumps and bumps, painful areas, or skin problems are all best dealt with sooner rather than later.

Hearts become inefficient

Some dogs want to play games for ever and ever. But does your dog tire sooner? Does it cough? Exercise tolerance naturally drops with age, but these can be symptoms of cardiovascular diseases, treatable conditions that are as common in older dogs as they are in us. I've mentioned valvular heart disease and cardiomyopathy (*see p.323*); conditions that develop during adulthood progress over the years, and the early stages are often picked up during annual health checks. Heart disease is the most common cause of death in older dogs, accounting for almost 23 per cent of fatalities.

Having been in clinical practice for a long time, I've seen ideas go full circle. Forty years ago, before modern heart medicines were available, some forms of heart disease were treated with the antioxidants vitamin E and selenium (although they weren't called antioxidants at the time). Some veterinary schools now incorporate marine fish oil – high in antioxidants – in their treatment of canine heart problems.

Keep track If your dog seems to be unusually thirsty, measure how much it's drinking. Start by making sure it can't drink from puddles, ponds, toilets or birdbaths, but keep the water bowl filled and accessible. Measure how much water you put in at the start of each day, and if you top it up, and then subtract what's left after a full 24 hours.

Digestion can falter

Lack of muscle tone in the bowels, reduced bowel activity, inappropriate diet, less exercise – older dogs suffer from constipation for many reasons. Regardless of cause, it means discomfort, even pain. Changing gut flora can lead to increases in gas-producing bacteria, and some old dogs become real bombers; when Liberty in her dotage cut one, even she left the room.

A range of conditions, usually treatable, can cause dogs to apparently forget years of housetraining. These include colitis, inflammatory bowel disease, sugar diabetes, bladder stones or infections, inflammation of the prostate, Cushing's disease, and kidney or liver disease. Medical conditions that cause pain or make it difficult for the dog to go outside to eliminate, including arthritis, anal sac disease, loss of vision, and some forms of colitis, can also contribute to messing indoors. Faecal incontinence troubles some elderly dogs and it amazes me when wonderful owners adapt to this unpleasant household problem. For most of these conditions, vets recommend a variety of diet changes and medications.

As dogs have got fatter, the incidence of sugar diabetes in older dogs has increased. It is usually diagnosed when an owner notices their dog is drinking more, eating well, but possibly losing weight. Most diabetic dogs need twice-daily insulin injections, but food management is equally important for minimizing fluctuations in blood sugar triggered by eating. If your dog is diabetic, avoid all semi-moist foods; these stimulate the greatest fluctuations. Starchy foods require more digestion, slowing the delivery of sugar into the blood. Barley is digested slowly, while rice is digested quickly, resulting in a blood-sugar "peak" and sudden, high insulin demand. Certain fibres, for example, carboxymethylcellulose (CMC), helps slow down stomach emptying, also slowing the delivery of sugar. The best diet for a diabetic dog is made from a fixed formula with consistent carbohydrate, fat, and high-quality protein. More than 40 per cent of the calories in the food should come from complex carbohydrate and less than 20 per cent from fat. Most major dog food manufacturers produce a range of diets to help dogs with diabetes.

Urinary problems

Loss of bladder control – urinary incontinence – occurs frequently in older females, who lose sphincter muscle control and dribble urine when sitting,

INCREASED URINATING HAS MANY POSSIBLE CAUSES

Increased urinating is often caused by advanced kidney failure, but there are many reasons why older dogs either drink more or urinate more, or both, including sugar or pituitary diabetes, kidney disease, liver disease, overactive adrenal gland, pain or fever, reaction to drugs or a dietary change. All of these conditions are either immediately or potentially dangerous, so if your dog is drinking more than the normal quantity of water it should be seen by your vet. Taking a recent urine sample along will speed up a diagnosis.

lying, or sleeping. This can be controlled or eliminated with one of several licensed medications in many if not most instances. Treating urinary incontinence in older male dogs is more difficult, but when licensed products don't work other drugs can be tried. Older dogs can produce a variety of different types of bladder (or kidney) stones, and there are specific diets for each type, with balanced minerals to produce urine of a very specific pH measurement.

Kidney filtration works surprisingly well throughout the lives of most dogs but kidney failure is not uncommon in very old dogs. Have routine annual blood tests: by the time symptoms appear, a dog has already lost most of its renal function. The target of dietary management is to minimize clinical signs of failure, help maintain the dog's well being, and (if possible) prolong life. You may have read that a low-protein diet is good for dogs with age-related kidney disease, but this is not so. Kidney failure is managed by reducing dietary phosphorus to maintain the nitrogen balance, and protein is a major source of phosphorus, but a low-phosphorus diet with moderate amounts of highly digestible protein is useful.

Supplementing the diet with omega-3 fatty acids probably protects the kidneys and possibly lowers blood pressure (not that hypertension is a problem with canine kidney failure, as it is with the feline or human equivalents), while too much omega-6 fatty acid probably damages the kidneys. A good diet for older dogs with impaired kidneys should also contain B vitamins, a good balance of the omega-3 and omega-6 fatty acids to reduce inflammation, and fibre to trap the waste products of nitrogen. All major manufacturers produce foods that are specially formulated for dogs with kidney disease.

Cancer accompanies old age

Cancer. We hate it when our vets say it just as much as when a doctor does. Tumours, and more specifically cancers, are an inevitable consequence of old age, so let me describe what they are. Tumours are abnormal growths, but many are benign. These get bigger, but don't invade surrounding tissue or spread to other parts of the body. Cancers or malignant tumours are abnormal growths that invade local tissue or spread to other parts of the body. Don't assume that all old-age lumps or bumps are cancers. Many skin lumps are blocked sebaceous glands, or cysts, common in certain breeds.

Others are unsightly but not dangerous warts called papillomas, which are technically tumours. The most common lumps I'm asked to examine on older dogs are fatty tumours called lipomas, almost invariably benign and common in older, overweight, medium, large, and giant dogs. Benign tumours are usually harmless and can often be left unless they're physically troubling the dog or will obviously cause problems in the future. If a dog lives long enough it will probably eventually develop a tumour, even a cancer. That doesn't mean this will be the reason it dies.

"Cancer" covers an extraordinarily wide variety of over 200 unrelated diseases. For reasons that aren't even remotely understood, cancers occur at twice the frequency in dogs than they do in people; they are the second most common cause of death in dogs, taking 16 per cent of our pets from us. This is not a new phenomenon. You may read that there is an increasing frequency of canine cancers, but it is proportional both to dogs living longer and to our increasingly keeping breeds with a higher than average risk of developing cancers. For example, six out of ten Bernese Mountain Dogs will die as a consequence of a cancer, while only one out of ten mutts will.

Dogs can develop the same tumours we do, but in significantly different frequencies. Tumours of the spleen called hemangiomas (benign) or hemangiosarcomas (malignant), are quite common in some large breeds but rare in people, while prostate cancer is common in men but rare in dogs. Canine tumours occur most commonly in skin, mouth, bones, mammary tissue, lymph tissue, and blood-related organs such as the spleen.

Malignant tumours, or cancers, are classified by where they originated: carcinomas develop from the tissues that line the external and internal surface of the skin and organs, sarcomas develop from within bones, muscles, and blood vessels, and lymphomas – which are among the most common and treatable tumours that I see in dogs – develop from lymph tissue, usually lymph nodes. My travelling companion Macy developed a fast-spreading carcinoma, with its origins in skin cells, that invaded her intestines, liver, and spleen.

There are almost as many causes of cancers as there are cancers. In the Bernese Mountain Dog there's an obvious genetic link, but it can be more complicated: some individuals inherit a cancer-producing gene, others inherit that gene but also a cancer-suppressing gene, and still others inherit a gene that suppresses the cancer-suppressing gene! On top of this, the genes are "switched" on and off by internal and external factors. Hormones trigger breast cancer in females and testicular cancer in males. Radiation and ultraviolet light from sunshine cause skin cancers. Injuries and infections may also predispose individuals to cancers, as do natural and manmade chemicals, but social stress does not cause cancer.

Cancer cells have a uniquely dangerous ability: they escape detection by the immune systems. They trick natural killer cells *(see p.246)* into not attacking and destroying them, evade the body's protective DNA policing enzymes, even produce chemicals called cytokines that suppress the immune system, and embark upon an eternal life of producing countless generations of cancer cells.

Double whammy Although cancer is related to old age, remember that what counts as old varies by breed. Some of the breeds with fairly long lifespans, like the Airedale, have a low risk of cancer, while a high risk of cancer is one reason for the shorter lifespan of other breeds. Mutts come out well, as they do on many health issues, with a low cancer risk and long life.

Reducing the risk

If you're a dog, one of the best ways to avoid cancer is to choose your parents wisely. According to pet insurance company records, there are breed differences in the risk of dying from cancer. Fortunately, the least susceptible breeds include many of the world's favourites, but remember, these are statistics. They apply to populations, not to individuals, so they are a likelihood, not a guarantee.

- LOWEST CANCER RISK: Border Collie, Cocker Spaniel, Mixed breed or mutts, German Shepherd Dog, West Highland White Terrier, Shetland Sheepdog, Yorkshire Terrier, Jack Russell Terrier, Collie, Bulldog, Welsh Springer Spaniel, Airedale, Irish Setter, Dachshund, Cavalier King Charles Spaniel, Beagle
- AVERAGE CANCER RISK: Dobermann, English Springer Spaniel, Labrador Retriever, Great Dane
- HIGHEST CANCER RISK: Bernese Mountain Dog, Irish Wolfhound, Rottweiler, Afghan Hound, Standard Poodle, Weimaraner, Staffordshire Bull Terrier, Boxer, Cairn Terrier, Old English Sheepdog, Golden Retriever, Flat-Coated Retriever

Whatever the breed, don't let your dog get fat. There's a correlation in dogs between obesity and certain cancers including breast cancer. Give your dog regular exercise: inactive people are almost twice as likely to develop cancer as those who exercise regularly, and the same probably applies to dogs. Even if your older dog appears perfectly healthy, have it thoroughly examined at

Poor prospects Surveys in the United Kingdom and North America show that almost half of all Bernese Mountain Dogs die of cancer, compared with a little over a quarter of all dogs. In spite of this health problem, the breed has greatly increased in popularity over the last decade.

least once a year, and twice a year once it's genuinely elderly. I can't tell you how often someone brings their older dog in because of something like bad breath and the diagnosis rapidly escalates from trivial to challenging. Thorough preventative examinations are the best way to catch problems when they're most treatable.

Diagnosis and treatment

We make great emotional investments in our dogs and in old age it's only natural that some of us instantly jump to the worst conclusion. Whether a dog is limping or drinking more, has diarrhoea or has a lump, we think of cancer. What's frustratingly true is that any of these changes can genuinely be a cancer symptom, but more likely causes are arthritis, kidney problems, scavenging, or benign tumours.

According to the American Veterinary Cancer Society, the ten most common signs of cancer are an abnormal swelling that persists or continues to grow; sores that don't heal; weight loss; loss of appetite; bleeding or discharge from any body opening; offensive odour; difficulty eating or swallowing; hesitation to exercise or lack of stamina; persistent lameness or stiffness; difficulty breathing, urinating, or defecating. This is a scary list, because it describes so many of the changes we all see in older dogs.

Two years ago I found myself taking my son's Labrador Inca then my own Golden Retriever Macy to veterinary neurologists for brain scans. Inca had developed seizures, while Macy's eyes had sunk back in their sockets with one facing northwest and the other southeast. In both instances brain tumours were part of the differential diagnoses, in which possible causes are eliminated until only one remains. Both problems turned out to have other causes, but only with MRI and CT scans could I know for sure. These very expensive diagnostic tools have spurred a gigantic leap forward in diagnosis and treatment of cancers.

Surgery remains the most effective treatment. If a cancer can be removed, it should be removed. If this isn't possible, some radiation-sensitive tumours can be shrunk, and pain can certainly be controlled with local radiation therapy. Radiation therapy is also useful when surgery removes most but not all of a skin cancer. Chemotherapy kills fast-multiplying cells, especially those that have spread throughout the body. I first used chemotherapy successfully in the early 1970s on a Labrador with lymphoma. The improvements since them have been literally breathtaking. I now expect permanent remissions for some lymphomas, although chemotherapy treatments for other cancers are still distressingly inefficient, especially when compared with the success rates in people. The reason for this is simple: humans can give informed consent to unpleasant but effective treatments, but vets make an ethical decision that the dog shouldn't suffer because of a treatment, or should suffer only very mild and short unpleasantness. Greater effectiveness may become possible with newer chemotherapies, including drugs that selectively cut off the blood supply to cancers, vaccines that stimulate the immune system to attack the tumour, or even gene therapies, in which a virus carries a tumour-destroying gene right into the cancer cells.

There's good evidence that if your dog has cancer, especially cancer of the lymphatic system, you should avoid feeding a high-carbohydrate diet. Carbohydrates give cancer cells energy. Evidence suggests that dogs with cancer benefit from diets high in fat and highly digestible protein, especially diets enriched with certain amino acids such as glutamine. Fortunately, this is exactly what an older dog enjoys. If a dog has a cancer, over half of its energy requirements can probably be met with fat calories. Dogs with cancer also need more micronutrients: a general vitamin and mineral supplement will do no harm, and a good balance of omega fatty acids may be useful. At least in theory, antioxidants may help to prevent cancers by keeping cells healthy, but they may also promote existing cancers by keeping cancer cells healthy too.

Sensory losses

Impaired hearing is very common in older dogs. Degeneration of structures deep inside the ear results in loss of both high-frequency hearing and general hearing. Eyesight also becomes poorer as the retinas lose rods and cones and the lenses lose elasticity and clarity. The loss of either one of these major senses can be terrible, although some dogs adjust well. But the loss of two is devastating. Unless you can guarantee to give twenty-four-hour-a-day, seven-days-a-week care, I have ethical problems with perpetuating lives of dogs that are both blind and deaf. Yes, of course an otherwise-healthy old

Visual cues It's a good idea to incorporate hand signals into training even for a dog with full hearing; for a deaf dog, it is essential. Your dog may learn with a speed that surprises you – remember that it instinctively watches your body language every moment, and build on that.

dog can satisfy its basic needs and carry out its body functions, and some dogs cope with these losses, but not many. In my experience, most become worried, even fearful. They are completely dependent on us to guide them to where food is, put them in their beds, protect them from harm. These overwhelming needs trigger a deep nurturing response in many of us: sometimes that human need stops us from seeing the reality.

Living with a deaf dog

Full loss often occurs very quickly, especially in breeds prone to age-related loss, such as Labrador and Golden Retrievers. Some owners feel that their dogs develop selective hearing, but more often than not this is genuine, even profound deafness. When Honey went deaf at 11 years of age, opening the fridge still brought her into the kitchen, even from the next floor. This was so reliable it was impossible for us not to question her hearing, even though I'd carried out a brainstem auditory evoked response (BAER) test and knew she had zero hearing. A dog's other senses – like Honey's sense of smell – are just so acute that they compensate. Older dogs can be more stubborn, more inclined to disobey, but they don't feign complete deafness. How your dog responds to hearing loss varies. With Honey, it was delightful that thunderstorms no longer upset her. Reactive dogs such as terriers might startle when unexpectedly touched, while laid back older dogs might just go "Huh?" A startled or disorientated dog may respond with a nip, but it's not difficult to train a dog not to be startled, as ever with food treats. Accustom your deaf dog to take a food treat from your open hand. Next, walk up behind it, gently touch it, and when it turns instantly offer the treat in your open hand. Once an unexpected touch is firmly associated with a food reward, put your treat-filled hand in front of your sleeping dog's nose. Just the smell may awaken it, but if it doesn't, touch your dog very, very lightly on the shoulder or back. Gently increase the touch to a stroke. As your dog awakens give the treat and continue stroking. As long as the brain is working well, it should take no more than three weeks to condition even a reactive dog not to nip if touched while sleeping.

Because dogs are acutely aware of your body language, deaf dogs quickly learn to respond to hand signals. I made up my own for Honey – the flat palm of my hand for "Wait", a beckoning arm wave for "Come", pointing my forefinger down and moving it towards the ground for "Sit". Both thumbs up, a smile, and a pat meant "Good girl". All of these can be taught in virtually the same way you teach verbal commands: just substitute the visual signal for the command. You need your dog's attention in the first place; we got Honey's attention by turning the lights on and off, stamping on the floor to create a vibration she felt, or throwing a food treat or tennis ball across her line of vision.

Old dogs, especially those who love food, easily learn to seek you out once taught that if they gaze into your eyes they get rewards. Do this only if you don't mind being constantly stared at by your deaf dog! Hide a treat in your hand, let your dog smell it, then bring it up to your nose so that its eyeline meets your eyes. Give a thumbs up signal, then the treat. Practice this until your dog routinely looks deep in your eyes before you reward it with the thumbs up and the snack. Now hold the treat half an arm's length away from you but don't give it until your dog impatiently looks you in the eye. Then give a thumbs up and the food reward. Vary where you hold the treat. You want your dog to learn that regardless of where the treat is, it gets it only after looking you in the eye. The website www.deafdogs.org has practical instructions for more advanced training of older deaf dogs.

When outdoors with a deaf dog, keep it on a lead unless you're in a fenced area. After a life off her lead responding to word commands, our deaf Honey was more relaxed when she walked on her lead, with a physical attachment to one of us. In the dark, a flashing light or laser light is useful.

Amend your dog's name tag with the word "deaf" just in case it gets lost. You can get collars that vibrate when you press a remote control. Look for the least bulky, weighing less than 90g (3oz), waterproof, with good battery life and a range suitable for what you want to do with your dog. It's quite basic to train your dog to look for you when the collar vibrates: simply get out the food treats, show them to your dog, trigger the vibration, then give the reward. Quite soon, your dog will look for you whenever it feels the vibration. Some collars have both vibration and tone, which is handy if you need to locate your dog; simply activate it and follow the ring tone!

Adjusting to loss of vision

All dogs develop cloudy lenses by the age of ten; this may look like cataracts but it's a tissue change called lenticular sclerosis. Older dogs usually retain a good ability to see slight movement at a distance of about 6m (20 feet) but something right under the nose is only a blur, and finding a ball in long grass now depends on the nose, rather than the eyes. Cataracts are also as common in dogs as they are in us. For many dogs, cataracts dramatically interfere with sight, but it takes years before they are so crystalline that they cause blindness. Some older dogs go blind because of medical conditions from hereditary cataracts or progressive retinal atrophy to sugar diabetes.

Regardless of the cause, it's now much safer for a dog to be on a lead except in enclosed areas where there's little possibility of injury. It gives your dog security and you peace of mind. Simple things may become difficult, especially if they involve depth perception at close range, like jumping up or down off sofas or beds or tackling stairs. A typical older dog becomes tentative when jumping up, not just because the joints hurt but because it has tried, missed, and hurt itself.

Some blind dogs cope amazingly well, others miserably. I once had a Yorkshire Terrier, Duchess, who became completely blind quite quickly at 12 years. Left alone she usually remained as rigid as a pine tree, seemingly fearful of taking a step in any direction. Once, on the shore of the lake we lived on, she walked into the water and in spite of my constant shouting started swimming for the far side almost a mile away. I had to swim after her to save her, and with heavy hearts we took her to be euthanized soon after.

Other blind dogs have a more laconic approach to their loss of vision. They quickly learn how to navigate familiar places, so don't rearrange your furniture or leave obstacles on the floor. A dog that may have enjoyed playing with fetch toys when it could see will now find squeaky toys and chew toys more valuable. Keep up your chatter with a blind dog. I've gone jogging with a client and his aged, blind Labrador Retriever, Amritsar. In the park Amri trotted and even cantered close to his owner's constant jabbering – "Attaboy Amri. Good dog. Keep going. Nice day. That's it. Good dog." But when his owner said "Amri. Dog coming!" Amri's tail went up to 12 o'clock high, his head perked up, his chest stuck out and he prepared himself for a dog-to-dog encounter. Here was a perfect role model for us, just getting on with life.

Bells and whistles You literally need to look out for your blind dog. Any sound that tells you when it's on the move allows you a bit more freedom of movement: you don't always have to be in the same place as your dog, as long as you're within earshot. Have your dog's collar tags and any microchips updated so the blindness is recorded.

Use your other senses more.

Amri and his dedicated but pragmatic owner were extra special. More commonly, blind dogs startle easily and they might nip when touched unexpectedly, just like reactive deaf dogs. Unexpected touches from people they know, let alone strangers, can be frightening, so ask people to offer a hand to be sniffed before touching the dog.

A blind dog should have a dog bed in each room and jingly things, such as gentle bells, on the collar to let you know when it's on the move. And you should learn to walk with heavy feet: your dog will hear your footsteps and know you're approaching, leaving, or just about anything else. Older blind dogs continue to respond well to verbal commands, but "Wait" becomes a much more important command – potentially life-saving – when a blind dog is off the lead.

Mental decline

Some dogs, just like some people, sail though old age without much brain decline; most of the dogs I see show signs of moderate decline if they reach or surpass the life expectancy of their breed, but a few show serious decline, what in us is called senile dementia. When this happens, behaviours that were minor nuisances become major problems. The more advanced the deterioration, the more truly senile a dog is, the more difficult it is to overcome those problems.

Seniors club With the hormonal highs and lows of youth long behind them, many older dogs meet and socialize with no jostling for position. Some become crankier and may not want to join the group, but it's worth keeping up with old friends in the park, even if you might now have to drive your dog there.

With time, a dog's brain shrinks, not only because cells die and cannot be replaced, but also because the remaining cells lose connections with each other. It may eventually weigh 20 per cent less than it did in its prime. Although the brain can't grow new cells, it can make new connections or reconnections between cells that remain. Mental activity helps to develop these connections and increases the cells' resistance to injury. Given a stimulating environment, more social activity with other dogs and people, and encouragement to play games and to solve problems, a dog's brain can actually increase in weight.

Yes, let sleeping dogs lie, but when they're awake offer mental stimulation; a food treat to work out of a hollow bone, a moving target to pin down. The longer any animal uses the brain, the longer it will take to lose it. New experiences are good: regularly replace old toys with new ones, try a new route to a new park, ensure regular off-lead meetings with new people and new dogs, because social activity keeps the brain sharp.

Even if your dog isn't friendly, routinely let it see other dogs, because even a growl is a social activity! Introducing a new pup into your dog's home can also help to keep an older dog physically and mentally active. The resident might at first hate the pup's rambunctiousness, but usually the terms of the contract between them will be set within three weeks and your old dog will be doing things you thought it would never do again.

Diet is important too, and I'm not just guessing here. Scientists at the University of Toronto and the University of California Irving carried out well-controlled studies lasting over three years of both youthful and older (nine- to twelve-year-old) Beagles. Old Beagles that were given a variety of stimulating tasks, the opportunity to play with other dogs, and a commercially available fortified diet performed better on cognitive tests and were more likely to readily learn new tasks than dogs not given these choices or supplements. Each factor alone could improve cognitive functions, but the greatest success occurred when all were combined. The diet fed to the Beagles was fortified with tomatoes, carrot granules, citrus pulp, spinach flakes, vitamins C and E, and two "mitochondrial co-factors", acetyl-l-carnitine and alpha lipoic acid (B/D). Mitochondrial co-factors may slow the rate of age-related damage to mitochondria, the power plants of cells, and reduce levels of free radicals. Free-radical damage is associated with age-associated learning and memory problems. If you have a cat too, don't use this for them! Alpha lipoic acid is toxic to cats.

In another, similar study, older dogs were given a commercial product called Aktivait, containing l-carnitine, alpha lipoic acid, coenzyme Q, vitamins E and C, phosphotidylserine, selenium, and omega-3 fish oils. They showed significant improvements in the areas of disorientation, social interaction, and house-soiling.

Behaviour changes

Even with the best care, the brain inevitably declines with age. It's a given. If a dog lives long enough – and most of those I meet now do – they end up with poorer memory, poorer judgment, poorer decision-making ability, a shorter attention span, interference with functions such as eating, urinating, or defecating, reduced cognitive function, and personality changes.

Dogs develop rational fears – of me, for example, because I stab them, prod parts that hurt, or squeeze their anal sacs. Rational fears protect dogs from threats or dangers. Stress is a natural part of life, and brief episodes of stress are not only normal but beneficial. When the thinking cortex communicates a stress to the rest of the brain, it triggers a cascade of chemical changes. In younger dogs this cascade is triggered only when necessary, but in older dogs it is triggered more easily – often too easily. An older dog is more likely to develop phobias, or irrational fears – of someone limping, or dressed unusually, or any one of a vast array of other non-threatening sights or sounds. Like a defective smoke alarm going off each time you light a candle, any stress leads to a sustained release of damaging chemicals. Something as simple as a change in your routine can be very unsettling to an older dog.

Never too old Play can be part of a dog's life right through old age. The games may be less boisterous – you might be rolling a ball across the ground rather than tossing it for a flying catch – but don't stop buying the odd new toy and playing to get your dog interested in it.

A dog in a stressful situation may lose its appetite, try to escape or destroy items, bark or howl excessively, mess inside the house, or develop compulsive behaviours, such as ritually licking, pacing, or barking rhythmically. It can suffer panic attacks, in which the muscles tense, the heart rate increases, and the dog hyperventilates.

Biochemically speaking, these events occur in the brain's limbic system (*see p.104*) and rely on neurotransmitter chemicals with a profound influence on an elderly dog's behaviour. In people, decreased levels of serotonin lead to depression, and some research in dogs suggests that serotonin is related to a feeling of confidence. Based on this research, selective serotonin re-uptake inhibitors (SSRIs) such as fluoxetine or Prozac are sometimes used in an attempt to calm elderly dogs when anxiety develops into panic.

When old dogs behave in new ways, the first question is whether the change is caused by an illness or disease or whether it's a consequence of the brain no longer doing what it once could. Cognitive decline in people is a continuum, and the same is true in dogs. In us, Alzheimer's disease is a form of senile dementia that occurs when people are still relatively young, for example in their fifties. Dogs rarely if ever develop very-early-onset dementia, but age-related "mild cognitive impairment" is common. According to the pharmaceutical company Pfizer, 62 per cent of dogs aged ten years and older experience some signs of geriatric senility or as they've called this condition, "canine cognitive dysfunction".

Annual service Symptoms can be misleading, especially seen in isolation. Full examination and a few tests might show that apparent mental decline has a physical cause, so regular health checks are vital for the ageing dog.

Diagnosing senility

We all recognize some typical symptoms of cognitive impairment, but these can only be diagnosed as the consequence of geriatric senility and a treatment recommended once your vet has ruled out failing senses and other medical factors. For example, restlessness at night could be caused by age-related brain changes, or it could simply be the result of a urinary tract disorder. Here's a short list of other age-related changes and the behaviour changes that they might cause. These are age-related behaviour problems, but not senility.

- REDUCED HEARING OR SIGHT: increased irritability, increased fear, altered sleep-wake cycle, aggression, increased barking, loss of housetraining, increased irritability or increased docility, reduced response to command, reduced learning.
- IMPAIRED HEART FUNCTION: reduced exercise tolerance, signs of senility, confusion, restlessness.
- LOSS OF MUSCLE MASS: house soiling and/or incontinence, decreased mobility, increased irritability because of pain, reduced tolerance of temperature changes.
- HORMONAL UPSETS: reduced tolerance of cold, decreased activity, increased irritability and/or aggression, behaviour changes associated with increased male or female hormone (such as urine marking, possessiveness).
- URINARY SYSTEM CONCERNS: increased drinking and urinating, incontinence, loss of housetraining.
- LUNG PROBLEMS: decreased energy and reduced exercise tolerance, apparent confusion.

Assessing senility

Jaime Rofina, a veterinary pathologist at Utrecht University in the Netherlands, found that the brain pathology in dogs with age-related declines (such as a loss of memory) was similar to that in humans. He was aware that many of the changes could also be caused by declines in other parts of the body rather than the brain, and produced the questionnaire and scoring system shown opposite to help diagnosis. The higher the score, the more advanced the senility is. Remember, vets use this *after* carrying out a full medical examination, so don't rush off and try to diagnose your own dog in the dark.

Variable signs All these areas of changed behaviour can be linked to mental decline; a dog may show changes in only one area of behaviour, or a broad spectrum of problems.

QUESTIONNAIRE

APPETITE

Normal	1
Decreased	2
Increased with diarrhoea	3
Increased without diarrhoea	4

DRINKING

Normal	1
Polydypsia	3

ACTIVE INCONTINENCE

Not incontinent	1
Urinates indoors	2
Urinates and defecates in the house	4

DAY-NIGHT RHYTHM

Normal sleeping	1
Increased	2
Sleeps during the day, restless at night	3

AIMLESS BEHAVIOUR

No aimless behaviour	1
Star gazing	2
Stereotyped walking	3
Circling	4

ACTIVITY/INTERACTION

Normal	1
Decreased	2
No contact with the environment/owner	4

LOSS OF PERCEPTION

No loss of perception	1
Collides into furniture	2
Tries to pass through narrow spaces	5
Tries to pass through the wrong side of the door	5

DISORIENTATION

No disorientation	1
On new walks	2
On daily walks	4
At home	5

MEMORY

Normal	1
No recognition of acquaintances	2
No recognition of the owner after a holiday	4
No recognition of the owner on a daily basis	5

PERSONALITY CHANGE

No change	1
Aggressive towards other pets and/or children	3
Aggressive towards the owner	4

Ageing gracefully The old age we hope for in our dogs is one of slight and gentle decline, a slowing down before the final halt. With luck and care, your dog can enjoy a relaxed and comfortable retirement.

Stress and anxiety problems

Most behaviour problems in most dogs have been learned and need to be "unlearned". In geriatric dogs, the same problems can be associated with the brain not working as well as it once did. They are more likely to develop in dogs with a susceptibility to anxiety. Older dogs are likely to have more problems with noises like thunderstorms or fireworks, more separation anxiety, more generalized anxiety disorders, more panic attacks, and of course more problems with learning and remembering. Behaviour problems in geriatric dogs are treated in the same way as in younger dogs, but there are special considerations. Learning and responding can be frustratingly slow in old dogs, because of brain degeneration.

Try to reduce unnecessary stresses: limit long trips and boarding, and if major changes are anticipated, make them as gradual as possible. Since older dogs don't handle stress well, a new puppy is not always a good idea, especially if the older dog is not mobile enough to get away from the puppy, is experiencing pain or cognitive dysfunction, or has poor hearing or vision. When sudden or major changes are unavoidable, and your dog is anxious or distressed, anti-anxiety medication may be useful.

Some older dogs become overly sensitive to noises. Cognitive dysfunction, immobility that makes it harder to get away from the source of the noise, and a decreased ability to manage stress can contribute to noise phobia. Identify which noises your dog is afraid of: it may be noises you can hear, such as thunderstorms, but remember that dogs hear sounds we can't. Try to relate your dog's behaviour to events. Once the sound is identified, treat phobias through desensitizing and counter-conditioning, using a commercially produced sound CD or DVD. Play the sound at a very low volume and reward your dog for showing no fear, gradually increasing the volume over weeks, or more likely months, and giving rewards.

Separation anxiety is perhaps the most common behaviour problem in older dogs. Any change might trigger anxiety and for some dogs, anxiety escalates into pure panic. The dog severely pants, shakes, and trembles. Heart and respiratory rates both skyrocket. The eyes are as dilated as they can get. A dog having a panic attack may run frantically from room to room looking either for you or for somewhere to hide.

Treating an older dog for separation anxiety involves changing the way you interact with it. Your dog must learn that it doesn't always get your attention when it wants, for example, when it comes over and asks to be touched. This is difficult, because not touching goes against our instincts, but your dog gradually gets accustomed to your absences, short at first and then longer. In older dogs this can sometimes only be achieved by using anti-anxiety drugs during the first few weeks of modifying behaviour.

Go back to basics. Teach your dog to relax. If it can learn to relax in a "Stay" for extended periods while you're there, it'll be more likely to relax while you're gone. Use all the same calming behaviour that you would use on a younger dog (*see pp.275–76*), but take extra care. Work out how long you can leave your dog before it gets anxious: it may be only seconds. If that's the case, shut the door and instantly open it again but avoid even looking at your dog, let alone talking to it. Gradually increase the time you're gone, always returning before your dog becomes anxious. Once inside, have your dog sit and only reward when it's calm. Be patient. This works, as long as your dog still has reasonable brain power, and the great majority of older dogs still do, but it takes at least three weeks, sometimes considerably longer.

Associate your departure with something good. As you leave, give your dog a hollow toy filled with soft cheese, peanut butter, or aromatic paté. The more powerful the food treat the more likely it is to distract. Make sure your dog is comfortable, with food and water. A sports or natural history channel on television, with moving balls or other animals, captivates some dogs. A television or radio also muffles some outdoor sounds and reduces the likelihood of frequent barking. Some dogs are more relaxed if they can see the outside world, others become more anxious. Some are anxious when left outdoors, and some feel safe in their crates, which reduces the risk of destructiveness. When Honey was 16 years old and becoming antsy if left in the house, she relaxed and snoozed for as long as I let her in my parked car, her personal crate on wheels. Find what's best for your dog.

Make your dog's day more stimulating. It may be less active, but if you're out during the day still have someone come in to let it out. Get advice from your vet. Anti-anxiety medications may initially be needed to break the cycle of separation anxiety. Medication alone, however, won't solve the problem. Work with your vet and an understanding dog trainer to develop a plan that will work best for all of you.

Aggression and biting

An older dog can become aggressive because of a medical problem that causes pain, because it startles easily due to diminished senses, or because it's less mobile and simply can't get away from that bouncy pup with the irritating zest for life. Anxiety or panic might also make an older dog more irritable and aggressive. In a multi-dog household, an older dog that once dominanted may be challenged by younger dogs. Although owners frequently tell me they think their dog has suddenly become aggressive because it has had a stroke, strokes are quite rare in dogs. Unfortunately, brain tumours aren't, and these may cause aggressive changes.

Determine what's contributing to aggression and eliminate or reduce it if you can. Have your dog thoroughly examined for signs of pain, and look for arthritis, dental disease, and ear infection. Treat any medical conditions. Watch your dog for signs of stress and remove it from stressful situations. Keep an older dog, especially one with reduced hearing or vision, on a lead and use a head halter such as a Gentle Leader or Halti. In some cases, a basket muzzle may be needed, but don't leave a muzzled dog unattended. If your dog has a sensory deficit, tell people to avoid approaching or touching it. If you think your dog might be aggressive, confine it to a safe, quiet area when you have visitors. Medication can be helpful in reducing aggression caused by fear and anxiety, but will not solve the problem. Your vet and a good dog trainer can help you work out a plan.

Grumpy old dog It can be really distressing when a dog that's been sweet-natured all its life undergoes a Jekyll-and-Hyde transformation in old age. Some causes need medical treatment, others will respond to an adjustment in the way you treat your dog.

Bark at the moon Changes in your dog's cycle of sleeping and waking can be hard to deal with even when they are relatively harmless to the dog. Once you know that there is no medical issue, confining your dog so you still get a good night's sleep may be all you can do.

Pointless barking and wandering

Some older dogs share their stress by barking, whining, or howling. Increased or pointless barking can also be associated with geriatric senility. Honey would lie on the floor in the living room in her latter years, staring into space, occasionally woofing pointless woofs.

Identify the cause of increased barking or howling and eliminate or reduce it when possible. If your dog is vocalizing to get your attention, what they're really doing is calling out "I'm here" or "Where are you?" Ignore it. You may need to drop a drinks can with a few coins in it to startle your dog into stopping, but don't let it associate you with the correction or it may increase the noise-making just to get your attention. Maybe you need to set aside more time to spend together, but do so on your terms, not your dog's.

Some older dogs become restless at night and stay awake, pacing through the house, whining, howling, or barking. Many medical conditions can contribute to restlessness, and you should only think of this as a behavioural problem after your vet has looked for signs of pain and eliminated medical causes. Remote corrections, such as infra-red buzzers that are triggered when your dog walks past them, may be needed. From my experience, it may be necessary to confine your dog away from where people sleep.

Loss of housetraining

I'm amazed and gratified by how so many owners are willing to put up with "accidents", assuming they are the inevitable unpleasant baggage of ageing. There are many medical conditions which result in an increased frequency of urinating or defecating, and one of these may be the underlying cause, so have your vet examine your dog. Before taking your dog in to the vet, observe the colour and amount of urine (or stool) passed, the frequency at which your older dog needs to eliminate, changes in eating or drinking habits, your dog's posture while eliminating, and whether the accidents only occur when you are gone.

Treat any medical condition that is diagnosed and control obesity if this is an issue. You may need to build a ramp to the outside so that an arthritic dog doesn't need to manoeuvre on stairs, or cover shiny, slippery floors with non-slip rugs. Intolerance of bad weather may also cause a dog to choose to eliminate indoors, as can separation anxiety.

Rid your home of odours that trigger messing indoors; use an enzyme cleanser on soiled areas. If your dog needs to urinate or defecate more frequently than your own schedule allows, find someone who can let it out at appropriate intervals when you're out; you know how you feel when you need to go and there's no toilet around. Stick to a regular feeding schedule and be consistent with both supervision and confinement. Avoid any punishment: it will make the problem worse or create others. A sharp noise given during the act to interrupt the behaviour is the only interactive correction that works.

Social problems

Young pups are full of boundless energy and love chasing, attacking, and biting other dogs. Most older dogs control exuberant pups through threats and inhibited bites, but some passive, fearful, or senile old timers will withdraw and hide instead. A few – very few – will become quite anxious

Two dogs or not Getting a younger dog can be a great idea, or it can be a terrible one. Many old dogs are shaken out of their lethargy by a bouncy young companion, but others, particularly those living with pain or cognitive problems, may be made worse by the change.

WHAT IS ALZHEIMER'S?

Alois Alzheimer, a German psychiatrist and neuropathologist, published his first article on senile dementia in a relatively young person, a 51-year-old woman, in 1907. This form of "presenile" senile dementia was named after Alzheimer.

Some veterinary authors call the similar condition in dogs "canine counterpart of the senile dementia of the Alzheimer type" because the pathological changes, fibrous tangles and plaques within dogs' brain cells are identical to the pathological changes that occur in Alzheimer's, but I disagree with this use of the name. The condition doesn't occur when dogs are relatively young, as Alzheimer's does in people, and the terms "canine cognitive dysfunction" or "canine geriatric senility" are more accurate for describing significant loss of thinking function in a dog's brain.

at having a new, young vibrant pup in the home. When this happens, the older resident may bark, urinate or defecate indoors, chew furniture and furnishings, or go off its food.

When an older dog is overwhelmed by a young pup, separate them whenever you are not around to supervise. Before allowing them to interact, provide the pup with enough exercise or play to reduce its exuberance, and then reward gentle play between the two. Keep a long lead on the pup for control and to apply light correction. Squeezing a squeaky toy or giving the occasional timely squirt from a water pistol may help distract a pup from play attacks.

Problems can also occur between dogs that have lived together without trouble for years. They happen when the older, more dominant dog declines in strength and assertiveness and the younger one, especially if it is of the same sex, challenges it for the right to greet you first, be fed first, own the toys, and choose the best places to sleep. We naturally tend to side with the older dog, but trying to help it to maintain its old dominant position only makes matters worse. Actively support the younger dog's dominant role instead, but be aware that it's difficult to convince some older dogs to defer, especially if the younger dog has been in your home for a shorter time. In these circumstances, you need to reaffirm you and your family's dominant role with both dogs.

Review and re-teach obedience commands to both dogs. Teach them that you have complete control over everything they need or want by requiring a response to a command before either receives food, treats, play, a walk, and especially attention. Whenever the dogs start to approach you, a guest, the doorway, or a food bowl, command both of them to "Stay!" and then release one at a time. Vary the order in which the dogs are released or receive attention each time. Establishing a strong dominant role for you reduces aggressive tension between the dogs. In some cases, muzzles may be necessary for safety.

Like us, older dogs get both wiser and sillier: wiser because they realise they don't always have to do what they're told, and sillier because even when suffering the ravages of time, they still like to chase a ball, play a game, act the fool. Sometimes it's both painfully sad and gloriously uplifting, like watching a grandfather do hops, skips, and jumps. Dogs grow old with immense charm and majesty.

CHAPTER THIRTEEN

A Dignified End

There's a natural, stoic dignity to the way dogs cope with the failings of old age. They seldom complain. When they fall, they simply get back up if they can and get on with life. Dogs don't look back at what they could do once: they concentrate on here and now, on what they still can do, and they do this remarkably well. That's why I respect them so much: they're perfect role models for how we should behave. But eventually, even the most noble of old timers is no longer able to cope or is living with constant pain. Then it's time to let go.

I think I speak for virtually all vets when I say I get more letters of thanks in a single year for ending lives properly than I've had in almost 40 years for saving lives. Euthanasia means voluntarily ending the life of an individual suffering from a terminal illness or other incurable condition, and the word comes from the Greek *eu*, meaning good, and *thanatos*, meaning death. For those who have watched a dog quickly fall asleep and then seconds later seen his or her heart stop, the procedure is aptly named. It *is* a good death. It's also the most common way dogs die in North America and Northern Europe. In the United Kingdom, 52 per cent of all dogs are euthanized. Another 42 per cent die from illnesses or diseases, 5 per cent die from accidents, and 1 per cent are put down because of behaviour problems.

An individual decision

Whether and how you and your vet decide to end your dog's life varies with every single dog and the circumstances of its life. Sometimes those circumstances are clear, sometimes they're cloudy. Let me, if I may, use some of my own dogs, all Golden Retrievers, as examples.

By the time Lexington was 13, she was having difficulty with the stairs and was unhappy with being helped up them. One day she suddenly lost her balance, collapsed on the floor with a head tilt, and vomited. Her eyes "ticked" in one direction. All these things appear when there is a "vestibular event" in the organ of balance in one ear. Almost invariably dogs recover, although recovery may take weeks. But Lex was also twitchy, and so deeply frightened that I profoundly sedated her. While she slept she was relaxed, but as the sedative wore off her twitchiness and apparent distress worsened. So I fed a long-acting anaesthetic through the intravenous line I'd set up. Every 12 hours I let it gradually wear off, but each time she was worse. Her eyes were ticking and rotating, and her moaning was pitiful. Whatever had happened – a haemorrhage, a tumour, I never knew – had happened in her brain not her ear, and her brain was getting more damaged. Her condition was dreadful and not improving. We had no difficulty making the decision to add a concentrated anaesthetic to her drip line and end her life.

By the time Liberty was 12 years old, she too couldn't make it up the stairs, but she was a confident, even flippant sparkler of a dog. When she wanted to go upstairs she had no trouble with issuing a short command

Right time to go Nobody knows your dog as well as you do, and in the end you are the one who will have to make the decision. It isn't always easy, but usually we know in our hearts whether our dogs are still enjoying life or not, and when we have to let them go.

bark: "Servant! Wheelbarrow me up the stairs!" We did this for years. During those years she had a genuine vestibular event, and within a week she was walking on her own again. Later she developed a thickening of the heart muscle, leaving little room in the heart for blood. Medication helped, but then she had another vestibular event and this time her heart failed. The circumstances weren't as black-and-white as they were with Lex, but we all agreed it would be unfair to her to attempt heroics, so her life was ended.

Honey seemed to go on forever, never experiencing a sudden or major decline. As with all big dogs, the stairs became a problem, but as long as she thought about them before hitting them and took the first step the right way, her momentum would get her up. She lived to 17, so long that she developed the senile changes I've already mentioned. Her decline was slow and gentle, but one morning I looked at her and thought she was no longer happy with life. It happened to be sports day at our daughter's school so I did the dad's sack-race and cheered Julia on in the egg-and-spoon race, then driving home told Julia that I thought Honey wasn't enjoying life any longer. Julia burst into tears and said she looked at Honey that morning and that's exactly what she too thought, but didn't want to tell me. When we got home I put Honey to sleep.

Macy was different. When she was just six years old, rather than charging ahead on a walk as usual, she unexpectedly walked beside me. I examined her and found a mass the size of a chicken egg in her guts. At the clinic, I found nothing unexpected in a blood sample, but knew I'd have to operate to investigate. That night, Macy came to our bed, anxious and panting; I gave her a painkiller and she relaxed. The following morning, when I operated on her, I found she had haemorrhaged in her abdomen. I found the site of bleeding and removed it, but there were other sites, filled with cheesy, pus-like material. Veronica and I operated for three hours, but there were simply too many sites to remove them all. After we finished I wondered why I had operated. I still didn't know the exact cause of her condition – pathology later showed it to be a wickedly fast-spreading cancer – but experience told me that the rest of her life would be short and probably uncomfortable. I didn't want to lose my dog, but I didn't want her to wake up either, so I increased the narcotic painkiller and took her home to Julia. I continued to add painkiller to her drip and, lying by the sofa, by the light of the fire, she died that evening, conscious, but without the distress of re-awakening.

Life lessons The life and care of a pet is a valuable part of a child's emotional education. The death of a pet, however much of a wrench it feels, is also part of that process.

Do dogs have moral status?

Do dogs have moral status, or moral rights, or both? Your answers will be intertwined with the moral values of your own culture and possibly religion. Jewish scripture advises that you should judge a man by the way he treats his animals; Mahatma Gandhi said one should judge a nation the same way. In Judaeo-Christian culture, the decision to euthanize an elderly dog is fraught with emotion, but still a morally simple choice. In other cultures or religions, where the value of a dog's "soul" is equal to that of a human's, euthanasia creates a moral dilemma. Rather than try to give universal answers, I'll recount where we've been heading in western culture.

Would I? One moral precept that turns up again and again in world religions runs along the lines of "don't put anyone else through something you wouldn't want to suffer". It's not a bad principle to apply to our pets as well: it takes a bit of imagination to put ourselves wholly in their position, but we do know what they're feeling.

All of us have ethical intuitions instilled by our parents and our societies. And like Pinocchio's nose, some just grow and grow. For example, when I was a veterinary student in the mid 1960s, I had no qualms about operating *on the same dog* every two weeks, but today, I feel terrible as I write that. How could I? How could I open up then sew shut that dog's belly one week, play with her for the next two weeks, then open her again and open and close her bladder, then play with her for two more weeks before opening her once more, removing her spleen, then play with her again while she recovered enough for me to operate on her yet again? My classmates and I were skilled surgeons when we graduated, but none of us questioned, at least not to each other, the deeply unpleasant and disturbing way we were acquiring those skills.

Empathy for animals isn't innate; it has to be learned. Once animals were regarded as morally insignificant, but in the 20th century, this attitude became increasingly less acceptable. In 1965, the Brambell Commission report on agriculture in Britain said that farming methods that failed to meet the needs and nature of animals were morally unacceptable. This was a turning point: a major government saying that animals, including dogs, had moral status. Today, humane education is part of the core curriculum in some places, and I'm sure that living with a dog helps kids on their journey from the self-centredness and egocentricity of childhood to an adult regard for others, including animals.

Western culture today accepts that animals have both moral status and moral rights, but exactly what those rights are is impossible to define. Each of us has a different answer, and as a dog nears the end of its life each of us can come to a slightly different conclusion. You have a "gut feeling" about what's the best thing to do, as Julia and I did with Honey, and this is often as good as anything that veterinary science or moral philosophy can offer.

Some dispassionate questions

With the help of your veterinarian, most of you too will eventually decide when and where your dog dies. It can be the most tormenting aspect of living with a dog, but in the 1970s, New York City veterinarian Dr Bernard Hershhorn devised the list of questions here to help you decide what's best. It may be over 30 years old, but it remains as practical today as it was when he wrote it.

- Is the condition prolonged, recurring, or getting worse?
- Is the condition no longer responding to treatment?
- Is the dog in pain or otherwise suffering, either physically or mentally?
- Is it no longer possible to alleviate pain or suffering?
- If your dog recovers, is he or she likely to be critically ill, invalid, or unable to care for him or herself?
- If your dog recovers, will there be severe personality changes?

Hershhorn said that if the answer to all of these questions is yes, then euthanasia is the honest, simple, and humane solution. I agree. But if you answer no to several of these questions, things are less obvious and you should ask yourself the following:

- Can I provide the necessary care?
- Will providing this care seriously interfere with or create serious problems for myself and my family?
- Will the cost of treatment be unbearably expensive?

Your dog is a member of your family. The decision is for you and your family, not the vet, although vets usually have personal and clinical experience that can help you with your decision. In my experience these are valid reasons for euthanasia:

- Overwhelming physical injury that is unlikely to repair well
- Irreversible disease that is causing your pet distress or discomfort that cannot be controlled
- Old-age wear and tear that has a permanent effect on your dog's quality of life
- Physical injury, disease, or wear and tear resulting in permanent loss of control of body functions
- Uncontrollable aggression with risk to children, owners, or others
- Untreatable disease dangerous to humans

When I was first in practice, it was easier to decide whether or not it was in a dog's interest to be kept alive. Today, just about any medical treatment that's available for us is also available for our dogs. That leads to many more questions for all of us, vets and owners. How far should we go? What treatments are acceptable? For example, it's possible to give a dog a kidney transplant. But who donates the kidney? Does that dog have a say? And what about the medical consequences of the transplant? What's the quality of life

Gone is not forgotten When a dog dies, the gap left can be every bit as large as when a human member of our family is no longer there. A dog may have been around for all of a child's life, making the loss more painful than it is for adults who have known life before that dog, or with other dogs.

Resting place Pet cemeteries may seem anthropomorphic – no other species buries its dead, after all – but we've spent tens of thousands of years humanizing dogs until they are part of the family. It's only natural that we use human rituals and places to remember them when they're gone.

for a dog on immune-suppressing drugs? How much should we spend on medical and surgical treatment for old dogs?

At least this last is an easy question to answer: I really don't care what you're willing to spend. That's none of my business. One family might choose to spend their income on a new car, another on flying their dog to a pioneering surgeon. My only concern is whether that dog will suffer from the treatment. But for most of us the time eventually comes when nothing that medicine can offer or money can buy works: decision time.

Euthanasia is simple

The anaesthetic pentobarbital is the most commonly used euthanasia agent. It's given intravenously at 200 times the strength once used for general anaesthesia. Some owners think their dogs know what's happening, but that's just our feeling of guilt. All a dog really knows is that someone holds a leg – something that's happened before when a blood sample was taken or a medicine given intravenously – and then comes a feeling of sleepiness. Your dog loses consciousness within seconds; within a few more seconds, the heart stops. Brain death occurs within seconds, but electrical activity in muscles can last for up to ten minutes, causing twitches. There can be a reflex contraction of the diaphragm producing a gasp, as if the dog were still alive. It isn't.

Until burial or cremation, the body is kept in cold storage at the vet's. We routinely cremate bodies individually, returning the ashes to the owner, unless they prefer burial. Some bury their dogs in their own gardens or in pet cemeteries. If you do this, make sure the body is wrapped in biodegradable material such as a cotton sheet, and dig the grave deep enough to prevent wild animals from digging it up, around 1m (39in).

Natural grieving

If you've read this book you probably have the same sort of feelings for your dog that my family has for ours. Non-pet owners sometimes find it difficult to understand how awful it can be when a smelly old dog with some pretty disgusting habits dies. We sometimes feel embarrassed that the death of a dog triggers raw, wrenching emotion, but grief is normal. This was a thinking, feeling being, and you've shared years together. Anger, denial, anxiety, all the emotions we experience when we lose a human friend are part of the grieving process when our dogs die. If you're an average owner, the stages of grief typically evolve for almost a year.

All of us grieve in our own way. Most of us eventually accept the loss, and balance the good that came from living with that dog with the heartache we felt when death came. In his *Philadelphia Inquirer* eulogy for his dog Marley, journalist John Grogan wrote "Marley taught me about living each day with unbridled exuberance and joy, about seizing the moment and following your heart. He taught me to appreciate the simple things – a walk in the woods, a fresh snowfall, a nap in a shaft of winter sunlight. And as he grew old and achy he taught me about optimism in the face of adversity, Mostly, he taught me about friendship and selflessness and, above all else, unwavering loyalty."

The response to his article spurred him to write the bestselling *Marley and Me*, which triggered a slew of similar titles. The week Macy died, I'd received one from an American publisher. *Merle's Door* is Ted Kerasote's intelligent and attractive tale of his life with a big yellow dog named Merle, inevitably including Merle's death: "Rocking back on my heels I wondered how this could be – his going off while I was cleaning his butt. Somehow, it seemed apt. A dog is always more interested in another dog's rear end than in its eyes. Half laughing, half crying at this thought, I suddenly felt all my joints lose cohesion, as if what had been holding me together had suddenly dissolved. 'My dog,' I said to the empty house. 'My dog.'"

But the subject isn't new. Fifty years ago, after his Basset hound died in a road traffic accident, Richard Joseph wrote an open letter 'To The Man Who Killed My Dog' to the *Westport Town Crier and Herald*, his local newspaper in Connecticut. It evokes an era but it's also timeless.

I hope you were going somewhere important when you drove so fast down Cross Highway across Bayberry Lane, on Tuesday night. I hope that when you got there the time you saved by speeding meant something to you or somebody else. Maybe we'd feel better if we could imagine that you were a doctor rushing to deliver a baby or ease somebody's pain. The life of our dog to shorten someone's suffering – that wouldn't have been so bad. But even though all we saw of you was the black shadow of your car and its jumping red tail lights as you roared down the road, we know too much about you to believe it.

You saw the dog, you stepped on your brakes, you felt a thump, you heard a yelp and then my wife's scream. Your reflexes are better than your heart and stronger than your courage – we know that – because you jumped on the gas again and got out of there as fast as your car could carry you. Whoever you are, mister, and whatever you do for a living, we know you are a killer. And in your hands, driving the way you drove on Tuesday night, your car was a murder weapon.

Saying goodbye Sometimes the end can come out of the blue, by accident or sudden illness. But with an old dog, you are usually preparing for the inevitable for some time before it happens.

Store of memories When you know the end is imminent, it may be tempting to make the most of your last days or weeks together by doing more things. It's fine to indulge yourself and your dog a bit, but make sure you don't inadvertently stress your dog – physically or mentally.

You didn't bother to look, so I'll tell you what that thump and yell were. They were Vicky, a six-month-old Basset puppy; white with brown and black markings. An aristocrat, with twelve champions among her forebears; but she clowned and she chased, and she loved people and kids and other dogs as much as any mongrel on earth.

I'm sorry you didn't stick around to see the job you did, though a dog dying by the side of the road isn't a very pretty sight. In less than two seconds you and that car of yours transformed a living being that had been beautiful, warm, clean, soft and loving into something dirty, ugly, broken and bloody. A poor, shocked and mad thing that tried to sink its teeth into the hand it had nuzzled and licked all its life.

I hope to God that when you hit my dog you had for a moment the sick, dead feeling in the throat and down in the stomach that we have known ever since. And that you feel it whenever you think about speeding down a winding country road again. Because the next time some eight-year-old boy might be wobbling along on his first bicycle. Or a very little one might wander out past the gate and into the road in the moment it takes his father to bend down to pull a weed out of the drive, the way my puppy got away from me. Or maybe you'll be really lucky again, and only kill another dog, and break the heart of another family.

The letter was reprinted in papers all over the country, and eventually it was even published as a short book, bound together with many of the replies that Joseph received.

My own experience

After my dog Macy died, to ease my pain, I wrote down how I felt. Six months later, when those feelings were no longer so raw, I sent what I wrote to a national newspaper. This is some of what I said:

When dogs are members of the family, when we know they have feelings and emotions so similar to ours, when we grieve for their passing as we do for any other beings we have formed bonds with, we need rituals to help us cope with the end of a life. Julia and I stayed with her body for a while, my fingers buried in my dog's hair for my comfort now rather than for hers, then I wrapped her in a sheet, put her on her bed in the back of the car and drove to Sussex.

At dawn the next morning, I started digging under a low, bushy bay tree where on hot days she had silently retreated for shade. The clay was as hard as concrete but this was a satisfying ritual I'd carried out before. I've got two more dogs, Liberty and Lex, buried in their favourite spots in that garden. It's a final service, a last "thank you" to an innocent. Rigor mortis had come and gone and as I carried her from the car to the hole I'd dug, her head lolled like a flower on an old stem. Mock me if you must, but I buried with her all the lost tennis balls that she'd found in the park during the previous month and proudly carried back to the car, 11 of them.

... Macy was the fourth dog we've had during our marriage, and certainly the most travelled. I've surprised myself by how cut up I still feel about her premature death. Maybe that's because she died young, or because I spent so many months on the road, travelling alone with her, sharing experiences with

her and no one else. Or maybe it's because she was my first digital dog. It seems that every time my screen saver comes on there's another random picture of Macy, among lingonberrys on the Russian border, ploughing through the surf of an empty Oregon beach, at Florian's café in Venice. The memories remain, but I know too that, inevitably and joyously, she will soon be followed by a fifth.

All of us, whether we believe in one religion or another or none at all, need rituals. My ritual was burying my own dog. I wanted the ritual to be mine, the sweat to be mine, to do something for her after she'd given so much to us. Writing about her was another satisfying ritual. I felt better when I put into words the feelings I had for her when she died.

Others will use different rituals. Some say prayers, others find comfort in poems. I recently went on a home visit to euthanize an elderly cat, and the owners had lit almost a hundred candles that twinkled throughout the room. My nurse and I broke into broad smiles we couldn't wipe away. We were just as soothed and warmed by that gloriously unexpected sight as the owners were.

Play it again Owners don't consciously set out to replace departed dogs – we know that's never possible, and to most of us it would feel like a betrayal – but most of us do end up gravitating towards the same breeds time and again.

The next dog

"Never again", I hear so very often after a dog dies. People tell me the pain is too much to bear. They'll never get another dog, they can't abide the thought of enduring that hurt ever again. But the fact is that three out of four of us bring another dog into our homes within a year, and so did my family. In that same newspaper, this is part of what I wrote six months later about the "new blonde" in my life.

Some readers may remember that when I wrote in these pages about the death of my dog Macy, I vowed one day to get a successor. I geared up for that by speaking to Julia, my number one blonde. "Let's get a brace of Jack Russells," I said. "We can use them as pillows when we read in bed." But Julia wasn't yet ready for either jokes or dogs. Death, even of a dog, is a real bummer and she needed more time to work through her emotions. And besides – how can I tactfully put this – she's a bit "breedist". Jack Russells are dogs. When she was ready, she didn't want a "dog", she wanted another Golden Retriever.

A few weeks later I told her about a retriever "with barking issues" at a rescue home. But Julia's a bit sexist, too, and he got vetoed for no more reason than the misfortune of carrying his reproductive articles externally rather than internally. Eventually The Chief relented. I'd made contacts in the curious world of Golden Retrieverdom and we acquired Lucca, a female pup.

After I wrote about my reactions when Macy died, many of you – all women – posted your thoughts on the newspaper's website. On the other hand, the majority of emails and letters I received were from men, who wrote privately and personally ... It seems that women don't mind others knowing how they feel, but guys worry they might be thought mushy, slushy sentimentalists. So let me tell you this, men: you may try to hide your tender emotions but you can never get rid of them. Love, care, compassion, tenderness – these emotions aren't simply the products of social change in the latter part of the 20th century, they're hardwired into the core of your being. Emotions and reason are not, repeat, not incompatible ... Talking about your dog, talking about your emotional attachment to your dog, is like admitting you watch soap operas. But let me nail my flag up: there ain't nothing wrong with being sentimental.

...When Lucca hops on to the bed, dive-bombs headfirst into my chest then stretches herself out between Julia and me, she's doing no more than triggering my biologically hard-wired tender feelings. Her large eyes, her still slightly clumsy movements, trigger an innate nurturing response. I can't help but want to care for her. As I write this, she's just trotted into the kitchen with my pyjama bottoms rolled up in her mouth. I don't know how she got them and I don't want her parading them around, yet my reaction to the pride in her walk is a feeling of disarming tenderness.

"Too much feeling, too little common sense," you say? You'd be correct to say that sentimentality can be excessive or misdirected, but there's nothing wrong if a book, or a film, or a television show, or an article in a paper, or a six-month-old puppy snuggling with you provokes your tender emotions. A sentimental world in which I let Lucca sleep with me, or I have a calendar made with photos of my dog, is not a distorted one. It's an emotionally more complete one. Loving your dog is not escaping from reality. If anything, it's the exact opposite.

Starting over After Macy died Julia was the only blonde in my life for the best part of a year. But if books furnish a room, dogs make a home, and the place just seems too still without one. It was inevitable that there would be another one, and sooner rather than later. Enter Lucca Bean.

For me and my family the circle has been completed again. Lucca Bean arrived in my home as a pup and will hopefully depart from it as a geriatric. A dog's life is a colourful series of ever-changing events, far less complex than the kaleidescope of human life, but in many ways more distinct, because the changes happen so quickly. A kid's childhood and adolescence each last for a decade (it can seem longer), but for the dog, infancy to adulthood can pass in just a year.

We love living with dogs for the whole range of reasons I've mentioned in this book, and one of them, a very important one, is that they bring a twinkle into our eyes. Whoever we are, dogs offer us uncomplicated, reliable, immutable fun, so let me finish by quoting some of the less serious things that have been said about them. You may have seen these floating around on the internet, but that doesn't make them any less true. Enough of me and my thoughts.

Dogs are better than women because:

- Dogs love it when your friends come over
- Dogs find you amusing when you're drunk
- The later you arrive home, the happier dogs are to see you
- Dogs will forgive you for playing with other dogs
- Dogs like it when you leave lots of things on the floor
- Dogs never need to examine the relationship
- Dogs enjoy heavy petting in public
- Dogs understand that instincts are better than asking for directions
- Dogs agree that you have to raise your voice to get your point across
- Dogs don't want to know about every other dog you've had
- Dogs don't mind if you give their offspring away

Best friend It doesn't matter whether your latest dog is your first or your fifth. They all give you less hassle than your children and less constructive criticism than your partner, and forget all those embarassing things your friends tend to remind you about.

Constant companion From long before recorded history the dog has been at our side. We tend to assume we've shaped it to our needs, but everyone who's felt owned by a dog must have wondered if it hasn't worked the other way too. They wouldn't be what they are without us – but equally we probably wouldn't be what we are without them.

Dogs are better than men because:

- Dogs don't have trouble expressing their feelings in public
- Dogs don't criticize your friends
- Dogs admit when they're jealous
- Dogs don't play games with you (except fetch)
- Dogs don't care how gushy the movie is
- Dogs don't feel threatened by female intelligence
- You can train a dog not to make a mess in the house
- Dogs don't have a mid-life crisis and look for younger owners
- Dogs don't care if you put your makeup on or not
- Dogs are loyal and faithful
- You can neuter dogs legally

Index

Page numbers in *italics* refer to picture caption

C

D

E

Acknowledgements

Sometimes, listening to the radio or watching TV or reading the papers, I hear or read that a writer has "writer's block". I know what that is. It's the need to hit a deadline when you don't want to and there are so many more interesting things to do. So my first thank you is to LL Bean, my dog. Whenever I found myself sitting at the keyboard, suffering from my kind of "writer's block", wondering why I was indoors staring at a screen, not outside doing something much more enjoyable, Bean just sucked up to my side with a "You're absolutely right. How about a good long walk" look in her eyes. Those one to two hour breaks were perfect.

Bean let me goof off from writing but as always it was everyone at my veterinary clinic who filled in so I could be away from "real work". Thanks to vets Veronica Aksmanovic and Grant Petrie and nurses Ashley McManus, Suzi Gray, Letty Lean, Hester Small and Angel Bettinson for your patience and help. That goes for my commander-in-chief Julia too. Julia knows I'm a sucker for excuses not to write and if I went off to the countryside on my own, I might take long walks with our dog but I'd also keep work hours I wouldn't if she were there. Thank you chief.

And finally thanks to the team that produced this volume, Georgina Atsiaris, Juliette Norsworthy and Helen Griffin and especially to my favourite "rent-a-brain", Candida Frith-MacDonald. Candida simply knows everything about everything that's ever happened. As she edited my text I'd get a gentle email, "Did you really mean to use the word 'always'" or "Are you sure the evidence is there? Have you read...?"

What a terrific back-stop. Thanks Candida.

Further info

If you are interested in more information on subjects in this book, and for all science results but especially those involving the canine genome visit: www.ncbi.nlm.nih.gov/pubmed/

For the results of the BSAVA/Kennel Club Purebred dog health survey visit: www.thekennelclub.org.uk/item/570

For a detailed list of 1000 canine diseases, visit: www.vet.cam.ac.uk/idid

For an English translation of the Zoroastrian Zend Avesta visit: www.avesta.org/vendidad/vd13sbe.htm

Photographic acknowledgments

Mitchell Beazley would like to acknowledge and thank the following for providing images for publication in this book.

a: above, b: below, c: centre, l: left, r: right

12a Moredun Animal Health Ltd/Science Photo Library; 12b Eric Isselée/Shutterstock; 13 Jack Fields/Corbis; 14a Marc Pagani Photography/Shutterstock; 17a Jane Burton/Warren Photographic; 19 DLILLC/Corbis; 20 Jane Burton/Warren Photographic; 21 Doreen Baum/Picani/Shutterstock; 22, 23, 24 Jane Burton/Warren Photographic; 25a Octopus Publishing Group; 25b Eric Isselée/Shutterstock; 26a Lisa A Svara/ Shutterstock; 26b Pieter/Shutterstock; 27 Jane Burton/Warren Photographic; 28a Octopus Publishing Group; 28b, 29a & b Jane Burton/Warren Photographic; 30l Waldemar Dabrowski/ Shutterstock; 30r Octopus Publishing Group; 31 DK Limited/Corbis; 32a & b, 33a Jane Burton/Warren Photographic; 33b Eric Isselée/Shutterstock; 34 Joy Fera/Shutterstock; 35 Eric Isselée/Shutterstock; 36l & r Jane Burton/Warren Photographic; 37a Don Mason/Corbis; 37b Jean Michel Labat/Ardea.com; 38a Jane Burton/Warren Photographic; 38b John Madere/Corbis; 39l Waldemar Dabrowski/ Shutterstock; 39r Wegner/Arco/Naturepl.com; 40a Dale C Spartas/Corbis; 40b Lew Robertson/ Corbis; 41a & b, 42a Jane Burton/Warren Photographic; 42b pixshots/Shutterstock; 43l Rick's Photography/ Shutterstock; 43r, 44l & r Octopus Publishing Group; 45 Eric Isselée/Shutterstock; 46, 47l Octopus Publishing Group; 47r, 48 Jane Burton/Warren Photographic; 49a Eric Isselée/Shutterstock; 49b John Daniels/Ardea.com; 50l Octopus Publishing Group; 50r Eric Isselée/Shutterstock; 51a & b Jane Burton/Warren Photographic; 52 Johan de Meester/Ardea.com; 53 Tracy Morgan/Dorling Kindersley; 54l & r, 55, 56r Jane Burton/Warren Photographic; 56l Shutterstock; 57 John Daniels/Ardea.com; 58, 59, 60l & r, 61r Jane Burton/Warren Photographic; 61l Rick's Photography/Shutterstock; 62 Ioannis Lelakis/Photographers Direct; 63 Jane Burton/Warren Photographic; 68 Shinya Sasaki/Neo Vision/Getty Images; 70 John Daniels/Ardea.com; 76 Roger Tidman/FLPA; 89a Arco Images/Alamy; 96b Yann Arthus-Bertrand/Ardea.com; 111r lemonlight features/Alamy; 113a Maksym Gorpenyuk/Shutterstock; 164 mediacolor's/Alamy; 176a Christie & Cole/Corbis; 186 Mike Buxton/Papilio/ Corbis; 187l Clouds Hill Imaging Ltd/Corbis; 187c Visuals Unlimited/ Corbis; 187r Science Photo Library.